ISBN 978-1-330-88480-5
PIBN 10116969

COLLECTIONS

OF THE

MAINE HISTORICAL SOCIETY

SECOND SERIES

DOCUMENTARY

HISTORY OF THE STATE OF MAINE

VOL. XIII

CONTAINING

THE BAXTER MANUSCRIPTS

EDITED

BY JAMES PHINNEY BAXTER, A. M., LITT. D.

PUBLISHED BY THE MAINE HISTORICAL SOCIETY, AIDED BY APPROPRIATIONS FROM THE STATE

PORTLAND
LEFAVOR-TOWER COMPANY

PRESS OF
LEFAVOR-TOWER COMPANY, PORTLAND

PREFACE

THIS volume contains correspondence of Thomas Pownall, whose prudent administration of affairs during his incumbency of the important office of Royal Governor of Massachusetts entitles him to an honorable place in our colonial history.

The publication of Charles A. W. Pownall's recent book "Thomas Pownall, M.P. F.R.S. Governor of Massachusetts Bay etc. etc., 1722-1805", in which he makes a notable addition to the controversy respecting the authorship of the Junius letters, which he believes should be ascribed to the Governor, will lend to this correspondence increased interest. A comparison of the hand writing of Governor Pownall with that of Junius strongly supports the claim of his kinsman, and we are obliged to pass unquestioned his assertion that the Governor's knowledge of political conditions especially fitted him for writing them. He says, "That no place in the province which this Governor worked so hard for while there, and had so deep an affection for always, derives its name from him. What is now Dresden on the Kennebec river, in the region which his expeditions opened for settlement was at first called Pownalborough, but at the beginning of the last century the present designation was adopted".

I was very glad to assure him that Governor Pownall has

not been forgotten, and that a thriving town in this State bears his name.

I wish to acknowledge my indebtedness and that of the Society to Mr. Edward Denham, New Bedford, Mass., for his invaluable services in preparing the index for this and former volumes of the Documentary History.

JAMES PHINNEY BAXTER,
61 Deering Street,
Portland, Me.

September 15, 1909.

CHRONOLOGICAL TABLE OF CONTENTS

DOCUMENTARY HISTORY

OF THE

STATE OF MAINE

Letter, Wm Millar to Lt Gov. Phips

Wallpolle September: 12: 1755

To his honour Spenchior phips Esqur Governer in Chiefe for the time preasente: Sir this Night I Recieved the Inclosed express from Cpt Lithgow & Cpt Goodwin to forward Estward Which I–Done & thought it my Duty to send this Coppy to your honour that you With the honourable Councle in your Wisdoms may act for the safety of us the Exposed Inhabitants in thies froonteers.

So I Conclude yours Honours most obeidiant

Humble Servent

William Millar

Letter, T. Fletcher to Lt Gov. Phips

These are To Inform, Your Honr that This Day, The Indians fell on us, Two Men were out A Small Distance from the Garrison, the Indians fired Upon Them, one Escaped, & the other is Missing, They began About Twelve of the Clock, & Continued fireing on The Cattle Till Almost Night, I imediately, Dispacht An Express To the Neighbouring Settlements, I judge There is a great Body of them, By their Appearance My Levt was on a March with Thirty Men,

But Happyly this Evening return^{d}, This Night, I Design To Go out & Try to Meet with them —

Being All at Present, I Beg To Subscribe My Self Your Hon^{rs} Most Obedient Hum^{bl} Ser^{t}

T: Fletcher

Message

Gentlemen of the Council & House of Represent^{ves}

Since your late Convention, I have received a Letter from the Penobscot Indians, in Answer to the Proposals made to the said Tribe in Conformity to the Resolutions of this Court for maintaining the Peace with them; Captain Bradbury is now in Town, and is able to give such Information of the Temper and Conduct of those Indians as may be of Use to direct our further Proceedings with them: I therefore desire you would consider this Affair as soon as may be and give me your Advice what Measures may be most proper to be taken by us in Relation to that Tribe.

S Phips

Council Chamber Septr 1755

Speech

Gentlemen of the Council
& House of Representatives

I was much pleased with ye Unanimity of your votes & proceedings in your late Convention and I hope that your Zealous Endeavours to promote his Majesty's service and the safety & prosperity of the British colonies will be attended with happy success.

You have had but little time at home for your private affairs, however as this is the day to which the court, before the late special meeting stood prorogued I was willing to see you again that so if any thing further should be thought necessary to be done for perfecting the rendering effectual your late votes and resolutions you might have an oppertunity for it.

During your recess I have constantly been employed in raising & sending away the new levies & I expect that in a few days the whole number will have marched to join their bretheren who have already bravely hazarded their lives in the Service of their King & Country, and defeated an army consisting of the French King's regular forces of Canadians & Indians Marching into that part of his Majesty's Territories to which his just right & title has never yet been questioned, to attack & destroy his subjects.

I congratulate you Gentlemen upon the welcom news of this seasonable, and important success. I hope it will animate our forces in the further opposition which we must expect they will meet with. I am sure it ought to fill the breasts of all ranks & orders of men among us with gratitude to almighty God the giver of Victory, and encourage them to place ther further dependanc upon his divine favour for every thing they still hope for.

I shall readily Concur with you in giveing all possible dispatch to such business as is of immediate necessity; other affairs it will be best to leave until we have More leisure to attend them.

S Phips

Council Chamber 24th Septemr 1755

Letter, Lt Gov. Phips to Capt. Wm Lithgow

Boston Sept. 27, 1755.

Sir

In Answer to your Letter of the 4th Instant referring to a Guard for Safe Conveying the Stores from Richmond &

Western to Fort Hallifax; I now send you my Orders to the several Commanders of the Marching Companies on the Eastern Frontiers to supply you with such Numbers of Men for that Service & at such time as you shall think proper to assign them; You will take Care seasonably to send these Orders so as that the said Soldiers may be got together at one and the same time when the Waters are sufficiently raised for the Passage of your Boats that so the Service may be done in the shortest time & the Soldiers return again to their common Duty.

Your assured Friend & Serv[t]

S Phips

Cap[t] W[m] Lithgow

Message.

In the House of Rep[ves] Oc[t] 3. 1755

Voted that the following Message be sent to His Hon[r] the Lieu[t] Gov[r] and Commander in Chiefe Viz

May it please Your Hon[r]

The House having taken into their Serious Consideration the Danger and Mischief the People of this Province especially in the Eastern parts, are continually exposed to from the Penobscot Tribe of Indians in their present Scituation who have appeared in open Hostility ag[t] us, or encouraged and abetted our other Enemies in Annoying us.

We do therefore earnestly request Your Hon[r] immediately to declare War Against the said Tribe.

T. Hubbard Spk[r]

Message

Gentlemen of the House of Representatives

It being one of his Majesty[s] Instructions to me not to declare War against the Indians without the Advice of his

Majestys Council I immediately laid before them your Message to me of this Morning for their Advice but their judgement not being in favour of the Motion you had maid It puts it out of my Power to Comply with your desire.

S Phips

Council Chamber Octr 3. 1755

Letter, Capt. Saml Goodwin to Lt Gov. Phips

Frankfort October ye 14th 1755

Sir/

if there should be any Forceses march up Kennebeck this winter Or next spring I shall be Glad to be ConCarnd and Dout not but I Can Rase a Rigement of men in thease Parts if your Honour & the Government Should want them for that Purpose &c I being acquainted here & with the River Kennebeck &c I am Sir as in Dute Bound your Honours Most Dutefull Sarvent

Samuel Goodwin

Sir/

NB. I shall be Glad to have Liberity of your Honour to Come to boston when the five months is out if I should be Continaued all winter here to make up the musterroal for my Compeny to that time ~ All Which is Humbly Submitted by your Honours most Dutefull Sarvent

Samuel Goodwin

Letter, Capt. Saml Goodwin to Lt Gov. Phips Oct. 14, 1755

To His Honour Spencer Phips Esqr Livetenant Governour Commander in Cheaff in and over His Majestys Province of the Massachssutts Bay —

Sir/

I Rece^d your Honours Orders of September ye 27th 1755 On the 11th of October 1755 —

and shall Chearfully Obay, that and all your Honours Commands, and Do Every thing in my Power to Sarve your Honour, and the Government in my Station, And as His Excellency Governour Shirley Gave, Capt. William Lithgow Orders, to Deliver Fort Richmond to me to take Care off, at his leaveing it. which he is now aDoing, and as Frankfort & Richmond is 16 & 17 Miles Distance from Fort Western. & 34 miles from Fort Hallefax on Kennebeck River and no Dout but the Indains will be Down on the Inhabitants nex Spring; if not in the Winter. to Cause a Deversion Else Where) and I being handy at any time to assist in Garding up Storers to Fort Western & Hallefax Therefore I Humbly Petition your Honour and the Honourable the Council &c to Continaue me and Part of my Compeny in the Province Sarvice at Frankfort for this Winter and so on as your Honour & the Honourable Court shall think Proper for the Bennefett and advantage of the Government in General and Settlements on Kennebeck River All Which is most Humbly Submitted by your Honours Most Dutefull Most Obediant and Very Humble Sarvent

Samuel Goodwin

Frankfort October ye 14th 1755

*Letter, Capt. Wm Lithgow to Josiah Willard Sec^y^*

Honble & Worthey Sir/

as an acknoligement for Sundery favours Rec^d^ of your Hon^r^ perticularly for Mr Flavels Workes, by which we are Sensible of your Kind Conserne for us, I send you a Barrel of Potatoas ℘ Capt Patterson and pray your Exceptence thereof, - being Informed ye government Intendes to Keep Two of ye marching Companyes In pay this Winter, or at Least part of them, if such a thing Should be I would with

Submission Recommend Capt Alexander Nichols Junr To your Hon^{r} for one of ye Two Companyes, or if any be Continiued that He may be one, as I Can Recommend Him To your Hon^{r} for a man of an Honoust principle, I speek from the knolige I have had of His behaviour ye Last Sumer, and I belive If His behaviour be examined Respecting His marching according to His Instructions, it will apeer much as I here Represent, -

I have had a most Trubelsom Time of it, for this Twelve mouthes Past, and I think was all the featigue and hardship I have under gon ever since I was Imploy'd by This government, which is now upwards of Twenty years (put to gather) it would not amount to more than I have undergon this year past, at Least I am not so Sensible of my former Hardships as what I am of those of this Year, we have ben hitherto presarved from falling Into ye Hands of ye Enemy by Gods grate goodness, notwithstanding According to ye Eye of Reason, we ware as much exposed as many of those that has fallen by ye Callemiety that attends on warr, we are going (as ever ye Watter is Raise Sufficient for our Boates) to Cary up Supplyes to Fort Hallifax which Fortress will be allmost finished this Fall, - S^{r} with all Due Regardes I beg Leave to Subscribe my Selfe your Honours most obedient Sarvent

Willm Lithgow

Richmond Octb^{r} 17th 1755

Letter, Capt. Saml Goodwin to Lt Gov. Phips

Frankfort October ye 17th 1755

May it Please Your Honour -

Sir/

as there is a large house of 80 feet by 40 & two Storey high built at Ticonnet with several block housses of hewed Timber

Which is Called Fort Hallefax And in hewing the Timber to a Joynt the uper Side of the under peace is hewed Hollow to bring them to a Joynt and in Driveing Stormes the Rane Drives into the Joynts and there Stands and being hid from the Sun Continaues weet for a long time: and Rotts the Timber very much Which is a Great Damage to such buildings.

Now Sir/ in my Humble Opinion I think they aught to be Covered ameditly Either with fether Eadge Boord so as to Break Joynts or Else Claboorded Which if Don Now will be a Great Saveing to the Province and Prevent a Great Destruction to the buildings there ~

And as the workmen is on the Spott now at said Fort the Province may Geet it Don Cheap by leeting it out by the Lump it being a Winters Job I Dout not but they may Save Near halfe) then they will to Transport New work men there to Do it Which must be Don Soon Or Else the work will Decay and Com to Nothing Witness Richmond Fort and all Timber Houses Not Covered.

Sir/ there is one Mr Aron Willard who has built the Large house there and that would Do it as Cheap and as well as any Person Whatever if your Honour and the Honourable Court Should Think Proper to Order it Don and if it Should be Left undon I am well assured the building would Receive more Damage then Double the Price of doing it now (in two years time) hopeing Sir/ you will Excuse my Freedom but Knowing it will be of Great advantage to the Province.

S^r I beg leave to Subscribe my Selfe your Honours most Dutefull most Obediant and Very Humble Sarvent

Samuel Goodwin

To His Honour Spencer Phips Esqr Lieutenant Governour Commander in Cheaff in and Over His majestys Province of the Massachssutts Bay ~

Letter, Capt. Saml Goodwin to Lt Gov. Phips

Octo^r ye 17th day 1755

May it Please your Honour two thirds of my Compeny is Imployed in Garding and helping up the Province Storers and the Moveing Every thing from Richmond and as they will always be wanting assistance It may be in the Winter as well as in the Summer and Early in the Spring to Gard the Vessalls up the River Kennebeck To Fort Western and I being handy I shall be Glad to have Part of my Compeny Continaued all Winter if aGreable to your Honour & the General Court but if not I shall be glad of your Honours Orders wheather I must Dismise them all on the 20 or 25th of November next or as longe before that that they may arive at Boston I beleave the Greatest Part of my Compeny would be Glad to Tarre with me and if any farther Sarvice should be Wanted they will willingly Goe with me next Summer if they should be wanted and if the Province should want more men next Summer I am well assured I Can Rase a Rigement of men in thease Part and would Do it if I Could Command them and should be Glad to be ConCarned if it should be aGreable to your Honour I shall be Glad of your Honours Favours to me and am as in Duty Bound your Honours most Dutefull and Verry Humbl Sarvent

Samuel Goodwin

Letter, Capt. Wm Lithgow to Lt Gov. Phips Oct. 18, 1755

May it Please your Honour/

I acknolige my Selfe Duty bound to Returne your Hon^r my Sincier Thanks In a most Humble manner, for ye grate Care your Honour has ben pleased to Shew us In ordring a Sufficent guard to Transpoart ye publick stores up ye River to Fort Hallefax, as the garrison there posted is most expos'd on account of it's daingerious Scittuation, of any of ye Forts on our Estern Fruntiers, as every one will alow that Considers it's Distince up Kennebeck River as also ye Deficualty and Hazad of going up s^d River., I hope your Hon^r will be made Sensible I shall be as Industerious as Circumstances of this River will permitt, and shall Do every thing In my Power to Dispatch ye guard that they may Returne to there Common Duty a greable to your Instructions to me,—

I have Dispatched your Honours orders to ye Sundery Commanders, as also have asigned them to send there Severel parties of men to Fort Western ye 22^d Instent, at which Time, I hope we shall be able to Cary up ye Stores, if ye River be properly Raised for ye Bo'ts —

with all Submission I humbely Beg Leave to

Subscribe my selfe your Hon^{rs} most obedient Humble Sarv^t Willm Lithgow

Richmond Octob^r 18th 1755

P-S —ye Inclos'd Scrip is a Calculation I Desired ye Carpnter to Draw of ye makeing Clapboards & Laying them to secure ye Building of Fort Hallifax &c — which I Humbely Recomend to your Hon^r for Considderation; and would Say if this piece of Work be not Dun, ye Stores will be very much exposed — In Bad weather as also ye buildings Themselves,— which will also Render ye officers & Soldiers quarters unComfortable

W — L —

["ye Inclos'd Scrip."]

Memorandom for Claboarding the Garrison at Halifax

To 10^m Claboards To be Large 6 inches wide @ 22£	220: 0: 0
To Laying 10^m Claboards @ 15£	150: 0: 0

To making 46 window Caps & Casing the Same to Receive the ends of the Claboards To Casing 32 ports & Look outs & 10 doors and making all weather boards Corner boards and water Tables and Casing 160 feet of a Jet	180: 0: 0
	550: 0: 0

Octo^r 17th 1755

Aaron Willard

Letter, Capt. Wm Lithgow to Lt Gov. Phips Oct. 20, 1755.

May it Please your Hon^r/

with Humble Submission onece more I would Intreat your Honour In behalfe of ye Soldiery of Fort Hallifax, that they may be Discharged this Fall as thay have ben Continued in ye Service for this 18 monthes Past thay say thay ware Listed or Impres'd only for ye Space of Three mouthes, which thay think is a grate imposition on them, In my Humble opinion ye best way to Remedy ye uneasyness of those Soldiers, to Send Down InListing papers for about 30 men, by ye help of which I dont know but it would be In my power to Engage a Sufficient Number to Tary a nother Twelve monthes, which will Save ye government ye Cost of Raising New men, and Dubble pay perhaps for Some Time, I will be accounteble to ye government for any money thay send for this purpose, and will Justely Returne, any that may be left —

I would pray your Honours Consideration on this, as it has ben with Dificulty I have Retain^d som of those men

I Remain Your Hon^rs Dutiful Servt

Richmond Octb^r 20th 1755

Wm Lithgow

the Reson why ye Soldiery of Fort Hallifax is so uneasy, is be Cause their Dutey is so much harder then at other Fortes, whare thay have their provisions bro^t^ to ye Door, without Truble, as also their Tower of Duty Coms Three Times as often at Fort Hallifax as at S^t^ georges whare thay have 45 men alowd and but one Fort to guard.
at Hallifax there is 80 men alowed and four postes to Defend vizt ye main Fort, Store House, and Two Redoubts which brings ye whole of ye 80 men on Duty every other Night there being Scattred at such a Distence which is not ye Case at georges Fort or others whare thay mount ye Night guard but once In five Nights, So that it's plane that 20 men is as sufficent for S^t^ georges Fort or any other neer ye See, as 80 men is for Fort Hallifax which is Seetuate 40 or 50 miles from Inhabitants which makes it more agreable to ye Soldiery

Wm Lithgow

[Superscribed]

To the Honourable Spencer phips Esqr
Lieu^t^ gov^r^ & Comm^dr^ In Cheif of His Majestyes
province of ye Masschusetts Bay N England

Message.

Gentlemen of the House of Representatives

The Present posture of Affairs with regard to the Indians is such as to make it necessary to provide for the Defence and Safety of our Exposed Frontiers. And as the establishment made in the May Session for the Forces to be employed in the Eastern and Western parts of the Province will expire on the 5th of next Month I must earnestly recommend it to you, Gentlemen, to make further Provision for their Defence

Council Chamber October 28. 1755

Letter to Capt. Saml Goodwin

Boston Novemr 6. 1755

Sir

You are hereby required forthwith to disband the Marching Company of Soldiers on the Eastern Frontiers under your Command, & to inform me of the Day of their Dismission & Allowing each man proper time to return Home and Making up your Roll accordingly. Notwithstanding, If any of your Men are still Guarding the Provisions &c to Fort Hallifax they must not taken off till that Service be done

Your Friend & Servant

Letter, Capt. John Lane to Josiah Willard, Secy

Bideford Novr ye 21d 1755

Honoured Sir

after my best dutey to your Honour I beg Leave to Acquaint you that thear is a number of the Solders that wass in my Company at Fort Hallifax which have bin in the Service Ever sinc Ginll Winslow went first Down and Cant gitt Clear notwithstanding the men that went Last winter are dismissed and gone Thay Have sent to me by the Baror Sergt Love Who is one of them to Beg your Honour will be so good as to use your Intrest to gitt them Clear the Baror will Informe your Honour more at Large I Must once more Beg your Honour Will Remember me when the Governour Cumes Home I Beg your Honours prayers for me,

And am your Honours Most dutifull and Obd Humble Servt John Lane

Letter, Capt. George Berry to Lt Gov. Phips

Falmouth Novbr 22nd: 1755

May it Pleas Yr Honour

Immediately upon my Receiving Yr Orders, in Obedience

Thereto I Dismis^{d} my Company of Soldiers, which was on the 17th & 19th Ins^{t} And shall Forward my Muster Roll and Journal as Soon as Possoble.

I am Y^{r} Hono^{rs} Most Obedient Humble Servt

George Berry

Letter, Capt. Thos Fletcher to Lt Gov. Phips Nov. 25, 1755.

To the Honourable Spencer Phips Esqr

May it Please Youer honouer having received No orders from youer honouer Concluded I must Conform to ye act of Cort — the time being Expired I have Dismised the men under my Command untill futher Orders from Youor honouor wich I Do not Expect.

Not that I pretend to Direct the honourable Cort but beg Leave to offer my opinion

I Do not think that thare has ben aney Indians amongst us Since the mischife was Dun ye 24th of September neither will be this fall or Winter and think It w^{d} be An Neadles Charge to Continew aney part of my Company Longer.

I Conclude beging Leave to Subscribe Youer honouers most obedient humble Serv^{nt}

Thos Fletcher

St Georges November ye 25th 1755

Letter, Samuel White to Josiah Willard, Sec^{y}

Brooklyn February 23 1756

Sir I am thankfull unto Almighty God who Preserves your Life unto an Old Age as I hope to be Ablessing in your day.

I have a fayour to Ask of your Honour for my Brother at Glossester he hes Ahopfull Son Living now at Saco falls at the Estward he was brought up at Colledge and is Now A Docter he is Averr Sensable Capeable Gentleman I have heard it Would be Agreat benifit to that people if His Excellency would Nomenate him for A Justice of the Peace for s[d] County I would beg of your Honour that yould Mention it unto the Governor before this Court Ends. his name is Sam[ll] White

So I remain your Honours most Obliging Ser

Samuel White

Message

Gentlemen of the Council & House of Represent[ves]

I herewith send you the Copy of a Resolve pass'd by the General Assembly of the Province of New York for a Gratuity to Cpt. Rogers of Fort William & Henry in consideration of his extraordinary Courage, Conduct & Diligence in His Majestys Service against the French & Indians at & about the French Fort at Crown Point.

And upon this Occasion I think my self obliged to lay this matter before you, & to let you Know that I apprehend it may be of great Service for the Common Cause, If we should likewise in some suitable Manner show our Acknowledgem[t] of Cpt Rogers's good service herein.

W Shirley

March 8, 1756. Province house

Letter, Capt. W[m] Lithgow to Gov. Shirley

Si[r] May it Pleas Your Excellency

I would Just Beg to Acquaint your Excellency that Cap[t] David Duning of Brunswick & Cap[t] Adam Hunter of Topsham were Boath Verry Ready in Relieving of this Fort in the Month of January 1755 when it was in a Verry Distressed Condition as Many of the Soilders here then being Sick having no beads Blankits Shoes hose or Scarce bodyly Cloathing to ware & but Little Provison in ye fort, then, ye Above two Cap^ts^ at that Time Came with Odd^s^ of twenty Men and being Joyned with ye few Soldiers then at Richmond in ye Space of three weeks halled by hand Sleads on ye Ice from Arousick beads Blankits Shoes hose &^ca^ as Also from fort Western about 200 Barr^ll^ Provision to Fort Hallifax I need not Mention the Distance or Severety of ye Weather as Your Excellency is a Perfict Judg; And as ye Above Duning & Hunter have not yet been Rewarded for there Extreordenery Service boath in Respect of there Raising those men & there Grate Travil up & down this River, I would with Submission Perpose if it may be Agreeable to Your Excellencys Pleasure that if there be Scouting Companys this Year Allowed as was Last On those Frountiers that Capt Duning have the Command of One of them and as Capt John Smith One of the Commanders of those Companys Last Year Shewed himself Verry Backward in Giving his Attendance when Ordered, and Also his withdrawing his Detachment from the Service of this fort in the midest of our Hurry & Danger which Gave me a Grate Deal of Trouble as ye unwarrantable Behavour of his Men Gave umbrage to ye Other Detachments —

I Beg Pardon for my Teadousness and Refer your Excellency to Capt Smiths Instructions and a Coppy of a Letter sent him on this Ocation as Also his Answer here Inclosed where he says he is Ready to Come at my Request with all his Company which if he had he might have known this would have frusterated the Designe of ye Court as it Appears there Intention was to have this work Carried on & ye frontiers Guarded at ye same time, and as Capt Duning

& hunter has been Servisable not only in ye Winter But Spring Also in Boating up Stores and as they are Men Verry Capable not only as Oficers for a Scouting Company but are as Capable & willing as Any Men I know of in the Province to Assist us in Gitting up ye Stores to this Fort is ye Cheif Reason why I Recommend Duning as Capt & Hunter as Leiv^t^ and humbly Submit it to Your Excellencys Consideration —

I Remain Your Excellencys Most Dutifull & Most Humble Sarv^t^ William Lithgow

Letter, T. Fletcher to Lt. Gov. Phips.

St Georges Fort March 24th 1756

This Morning three men went to the mill to Git Smelts the Indians Killed 2. wounded and Scalped the third the men are R^b^ Key hennary hendly and J^o^ hennary we found a Live and he says that as soon as thay saw the Indians J^o^ Laid Down his Gun and asked Quarters but thay wo^d^ Give them none thare is Litle hope that henary will recover he is Shott through the Belley.

You will Communicate this to the Govrnouer if You think proper for I shall not rite to him the men went out without My knowledge henary says that thare ware about 10. Indians

I am Si^r^ Your humble Searvent

T. Fletcher

Letter, Capt. Alex^r^ Nikels to Gov. Shirley. March 26, 1756.

To His Excelencie William Shirly Esqr: our Governor and Comander in Chief in and over His majestys province of the Masachusets Bay in New England

Inclosed I have sent you the Express I received yesterday from Leftenant flatcher at St: Georges by which your Excellencie may see the Emenent Danger we are in at pressent and begs your Excelencie would be pleased heasten Down orders for men to be raised to goe out against them and your ready Complyance with the above requist will very much oblidg your loveing frient and servant at Comand

New castle March the 26th 1756

Alexr Nikels

I have sent a Copi of the said Express with all the speed I Could allong shore to Kenybek river

[Superscribed]

To His Excelencie William Shirley Esqr
our Governor and Comander in Chief

Message.

Gentlemen of the House of Representves

I have received Applications from the Inhabitants on St Georges River for a few Soldiers for their Defence against the Indian Enemy. The People in those Parts seem to be in a peculiar Manner the Objects of the Enemys Fury & Resentment And the Terror thereof has made such Impression upon the Inhabts there, that there seems to be great Danger that without immediate Relief the Place will be wholly abandoned (excepting the Province Fort there,) And as one Mr Burton has erected a commodious Fortification round his House, And I am inclined to think the Inhabitants would be easy to remain there if six or eight Soldiers were posted at that House, Therefore I must recommend it to you to make Provision for the Pay & Subsistence of such Soldiers there to be posted accordingly.

W Shirley

Province House April 7, 1756

Broad Bay. Vote.

In the House of Represent^s April 8, 1756.

Whereas it appears to this House Necessary for the safety of the Inhab^ts of Broad Bay & those near Henderson's Fort near pleasant point & Burton's Block house, That there be a Number of Men Ordered for their Defence: —

Therefore

Voted That there be a Detachment of fifteen Men made from the two lowest Scouting Companies on the Eastern Frontiers, to guard the Inhabitants of Broad Bay during their Seed time & Harvest, And on other necessary Occasions; And for the Safety of such Inhabit^ts as are at or near Henderson's Fort at pleasant point & Burton's Block house, That six Men including a Sergeant be posted at each of those places, six of the said Men to be draughted from the Garrison at Fort Frederick And the other Six to be inlisted from amongst the said Inhabitants; & That his Excellency the Capt General be desired to give Order accordingly: — And That the Establishment for the Wages & Subsistence of said twelve Men be the same as is allowed for other Garrisons on ye Eastern Frontiers For the Term of two months

Sent up for Concurrence T. Hubbard Spk^r

In Council April 10th 1756 Read and Concurr'd

Thos Clarke Dp^ty Secry

Consented to W Shirley

Message. April 9, 1756

Gentlemen of the Council & House of Represent^ves

It seems to me that Providence has put a peculiar Advantage into our hands for effecting that which probably would be a singular means of strengthning our Eastern Frontiers against the Attacks of the Enemy, I mean the building and garrisoning a Fort upon Penobscot River; A time of War with the Indians has been thought the only proper Season for Attempting this Design; And if our repeated Advices of – late Effects of the Small Pox among the Penobscot and St John's Indians whereby their Numbers are much lessened, have any good Foundation; This Circumstance may tend much to facilitate the Enterprize.

If a suitable Fort should be built there the Garrison at and Fort on St George's River might be reduced to a few Men, & the Fort left principally for a Retreat to the Inhabitants in time of Danger.

If it should please God to restore Peace to us; this projected Fort would be in a Place much more suitable for carrying on the Trade with the Indians, as it would not draw the Indians into our Settlements, It would prevent those Contentions and Quarrels which have generally laid the Foundation of our Wars with them; And a good Part of the Forces raised for the Security of the Eastern Frontiers may be employed in covering the Workmen in building this Fort.

I doubt not but that if we should undertake this Affair, and accomplish it, His Majesty would be easily induced to order the Building of a strong Fort near the Mouth of St John's River, And by that means by the Blessing of God the whole Eastern Coast, even up into the Bay of Funday might be secured against the Attacks of the French be a great Restraint upon the Indian Enemy.

Gentlemen, I must earnestly desire you would enter upon the speedy Consideration of these things, according to their Importance, And come to such Resolution thereon as may be most for the Safety of the Province.

W Shirley

Province House April 9th 1756

Gov. Shirleys Message "March 1756."

Gentlemen of the Council & House of Representatives

It was a Part of the general Plan for the Operations of the advancing Year that a considerable Force should be sent up the River Kennebeck, to spoil & break up the French Settlements upon & near Chaudiere [River] & to give an alarm to Quebec: I find that a body of Men sufficient for this Purpose cannot possibly be spared from the Forces of the Several Governments raising for the Service against Crown Point: I despair therefore of our being able to employ so great a Number of Men up Kennebeck River as was at first intended. However Gentlemen, there are many Advantages which may arise from a small Party of Men well spirited for the Service, & under an Officer of Courage & Discretion; Such a party might do great damage to the French Villages, it would be in less Danger of being discovered & would make a quicker Retreat than a larger Body, and yet might be sufficient to keep that part of Canada in an Alarm, and to oblige the French to retain part of their Strength there; but I have in view a further Advantage & it shall be the Business of one or more skilful persons whom I would have to accompany such a party to make the most accurate Observations of that Country, which at present we are too little acquainted with, and I cannot but think that if we can gain a thorough Knowledge of those parts it will be found that an Army may march against Quebec by this Route with greater Safety & less Expence than by any other Way whatsoever. I do not desire you, Gentlemen to lay any additional Burthen on the Province, I think that part of the Forces raised as a Guard for the Eastern Frontier may be employed in the Service I now propose to you & yet that Frontier be as secure in the mean time as if those Forces were kept within the Limits to which by your Vote for raising them you have desired me to retain them.

I therefore recommend this Affair to your immediate Consideration & desire you would do what may be proper on your part to enable me to employ in the proposed Service one or two hundred of those Forces as shall be found most convenient & that you would make all necessary provision for executing _ Design to the greatest Advantage that may be.

W Shirley

Province House April 14, 1756

Letter, Capt. George Berry to Lt Gov. Phips

Falmouth 17th April 1756

May it please yr Honour

As my Orders from his Excellency Governour Shirley were (in Case of Mischief done) to send him the Accot thereof would now in his Absence take the Freedom to acquaint yr Honour that las Fryday a Party of about Seven or Eight Indians at a Village called New Marblehead way lay'd a Field where the Inhabitants were at work and kill'd one Man and wounded another. my Lieut at that Time, being in the Borders of sd Village with a Detachment of men immediately ran to their Relief, and had the Opportunity of discharging once or twice at the Enemy, but could recover Nothing more than five of their Packs, which they quitted to facilitate their Escape and immediately made the best of their way off —Last Warr I transported three Whale Boats into Sabago Pond by means of which I went to the Head of their Transport, burn't Sundry of their Canoes, which they perceiving & discovering may Signs of our being there deterred them from ever coming that way again, during last War, and beg leave to mention to yr Honour that I might have two Whale Boats allow'd me now, whereby I might proceed to their highest Transport, & from thence over into Ammoscoggin River, (which is the usual Way of their making a Descent upon us at this Time) and thereby I doubt not prevent their returning that Way again, and very probably by Ambushments cut some of the Enemy of either in their Descent or Retreat, but without Whale Boats cannot possible penetrate so far into the Country —

When I rec^{d} my Orders & Com̄issions from Governor Shirley I immediately enlisted my Company, which by my Com̄ission consisted of Sixty Men, & proceeded upon Action, but have never rec^{d} the Bounty for each Soldiers inlisting or any part thereof, humbly your honour would please to Order it to be sent by Capt David Stickney, who will give any Security required for his Safe Delivering it here —

I am y^{r} Honours most Obed^{t} Hum^{l} Servt

George Berry

Letter, Sir Wm Pepperrell to Lt Gov. Phips

Kittery April. 30th 1756

Sir

I am Honour'd with your Letter of ye 23^{d} inst with a Blank Commission. and acopy of a Letter from Capt Berry, it is impossiable for me thouroughly to consider this affaire to do any thing that will serve the Eastern Frontiers without I go there, wch I designe to set out next monday.

I Should have don it before this time but have ben hurry^{d} raising men for the Crown Point expedition, having but two days time given me to raise. 70. men and no Commissions sent with the warrant, here has ben one Capt Lane raising men for said expedition but he has not made any return of ye number he has rais'd in my Regiment. but I heare upw^{ds} of forty, and now Capt Joseph Holt brings wth him self makes 70: more. I think it hard to take so many from hence as there is Scarce an Inhabitant But is exposed to the Enemy both by Sea or Land or both

with much Esteem I am Your Honours Faithfull and Most Obediant Humble Servt

Wm Pepperrell

The Honble Lt Govr Phips

Letter, Capt. J. Freeman to Lt. Gov Phips

Georges May 15: 1756

Sir

This day I Rec^{d} your Honorse Order for my detacheing Six Men And one Sergeant out of my Company to guard the inhabitants of Broad Bay; as also the Votes of the general Court Shall agreeable thereto with the leave of Divine providence perform the Same Early on the week following (this being Saturday). The Indians have discovered by the inhabitants of this place at Sundry times Since they did the dammage at the Mills Near the Fort a Short time ago. viz On the Tenth day of April last there wass One Seen from the Fort at Som Small distance on ye Twelfth day there wass one Seen about Two hundreed y^{ds} from the Block House on the Sixteenth day there wass one Seen a Small distance from the Block House at Pleasant Point On the Seventh day of this instant One wass Seen by Capt Fletcher And Sundry of his Company Early in the Morning Near the Fort about Two Hours after there wass Two Seen About two Mile down the River And on the Eleventh Instant there wass One Seen about Three Miles down the River from the Fort. I Have been out with My Company And Sundry times have had part of Capt Fletchers Company after them haveing Traveled by Night Sundry times in order to way lay those Places that we thought Probable they Mought Travell And we thereby to be undiscovered by them; but have not ass yet the good luck to see them when our Company wass together; we have Not at Any one time in our Traveling after them discovered more then the Tracks of Three at once. Haveing Not ass yet Rec[d] our Stores to March but Expect to Receive them on Munday Next Cap[t] Sanders this day Ariveing And Bringing Supplies for the Fort Cap[t] Fletcher hath given Me inCourageMent that he will Supply us for the Present Am — S[r] your Honors Most Obedient And Verry Humble Serv[t]

Joshua Freeman

To the Honorable Spencer Phips Esq[r] Lieu[t] Gov[r] &c

Letter, John Minot to Gov. Shirley

Brunswick May 20th 1756

May it Please your Excel —

I am Desired by the Selectmen & Others Prinsipall men in this Town) to begg the favour of your Excel. that 3 or 4 men or as many as your Excel. sees meet be placed at M[r] Spears Garrison out of Some of those marching Companyes his Garrison is halfe wayes betwene ffort George & Maquoit, no house within amile & a halfe of it, he an old man upwards of 80 years & but One son with him who uppon the late murders Committed by the Indians) if they cannot have some men allow'd are going to leave it We ask this favour for this Garrison only I know of none in the County so necessary to be kept it being a Common passage for Travellers and soldiers in their march from Kennibeck river to this Bay —

I am Yo[r] Exel[s] most Obed[t] humb Serv[t]

John Minot

Letter, Capt Matth^{s} Remley to Lieut. Gov. Phips 25 May, 1756.

Honble Sir

I rec^{d} the Order past both the Honble Houses for 15 Men to be allowed, out of the Two Lowest Scouting Company's, for the protection of the inhabitants of this place. Capt Freeman and so Capt Goodwine, have According to the Order from Your Hon^{r} each sent 16 Men and a Sergant, wch onely makes 14 Men, in Lew of 15, and as the said Sergants are only to observe the Orders of their Cap^{ts} and are Strangers and Unacquainted with the Situation, or the Business of this Place, therefore beg Leave to pray Your Hon^{rs} Order on that head as well on Acc^{tt} of fifteen Men who is wanting yet.

I in Duty bound subscribe myself

Your Hon^{rs} most Humb^{le} & Ob^{d} Servt to Com^{d}

Matt^{hs} Remley Capt

Broad Bay 25th May 1756

Phillipstown, Petition

Province of the Massach^{tts} Bay

To His Excel^{cy} William Shirley Esqr Capt Genr^{l} and Govern^{r} in chief of His Majesty's Province aforesaid The Honble his Majesty's Council & Ho_ of Representatives in Gener^{l} Court assembled May 26th 1756

The Inhabitants and settlers of a place called Phillips-town within the County of York most humbly shew

That the Proprietors of a Tract of Land of Eight Miles square situate at the Inland head of the Town of Wells in said County and commonly called Phillipstown bounded viz beginning at a Pine Tree standing upon the North Corner of said Wells Township & on the South West Side of Kennebunk River upon the North end of a Rockey Hill which Tree is marked ~ four sides, from thence South West by Wells Bounds Eight Miles to a Pitch Pine Tree mark'd four Sides standing on the West side of Merryland Meadows so called, thence North West Eight Miles to a Hemlock Tree mark[d] four Sides standing to the Northward of Bonnabeag Hills, thence North East Eight Miles to a White Oak Tree mark[d] four Sides & thence South East Eight Miles to the place began at. In Order to bring forward the Settlement of the same Did Grant to your Petitioners & others Forty Lots of Land part of said Tract consisting of 130 Acres each upon certain Conditions of settleing them most of which are already fulfilled the others in a fair way so that there are now about Thirty Families and upwards of 150 Souls Inhabiting there most of whom thro' the good Hand of Providence & by means of the help and assistance of this Province have been enabled to defend & keep their Possessions and Improvements during the last Indian War without the loss of so much as one person, not only to the Interest and safe Guard of the Sea port Towns of the s[d] County in special As being the Barrier to them, but the Province in Gener[l] which has given great Incouragement to others to settle there, & a Hopeful prospect of a Flourishing settlement & Town in a Short Time, if suitably Incouraged —

That the Greatest Obsticle and Discouragement in their Way of settling a Town is their being under no proper Regulation of an Incorporated Town or Precinct and so have not the Power and Priviledge (as such) of raising Money in an equitable manner for the Support and maintenance of the Gospel there, so necessary for the Prevention of Irreligion & profaneness, as well as for the Edification of such as are Religiouss and well Dispos'd, nor Adjusting the repairs of High Ways or managing any other their Prudential Affairs or having proper Officers for keeping up good Order and Discipline ; Inconveniences which this Hon[ble] Court can't but see are Ruinous and Destructive to a good settlement, Tending to the Youth's leading Loose and Deprav'd Lives and liable to all Disorder and confusion —

Wherefore Your Petitioners most humbly pray this Court to take the Premisses under consideration, And of their Wanted Goodness & Parental Care of such Infant settlements Incorporate them into a Town or Precinct by the meets and Bounds aforesaid, or such others as may be Judg'd fit. And Grant them such Powers and Priviledges as have been usual for such, Or provide such other Way and Method for Redress of the Inconveniences aforesaid, And the Incouragement of the settlement as this Court in their Wisdom shall Judge most fit & reasonable And Your Petitioners As in Duty bound shall ever pray &c

Daniel W	Naphtali Harmon	John Harmon
Joshua W	Jonathan Adams	Joshua Cane
Robert Miller	John Garey	Sam^{ll} Wilson
Nicolas Cane	Jos Stanley	Jonathun Johnsan
John Miles	John Thompson	Sam^{ll} Cane
	John thompson Junr	John Stanyan
	Eph	John Chadbourn
	John C	Joshua Chadbourn
	Benj^{a} Harmon	Thomas Wasgatt
	Benjamin Harmon Jun	Jesse Thompson
	Edward Harmon	Edward Whitehouse
	John Staple	Jonn: Johnson
	Eben Staple	Samson Johnson
	Benj: W	James Garey
		Jonathan Swett

In the House of Rep^{s} June 4, 1756

Read and Ordered, That ye Prayer of the Pet^{n} be so far granted as That ye Pet^{rs} notify the non resident Proprietors with this Pet^{n} by leaving an Attested Copy thereof with the

Clerk of the Proprietors of s[d] Land, y[t] they shew Cause (if any they have) on the second Wednesday of the next sitting of this Court, why the Prayer thereof should not be granted

Sent up for Concurrence.— T. Hubbard Spk[r]

In Council June 5 1756

Read and Concurred J Willard Secry

In Council August 26 1756. Read and Ordered that the Consideration of this Pet[n] be referred to the second Wednesday of the next sitting of this Court

Sent down for Concurrence Tho[s] Clarke Dp[ty] Secry

In the House of Rep[s] Aug[t] 28 1756

Read and Concurred T. Hubbard Spk[r]

Brunswick. Petition

Province of the Mass[a] Bay

To the Hon[ble] Spencer Phips Esq[r] L[tt] Governour & Commander in Cheif. The Hon[ble] His Majestys Councill and House of Representatives in General Court Assembled May 26. 1756

The Petition of the Select Men of the Town of Brunswick Humbly Sheweth.

That the said Town for many years past has been exposed to the Incursions of the Indian Enemy and many of said Indians killed and captivated; and that very lately they Surprized three of the Inhabitants in their return from the place of Publick Worship one of whom was taken and carried away the other very narrowly escaped: At the same time near the Borders of said Town Another Family was surprized, One Man Killed & his child at the Breast of its Mother who was dangerously wounded this necessarily Alarmed the Inhabitants, obliged them to Neglect their Husbandry and to retire into Garrisons where they are at present confined by reason of the Enemy. Therefore your Petitioners humbly represent their distressed Circumstances at this day and earnestly pray the Compassionate Regard of this Honble Court so far as to Allow a few Men to be posted at a Garrison situate in the Centre of said Town near to the Meeting house, on the Main Road from Maquoit to Fort George so necessary and convenient for Travellers & others, which has hitherto been Maintained at the Expence of the Owner Mr Robert Spear, but he is now greatly Advanced in Years, Lame and without any help except one Son and he must necessarily quitt the Place unless some Releif be afforded –

Your Petitioners humbly hope that your Honours would be pleased to take this into your Consideration and afford them this necessary Releif at this so Critical Juncture And Your Petitioners as in duty bound shall ever pray &c

Thos Skolfield	}	Selectmen
Sam^{ll} Standwood	}	of
Isaac Snow	}	Brunswick

In the House of Representatives May 28. 1756 —

Read and Voted That his Hon^{r} the Lieu^{t} Governor be desired to give Orders that fourteen Men belonging to the Scouting Company under the Command of Capt Samuel Gooding Continually Scout on the back of the Inhabit^{ts} from Fort George to Macquoit, untill the further Order of this Court.—

Sent up for Concurrence T Hubbard Spk^{r}

In Council May 29. 1756 Read and Concur'd

Thos Clarke Dp^{ty} Secry

Consented to S Phips

In the House of Represent^{s} June 4. 1756.—

Whereas it appears to this House That it would be of great Service to have a suitable Number of Boats in

Sabago Pond for transporting Men thrô the Same to Amascoggin River in Order to Cut off the Indian Enemy in their descent upon or retreat from the Inhabitants on the Eastern Frontiers;

Voted That the Commissary General be directed to provide as soon as may be two Good Cedar Whaleboats for the Use of the Scouting Companies on the said Frontiers as Occasion shall offer the said Boats to be delivered to the Order of the Commander in Chief.

Sent up for Concurrence T. Hubbard, Spk[r]

In Council June 5. 1756 Read and Concur'd

Tho[s] Clarke Dp[ty] Secry

Consented to S Phips

New Gloucester, Petition.

To the Honourable Spencer Phips Esq[r] Lev[t] Governer & Comander in Chief in and over his Majesties province of y[e] Massachu[ts] Bay in New England

The Honourable his Majesties Counsel & House of Representatives in Generall Court assembled on the Last Wednesday in May 1756 —

The Memorial of philamon Warner & Nath Allen of Gloucester in the County of Essex, in behalf of themselves and severall other persons Humbly Sheweth

That some Years past the Grate & Generall Court made a Grant of a Township (called it New Gloucester) to A Number of the Inhabitants of Gloucester, Soon after s[d] Grant we built near Twenty Houses, and A Saw Mill, but the last Indian War they were destroyed, in the years 1755 & 6 with grate Difficulty We Built a Block house verry Comodiously situated, and picketed round One hundred & ten feet square, with Watch Boxes in s[d] Blockhouse & on y[e] pickets — There is Now about Twenty Men att s^{d} New Gloucester A Number of wch have Famely^{s} & some small stock of Cattle, and much Expos'd to A Cruel Enemy, & as we have been att grate expence in so far setling s^{d} place Your Memo^{sts} humbly pray that a number of the Inhabitants of s^{d} New Gloucester, may have pay from the province, or relieve us in any other way as your Honours Grate Wisdome shall see resonable & as in duty Bound Your Memo^{sts} shall ever pray

Phile^{m} Warner
Nathaniel Allen } Comitt

In the house of Representatives June 5, 1756 — Read and

Voted, That such of the Inhabitants of a place Called New Glocester in the County of York as are effective for ye service (one of whom to be a serjeant) be put into the pay & subsistance of the Governm^{t} vizt Ten only at the same time, The s^{d} Ten to be employed in scouting for the protection of said Inhabitants, till the last day of October next, And

That his Honour the Lieu^{t} Govr & Commander in Chief be desired to give Directions Accordingly.

Sent up for Concurrence T. Hubbard Spk^{r}

In Council June 7, 1756 Read & Concur'd

Thos Clarke Dp^{ty} Secry.

Consented to S Phips

Letter, Saml Howard to Gov. Shirley 12 June 1756

May it Pleas Your Excellency —

As I am in Duty Bound I here Send you the Mallincolly Account of two Men's being Mortally Wounded by ye Indians whose Names are Robert & Samu Barrett, as they were ketching a few fish at ye falls, four Indians fired upon them & one of our Men Returned ye fire though wounded, and says he wound one Indian our Men Isued out so Quick that they had nō Time to Scalp them, there is no hopes of one's Recoverry y[e] Other may Possibly Recover but its Verry Doutfull, I shall at Presant Trouble Your Excellency Nofurther But Beg Leave to Subscribe my Self Your Most Dutifull Humble Sarv[t]

Samuel Howard

Fort Hallifax 12 June 1756.

Letter, L[t] Gov. Phips to Capt. Sam[l] Goodwin

Cap[t] Samuel Goodwin

Boston July 23, 1756

It having been represent[d] to me that there is a Considerable Inconvenience attending the Company under your Scouting to the Westward of Kennebeck River and Cap[t] Nicholss C[o] to the Eastward as are obliged to March a Number of Miles before they come to the Bounds in which they are to Scout I therefore direct you for the Future to Scout between Fort Shirley and Amariscoggin River

I am Your Friend & Serv[t]

S P

Letter, L[t] Gov. Phips to Capt. A. Nickels J[r]

Cap[t] Alex[r] Nickels jun[r]

Boston July 23, 1756

Upon Application made to me by a Number of Soldiers in the Scouting Comp[a] under your Command in the Eastern Frontier I have issued my Orders to Cap[t] Samuel Goodwin to Scout with his Company between Fort Shirley and Amariscoggen River and do direct you for the future to Scout between Fort Shirley and Damariscotta River

I am Your Friend and Servt

S P.

Letter, Enoch Freeman to Lt Gov. Phips

Falmouth July 26th 1756

Sir

I have made it my Business to look into the Situation of the Scouting Companies in my District and instead of Scouting in their old Tracts, have orderd them i e ye Captains to divide their Companies into small Parties and ambush ye most likely Places round ye Most expos'd Fields when the Inhabitants are at work; that their Ambushm^{ts} go out in the Night, and place themselves to ye best Advantage, without being Discover'd by the Enemy & there lay till Noon next Day, that if there shou'd be any Indians lurking about Endeavouring to get a Shot at our People in such Fields they must unavoidably fall into the hands of our Ambushes, and I am persuaded if that shou'd be the Case, once or twice, it would stricke such a panick into the Indians in general, that we should hardly ever hear of 'em again in that Manner on our Frontiers; and I hope the Method will meet with your Honour's Approbation.—

I dont learn there has been any late Discovery of the Enemy this Way, & am persuaded, the numbers of men, we sent into the Woods, on their first Arival, and having the Brush with 'em at New Marblehead &c. Occasion'd them to draw off.

And agreable to ye vote of ye General Court I have taken the best Advice I can, as to placing the Stores and it being agreed on all Hands, that it wou'd be most convenient for y^{e}

Stores for Cap[t] Berrys Company to be plac'd at Gorhamtown, I recommended it to M[r] Wheelwright the Commissary General, Accordingly; but he declines doing it, and writes to his Sub-Commissary here to consult Capt[a] Berry, to know if it would be best &c. and I shou'd be glad to know whether the Court will Insist on their Vote being Comply'd with or not, I appeal to every one, that it is the most Convenient Place; and unless the Commissary is oblig'd to Obey y[e] Orders of the Court, it seems in vain for them to come into any Resolves about the Stores, or for Your Honour to appoint Officers to put the Orders of Court into Execution; and this I thought Necessary Your Honour shou'd be acquainted with, lest Mischief being done while the Soldiers were gone to fetch their Allowance, the Blame shou'd lay upon me that the Stores were not sent to the most convenient Place &c.

The ten Garrison Soldiers at Hobs & Pearson Town, for want of Money, are destitute of Ammunition, & being desir'd to acquaint Your Honour with it, beg Leave to recommend it as convenient if not necessary, that the Commissary be directed to Supply them with a Suitable Quantity, either on the Province Charge, or to be deducted out of their Wages.

I am Your Honour's Most Dutifull & Obed[t] hum[l] Servt

Enoch Freeman

The Hon[l] Spencer Phips Esq Lieut[t] Gov[r] &c[ra]

Letter Enoch Freeman to L[t] Gov. Phips

Falmouth Aug[t] 6th 1756

Sir

I have a pretty good Accô from Hunters & Captives that Amascoggin River is passable with Whaleboats for above a hundred Miles about NorthWest towards Canady and that the upper Part of s[d] River, & between said River and the Western Branch of Kennebeck River whereon stands New Noridgewalk is the constant Hunting Ground of the Indians, and the way y[e] french Indians take to come down on our Frontiers, and as some of the Soldiers in the Scouting Companies, are desirous of proceeding up said Amascoggin with Whale Boats to carry Provisions, as far as they can, & then to take their Packs & range that Part of the Country whereby they Apprehend they will stand a good Chance of not only destroying some of the Enemy, but of Surprizing them in such a Manner, as will prevent their Scouts coming down upon us again this Fall, & also of making a good Discovery of the Rivers Ponds &c so far back, which may be of Service to facilitate some greater Design against the Enemy, y[e] Government may hereafter form against them, and it is my Opinion four whaleboats will be necessary, which will carry 13 men Each & their Stores; two whaleboats y[e] Goverm[t] have already, in May Sessions, granted, tho' not yet come down; and I wou'd beg Leave to desire (if your Honour approves of the Design) to recommend to y[e] Court, their furnishing two more, either by their being purchas'd here or sent down from Boston, where I beleive they may be had cheapest, in Case it may be done in Season, that is in three Weeks from this Date, or thereabouts, for by that Time it seems they ought to set out; Cap[t] Berry & Cap[t] Smith offer to go on this Rout, One or both, as your Honour shall think best, and I am persuaded their going will have a good Effect.

I submit y[e] whole Affair &c & am,

Your Honour's most Dutifull & Obedient Serv[t]

Enoch Freeman

To Hon[ble] Spencer Phips Esq. Lieut[t] Govern[r] & Commander in Chiefe &c

Message.

Gentlemen of the Council and House of Representatives.

This accompanies a Letter I rec^{d} from his Excellency Governor Lawrence concerning the Return of the French Inhabitants of Nova Scotia lately sent from thence and dispersed among the English Colonies representing the Pernicious Consequences of it. W^{ch} are so clearly set forth in his Letter that I need add Nothing on that Subject; Except that, as I shall soon return to Great Britain nothing shall be wanting on my part to represent what you shall do for prevent^{g} this Evil, to his Majestys Ministers in such a light as may I hope, induce his Majesty to have a favourable Consideration of it.

W Shirley

Council Chamber August 16, 1756

Letter, Gov. Shirley to Maj. E. Freeman

Boston August 26, 1756

Sir,

Agreeable to your Motion for a Scout going up Ameriscoggin River in Whale Boats, the Gen^{ll} Court have ordered that Whale boats should be provided for that Service;

And I do hereby desire & direct you as soon as you shall have the Boats to take effectual Care, that the s^{d} Scout (to consist of the most suitable Persons) be sent up the River of Ameriscoggin to pursue the Affair according to your own Scheme —

I am Sir, Your assured Friend and Servant

W Shirley

To Maj^{r} Enoch Freeman

Message.

Gentlemen of the Council & House of Represent^{ves}

I herewith send you the Petition of Captain William Lithgow Commander of Fort Hallifax, to this Court, which appears to me so seasonable, that I must earnestly recommend it to you to make him an allowance suitable to the extraordinary Services he hath set forth in it, for I think it by no means safe for so good an Officer and one in so important a Post to want proper Encouragement; And therefore desire you Gentlemen of the House of Repres^{ves} to make Provision accordingly.

W Shirley

Province House August 26, 1756

Message. Aug. 27, 1756.

Gentlemen of the House of Represent^{ves}

I must put you mind, "that in April last the General Court "Voted the Discharge of those Soldiers, who had serv'd "upwards of one Year at Fort Halifax under the Command "of Cpt^{n} Wm Lithgow, and that he was directed by the "Lieuten^{t} Govr to give him an Account of such Soldiers as "were intitled to their Discharge by Virtue of said Vote, "which he informs me he did; But that the Court hath done "nothing yet for their Dismission;" and he apprehends — Soldiers will be very uneasy, and fears many of them will depart, & possibly go off forcibly, as some have already threatned (if they should not be discharg'd) which would indanger the Loss of the Fort:

I must therefore desire you, Gentlemen of the House of Represent^{ves} that you would forthwith take this Matter under your Consideration, and make such Provision on your Part as the Honour of the Government, the Safety of that

Fortress, & Compassion and Justice to the poor men detained against their Will, and not agreably to the publick Faith, requires; and if there be not a sufficient Bounty granted for such as may inlist, I must have Resort to the only Method in Reserve, which is to issue my Warrants for impressing a Number of Men for the Discharge of such as are intitled to it.

W Shirley

Province House Aug[t] 27, 1756.

Message. "Sept[r] 7, 1756."

Gentlemen of the House of Representatives,

The Secretary will lay before you a Letter which I received by the last Post, from Sir W[m] Pepperrell; Wherein you will find (among other Representations of the exposed Condition of the Eastern Frontiers) he informs me that he apprehends, from the Indians Lurking about that Frontier, that Fort Halifax and Fort Western are in great danger of falling into the Enemies Hands.

Gentlemen, I desire you would consider the unavoidable Consequence of such an Event if it should happen, and that you would do your Part to prevent it, by providing for my strengthning the Garrisons there without delay.

I must desire, Gentlemen, that you would keep your House together till the publick Business of the Province be dispatched.

W Shirley

Vote.

In the House of Representatives, Sept[r] 9, 1756 Voted, That his Excellency the Govern[r] be desired to give orders, to some suitable number of men, not exceeding fifteen in the whole, to be one Company or more as shall be Judged best to discover by actual observation on the spot the distance & quality of the way from the head of Kenebeck River, the nearest practicable way to the head of Chaudier & by or near Chaudier, down to the River St Lawrence & make report to this Court with an exact Journal on oath of their proceedings containing an acco^t^ of each days doings, with every observable occurrent tending to give a good knowledge of that way to Canada, to be laid before this Court by the 25th day of November next, to be paid Each Man at the Rate of Six Dollars per week, they providing wholly for themselves, [and] they going down on or near Chandier to the mouth of that River, unless prevented by some unavoidable obstruction, one weeks pay to be advanced by the Province Treasurer to them, at their setting out. And As a further Encouragement, they shall be entituled to the full preemium for Prisoners & scalps

Sent up for concurrence T. Hubbard Spk^r^

In Council Sepr 11, 1756 — Read & Concur'd

Thos Clarke Dp^ty^ Secry

Consented to W Shirley.

To the Hon Sr Wm Peperel B^t^ & Saml Waldo Junr Esqr

The Great & General Court having made Provision for Transport Vessels to carry the Men rais'd in ye County of York to Albany by Water, I do hereby Authorize & Appoint You to take up & agree for Vessels for the said purpose allowing one Ton & a quarter for each Person.

As ye Service is attended with little difficulty & little Risque I do expect that ye Price of ye Hire of ye Vessels be accordingly.

If the Vessels when loaded draw more than six feet _ Water

there will be great Risque of their getting up to Albany; You will therefore conduct yourselves accordingly.

I do further recommend it to You to hire them for ye Voyage rather than by ye Month as that may prevent delays, but if you think it will be cheaper and will not be occasion of such delays to hire the Vessels by ye week or month You may use your discretion.

Merryconege Neck, Petition

To His Excellency, William Shirley Esq. Capt Genl Governour, & Commander In Cheif: The Honble his Majesties Council: and House of representatives —

The Petition of the Inhabitants Settled on Merryconeege Neck Humbly Sheweth y^{t} their are Settled on s^{d} Neck to the Number of Sixty Families, & Upw^{ds}: who are Embodied In A Church State; and have regularly Ordained A Minister of ye Gospel, to our General Satisfaction: under, this hopefull prospect the Inhabitants on s^{d} Neck, w^{ld} be Greatly Increased: If this Honble Court would Please to Encouridge s^{d} Infant Settlement. for wch Purpose, we Humbly ask Leave to represent to you, our Present Difficulties; y^{t} we may be remedied; as, You In Y^{r} great Wisdom Shall Seem Meet The Extent of said Neck of Land: Being about Ten Miles: and in many Places not above a Mile wide; the Uper Part Adjoyns the Township of Brunswick: and is not Included In the Bounds of Any Town: But ye Lower half of s^{d} Neck; by the Large Extent of North Yarmouth. South East Line not Included within the bounds of N^{o} Yarmouth at which place they have for many years Past, been Subject to many Inconveniencies, with respect to as to any Town priviledges: we are not Capable of receiving the Least Benefitt & advantage, on Many Accounts and by Reason, of the great distance, Either by Land or Water. of wch Hardships, and Great Difficulties ye Ihabitants on sd Neck, have for many Years Complained, and, this Hond Court; In their Great goodness Some few Yrs since; was Pleased to ease them in Part, on Account of the Ministry, and sett us off as A Precinct: But ye other Hardship remains A Grevious Burden on us to this Day: Wherefore yr Petitioners, Being Now Arrived to a Competent Number, and daily Increasing; Bt find themselves Incumbered wth the Burden of Paying Taxes to ye town of No Yarth more than our Proportion most Humbly Address this Hond Court, for ye remedy thereof: and for the Encouragement of the Gospel settled Among us; yt ye whole of sd Neck of Land; togeather with ye Islands Belonging to ye Precinct May be Incorporated into A seperate Township, or District and vested with the powers, & Privilidges Enjoyed by other Towns. all wch is Humbly Submitted, to ye wisdom & Justice of this Hond Court, and we Yr Humble Petitioners, as, in Duty Bound; shall Ever pray

David Curtis Lemll Turner Jonathan Flint William Alexander Alexr Willson Henry McCausling	Committee chosen by ye Precinct to Act In this Affair

The Inhabitants on Aforsd Neck Being Desirous of the good Welfare, and Increase of the Place, Most humbly Beg of this Hond Court to grant us a Penny Tax upon the Dormant Land Belonging To the Precinct; In ordr for the Defraying of Charges among us: Gent, The parish is Bt A New Settlemt, and their are many Opinionists* Settled among us wch is a Great Damage to ye Parish; and we have Been at very Great Charges of late respecting Some Publick Affairs and those Oppionist will not in ye Least Strive for ye Promotion of sd Parish; or in ye least to Pay Prect Charges. This and wt ever Else we have offered is wholly submitted to ye Wisdom, & Justice of this Hon^d Court; we y^r Humble Petitioners as In Duty Bound Shall ever Pray.

	David Curtis	Comm^tt
	Lem^ll Turner	
*Quakers	Jonathan Flint	to Act
	William Alexander	
	Alex^r Willson	In this
	Henry McCausling	Affair

P. S. The Inhabitants of s^d Neck Desired to be Incorporated into a Sepperate Township by ye first prec^t In ye Town of N^o yarmouth and Sett them of_ free & clear from Any Charges Paying to them wch they refused to grant us (wch You May please to see In ye Coppy of N^o yarmouth Vote) wch we think is A great Abuse to this sec^d Parish: Gen^t we ye Inhabitants of ye Sec^d prec^t are Oblidged to Help Maintain ye County Road B^t here is ye Case. Y^e County road of N^o yar^th & Town Road is one & ye same and we think is Injustice for to help Maintain, Considering we have no Benefit in ye Least Either of ye County or Town road For our whole Passing is by Water.

In the House of Rep^ves Octr 13. 1756

Read and Ordered that the Pet^rs serve the Town Clerk of North Yarmouth with a Copy of this Pet^n that so the said Town may shew cause (if any they have on the second thirsday of the next sitting of this Court why the Prayer thereof should not be granted

Sent up for concurrence T Hubbard Spk^r

In Council April 23. 1757. Read and Ordered

That the consideration of this Petition be referred to the second Wednesday of the next May Session.

Sent down for concurrence A Oliver Sec^r

In the House of Rep^rs April 23. 1757.

Read and Concurred

T Hubbard Spk^r

In Council June 14th 1757 Read together with the Answer of the Town of North Yarmouth and Ordered that Richard Cutts Esqr with such as the Honble House shall join be a Committee to hear the Parties, consider of the Affair and report what they judge proper for this Court to do thereon: And that the Parties appear for that Purpose on the second Friday of the next Sitting. Sent down for Concurrence

Thos Clarke Dpty Secry

In the House of Reprs June 14. 1757

Read and Concurred, and Mr Sparhawk and Mr Bradbury are joined in the Affair

T Hubbard Spkr

Decr 2: 1757. Voted yt Mr Flucker be of ye abovesaid Comtee in ye room of Mr Sparhawk who is absent.

Letter, Lt Gov. Phips to Maj. Freeman

Boston Octr 26, 1756

Sir,

I herewith send you a Copy of a Vote of the Genl Court for a March of 150 Men to the Indians Hunting Grounds between the Eastern Frontiers & Canada, with a Set of Commissions for three Companies for this Services, which I leave to you to fill up with the names of such as shall be willing to undertake this Service & most suitable for it, giving Preference to such Officers now in the Service or your Frontier, as are best qualified.

You must use all Care & Diligence that this Service may be promoted & forwarded that the several Companies be furnished with all necessaries for rendering the same more easy & succesful & Let as many good Men be inlisted out of the Soldiers to be dismiss'd as may be obtained: You must give the Commanders such particular Orders as you shall find requisite consistent with my Instructions to them

I am Sir Your Assured Friend & Serv[t]

S P.

Maj[r] Freeman

Letter, L[t] Gov Phips to Cap[t] Freeman and others.

Boston October 26. 1756

Sir,

I hereby direct you to dismiss [one of] the Scouting Company under your command upon the first Day of Novem[r] next, or as soon after as this Order shall come to your Hand, first allowing them to inlist into the Marching Service under such Officers as I shall appoint & upon such advantageous terms as shall be proposed; And the other Half of your Company you must retain in the Service & employ them in the same duty as heretofore until the 20th Day of Novem. w[n] they are to be dismissed unless you shall receive my Orders or some extraordinary Danger necessarily require their Continuance in the Service for the Defence of the Inhabitants.

I am Your Assured Friend & Servant

S P

that part of the above Letter with a Line drawn under it except what is Contained in the Crotchet was sent to Cap[ts] Gerrish Berry Smith and Goodwin
Cpt. Freeman & Cpt. Nichols

Letter, Enoch Freeman to L[t] Gov. Phips

Falmouth Nov[r] 1st 1756

Sir

Cap[t] Berry is return'd from his Rout up Amascoggin River, he took the Courses & Distances of y[e] River for about

Eighty five Miles up, & there the River is also as below, large and about twenty Rods Wide, which makes him beleive he did not go near the Head of it, but the Water being very low in the Rivers this Season of the Year, there was so many Riflens, that retarded his course, and he was oblig'd to return; he went about fifteen or twenty Miles above a Place call'd Rockomeekook, an old large Indian Settlement some hundreds of Acres of clear'd Land, & great Quantities of rich Intervale, from thence all the way down to Brunswick, is a fine Country for Land, many beautifull levell Islands of good Land in the River, but I cant describe it so well as by a Plan of the River &c which I am about getting Done & shall send it to Your Honour —

Several Captains of y[e] Scouting Companies, have asked me when they must dismiss their men I told 'em the first of November they Expected, they said, to have orders for doing it, I told them it was voted, and I look'd for the Orders every Moment; And as y[e] Season of the Year Advances, Your Honour will hasten down as soon as possible Orders respecting y[e] Inlisting y[e] 150 men to Scout this Fall; I wou'd propose their being divided into five Companies of thirty men Each; and I purpose to send one up y[e] Western Branch of Kenebeck, One over to Chaudier River, One to the Head of Amascoggin, One to the Head of Saco, and One from Berwick to find y[e] Head of Connecticut River, if Your Honour likes the Scheme; so that it will be necessary, there should be five sets of Blank Commissions sent down, with listing Orders, & the Sooner y[e] better and also that y[e] Commissary General send me y[e] Snow shoes for the men, if he has 'em by him, if not that he or some other Person, get 'em made Immediately, I cou'd get a good many here, I shou'd Esteem also y[t] a Copy of y[e] vote of Court and Your Honours Directions which I shall take a Pleasure in Executing in y[e] best Manner possible and doubt not some Discovery will be made &c that will compensate ye Charge, and I am very sure it wou'd be worth while for ye Goverment to be at ye Charge of a good Surveyor to go with Each Partie, & hope Your Honour will give Orders accordingly —

I am Your Honour's Obed^t^ humb^l^ Servt

Enoch Freeman

Honble Spencer Phips Esqr Lieut^t^ Govr &c

Letter, John Greenleaf to Lt Gov. Phips

Newbury Novr 2^d^ 1756

May itt Please y^r^ Hon^r^

I Receved Orders Sometime past to inlist Men for to Reinforce Generall Winslow or to March for the Assistance of ye Frontiers if Either should be attacked.

I find the People in Generall backward to inlist As itt is late in the fall & wee have News from time to time of Our forcess returning home — Many of the Hampshire forcess as well some of Our Own I am informed Are Already returned & more upon their March Home — I have Notwithstanding Ordered Severall of my Captains to be in readiness in Case of an Attack on Any of Our frontiers &c & trust there will A Considerable Number be ready to March immediately if Occasion should Call Although att this Day Our Meen Are Exceedingly drained of.

I am with the Greatest Respect

y^r^ Hon^rs^ Most Obed^t^ Humb^l^ Servt

John Greenleaf

Letter, Jabez Bradbury to Josiah Willard Secy Novr 23^d^ 1756

Honner^d^ Sir

It was Surprising to me that Jest at the Governors going of, or perhaps after he was gon, (by filling up a blank) there should a Commission be Sent here to one Mr Burton to be my Lieu^{t} when the Governor had so freely told Mr. Fletcher he Should Sertainly return to his post, as L^{t} when his marching Company were dismist, and he realy did so; otherwise he wou^{d} not have taken a Commission for marching in the woods. he is a Sober Sencable man, one that may be Confided in, (has bin the L^{t} here almost Seven year,) I wish I Could Say as much of Mr Burton but.—

I should take it as a very great favor if your honnor would prevail with the Lt Governor to give Mr. Fletcher a Commission for this Garrison as formerly, and if Mr. Burton must be again helpt by the Govr^{t} that it may be at som other place & not here, for I shall not think, my own affairs here, safe if at any time I should Leave the Fort, as I shall be oblig^{d} to do, if I Live till the Spring, my business then Calling me to Boston. I now intreet your Honnors Excuse for troubleing you with this, and subscribe my self your Honnors

Most Obedient Humble Servt

Jabez Bradbury

St Georges Novr 23^{d} 1756

P. S for Every Day m^{r} Burton has Serv^{d} the Government, I am Suer Mr. Fletcher has Serv^{d} them Ten.

Am as above J. B

[Superscribed]
To the Honnorable Josiah Willard Esqr
att Boston by Capt Sanders

Letter, John Rous to Lt Gov. Phips 17 Dec. 1756.

Sir

Upon my Arrival here from Casco Bay I found Commodore Holmes had saild for England with several other Ships, leaving behind him only the Nottingham of 60 Guns, & the Baltimore & Vulture Sloops, which with the Success is all the strength here at present & which I intend shall be got ready for the Sea as early in the Spring as the season will admit —

I have just receiv'd intelligence of one or two small French privateers cruising to the Westward of this Harbour to intercept our provision Vessells & as his Majestys Ships are not in a Capacity to cruise in the Winter season, I have taken a Large Schooner belonging to the Town, Mann'd and Arm'd her with twelve Carriage Guns & 100 Men, which I intend to keep cruising to protect the Trade till some of the Ships can be got ready; I shall be oblig'd to you for what ever Intelligence relating to the Enemy you may have & will always be ready to Join with you in doing every thing that may be thought for the good of his Majestys Service —

I am Sir Your most Obedient & most Hum^l Servt

John Rous

Success in Halifax Harbour.

17th December 1756

The Honble Spencer Phips Esqr

We the Subscribers do hereby Certify that We Severaly Served his Majesty in the Years Expeditions and under the Command of those Set against our respective Names Viz^{t}—

Persons Names	Year	what Expedition		Name of the Commander
Stephen Jones	1757	[illegible]own point	Col John Frye	[illegible]t Ebenezer Leonard
Isaiah Foster	60	Canda		Capt [illegible]hl Engersol
Arthur Dillaway	61	Canada	Col Hoar	Capt James Saward
Benja	59	Crown point		Major Rogers
Jones Dyer	59	Crown point		Major Rogers
Benja Foster Jur	58	Crown point	Col Pebble	Capt John Libby
Morris Obrion	45	Louisbourg	Sir William Peperil	Capt Peter Staples
John Crocker	58	Crownpoint	Col Pebble	Cap James Gowing
Enoch Sanborn	4–	Louisbourg	Col More	Capt Edward Williams
Isaac Larrabee	55	Kennebeck		Capt John Lane
Sivanus Scott	55	Kennebeck		Capt Joseph Engersol
James Dillaway	60	Canada	Col Engersol	Capt Johnson Molton
Daniel Hill	58	Crown Point	Col Pebble	Capt John Libby
Ephraim Andrews	47	Cannada	Col Noble	Capt [illegible]as Perkins
Saml Kenny	56	Crown point	Col Dwight	Capt John Lane
Ezekiel Foster	58	Crown point	Col Pebble	Capt John Libby
Joseph Munson	45	Louisbourg	on Board His Majesty Ship Laybeme Capt Gayton	
Bartholomew Bryant	58	Crown point	Col Pebble	Capt John [illegible]bby
Joseph Getchel	58	Crown point	Col Pebble	Capt John Libby
[illegible]d Jones	45	Louisbourg		[illegible]er of a Hospital Vessell
John Bohannan	1759, 60	[illegible]ec		Admiral [illegible]ders & Lord
James Horn	1759, 60			Colvil —

Letter, Sir Wm Pepperrell to Lt Gov. Phips

Sir

As I came here this day am inform[d] that the hundred & fifty men were gone out from this County agreable to your Honours Orders to See what Discovery they could make on the Indians hunting ground & that there design was when they got there to Divide into Several Scouts and on their return some was to goo so far westward as the back of the Town above Berwick: if this is matter of Fact w[ch] I shall as Soon as Possiable make inquirey into it will answer the End that y[e] hundred Men would do that you gave me orders to raise; & Save y[e] Province that charge; and if Your Hon[r] would be pleased upon their return to send your orders that one hundred of them be Divided into foure Quoties to Scout above the heads of Each Town in this County untill the tenth day of April next it might answer the design of the last Vote of the General Court for the hundred men, this I tho[t] it my Duty to let you Know and shall wait for further Orders w[ch] shall be Strictly observed.

I am now sending out yo[r] orders to inlist Sixty Eight men belonging to this Regiment and I hope the Second Regiment in this County will soon inlist the same number of good men w[ch] will be much better then an impress, for the name of an impress here will drive the Young able body[d] men great part of them out of this County to Sea or into the Province of New Hampshire as it did the last year and you are Senceable that this County lays much Exposed to the Enemy both by Land & Sea.

I shall give out your promise that the officers where no Objection can be made that are recommend[d] to your Hon[r] from hence you will Commission them as there is one hundred & thirty six men to be rais'd in this County I hope you will reserve to command them one Cap[t] three Lieu[ts] & one Ensign —

I am with much Esteem Sir

Your Hon[rs] Faithfull and Most obed[t] Humble Servant

W[m] Pepperrell

Kittery March 3[d] 1757

Letter, Sir W[m] Pepperrell to L[t] Gov. Phips

Sir

Your Honours favour of the 9th ins[t] I received, as to the hundred & fifty men heretofore order[d] out upon the Eastern Frontiers, if they return before the 10th of April next Your orders shall be Strictly Observed.

and as to send your Honour a particular acco[t] of the Shipping in y[e] harbours in this County by this Express that are fit for Transports at this time is not in my power, but by what inquirey I could within time make there is in Berwick a Brig[a] of one hundred & thirty Tuns one Deck & half & a Single deck Sloop of about one hundred Tuns.

in the Town of Kittery two Single Deck Vesels of about Sixty Tuns another of about Eightty a new Schoner fited for y[e] Sea of one Deck & half of about ninety Tuns.

in York Seven Single Deck Sloops from about Eighty to ninety Tuns Each a Schoner of about one hundred & thirty and in Wells two Single Deck[d] Vesels of about Ninety Tuns Each in Arrundel two more of the Same Burthen, in Bediford the Same number, in Scarborough the same number, in Falmouth I am not certain but I beleive as many as in all the rest of the County

I am Sir Your Honours Most Obed[t] Humble Serv[t]

W[m] Pepperrell

Letter, Capt. Wm Lithgow to Lt. Gov Phips March 15, 1757

May it Please your Honour

the Spring being near att Hand In which season it hase ben usual, and is the most Convenient Time for Supplying Fort Hallifax with Twelve months Provisions, and as I apprehend this Time of y[e] yeare generely to be attended with as Grate Dainger from either the French or Indian Enemy if not grater then any other Season of y[e] year, as then the Ponds & Rivers will be all Cleer of Ice, and Consiquently an easy Transportation for them in Birch Cannooes and also Good Hunting for Beaver or Inglish Inhabitence, all which I apprehend to be Inducement to Draw the Enemie towards our Frountiers, which I apprehend your Hon[r] Is not unsensible off —

therefor I would Humbely Intreet Your Hon[r] Supply us with such a guard and In such manner as your Honour may In wisdom Judge Sufficient for the above Sarvice all which I most Humbely Submitt to your Honours Wise Considderation —

what ever guard your Hon[r] Is pleased to order I would pray thay may be at Cusnock or y[e] Store house the middle of april at furthest as that Is y[e] most Suitable Time for y[e] above Sarvice. haveing nothing farther to advis your Hon[r] of at present then that y[e] Gerrison by y[e] Divine Goodness is Generaly In good Health &c[a] —

I humbely beg Leave to Subscribe my Selfe

Your Honours most obedient & most Humble Sarvent,—

William Lithgow

Fort Hallifax march y[e] 15th 1757

Letter, Ezkl Cushing to the Council

Falmouth April 12th, 1757

May it please your Honours

The enclos[d] accounts your Honours will see the one for

Stores for the Soldiers while here which I were oblig^{d} to gett for their Subsistance untill the Province sent for them, tho I had no orders from the Province so to do yet the Circumstances of the Soldiers here rais^{d} requiring it I hope it will be Look^{d} upon in such a Light as to vindicate me in so doing — The other account — Viz^{t} Capt Joshua Bangs's — I look upon it as a reasonable one Considering the Severity of the weather the most of the Time after the Soldiers were rais^{d} untill their embarkation for Boston — Such a Number of Soldiers in so severe a Season must certainly Consume a Considerable Quantity of wood — The family Utensils for Cooking among so many persons must be worth something the whole of His Trouble house room & all. as he has Desir^{d} me to mention it to your Honours will have that weight as that your Honours will Look upon his account just & reasonable & grant the same — I should have sent the account from the Commissary by the Vessel that Carried the Soldiers from hence to Boston, but could not gett it untill the Day after their Departure from hence —

Since beginning to write the above an account offers from Major Enoch Freeman as Comissary for four Blanketts rec^{d} by four of the Soldiers, as your Honours may See p^{r} the account enclos^{d} which hope will be allow^{d} The other paper is a List of the Soldiers enlisted & an account of what each person is entitled to agreeable to the proclamation as also what each person has rec^{d} —

I would here beg Leave to inform your Honours, that after the men had inlisted they would not upon any means be prevail^{d} upon to goe for Boston untill each had rec^{d} what Bounty they were entitled to according to the proclamation — what to Doe I could not tell — I had rec^{d} no money from the province to enable me to fullfill what the proclamation promis^{d} to those that should inlist, neither any orders for Drawing any money from the Collectors or Constables to enable me to pay the full Bounty I were oblig'd at Last rather than the province should Suffer by the men's rais'd not being Sent to boston, to get of the Collectors the several Sums your Honours will by the enclos[d] see & pay each person what is respectively sett against their names, before they would embark. I hope my Conduct in this affair as it Concerns the province will be Look[d] upon in a just Light, as that the Treasurer will answer the orders I drew upon him in favour of the Collectors who I rec[d] the money from —

I remain yours Honours most Obedient Serv[t] to Comand

Eze Cushing

Letter, The Council to Col. Ezkl Cushing

Boston 15 Apr[l] 1757 —

Col[o] Ezek[l] Cushing

S[r]

It appears that there is a deficiency of seven men in the number you were directed to raise for his Majestys Service under the Command of the Earl of Loudoun. The council expect that you immediately compleat the number of Men assigned You and send them up to Boston. And as the Council are informed that five of the afores[d] Men were to be raised by Cap[n] Alex[r] Nichols, and that he is wholly deficient in his duty, they have directed him to come up to Boston to Answer for his neglect. The order comes to you open, that in case he shall have complied with his Orders before this reaches your hands, and you shall be satisfied with his Conduct, you may forbear delivering the said Letter, and send it back with your next return.

Letter, The Council to Capt. Alex[r] Nichols

Boston 15 Apr[l] 1757.

Cap[n] Alex[r] Nichols

The Council being informed that you was ordered to raise

five Men for his Majesty's Service under the Command of the Earl of Loudoun, and that you have wholly disregarded your Orders and returned none of the Men assigned You.

The Council direct you forthwith to attend them at Boston to make Answer for your Neglect.

Letter, Benj. Burton to the Council. April 15, 1757

May it please your Honours, This morning about Eight of the clock there appeared at a small Distance from the fort four Indians with a flag of Truce, Three of which being Penobscut's, the other a St John's we hoisted one in the fort and then they came in, Asked me by the Interpreter if there was any answer come to their Letter Sent up this winter to the Govr I told – there was no positive answer come as yet, Only what was Contained in a letter I had received lately Sent by the Govr to Capn Bradbury, wherein he gives his Opinion "That he did not see how they open a trade with them at presant. But if the Indians would come and live amongst us That he did not doubt but that the Court would make provision for them during the war," To which they replyed, they could give No Answer till they talked with their Old men, I told them if they desired to live in peace with us they must come in directly for our Scouts would be out, and could not distinguish them from other Indians, They said that was true, and promised me to be in Ten or fifteen days hence at farthest, with a full answer from their tribe ——

I then asked them if they thought themselves safe to come and trade with us here when our Scouts were out after other Indians They said No, ——

After they went Out of the room, One being the St John's Indian Came in – told me by the Interpreter Aduakinque's

Brother was comeing on us with Ten more Ind[s] so soon as the Snow was off the ground or at farthest in One moon I asked him if the penubscutts would Joyn said Number he said he could not tell how presants might prevail on them, and that he did not know but that a large body would come, To this he held up his hand and said God knows it to be true, true, true, Beg'd not to let the other Indians know what he has told us for they certainly would cutt off his head, they would surely kill him if they found he had told us. This is what has been delivered me from the Interp[r] as he can attest to the truth of the above:

I remain your Honours most obedient & faithfull ser[vt] to Command

Benj[a] Burton

Fort S[t] Georges April 15th 1757.

P S The above S[t] Johns Indian told me further that there was a Great body of French Lived all this winter up S[t] Johns River

Letter, Andrew Oliver to Col. Cushing & Major Freeman

Boston April 28, 1757.

Sirs,

I send you by directions of the Council Extract of a Letter which come to hand yesterday from Lieutenant Burton.

You will judge what Credit is to be given to the Indians Account; the Council think it ought to carry so much weight at least, as to put the Inhabitants of the Eastern Country upon their Guard: they therefore direct that you send the Intelligence across Maquoit to some proper person to be handed along from place to place till it shall reach Fort Halifax, and to such other places as you shall judge requisite.

If this should overtake Major Freeman on the Road homeward, so as to give him opportunity of conferring with Sir William Pepperrell it would be best to consult with Sir William upon measures proper to be taken on this Occasion.

I am Sir Your hum^l Sert

And^w Oliver

Col^o Ezekiel Cushing
Major Enoch Freeman

Letter, Andrew Oliver to Sr Wm Pepperrell

Boston 28 April 1757.

Sir

The Council yesterday received a Letter from Lt Burton dated Fort St Georges April 15 and by their direction I send you copy of the essential part of his Letter under cover herewith; Whether full credit is to be given or not to the Indians relation yet the Council judge it a sufficient Ground for them to proceed to notify the Inhabitants of the Eastern Country of the Intelligence received so that they may be on their Guard.

You will therefore S^r be pleased to take the most proper measures for this purpose.

the express has another Letter for Col^o Cushing and Major Freeman, which the council desire you would order to be sent forward by Express or by any other as you shall judge best, they are directed to send the Intelligence across Maquoit so as to be handed along from Place to Place till it shall reach Fort Halifax. If you should see Major Freeman after receipt hereof upon his Return home, you will please to give him best Advice for his Government

I am Sr Your most Ob^t humb Servt

And^w Oliver

Letter, Sir Wm Pepperrell to the Council

Kittery May 2^d^ 1757

Honourable Gentlemen

The inclosed Letter came to me by Express from Hampton, wch I have paid for.

I take it to be an answer to a Letter I sign^d^ as president by order of the Council when I was in Boston ever Since I have been from thence, have been indeavoring to get the Front^rs^ in a post^r^ of Defence, as I expect soon to heare of the Enemy. I wish your Hon^rs^ would hasten the Commissary to send Provishon for the Marching Scouts that they may be upon Duty. I am this day about Delivering some out to Capt Gerrishes Companny out of my wharehouse that he may be on the back of ye Towns to prevent the Enemy doing damage and I hope will destroy some of them

I have the Hon^r^ to be Your Hon^rs^

Most obedient Faithfull Humble Servant

Wm Pepperrell

The Honble His Majesty's Council

Letter, C. C. Leissner to Sr Wm Pepperrell

Broad Bay May 9th 1757

Honble Sir

I beg Leave to sent Your Hon^r^ inClosed a Copy of my Journall what Trouble and Barbarety hapned since my Last.

A Waile Boat would be a most Necessary thing for this place, as I can't come to the Assistance of the inhabitants on each Side of the river, with out going round the Falls wch will take near a Day should therefore be Glad if Your Hon^r^ would please to Order One

Scarceness of time Obliges me to breake of so

Subscribe my self Your Hon^rs^ most Submisfull Servt

C. C. Leissner

P. S. I have as yet no Orders how to Act with the Men but in the mean while do the best I can.

[Superscribed.]

On his Majestys Service To Sir William Pepprill Kn^t^
p^r^ Capt Kent att Boston

*Letter, Col. Ezkl Cushing to Andrew Oliver Sec^y^*

Falmouth May 10 1757

Sr Having lately rec^d^ the Goverments Orders to Compleat Seven men more for His Majestys Service accordingly have Compleated the number including one man Capt Nichols Sent to Boston out of the Quota assign'd him to raise the remainder of his s^d^ Quota he Dl^d^ to me in Falmouth which I hope will be sufficient to excuse his not coming to Boston as he has Compleated the number assigned him to raise — just as I were embarking of the men to Send to the goverment one of them Deserted I cannot here nor find any thing of him so as to Ship him on board of Capt Hodgkins — with the other men rais^d^ neither is it possible to gett another man in the Deserters room to Ship on board of Capt Hodgkins by reason of his so Sudden Departure. I shall use my utmost endeavours immediately to find & send the man to the Government. S^r^ I cannot find by the List I have by me of the Number assign^d^ me to raise how seven Should be wanting I Sent fivety nine men by my Son one p^r^ Capt. Cox & three went by Land. is Sixty three men & the Quota assign^d^ me being Sixty Eight I rest this matter with your Honour —
& am S^r^ your most Humble Servt

Eze Cushing

A List of the Mens Names Shipt on board Capt Hodgkins for His Majestys Service —
inlisted March 21. 1757 Cornelius Keff —
impress^d^ Benjamin Parker in room of an impress^d^ man

David Welch Ditto James Braman Ditto Samuel Green — Ditto

The above Cornelius Heff rec^{d} a fall that hinder^{d} his being to Boston before this opportunity. Loring Cushing in behalf of my father Ezekiel Cushing

[Superscribed]

To The Honourable Andrew Oliver Esqr
Secretary of The Province of Massachusetts Bay ~

Letter, J. Tasker & J. Fowle to A. Oliver Sec^{y}

Marblehead Wednesday Nine in ye Evening

Sir

This moment came in a Schooner intended for Boston, as a Flag of Truce from Louisbourg: wch place she left Eight days ago; commanded by Monsr Larchez having on board Seventy English Prisoners: & navigated by seven French men: a proper Guard shall be placed for their security till farther Orders. & ye most Intelligent of ye English sent up Early in ye Morning to Boston. no more than one Vessel by their Acco^{t} was arivd from France this Spring, the Garrison in a poor Condition the Soldiers & Inhabitants murmuring & in great Want of Provisions not one ship of Force there & few others. the News of the Attempt made on ye French King's Life created a generall Pannick.
these are ye particulars wch Time permit us to collect

We are wth great Regard Y^{r} most Obed^{t} Serv^{ts}
John Tasker
Jacob Fowle

P S:
we find they are Come for Observation, & that there is some Gent^{n} of Distinction on board
To the Secretary of ye Province to be communicated
to his Maj^{teys} Council.

Letter, John Tasker to A. Oliver, Sec^{y}

Marblehead Monday Morning

Sir

I Wrote you last Night by an Express acquainting you with the Arivall of a Flag of Truce. since which I have been on board & talk'd with Mr Larchez, ye Person Commissioned to treat with ye Governour of this Province to whom I think he told me _ had Letters, wch no doubt you'll be desirous to see that Lord Louden may as soon as may be acquainted wth his Errand. & what ever else may be thought of Use. I have conversd with sevrall of ye Prisoners & find one Bragdon capable to give Information of what is passing at Louisbourg, whom shall Instantly despatch that he may be at Boston as Soon as ye Council can be Assembled.

I am of Opinion it will be best y^{t} the Vessel be orderd from this Exposd Defenceless Harbour. and ye Commissioner who resided at Roxbury Seven Years ago & well Known to Mr Lovel & many others be sent up by Land.

wch Submit to your better Understanding & am

wth great Regard Sir Y^{r} most Obed^{t} Servt

John Tasker

To Andrew Oliver Esq to be communicated to his Maj^{tys} Council

Letter, John Osborne to Lord Loudoun

Boston 12. May 1757.

May it please your Lordship

The Council received very early this morning by Express from Marblehead an Account of the Arrival of a Flag of Truce in eight days from Louisbourgh.

As the Accounts from thence appear very favourable to

your Lordships designs We thought it our duty to transmit them immediately to your Lordship by Express, forwarding herewith copy of the Letter from Marblehead and what further information we could collect from One of the Prisoners who is just come to Town as declared before the Council. We shall give Orders for securing the French men, and their Vessell till we hear from your Lordship, and in the mean time treat them with that civility which is otherwise due to the Character they are come in.

We received Intelligence yesterday Noon of a Sloop about 25 Leagues to the Eastward of Cape Ann giving chace to a Vessell arrived at Marblehead, upon which the Council gave Orders for the Province Snow Prince of Wales Capt. Dowse to go out upon a Cruise after her; He slipt his Cables at 6 in the Evening having seventy five stout Seamen aboard, and has probably run the distance by this time, He is there to cruise twenty four hours, and if he makes no discovery, nor gains any further Intelligence he is then to return, and take the Fishermen and Vessells for Halifax under his Convoy.

One of our Vessells inward bound discover^{g} a Vessell ashore about 3 weeks ago on the Isle of Sables went to their Relief: it proved to be an Eng: prize Ship fr. Portugal having 13 Hands aboard which the French had taken off Virginia; the French Man secured the Vessell & her Crew which came to their Releif, and proceeded therewith for Louisbourgh, in their way thither they took another small Vessell, and having more English men aboard than they chose to trust themselves with, they put most of them aboard the last mentioned Vessell, which is since arrived at Cape Ann, but we have seen none of the People.

We are endeavouring that some of the Prisoners which came in the Flag of Truce shall proceed as Seamen in some of the Transports bound to New York that your Lordship may have the oportunity of gaining more direct Information —

We are with very great Respect

May it please your Lordship your Lordships

most obedient and most hum[l] Serv[ts]

I O in the name and by order of the Council. By this Express We send your Lordship the rest of the returns made Us, of the Troops of this Government, raised for his Majestys Service, Who are all Marched agreeable to your Lordships Directions.

Letter, Joshua Freeman to the Council.

S[t] Georges May 17 : 1757 —

Gentle[n]

May it Please your Honnors There Came in Yesterday Morning Frounteer Indians To Treat with Capt Bradbury under Awhite Flag —

what they had to say I understand he hass Acquainted y[r] Hon[s] About Three in the After Noon they went of with there flag About Foure a Clock Som of My Company Unbeknown to me went out after the Indians And Brought in One who they say they found Alone the rest being gone out of Sight And ass they found him alone And No Flag with him They Thought he wass a Lawfull prize. I Told them I did Not Approve of there Conduct in bringing the fellow back And that they must immediately let him go — And Accordingly After Som debate he wass Dismis'd And Care taken that he got of Clear —

Betwen Four And five A Clock there Came a Single indian in to the fort with a flag but Tarry'd but a few Minutes And

Went of with the Indian that wass brought back in the Evening Wm Killpatrick Came over from the fort And told that the Indian that Came in last Informd that there wass Twenty Six Indians belonged to there Company And that there wass Thirty More Expected in toMorrow but ass there was No Likelywhood of the Truck to be Opened to them they would be Stopt Upon which Our People Said that it wass likely the Indians would do dammage before they went of there being Such A number together And No Expectation of any Trade in the province which I thought Reasonable They Mentioned that they thought it wass Necessary that a Company of Men Should go out in the Night And Indeavour to Make all the Discovery they Could that the Indians Should Not have Any Advantage on Us Accordingly I Consented that Twenty Men Might go out And if they found their wass Any Indians Lurkeing About that they would send A man in And let Me know of it y^t we Mought be upon our guard And likewise Ready to Attack them —; Betwen Ten And Eleven a Clock Twenty of My Men went And about a Mild from the Block House they Came upon a party of Indians And Fird on them And Hussay'd the Indians Immediately Returnd the fire on both Sides of them And Yel'd After Exchainging Sundry Guns at Each Other Our People Came of with One Scalp which they Recovered haveing Rec^d but little Dammage on our Side one Man being Slightly wounded in the hand and his gun Part of the Stock fir'd of a little before break of Day our People went out again — Discoverd three Indians fird at them but Could not Recover any of them on there Return back to the Place where they had the dispute the last night they found Seven Gunns a Small Quantaty of Beavour Feathers

Am your Honners Most Obedient And verry Humble Servt

Joshua Freeman

To the Honnorable his Majestys Councill for the Province of the Massachusets Bay in New England

Letter, James Howard to the Council

Fort Western 18th May 1757

May it please y^r^ honours Capt Lithgow Sent down a boats Crew consisting of ten men as far as Brunswick to fetch up Lieu^t^ Moody in order to mend our Boats, and this morning about Seven o Clock Ensign Petee was returng home and we thought it best to Send two men by Land as an Advance Guard, and the other eight on the boat and when they were about Seven miles above the fort then the two men on the Shore who kept Just about three or four Rod before the Boat, Discover'd a Scout of Seventeen Indians Close on the Shore and fired on the Boat three times not being more than fifteen yards distance, and our people returnd the fire three times out of the boat and as they could not recover the Indians side of the River they put a cross the river recoverd that Shore a fired Several Guns, one of the men that were on the Shore Lept into the river and Swam across the river tho' the freshet is very high, and the other was Seen under a Root and we hope the enemy has not found him but he is not return'd yet it is now about two hours Since the action. There is two of our men wounded but I hope they are not mortal, all our people declare that they saw the Indians Carry off two dead or wounded of their own party.

I conclude with begging Leave to Subscribe myself y^r^ Honours most Hble Servt

James Howard

Letter, from Samuel Goodwin

Frankfort on Kennebeck River May ye 18th 1757

May it please your Honours ——

this day as Insigne Ezeekel Patte was agoeing from Fort Western to Fort Halifax in aboat with nine Men & himself he Put two Men ashoar as aGard and about 7 miles up from Fort Western those ashore Discovered a party of Indains of 17 which they Counted & howmany more they Cant say and being within 15 or 20 yards of them & y[e] Boat, those ashore Cryd out Indains Indains upon this y[e] Indains Rise and fiered on them in y[e] Boat our men Returned y[e] fire several times and suppose they Kell[d] or wounded two or more for they see them Carry away two on there backs. one of our men ashore Escaped by Sweeming over y[e] River y[e] other they Left under y[e] Bank wheather Deed or alive they Could not Tell, two in y[e] Boat was wounded, one of them hath abullet Lodged in his Leage & slightly wounded in several places in his body & head y[e] other in his Shoulder & Cheake Lieutenant John Howard Came here with them about 5 o Clock this afternoon, I haveing y[e] Remains of a Docters Box which I Gott Last year of my own; I Dressed them in the best Manner I Could ——

Gentelmen if y[e] People Could have Provision only to Sarve them while in y[e] woods I Could have a Number of men to Goe out on any Sudden Disturbance or ocation What Ever and the Expecttation of aNumber of Indains if not Frinch to fall on thease parts Give Great uneasseness to many and the People are Short of Provision in thease parts so they Could not Support themselves if obliged to Goe out I thought it my Duty to inform your Honours and with the Greatest Submission Begg leave to Subscribe myselfe your Honours Most Dutefull Most Obedaint and very Humble Sarvent

Samuel Goodwin

To There Honours His Majestys Council of the Province of the Massachssutts Bay

NB I have supply[d] y[e] sick and lame marching soldiers two years past with meadssons & if aDocters Box was to be Lodged here or any allowanc for what medeasons I have

Expended I might be of service to some who might meet with ye Lieke misfortin ——

Copy of record.

At a meeting of the freeholders & other Inhabitants of the Town of Northyarmouth Convened Held at the Meeting House in the first Parrish in s^d Town and Continued by adjournment from may ye 18th to May ye 24, 1756 The Petition of the Second Parrish (praying the consent of the first Parrish to be Set off a Separate District &c) being Read and Considered: and where as the Intrest of the s^d Second parrish may be advanced by their being Set of_ & Vested with ye privalages y^t Towns Do Enjoy &c: But the County Road Runing through the Town of Northyarmouth to Brunswick at a Considerable Distance from the Second Parrish which has been and Ever will be a very great Charge to the Town & too heavy a Burthen for the first Parrish alone and also the first is and must be at Vast Expence other than the County Road as to Roads to other Towns Setleing on the Back of them &c: from which Like Expence the second parrish is Ever Like to be freed being a narrow neck of Land and Islands adjoyning Therefore Voted That tho s^d Second Parrish Have the Consent of the first Parrish to be set off a seperate District agreeable only to the Boundaries of s^d Second Parrish, provided that they at all times bear their proportionable part of the Charge of the County Road and Bridges thereon.

A True Copey taken of_ from Northyarmouth Town Records and Examined

p^r Barnabas Seabury Town Clerk

Copy of record

At a Legal Meeting of the Inhabitants of the first Parrish in North Yarmouth on the thirteenth of December 1756 —

Voted that Jonas Mason Esqr Messr^s^ Andrew Gray and John Lewis be a Committee to draft an Answer to the Petition of the Inhabitants of Merriconeag Neck according to the General Courts order

Voted that Jer Powell Esqr be an Agent to Prefer said Answer to the Great and General Court

Voted that the Agent and the Charge of Prefering the Said answer be paid by the Parish — —

The above is a true Copy Transcrib^d^ from North Yarmouth First Parish Book of Records Fol^o^ 20

Att^r^ Thos Scales Parrish Clerk

North Yarmouth May 23^d^ 1757

Letter, Capt. Wm Lithgow to the Council

Fort Hallifax May ye 23^d^ 1757

may it please your Honours

these may Sarve Just to Informe that we have this Spring Boated up Stoors Sufficent for one year, for the Supplye of ye garrisson att this place - and that som Hunters In there Returne from Hunting heard a grate yaling of Indians five miles above this Fort. thay Supposed ye Number to be Considderable by the Noise the Indians made. - the aboves^d^ hunters left five of there Companions In ye Woods which they parted with Som Time before which Is Supposed to have fallen Into ye Indians Hands as thay have not yet Returned — we have Discovred Raftes Driveing by this Fort which I Suppose ye Indians made use of to ferrey them over ye River, and I amagin thay may have gon dowen amongst ye Inhabitince to Doe mischeif all which I have Duely warned ye Inhabitence off, the Boate which I Sent this Intelligeance by was attacted In there Returne up this River Ten miles below this fort, by 17 Indians ye boates Crew

Consisted of an Ensigne & nine men, the Indians had ye first fire within 20 yards of ye Boate only wounded 2 men, one in ye Lege. & Side, the other In ye Head, I hope ye men will Soon Recover as I amagin there wounds is not mortal being only fleash wounds, I think the officer and his Crew behaved very gallent'ly as thay immedietly Returned the fire on the Enemie which ware all in fare view Kill'd one Indian which fell on the bank and lay in view Duering ye action, which Continued very furious on the Boat till She Retreeted to ye other side of ye River, In which Time Saverel of our men Discharged there guns Three Times after our men got over ye River which is but a bout a hundred yardes a Cross or Rather less thay left ye Boate and Shaltered them Selves behind ye Trees. & so Continued there fire on ye Indians till thay with Drawed at which Time Two of them took up ye above Dead Indian that lay on ye bank and Caryed him off. as also one more which was Caryed of by one Indian his armes around his neck but Could not walk, ye Indians ware obliged to Retreet over a hill or Rather a long Ridge of Cleer ground. So that our people Could easely Count them and give this account which I had from ye Ensigne which I give Credit too, as I have always found him to be honoust and Just in other accounts.—

I Remain with all Due obediance your

Honours most Dutifull Humble Servt

Wm Lithgow

Letter, C. C. Leissner to Sr Wm Pepperrell May 28, 1757

Honorable Sir

Your Honrs humanety, and wonted Goodness toward the distressed, has been made Known by Coasters and Masters of Vessells to the Settlers of this Place: and as I am their directer, they have desired me, to inform Your Hon^{r} of their distresses, and deplorable situation.

Yesterday in the morning about 9 of ye Clock, one Cassemir Losh, an inhabitant of this Place, being at his Farm at Work, close by a Garrison, was Shot by the Indians, whereupon Larm was fired; I went immediately with Fifteen Men in the Woods, and took around to the Place where the Damage was done, we found the body laying a burning, with the Hatched Sticking fast in his Skull, he was Shot under the right Ārm, and Stabbed with a Knife in a most barbarous manner, his Wife being at the time the Murder was done, at the House and Saved her self by flying to the Garrison.

This Day again all the Cattle comes a flying out of the Woods, and no person Capable, to drive them back again, which is a certain Sign of the Enemies being near at hand. there are Sixe Coasters a Loading in the Place, and desire Guard, I have Sent them One and Two Men each according to the danger of the Place, but they Seem displeased, and threadne to Complain; the Generall Court has been pleased to allow Eighteen Men for this place which is Settled ab^{t} 9 Mile, in the lenght. the Number of the inhabitants ab^{t} 140, and Some times ab^{t} ten and twelve Coasters aloading, it is therefore an impossibility with 18 Men to protect the Coasters; inhabitants and to take care of the Garrisons, this being the onely Place which provid's the Western Towns with fire Wood, and no more being hawled at present, the 18 Men not Capable to Guard every were Consequently the Coasters must lay up their Vessells, the settlement is ruined, and such a Vast Number of poor people, will come to destruction

The inhabitants therefore Humbly implore Your Hon^{r} and his Majestys Hon^{rble} Councill to Consider their Deplorable Situation, and onely to allowe to 18 men more provision, which 18 Men will do Duty as well as the 18 allready in the Service, and will divide the pay with them, so that onely 18

Men will be paid, and 36 be Victualt, and the place then Sufficient protected that Coasters can be provided, and Safely Load.

I remain in Duty bound Your Hon[rs]

most Submissfull Servant

C. C. Leissner

Answer of the First Parish of North Yarmouth

To the Hon[ble] his Majesties Council & House of Representatives, in General Court Assembled. June 1st A. D. 1757 — The Answer of the Inhabitants of the first Parish in the Town of Northyarmouth to the Petition of the Inhabitants of y[e] Second Parish (settled on Merriconeag neck) in said Town, humbly Sheweth.

That whereas the said Inhabitants in their Petition, complain of their being burthen'd with paying Taxes to the Town of North Yarmouth more than their proportion. We say we See no cause at all for Such complaint, for from y[e] early days of their Settlem[t], they have been excus'd from paying to the Minister. And a Vote was past by y[e] Town, that if they provided themselves a School, they Should draw out of the Town Treasury yearly their full proportion of Money rais'd in y[e] Town for a School According to the Taxes they paid, which they have done accordingly. And they have never paid one farthing towards laying out, Clearing or amending any of y[e] Private ways for y[e] use of s[d] Town in the first Parish: all they have been Taxt for, is their proportion of y[e] Province Tax & pay of a Representative, the County Tax & Repairs of y[e] County Road. And in making their proportion this has been y[e] Constant method. There has been Yearly one of themselves chosen a Select-man & Assessor, & from him we have had a List of their Polls & Rateable Estates, which was put into y[e] Valuation List with y[e] other part of

ye Town, & the whole of ye Rates proportion'd according to ye Valuation List.

In answer to what they Say respecting our refusal to set them off free & Clear from all Charge &c we acknowledge y^t for Some reasons we refus'd, which reasons we humbly ask leave to offer to this Honble Court, praying you would take ye same into your wise consideration & Order thereon as to you in Your great Wisdom & Justice shall seem meet. And first, as to ye County Road, considering them as a part of ye Town of North Yarmouth, and so situated as they are, we think it highly reasonable they ought to help maintain ye County Road, or to do ye whole of y^t part y^t lies to ye Eastward of Our Settlement, it being next to them. And whereas they say, "The County Road of North yarmouth & Town Road is one & ye Same &c and that they have no benefit in ye least either of County or Town Road, for all their passing is by water," we say y^t this is ye true State of ye Case between their Parish & Ours respecting Roads. The County Road leading from Falmouth to Brunswick, runs thro' ye whole width of ye Township of Northyarmouth, but _ bigger part thereof is laid above & to ye Eastward of ye Settlements of Our Inhabitants & runs thro' a wilderness y^t is not like to be Settled these many Years, And this ye only Road that leads to their Parish, & was laid out made & repaired purely to accomodate them & ye other Settlements to ye Eastward of us, to travil to ye Shire Town in ye County & not for any benefit or Accomodation to this part of ye Town, and tho' its a nearer Cut for them to go by Water to this Parish or to Falmouth & then take ye County Road, yet there are Some Seasons wherein it may be altogether necessary for to travil to them & they to travil s^d Road when there is no passing by Water, So that as they lie to ye Eastward of us, & ye half of ye Road at least lies to ye Eastward of Our Settlement, it's altogether probable y^t they will have more benefit of that part of ye Road than ye most part of ye Inhabitants of this parish ever will. This is also a Very chargeable Road, for besides some Caswaying & many Smaller there are two Large Bridges to maintain, And as to private ways ye Charges always have & will be very heavy on this Parish, which they ye Second Parish have been & will be exempt from, for we have here Six private ways for ye Towns use, that have for Years past & are likely always to be very Expensive, & their Parish have never been at any Charge of them, for we have bro't ye Charge of Our Roads yearly into a Rate & ye Surveyors have always kept a seperate Acc^t of ye Charge, & only ye Charge of ye County Road was bro't into the Town Rate, but we have born Our proportion of ye Charge of laying them out a Road ye length their neck, so far as lay in North yarmouth bounds, which considering ye narrowness of their neck & situation of their Lots is all ye Road perhaps they will have occasion for, for ye Road thro' their neck will lead them to Brunswick line. & then ye Town of Brunswick must make them a Road to ye County Road. So y^t they will be at no cost at all towards ye County Road if excus'd doing their part with us. Moreover we in this Parish have this fall open'd a Road to ye Townships of New Boston & Glocester Seven Miles at least into ye wilderness & built a large Bridge thereon Over Royalls River, which this Parish must be at ye Charge always to maintain. We in this Parish are ye more unable to wade thro' Charges in respect of ye War, as we are many of us expos'd to Garrison & move off from Our places &c, from which charge & hindrance they are, by their Situation wholly Exempt. We also tho't that considering their & Our present Circumstances they should unite with us in sending a Representative. On these Conditions viz That they bear their equal proportion of maintaining ye County Road, their part to be set off as they & we, or Indifferent persons for us shou'd agree & appoint. and y^t they unite with us in Sending a Representative, we were & are entirely willing they should be Set off from us. all which we chearfully offer to ye Consideration, Order & Appointment of this Honble Court, as in their wisdom & Justice Shall seem meet. And we as in duty bound shall ever pray.

Jonas Mason
Andrew Gray
Jno Lewis
} Com̃tee chosen by ye Părish to prepare an Answer.

To The Honble Genl Court

Most hon^{ble} your most Humble Petitioners of The Second Parish in the Town of Northyarmouth, most Humbly ask Leave to renew our request To This hon^{d} Court, To Have The Petition Granted wch your Humble Petitioners, of The sec^{d} Parish In S^{d} Town, Pray'd for; and we have Received Cognizance That The Ven^{ble} Lower House has Granted us Faviour; w^{ch}, we humbly Pray may be Granted, & Confirm'd by ye Honble The Upp^{r} house We have Intelligence y^{t} ye first Parish In afors^{d} Town of N^{o} Yarth, has Chosen a person (as Agent) To App^{r} att The Genl Court, at Boston In Ord^{r} To prevent The prayer of s^{d} Second Parish being Granted, wch we Humbly pray This Hon^{d} Court would not hearken To; we Y^{r} Humble Petitiones, Think it a Great Imposition on us by the first parish In s^{d} Town Their Oblidging us to Help Maintain Their County and Town Road, Representative, wch we Have no Benefit In The Least of; From The Center of Afors^{d} Neck, it is Between Twenty & Thirty Miles Before we can Come Into The Road of N^{o} Yarth The Upp^{r} Part Adjoins To The Township of Brunswick, & we Must go Through The Town of Brunswick Before we Can Come Into

The Road of sd Town of No Yath and by Water its Upwards of Eight Miles, wch is a Large Bay To Cross over, and we have Likewise got a Road Laid out Upon The Neck, & The First Parish In sd Town Utterly Denys us Their aid Respecting The Cultivation Theirof and we ye Secd Parish have Upwds of Twenty Yrs by The Oblidgmt of No Yarth help't Maintain ye County & Town Road of No Yarth Their Representative. Which we The Inhabitants of ye said Parish Have not The Least advantage Theirof which is a Great Charge Yearly To us wch we are Very Unable To Bear, Being In our Infant Settlement.

All wch is Humbly Submited To The Wisdom & Justice of This hond Court and we Yr Humble Petitioners as In duty Bound Shll Ever pray.

David Curtis
Lemll Turner
Jonatn Flint
Willm Alexdr
Alexdr Willson
Henry McCausland
} Comtt

Superscribed,
To The Honble Genl Court at Boston
To be Communicated pr his Honr Thos Hobart Speak'r

Declaration of Joseph Cox & others June 2, 1757.

We the Subscribers with four Others on the 20th of April last past took our Departure from Falmouth with Design of Captivating and Killing the Indian Enemy, upon the Encouragement of the Government by their Resolve in June 1756, and having made various Attempts by Sea and Land, up Penobscut River at Isle of Holt, Burncoat Island, Long Island, Mount Desert, and the Gull Rock, about a League to the Eastward of Mount Desert where we lay about Ten

Days, and on Thursday the 26th of May last, we departed from said Rock (leaving there our Whale Boat and part of our Company) and proceeded in our Schooner to the Northward up the Bay about five or six Leagues, and on Saturday Morning the 28th of said May about Seven of the Clock, as we were sailing by a certain Island in said Bay, we espied two Indians in a Canoe, padling off said Island we soon came near them, and having called to them once and again and offerred them Quarter, which they refusing and Striving to get from us, we fired upon them, killed one of them in the Canoe, the other still Striving to get away we continued fireing at him, and He fired at us, and wounded two of us, but at last we perceived we had Shot him through the Body, however he padled on Shore, took his Gun, and went in to the Woods, where having pursued, we found him dead— We Scalp'd the sd Indians, and return'd to Falmouth this Day.

Falmouth June 2d 1757

Joseph Cox — Joseph Bayley Jr
Benjaman trott — William Cotton Jr
William Bayley

York ss. Falmouth June 4th 1757

the above named Joseph Cox, Joseph Bayley Jur Benjn Trott Wm Cotten Jur and Wm Bayley appeared Before me the Subscriber one of His Majestys Justices Peace for sd County and made Oat to the truth of the foregoing Declaration By them Subscribed.

Moses Pearson

Letter, Ezekl Cushing to the Council

Falmouth June 3d 1757—

May it Please Your Honours

Inclos'd is the Deposition of Part of a Company of nine men, that about the 20th of April last, went in quest of the

Indian Enemy, having left their Names with me in writing signifying their Design, agreable to the Resolve of the General Court in June last Year:—

The Laudable Enterprize of these resolute Indefatigable Young men, doubtless will meet with Applause, and I cant but rejoice at these beginnings of Success; we have this Spring had, against our horrid Indian Enemy; and God grant that it may Stimulate more of our young men to do the like, till our Enemies shall be forc'd to be at Peace with us.

I doubt not the Bounty will be Immediately paid, and ye same renew'd for another Year.

I am Your Honour's most Obed^t^ huml^l^ Servt

Eze Cushing

To the Hon^r^ his Majesty's Councell

Falmouth Petition June 6, 1757.

To His Excellency Thos Pownall Esqr Govern^r^ the Honble His Majesties Council of the Province of the Massachussets Bay & house of Representatives In Gene^ll^ Court Assembled

The Petition of the Select Men of the Town of Falmouth In the County of York Humbly Sheweth

That Whereas John Clark of a Place Caled Hobbs & Pearson town, Without the bounds of any town but within s^d^ County for about three Months Past has been Confined In York Jail for Supposed Murther And his Wife And daughter for the Same Space of time in the Jail in this town for Supposed Accessorys In s^d^ Crime; by Means Whereof two young Chilldren of s^d^ Cleark have Ever since been supported by the said town of Falmouth; Upon Which your Petitioners Requested the Court of General Sessions of the Peace at

April Term last to Releive them in that Case Whereupon the Court of Sessions Appointed three Gen^t overseers of the same according to law: And the s^d Gentlemen having done their utmost to bind out s^d Children Apprentice, Could Not find any Person that Would take them by Reason of their beaing so Young, and therefore left them on the hands of your Petitioners, And as they do Not belong to this town Any More than Any town in s^d County your Petitioners think it Not equal that s^d Town of Falmouth should bear the Burthen of their Support alone; And therefore humbly Pray your Honoürs they may be Releived In that Case And that the Charge of Supporting s^d young Children may be Proportioned on the Province In general or at least on the Whole County of York And your Petitioners as In Duty bound Will Ever Pray

Falmouth 6th June 1757

Christo Strout
Isaac Ilsley
Joseph Tompson
William Cotton
} Select men

In _ H of Rep^rs March 17th 1758 Read again & Voted,
That this Pet^n be Revived:— And,

Whereas it appears to this Court that the Maintenance of the Children mentioned is properly a County Charge,—

Ordered, That the Justices of the General Sessions of the Peace for the County of York, be and hereby are directed & enjoined to provide for it accordingly, till the Children can be bound out or taken Care of by their parents.

Sent up for Concurrence T. Hubbard Spk^r

In Council March 18. 1758 Read and Concurred

A Oliver Sec^r

Consented to T Pownall

New Castle — Petition.

To the Honourable Counsel and the house of Representatives In General Court Assembled

The Petition of us the Inhabitants of New Castle residing and Living upon Sheepscut and Damerscotty River Humbly Sheweth

That your Petitioners have Esteemed themselves very happy under the care and protection of this government for these years by past while much Exposed to the rage and Cruelty of the french and Indians being A frontier and have Suffered exceedly by the Enemy. Last war we had more people killed and C̄aptivated & wounded than all the rest of the Eastern parts. We think to the best of our Remembrance we had about thirty persons killed Captivated and wounded During said war besides five Captivated since ——

That your Honours have thought proper not to grant us this year the protection which formerly Enjoyed by having a Company of Soldiers Stationed in our town which we heartily Lament as that we fear will probably prove very fatoll to us for the Enemy have already appeared by firing upon a Crew of hands going up to fort Hallifax in a Boat; and wounded two which men Belonged to Capt Lythgows Garrison and all the men that hath Been out a Hunting Discovered Indians in Different Parts they have brought in that news which hath so alarmed us that we are afraid and Expect them to fall upon some of us Every day. We are all obliged to flee into Garrisons for there is not one man appears amongst us for our Defence. Notwithstanding the many Dangers and Difficulties we have not as yet fled from our habitations but have maintained our ground paid our province Rates and found our quota of men for the present war; But for want of a Company station'd here as aforemention'd all our young men and they that have no families are a going to Leave the place while we with our families are thus Expos'd, Likewise We Beg Leave to acquaint your Honours that Officers and Soldiers from the westward are very Slow in their Motion towards us and when they are arrived here they have not the Same motives to Excite them to a Vigilance and activity and to Risque their Lives in the Defence of the Inhabitants as those we have their all in these parts; In Case we should Be attack'd By the Enemy at any time we have no where to go or send for Relief nearer than ten miles; So that we may Be all Destroyed Before we Could have any left; Therefore we pray that your Honours would take the premisses into your wise Considerations And in your Wisdom and Goodness to order one of the Marching Companies to have their head quarters at New Castle and your Petitioners as in Duty Bound shall Ever Pray.

Bartholemy fouler	Alexr: Nickels
Davied Given	Joseph Jones
John givin	Thomes T Morly
Samuel Nickels	Samuel Hall
Robert Coheran	Adam C
Willem Coheran	Patrick Loggon
Robert Givien	Nathanael Rolings
Joseph Danel	Kenelm Winslow
Robert Houdg	Samuel Hall
Samul Bougs	John Mc N
Chaisteford Hopkins	Samuell Kennedy
Robert Flagg	Willam Kenedy
William Cuningham	Joshay Linscot
James Cuningham	Samuel Anderson
Davd Hopkins	William Kennedy
William Hopkins	Henry Little
William McCleleland	James Little
John Cuningham	James Griffen
Joseph Anderson	

In Council June 7th 1757 Read & sent down

Letter, Israel Herrick to the Council. June 15, 1757

To there Honours His Majesty[s] Council of the Province of the Massachssutts Bay —

Gentelmen/

as your Honours was pleased to Honour me with a Commission to Command a Compeny of Rangers of 40 men for the Defence of the Eastern parts to Continue three months from the first of April 1757 & no longer Except further orders I therefore begg your Honours to Give me Orders Wheather I shall Dimiss said Compeny under my Command at the Exparation of said Term or Continew Longer as I shall with the Greatis Chearfullness Obay your Honours Orders and begg leave to subscrib my Selfe your Honours Most Dutefull most Obedeant and Very Humble Sarvent

Israel Herrick

Fort Shirley at Frankfort June y[e] 15th 1757

Letter, Enoch Freeman to the Council

Falmouth June 17th 1757

The 6th Inst[t] in y[e] Night there came ten or twelve Indians on Muntinicus Island, on Tuesday Morning they, attempted to brake open Eben[r] Hall's House, but Hall perceiv'd them and knock off a board from y[e] Roof, to prevent their firing the House w[c] some of them were Endeavouring to do at y[e] same Time, and Hall fir'd thro' a Loop Hole and said he had kill'd One, but they return'd y[e] Fire, and so continued y[e] Engagment till Thursday following about 12 o' Clock, when as Hall was raising his Head over a sort of Breast work he had prepar'd for ye Purpose to get a shot at ye Enemy, they sent a Ball through his Head and kill'd him dead on ye Spot, & then his wife call'd out for Quarter, whereupon Hall's son in Law who gives this Accô jumpt out over ye wall of the House and Hid in the woods, and thereby Escapt and ye Indians took said Hall's Wife, one Benj^a Mortgaridge, and five Children and Carry'd them off; the Next Day ye Young Lad that gives me this Accô says he paddled about two Leagues off in the Bay in a Float, and was taken up by a small Fishing Schooner belonging to Brunswick the next Day a Saturday, the said Schooner Went on shoar on s^d Island & found said Hall scalpt, and bury'd him, this Young Lad is about fifteen or sixteen Years Old, & says they kill'd several of his Father's Cattle Empty'd ye Fether beds and carry'd off ye Ticken and every thing Else they cou'd in said Hall's fishing Boat, he further says a Day or two after his Father was Bury'd, the Skipper he was on board off went into Madumpkook where the Indians had Engag'd one Jacob Elwells House in ye Night sot fire to it, but a sudden Rain, put it out, and Elwell's wife shot down one Indian with a Pistoll thro' a Small Port Hole, and another was wounded & then ye Enemy went off and at Broad Bay the Indians kill'd a Man & Woman one Smith & his wife who was a Granny as he heard 'em say at Madumpkook ——

taken from Joseph Green's own Mouth the Young Lad abovemention'd

p Enoch Freeman

To the Honble his Majesty's Councill May it Please Your Honours

I thought ye Acco^t Inclos'd of the Destruction of m^r Hall's Family at Muntincus &c wou'd not be disagreable to Your Honours and therefore have inclos'd it as I just now took it from the mouth of ye Young Lad that made his Escape;

I am Your Honour's Most Obed^t humble Servt

Enoch Freeman

Falmouth June 17th 1757

Letter, Sr Wm Pepperrell to the Council

Honourable Sirs

Since I came from Boston have indeavour'd to put this part of the Province in as Defencable a manner ag^{st} the Enemy as was in my power, and have sent to C^{olo} Cushing that if there should appear five or more Ships on this Coast at one & the same time that he would immediately send an Express.

Some of the officers of the Scouting Companys have made Complaint to me that the men Enlisted did not care to proceed any further as they Sayd the time they inlisted for was out and they had never received the two Dollars $promis^d$ them by the General Court the Bounty to inlist, but this think I have $Settel^d$, we have no news of any damage being done by the Indians since their killing Mr Hall on Mintonicus Island. & Captivated His Family.

I hope soon to wait on your Hon^{rs} in Boston and shall take a pleasure at all times to Execute Your Commands

I am with Due respects Honble Sirs Your Faithfull and Most Humble Servant

Wm Pepperrell

The Honourable His Majestys Council

Letter, Boyce Cooper & others to Sr Wm Pepperrell
13 July 1757

To the honourable Sr Wm Pepperell

S^r

We your hum^l Subscribers beg leave to send this our request to your $hono^{le}$ soldiers of pemaquid fort. ~ ~ being Deeply Sensible of your Willingness & Readiness to Grant any reasonable favour, Consistent to the Wellfare & advantage of y^e people under your Wise administrations, humbly beg the favour that we may be allowed to Gett in our hay from y^e Meadows & Else where this Season. and as our absence from the fort will be but a few days Reterming home Every Night Do humbly presume you will readly Grant us the Liberty, & as it will not only be the Means of preserving the Lives of our Creatures (through the Ensuing Winter) but add also to the main benefit of our familys subsistance, We requested of our Capt the favour but was refused, & he knowing the great Injuries done him of Late by Malicious Enemies Complaining against him &c) dont in the Least blame him,

But by his advice to us have taken this Method of applying to your honour for the Liberty aforesaid and in Granting of which request we shall ever in Duty bound remain your faithfull Soldiers & very humble Servants

Boyce Cooper
John M^c farland
Robt m^c Slattery

Pemaquid 13th July 1757
Consented to ꝑ John North

"Inhabitants of Pearson Town's Petition." July 20, 1757.

Province of the Massachusetts Bay

To His Excellency Thomas Pownall Esqr Govr in chief of his Maj^s Prov: of ye Mass Bay in New Eng^d the Honble his Majesties Council & House of Representatives in general Court Assembled Augt 1757

The Petition of the Inhabitants of a New Township in the County of York lately granted to Cap^ts Humphry Hobbs and Moses Pearson and others Humbly Sheweth

That they live more exposed to the Indian Enemy than any other Part of the Eastern Country, and that there is no Settlement so far removed into the Wilderness by Eight Miles as they are by Reason whereof they could by no means subsist in Time of War, unless they were help'd by the Government the last Year as well as this, which Favour they are in Duty bound to acknowlege & Return the Honble general Court hearty Thanks for the Same; but as their Number is now increas'd to Sixteen Families and the Honble Court have as yet been pleas^{d} to put but Ten of the s^{d} Inhabitants into Pay, and being quite a new Country & they not being able to cultivate and improve their Lands in Time of War have had nothing, or very little else to subsist on this Spring and Summer than what those ten Inhabitants in Pay of the Province have rec^{d} from the Province, divided among the Sixteen Families, by means whereof most of their Families have been in a Suffering and at Times in a Starving Condition and must inevitably quit the Settlement to avoid Perishing with Hunger —

Wherefore your Petitioners humbly beseech your Hon^{rs} to take Pity on them in their distressed Condition, especially as they are so remote from the utmost Frontier of any other Settlement in the County, and give Orders that Sixteen of said Inhabitants be put into Pay and Subsistance and your Petitioners as in Duty bound will ever pray

Pearson Town July 20th 1757

Thomas Stevens
John Walker Samuel Knowles

Directions to Sr Wm Pepperrell 8 Aug. 1757.

Province of the Massachusetts Bay

To Sir William Pepperrell Baronet Major General of his Majesty's Forces, and Lieutenant General of the Province aforesaid,

You are forthwith to Repair to Springfield or any other

part of the Frontiers of the Province where the Service shall require, and there to collect the Forces now to be raised for the necessary defence of the Country. Those Forces or such a number of them as you shall judge necessary you are as soon as may be to send forward to Reinforce the army now under the Command of Major General Webb, or any other Body of his majestys Troops that shall be opposed to the Enemy, But if such reinforcement shall by any unfortunate Event be rendered impracticable, or there be no where now remaining or Collected any such Body to oppose the Enemy (which said Event may God forbid) You are then to dispose of the Forces under your command in such manner upon the Frontiers of the Province as you shall judge best for the security thereof, and most conducive to his Service.

You are likewise hereby authorized & directed by yourself or by any person or Persons under you and specially impowered for that purpose to furnish Provisions or to contract with any Person or Persons for the victualling the Forces on the most advantageous Terms for the Province, and as you shall from time to time find it necessary, and also to appoint a Commissary or commissaries for the service of such Forces.

For the Encouragement of the Militia You may assure them that they shall be at liberty to Return home immediately after the withdraw of the Enemy and that they shall be kept a distinct Corps as Militia, not Troops, agreeable to the 11 Section of the Mutiny Act, and under their own Officers acting in Aid and assistance to his Majestys Regular Forces.

You have my Liberty to open any Pacquetts by any Express directed to the Governour or Commander in Chief from any Officer or Officers of the Army, or which you may have reason to think contain intelligence of the circumstances of the Army, or those of the Enemy, causing such Pacquetts to be resealed with your own Seal and sent forward without delay. You are to keep me constantly advised of your proceedings.

T Pownall

Boston 8th August 1757.

Extract of a Letter from Col° Partridge to Govr Pownall dated Hātfield 10th Augst 1757.

I am inform'd that a Scout of Col° Whitings men from N° 4 discover'd a few days since a Body of the Enemy coming down on the Frontiers of Connecticutt River suppos'd abt 150. I have ordered two Companies to proceed as far as Deerfield Expect every hour to hear some part of this Frontier is attack'd

I have Wrote to Govr Wentworth (who wrote me word that he had 200 Men ready on horseback) to send up Reinforcements to N° 4.

I have acquainted Sr Wm Peperel of this

T Pownall

Letter, Gov. Pownall to Sr Wm Pepperrell

Boston Augst 10, 1757.

Sir

I can only Repeat and do most earnestly that you will send off all the Men that you can possibly get to go, and that on Horse back to the aid and assistance of his majestys forces, and that you will use your utmost endeavours to expedite them that may not be too late and that you will for their more safe and regular march put them under the care and lead of Sir John St Clair who will by your direction exercise no other Power over them but what is consistent with a Body of Militia voluntarily Marching out of the limits of the Province and yet will on the other hand prudently exercise every command that is necessary for their safety and for the Service they are going upon, however if there be any difficulty among the People on this head you must send them in the manner as you can get them to go, and that without delay. You will be so good as to Communicate this to Sir John St Clair who as a good Servant to his majesty and the Public will be more Sollicitous for the good of the Service than to Start difficulties about Military Rank and Command which must Hurt it, and I trust no difficulties will arise on his part as we intirely agreed in our sentiments upon this head when he went off with You.

T Pownall

Letter, Gov. Pownall to Sr Wm Pepperrell

Boston 13th Augt 1757

Sir

Since I wrote you in the morning the Council have advised me to Order up to the Western Frontiers one fourth part of each Regiment in the Province excepting those in the Counties of York Nantucket & dukes County: And I have issued my Orders accordingly.—

The Council have likewise advised to the forming a Train of Artillery of eight pieces of Cannon under proper Officers, which I shall put in Execution and send thither also as fast as possible: and I desire that you would advise Capt Christie what I am doing, and that you would give the Necessary Orders for provisions for the people

Your Most Obed^{t} Ser^{t}

T Pownall

Letter, Gov. Pownall to Sr Wm Pepperrell

Boston August 13, 1757
¾ after 12 Noon

Sir

I have just now reciev'd your Letter and the Packet you forwarded, I have sent the inclos'd Orders to all the Reg^ts^ that have Troops. I am endeavouring to form a Field Train. I send this by Lt Col^o^ Murray whom I must Recommend to Your Honour for his Services. He comes to assist you in the matter of Provisions. I must desire you will form a magazine at Springfield. If the Enemy should approach the Frontiers you will order all Waggons West of Connecticutt River to have their Wheels knock'd off, and to Drive the said Country of all Horses; to order in all Provisions that can be brought off & what cannot to destroy, and you will recieve this as my order not to execute but in such case of necassity, and then not to fail to do it.

T P

Boston Augt ye 14th 12 o Clock M.

Sir

You will before this Express arrives receive an Account that I have order'd up all the Troop of Horse and a fourth Part of the Militia to put themselves under your Command, this will not only enable you to secure the Frontiers but send off such further Reinforcements as shall be necessary, Governour Wentworth having wrote me that he had 200 Men ready to send off I have desir'd him to send a Reinforcement to N° 4, I am forming a Train of eight Peices of Cannon which I shall forward as soon as Compleated.

Sir William I must in a most earnest Manner recommend to your Care the Articles of Provisions and especially Bread for the Number of Men you will have with you, & must beg you will write to Mr De Lancey the measures you have taken and are taking for I am amazed to find that none of our Troops had reached Albany on the 11th Instant

Your Honors most Obedient Friend & Servant

T. Pownall.

To Sr Wm Pepperrell Lt General of the Province

P. S. I shall send up Genl Winslow to your Assistance & I have Appointed Col. Hatch Brigadier of the Horse.

Springfield August 15th 1757

Sir

Since I wrote your Excellency Eairly this morning by the Albany Express, I am favourd with yors of the 13th inst— I observe you mention the Advice the Council gave you of ordering the fourth part of most of the Regiments in the Province up to the western Frontiers.

Since Colo Israel Williams & Colo Ruggles are returning if they and Colo Whilders Regiment should hold them selves in readiness on any Emergence I should think with great Submistion that it would answer, for I cannot think that any body of the Enemy will attack any of our Frontiers at present and as the Indians return to their homs — I apprehend will be the danger in Small partys, as I before hinted to Yor Excellency That if Govr Wentworth would well Garrison No 4 wch is in His Government it would be a considerable Barrier to His & our Frontiers, and they might be implyd in Scouting from one place to the other on the back of the Setlments to make discovery if any Enemy was Approaching, to give the Alarm.

I have hitherto advised Capt Christie of Yor Zeal in forwarding the Militia for their releaf and Shall Still continue to do the Same.

as it is an exceeding buisey time with the Farmers it will be a great damage to take more People then are of necessity I am Sir Your Excellencys Most obedient and

Most Humble Servant

Wm Pepperrell

His Excellency Govr Pownall "Rec^d^ Aug. 17 8 o'clock A. M. 1757

Letter, Col^s^ Williams & Ruggles to Sr Wm Pepperrell Aug. 15, 1757.

"Letter Colonel Williams & Colonel Ruggles to Sr Wm Pepperrell B^t^

Giving an Account of their Proceeding to the Aid and Assistance of Genl Webb according to his Excellency Gov. Pownall's Order & the Reasons of their Return after the Surrender of Fort Wm Henry.

— Copy —

transmitted to his Excellency by Sr Wm Pepperrell Augt 16 – Rec^d^ Augt 17th at Night

Sheffield Augt 15th 1757.

Sir William,

We wrote Govr De Lancy from Kederhook, That we were there with Part of our Regiments pursuant to his Excellency's Orders, That we were ready to proceed to Fort Edward to the Aid of the Forces under Generall Webb, and desired him to let us know the true State of Affairs that we might be able to form a Judgment how to conduct our selves.

To which that Gentleman gave us the following Answer. Viz^t^

Albany 13th August 1757

Gentlemen,

I receiv'd your Letter of Yesterday at two of the Clock

this Morning acquainting me that pursuant to Order rec[d] from Governour Pownall you had march'd to Kenderhook part of your Regiments and desired my Opinion whether you should proceed to Fort Edward.

By a Letter from Gen[l] Webb of the 11th Ins[t] I learn that he has receiv'd Intelligence which he is certain is true that the Indians and Canadians were to go off from Fort William Henry that Day. Therefore I am of Opinion that the Militia should march up to General Webb's Assistance that he may be in a Condition to take Advantage of the Absence of the Indians & Canadians and endeavour to drive the French back out of Fort William Henry.

This is my Opinion and in this Account my Desire is that you continue your March, which I hope you have already begun this morning — As to Provisions they are to be had out of the King's Stores at this Place, Half Moon, Still-waters, Saratoga and Fort Edward, so that there can be no Difficulty on that Head.

I am Gentlemen Y[r] Most Humble Serv[t]

James Delancy

Col. Williams
Col[o] Ruggles

To which after mature Deliberation & Consultation with the Field Officers with us we wrote M[r] Delancy as follows, and then Order'd our Troops to return.

Kenderhook Aug[t] 13th, 1757.

Sir,

We received your Favour of this Day in answer to ours of Yesterday — We don't dispute your Honour's Opinion of what may be the best Measures for Gen[l] Webb to take at this Critical Juncture being now join'd by such a large Body of Troops —

But inasmuch as our March was order'd to continue only for the Aid and Assistance of the Forces under the Command of that Gentleman attack'd by the Enemy, & not to assist in Expeditions that may probably be projected in some future Time, We can't be of the Opinion that its consistent with the Orders we are under to proceed to Fort Edward the Canadians and Indians being withdrawn and the Troops at that Place not attack'd nor in immediate Danger of being so.

We are well inform'd of a large Party of the Enemy turu'd of Eastward from Fort Edward with a Design as it is conjectur'd to attack our own Frontiers. Apprehend it our Duty to make all possible Expedition to their Relief, least a Delay should prove their Destruction.

We are Your most Obedient Humble Servants

I^{l} Williams

J^{o} Ruggles

We have Nothing material besides what your Honour will be appriz'd of by the Expresses before this reaches You.

There was doubtless a most horrible Massacre of our People, but we hope not so many murder'd as was at first represented. Numbers being come in suppos'd to be slain.

One Lt Farnsworth who was taken Captive at N° 4 in April last is now with us on his Return. He says he left Montreal twenty one Days since, that the French Army he was told by Maj^{r} Larose consisted of above Eleven Thousand made up of Old & Young, that they sent over the Country for Provisions for their Army, and that Those that did not hide their Wheat had no Bread for their Families, that the French said there was a large Supply of Provisions at Fort William Henry and by that they expected Relief. If their Army did not succeed they must give up for this Year.

That there was fifteen Hundred Utawas in the French Army which they told him they intended to keep out upon our Frontiers. That the French expected Loisbourgh would be invested by the English that they supposed the Siege was begun, and doubted not but the English would get possession of it, That he had diverse Times heard of two large Fleets one of Twenty Vessels, the other of twenty four that were arriv'd at Quebec with Provisions which he believed was false. And that after their Army had left Montreal a Scooner came there and took Provisions out of the King's Stores to carry to Quebec, and he could not learn that more than two Ships of War were come to Quebec this Year. That they said the English would not come to Canada this Year; That they were like to have exceeding good Crops this Year.— The foregoing is the most material of his Narrative.

When our Troops were returning and had march'd thirty Miles and more we receiv'd your Honour's Advice to continue our March to Fort Edward, but as you was unacquainted with what we had receiv'd from Mr Delancy (which if you had known) we presumed you would not have directed us as you did, and therefore we did not Countermand our Troops.

One Thing we omitted, Viz^t^ That Evening we arriv'd at Kenderhook we met one Company of his own Militia which they told us Govr Delancy had order'd back for a Protection of that Place upon the Intelligence he had of the Indians being come out. We are Your Honour's Most obedient Humble Servants

Is^l^ Williams
Tim^o^ Ruggles

Letter, Sr Wm Pepperrell to Gov. Pownall

Springfield August 15th 1757.

Sir,

Your Excellency's Favour of the 13th $inst^t$ I received.

Last Saturday Morning the Remainder of Col° Chandler's Regiment went over this River to hasten to Fort Edward, and my Design was to follow them to hasten them forward, but finding that the Enemy did not intend to come down lower than Fort Wm Henry I could not see any Good End it would answer.

Many of the Militia that brought Loaf Bread with them, before they got here was damnify'd by the very heavy Rains that was oblig'd to take the Flower lodg'd in this Town by Mr Kilby and to set the Women baking Bread for our Men.

Your Letter of the 10th Ins^t to me which you directed to be communicated to Sr John St Clair I immediately wrote him and inclosed a Copy of your Letter. You have here inclos'd a Copy of the Letters wrote Captain Christie: As the French and Indians are returning cannot think there can be any further Danger from that Quarter all the Danger at present which I apprehend that as the greatest Part of the Eastern Tribes of Indians was there, upon their Return to their Homes may fall on our Frontiers.

I cannot see that I can be of any further service in these Parts, have thoughts of returning.

I am Sir Your Excellencys most $Obed^t$
and most Humble Servant
Wm Pepperrell.

Sir

As I was Sealing this Letter some of Col° Ruggles's Men return'd and inform'd me his and Col° Williams's Regiments had Directions to return back. As I would not delay this Express I beg you will excuse what is Amiss.

Letter, Sr Wm Pepperrell to Capt Christie

Springfield Aug[t] 15th 1757.

Sir,

Having Governour Pownall's Directions to unseal and examine the Contents of the several Letters sent him by Express on His Majesty's service. I find by Governour De Lancy's & Y[r]s of the 12th and by the Copy of Gen[l] Webb's of the 11th to Him that he has pretty certain Intelligence that the Enemy purpose to return without making an Attempt on Fort Edward.

If this should by any further Advices be more Confirmed, I suppose General Webb will soon think of dismissing such of the Militia of this Province as may be with him at Fort Edward.

I hope, Sir, sufficient care will be taken that those Men who were earliest in their March (to relieve the Garrison in its Distress) & so will be last in their Return will be properly supply'd with Provisions necessary for them therein, and of this I can't in the least doubt as the People pushed away in great Haste & therefore illy provided and many of them without Money or opportunity to purchase Necessaries on their March — And as this at least will be necessary to preserve in them the same good Disposition readily to give their Assistance on any like unhappy Occasion hereafter.

And as it is the Midst of Harvest, and the People left their Business in great Confusion and Disadvantage at Home I trust Gen[l] Webb will dismiss them as soon as possibly he can with Safety.— While I am writing I am told by some Soldiers returning that Col[o] Ruggles and Col[o] Williams have ordered the Return of their Regiments apprehending the Danger to be over on Hudsons River, and suspecting that like Scenes of Cruelty and Barbarity may soon be in Connecticut (which God prevent) I suppose they had the Advice of some Gentlemen with You on this Head.

And as I now Conceive I can be of no possible Service on the Western Frontier, and suspecting that the People in the Eastern Part of the Province (who if any deserve my particular Concern) May be soon attack'd, I think of returning thither from hence instead of proceeding Westward as I design'd

I am Sir Your most Obed^{t} Humble Servant

Wm Pepperrell

Capt Christie

Letter, Sr Wm Pepperrell to Col. Jno Worthington

Boston August 25th 1757

Col^{o} John Worthington

Sir

Yours of the 22^{d} ins^{t} Col^{o} Murray communicated to the Govr & Council who have directed me to write to you to dispose of the twenty Eight Cattel left under your care as you Shall think best for the intrest of the Province if Mr Lyman will purchase them for Mr Kilby he may draw on his Agent Col^{o} Jarvis for the money, the affair is left with you inclosed you have Acco^{t} of the cost I am with much Esteem S^{ir} Your Most Obedient Humble Servant

Wm Pepperrell

Petition of Richard Cutt & Timothy Gerrish Adm^{ors}

To His Excellency Thomas Pownall Esqr Captn General & Com^{r} in Cheif in & over His Majestys Province of the Massachusetts Bay The Honble His Majestys Council & House of Representatives In General Court Assembled this 16th Augst 1757

The Petition of Richd Cutt and Timothy Gerrish Adm^{rs}

on the estate of Samuel Mitchel late of Kittery in the County of York mariner dec^d^ Humbly Sheweth

That the Creditors claims on s^d^ estate amount to forty three pounds eleven shillings & four pence more than the personal Estate of s^d^ dec^d^ and the Land Sold by order of the Superiour Court at York 1756 which will appear by the Register of Probates certificate herewith exhibited.

That s^d^ Claims were not compleated until since the sitting of the Sup^r^ Court in the County of York in June last; So that application could not be made in that Court for a further sale of lands. That it will be ten Months before the Sup^r^ Court will be held in the County of York again —

Your Pet^rs^ therefore pray your Excell^y^ & Honours to Impower them to make Sale of So much of the dec^ds^ Real Estate as will pay the sum afores^d^ & the Charges that may Accrue on the Sale thereof; and Your Pet^rs^ as in duty bound shall ever pray ~

Richd Cutt for himself and in behalf of s^d^ Gerrish

Letter, Gov. Pownall to Sr Wm Pepperrell

Boston Augt 17th — 57.
8 o Clock A M

Dear Sir William,

I this Moment receiv'd Yours dated Springfield August 15th — I do suppose that before this You will have receiv'd my Letter acquainting You that I had wrote to Governour Wentworth to send up Reinforcements to N° 4. I did it from my general Idea prior to any particular Information, knowing the Danger of that Part of the Country, I did it also as his Excellency had wrote me Word that he had 200 Men ready to send off on Horseback, but did not know how he should provide for the Expence, I thought the two

Hundred so inconsiderable a Reinforcement that I thought such would be better employ'd at N° 4.—

I received Yesterday the Packet your Honour forwarded, I will ask the Opinion of the Council & give immediate Orders thereupon & in the mean while I shall send up Major General Winslow to Worcester with Orders to forward or send back the Troops now under Marching Orders as the Case shall require & You will give him Your Orders accordingly—I order'd those Troops up upon the Idea that the Frontier Country was left naked So many being gone forward out of the Province, as also that you might have with you a sufficient Number out of which to send off more, should more have been necessary—I agree with you that as the Regiments are returning back to the Frontiers, the same Necessity for the Inland Regiments Marching up to the Frontiers does not subsist. But the Necessity of being provided against the Enemy till we have a certain & absolute Assurance that they are no longer in the Country does still subsist, and as they are now march'd and upon the March a Day or two will make no great Difference with them but may be of the utmost Consequence to the Country should we hastily and too securely take any wrong Measures.

I beg Sir William, That you will In Form Give my Thanks to the Gallant Officers & Men who have on this Occasion so chearfully turn'd out to serve their Country—I shall alway retain a very high Esteem and Honour for Them and do every Thing that falls within my Power to make them Amends for the Fatigue & Expence they must have undergone.

Sir William as soon as I can be able to form any determinate Judgment I will write further to You, In the mean Time You will go on to act upon your own better Judgment & Intelligence.

None of the Eastern Regiments march'd I have exempted

them from the General Order on Account of the exposed Condition of that Country.

I have ye honor to be Sir Your freind & servant

T Pownall

P: S: Tho' the French did not advance upon F^{t} Edward when They found Reinforcements coming up to Genl Webb & that He was likely to be Strengthen'd: Yet If the Reinforcements return home & leave him weakend & Defenceless As He complains, Will They not then come upon him.

Petition of Capt Moses Pearson

Province of the Massachusetts Bay

To His Excell^{y} Thos Pownall Esqr Govr in Chief of his Maj^{s} Prov: of Massa: Bay To the Honourable His Majestys Council And House of Representitives in General Court assembled Augt 1757 —

The Petition of Moses Pearson of Falmouth in the County of York Humbly sheweth: that Your petitioner with a nomber of Others to Whome was Granted By the General Court a tract of Land at Sabago pond in s^{d} County. on Which the Grantees have At a Considerable Expence Cleared Roads made Bridges and Erected a Good Garison. and setled a nomber of Inhabitants suplyed s^{d} Garison with one small Carage Gun and two wall peaces, and a small quantety of ammunition for larram in Case of an attack.—

Your Honours have Been pleased to put into Y^{r} pay and subsistance ten of s^{d} Inhabitants to inable them to Keep that part of the Fronteer which favour shall allways Be acknowledged by y^{r} Petitioners —

But so it is there haith not as Yet Been any alowance Of Guns or ammunition made for s^{d} Garison the want of Which in case of an attack by any Considerable nomber of the Enemy. May Be the loss of the place and people. Therefore Your petitioner Humbly Prays Yr Honours Wold Be pleased to suply s[d] Garison: With some swivel Guns and a quantety of ammunition as in Yr Known Wisdom and Goodness shall see– meet. and yr petitioner as in Duty Bound Shall Ever pray In the name and Behalf Of s[d] Grantees —

Moses Pearson

Broad Bay Petition "August 1757."

May it Please Your Houners

To receive in thes few lines, an Account of the Griefances, of the most part of the Settlers at Broad Bay.

The Continuation of the Warre, and the cruelty of the Indian Enemy Used here, has been a terror to us and been a Great hinderance to our Labour; Tho we bare all that with patiece, as long as we were Capable to mentain in some measure, our large Famelys, but now with Tears in our Eyes, must Acqaint Your Hon[rs] that our harvest is so miserable, as ever been Known by Man Kind, so that the most of Us will not be able to reap the Seed, which we Sowed with hard Labour, and in danger of our lives, owing to the deep Snow, which lasted till the middle of May, and then the Great drought which followed: We See no way to Keep us, and Large Famelys from Starving (as the respective Towns in the Western parts, refuse to receive any of Us,) We therefore hope Your Hon[rs] will be pleased to take our deplorable case in to Consideration, what Damage it would accrue to the Eastern parts, in case such a Number of Famelys should be forced to breake up, as we are at the borders of the Enemy, certainly the rest of the Settlements, betwixt this, and North Yarmouth would be Obliged to follow Us, as they then would be exposed and incapable to Stand their Ground, and such Number of Famely's, would certainly become a Great Charge and Trouble to this Provinz: We therefore Humbly implore Your Hon^{rs} mercy; to allowe onely an Allowance of Provision, for three months, to each of Us, which with the roots we perhaps may raise, would in some measure make us able, to cutt Wood, and other Lumber, against, and during the Winter, to provid_ for us and poor Famelys, till a further Harvest; Which would prove a Great benefit to the Country in Generall by Keepeing the fronteers Strongly Settled, and Save a vast Charge, and Trouble, which would come upon the Provinz; by the Multitude of so many poor Souls, also a benefit to the Westerd, by Supplying that part with fire Wood, and other Lumber.

— We Humbly repose our Self's, unto Your Hon^{rs} Mercy, and shall in Duty bound for ever Pray

M—, Johannes, H—, g—, J—, Mat—, S—, Jacob, Jacob, J—, J—, Jacob, Jo—, Jo—, M—, S—, P—, L—, E—, Johannes, Johan—, J—, Johannes, Anthon—, A—, J—, Johann—, M—, J—, Jorg—, Johann—, P—, Johann—, Frank, Balthesar, L—, O—, Paulus, David, M—, Conrad, Jo—, Johannnes, F—, C—, Johan—, J—, K—, S—, Jakob, Jakob, T—, J—, Jacob, Paul, S—, Johan—, P—, G—, D—.

That the Circumstances mentioned in this Petion being the truth we do hereby Certifie

C. C. Leissner, Com^{dr}
Math^{s} R town Capt
Joseph Kent

Lebanon, Petition.

To His Excellency Thomas Pownall Esqr Captain General & Governour in Chief in & over His Majesty's Province of the Massachusetts Bay in New England, The Honble His Maj^{ts} Council & House of Represent^{ves} in General Court assembled at Boston August 18 1757

The Petition of the Inhabitants of the now Township at the Head of Berwick in ye County of York called Lebanon, most humbly Sheweth

That the Said Township was granted by the Great & General Court of this Province more than twenty Years Since to Sixty persons und^{r} the Conditions of clearing a certain Quantity of Land and building Houses thereon, and inhabiting ye Same and Settling an Orthodox Minister &c., within Seven Years from the Date of said Grant as may more at large appear on the Records of this Honble Court.

But so it was that most of the original Grantees Sold their Rights to other persons, some of whom have sold their home Lots containing about 25 Acres each, to ye present Inhabitants (reserving their Interests in the future Divisions to themselves) the S^{d} Inhabit^{ts} consisting of about twenty Families; And ye present Proprietors being generally men of large Estates many of whom live in New hamps^{r} do not need Settlem^{ts} for themselves, nor will they Sell at so low or cheap a Rate as that a poor Man can purchase. And thus by the Merchandize or buying and selling the Rights in this, as well as other Townships ye Number of Inhabit^{ts} continue Small & are like so to do unless remedied by this hon^{ble} Court.

The said Inhabitants would further Shew or inform this hon^{ble} Court that they have no Settled Minister nor are they able to Support the Gospel among them and that the Propriet^{rs} deny to do any thing tow^{ds} the Settlem^{t} of a Minister. And they live about Six Miles from Rochester ye nearest place of publick Worship, & a River to pass over, So that they can't but Seldom attend _ publick Worship.— That they have not a School for the Children althô a Lott for the first Settled Minister & a School was allowed by said Grant.

That they have not a Grist Mill in S^{d} Township. And the Said Prop^{rs} deny to grant them the Priviledge of the Stream or River althô it was laid out and reserved for that purpose, and are obliged to carry their Corn as far as Berwick which is at least Ten Miles & in which they spend so much time as to be a great Hindrance to their Husbandry.

Your Petition^{rs} would farther represent that they have not been allowed Soldiers to guard them in this War, and conceive that they are not any better protected by ye ranging Company allowed by the Governm^{t} being in great Danger of their own & Families Lives while upon their Necessary Business abroad.

Wherefore your Petitioners humbly pray that this Honble Court would be pleased to take the Premisses under your wise Consideration and either Declare the Rights of such of ye Propriet^{rs} or Grantees (who have not fulfilled the Conditions of the Said Grant) forfeited, and grant the Lands not Settled to Such as will Settle the Same within a Suitable Term Or grant the Inhabitants of Said Township (or Some other meet persons) power & Authority to lay a Tax of one penny p^{r} Acre p^{r} Annum on all the unimproved Lands within the said Township belonging to the non-resident proprietors. And the Money so raised to be applied to Settle & Support the Gospel among the Inhabit^{ts} of said Township, and also a School for their Children. And that this hon^{ble} Court woud also grant them a Suitable place within said Township to buld a Grist Mill. and order that a Number of Soldiers may bē Sent to Guard the said Inhabitants. and that yor Excellency & Hon^{rs} would so far compassion^{t} their difficult Condition & Circumstances as to grant such further or other Relief in the Premisses As to your great Wisdom & Goodness shall seem meet.

And your Petit^{rs} Shall ever pray &c

Benjaman Tibbets Henry Bickford Ephraim Blasdell

Dodge	Joseph Farnam	John grindle
Edward Burrows	Solomon Tebbets	John door
Beiaman ash	Jacob Hassam	Samuel fall
John Cloutman	John Whitehouse	Samuel Denney
Paul Farnam	Phillip Door	Richard Door
Ruben Hussey	Benjamin furbish	Joseph Rankens
William Tebbets	Ebenezer Tebbets	

In the house of Rep^{s} Decr 16, 1757 Read and Ordered That the Consideration of this Petition Be referred till the Next Setting of this Court; and that the petitioners serve the Clerk of the Propriety of said Township with a Copy thereof and that said Clerk be & is hereby Directed to return a List at s^{d} Session of all the Lotts that are not Settled within said Township pursuant to the order of the General Court when the Original Grant was made as also an attested Copy of all the Votes and Grants of money made by the Grantees: (or proprietors) Towards forwarding ye s^{d} Settlement

Sent up for Concurrence T. Hubbard Spk^{r}

In Council Decem^{r} 16. 1757

Read and Concur'd . Thos Clarke Dp^{ty} Secry

Answer

In Council Augt 19, 1757.

Read & Ordered that the Prayer of the Petition be granted, and the Petitioners are allowed to sell so much of the Real Estate of the said Deceas'd as shall be sufficient for the Purpose within mentioned, to such Person or Persons as shall give most for the same And that they account for the Produce thereof with the Judge of Probate for the County of York; Provided, before such Lands be sold they post up Notifications thereof agreeable to the Law for impowering Execrs & Adminrs to make Sale of Real Estate.

Sent down for Concurrence Thos Clarke Dpty Secry

In the House of Reps Augt 19. 1757.

Read and Concurred. T. Hubbard Spkr

Consented to T Pownall

Letter, Col. John Worthington to Col. Murray

Springfd Augt 22d 1757 ~

Sir

Last Evening Mr Com̄issary Lyman was here to see if ye Cattle you had purchassd for ye Governmts might be purchassd for Mr Kilby. Sr Wm refer ye Matter wholly to me I fully Concluded ye Governmts had no present Occasion for 'em That they would be a growing Charge, Pasturage Scarc &c & that it wd be best he shd have 'em but Nothing Could be done as no Orders were for disposing of 'em nor any Price Known. Mr Lyman will want 'em if he can have about 8 or Ten days Hence perhaps sooner he desird me to write to Know if they might be had and at what Price That he might Know if it would answer for Him to have them.

If you have dischargd your Self of 'em wholly & they now lie on the Province I think you would Continue to serve ye Publick if you would Advise 'em Hereof and send word if they may be Sold & the Terms.

I proposed to Him to have 'em At ye Price you gave & pay the Bill of Charge but tho he did not refuse that he would not Conclude to do it without knowing the Original Price & ye Consequent Cost

You will on this Advice do that in this Affair that you shall Apprehend will best serve your Province to Contribute a Little also to which is ye Motive I have in writing you this

I am Sr most Sincerely Your Assurd Friend &

John Worthington

Letter, Sir Wm Pepperrell to Gov. Pownall Aug. 24, 1757.

Sir

Psuant to your Excellencys orders upon your hearing of Fort William Henry being invested by the Enemy I hasten^d to Springfield and to anoy the Enemy but upon my Ariving there, found the Garrison was delivered to the Enemy —

I would observe to yor Excellency that those Regiments in the Lower part of the Province that you ordered one quarter part of the men in the Train list to March up to be under my direction gave me pleasure to See such a brave English Spirit as appear^d in them ready to resque their Lives in the Service of their King & Country, But there was but one field officer came with them, and maney detachments that was draught^d out of Several Compannys no Commission officer was Sent with them and while some of them so came I expected immediately to have ben in Action, and Your Excellency must be Senciable that at such time the Commanding officer could have but Little time to Regiment them nor is it Likely that proper persons could be found amongst them to take the places of Field Officers, If there Should be the like occasion as we may Expect in a time of Warr Alarms if there was a number of able body'd men draughted out of each Regiment with Proper officers able to Travel & proper to Command them to be at an hours warning to March to any place invested by the Enemy it might be of gread Service to this Province and Save considerable expence

I am Sir Yo^r Excellencys Most Humble
and Most Obedient Servant
Wm Pepperrell

Letter, Sr Wm Pepperrell to Gov Pownall

Kittery Septr 16th 1757

Sir

Since my coming here I would let Your Excellency know

that there has been Several Small parties of the Enemy discovered Sculking on our back Settelments I have sent to the Commanders of the Scouting Compannys to be Very carefull & dilligent and have wrote them some Schems wch if followed I hope will be a means of taking some of the Enemy, and as soon as my health will permit my design is to goo to the most expos^{d} places and see that the Inhabitants are on their Guard, who I am inform^{d} are reatch^{d} careliss — in Queen Anns war we had five Towns in this County destroy^{d} in one day, and I am afraid that the People being so Careless that it will be a means of bringing the Enemy upon us as every part of this County is a Front^{r} in the three year Warr so call^{d} there was a Law made that oblig^{d} the Inhabitants to Garrison the most proporest Houses to guard them and the others to go & do Duty there without any great cost to the Publick by wch ye People made a Stand

If there was a Law made to oblige those that Live in the Frontiers to carry their Arms & ammunition with them when they went from their own Houses it might be a means of detering the Enemy when they See we were provided to meet them,

I beg you will be so good as to Excuse my being troublesome, these are my present tho^{ts}

I am with the Utmost Esteem S^{ir} Your Excellencys Most Obedient and Most Humble Servant

Wm Pepperrell

Certificate.

These Certifie That I have for a number of Years past paid out of my Office, to the Second Parish in this Town their proportion of Money rais'd for a School upon their certifying that they had provided a School for themselves this being agreeable to a Vote of the Town.

North Yarmouth p Gilbert Winslow Town Treasur^r^
Octr 17. 1757.

Petition of David Butler Adm^or^ & Martha Hatch, Widow.

To his Excellency Thomas Pownel, Esqr Capt General & Comander In Chief in & Over his Majesties Province of ye Massachusets Bay to The Honor^ble^ his Majestie Councell and House of Representatives in General Court assembled November 23, 1757

The Petition of David Butler of Falmouth as he is administrator to ye Estate of Benjamin Hatch late of said Falmouth Deccas^d^ and Martha Hatch wido_ of sai^d^ Deceas^d^ Humbly Sheweth That The personal Estate of sa^d^ Deces^d^ Falls Short of paying his Just Debts & charge of Administration the Sum of Nineteen pound Six shilling. & 8^d^ as appears by Certificate herewith Exhibated whereby it becomes Necessary that part of ye Real Estate be sold for payment of Said Debts and in as much as ye Estate of ye Decesed is but Small being apprized at Sixty two pounds 13/ and So Scituated that if part onely be sold will in a Great Measure Spoil ye Sail of ye Remainder and no part thereof Sell for So much in proportion as ye whole would Do if sold Togather Therefore Your Petitioners Humbly Pray That You_ Excellency & Honours would Enable Them to Make Sale of ye Whole of ye Real Estate aforeSa^d^ The wido of Sai^d^ Deceasd Giving sufficient Caution to ye Judg of Probate for ye Count. of Barnstable for one third of the Principle sum ye sa^d^ Estate shal be sold for and your Petitioners as in Duty bound shall Ever Pray.

David Butler } Administrator
Martha Hatch }

Report.

The Committee to whom was referred the Petition of David Curtis & others a Committee chosen by the 2 Parish of North Yarmouth praying they may be made a Town or district &c beg leave to report that we are of opinion that y[r] prayer is reasonable & that the same be granted, & that the Petitioners have liberty to bring in a bill for erecting them into a district

by order of y[e] Committey

Richd Cutt

In Council Dec[r] 6. 1757

Read and Accepted. And Ordered that the Petitioners have liberty to bring in a Bill accordingly.

Sent down for Concurrence A Oliver Sec[r]

In the House of Rep[s] Dec[r] 8. 1757

Read and Concurred. T. Hubbard Spk[r]

Letter, Lord Colvill to Gov. Pownall Dec. 7, 1757

Sir

The inclosed Letters were sent me from Lunenburgh,/ about 12 Leagues to the westward of this/. The Vessel which was carrying them to Boston put into that Place, and has continued there ever since. As we have nothing here, belonging to the King, fit to guard this Coast in the Winter Season; I have borrowed the Monkton Schooner of 60 Tons, from Governour Lawrence, have fitted her as a Cruizer, have given the Command of her to Leu[t] Cosby of the Orford with 45 Men, and have appointed her to Cruize between the Capes Sable and Sambrough, for the protection of our New England Trade.— My Regard for a worthy People, among whom I spent the only three years of my Life, of which I can truely say I lived, makes me exult in this weak Effort of my Desire to serve them.

As I have Dispatches of considerable Moment for the Lords of the Admiralty, I have directed M[r] Cosby to push over from Cape Sable to Piscataqua, and deliver them, together with this Letter for you to Captain Donkley of the Enterprize: After which he is to return to his Station without a Moment's loss of Time. I am Sir Your

Excellency's most obedient humble Servant

Colvill

Northumberland Halifax

Merryconeeg Neck incorporated into a separate District. 1757.

Anno Regni Regis Georgii Secundi 31.

An Act for incorporating a Neck of Land called Merryconeeg Neck & Certain Islands Adjacent, in the County of York, into a Seperate District by the Name of

Whereas the Inhabitants of said Merryconeeg Neck, & the Islands Adjacent have humbly represented to this Court the Difficulties & great Inconveniences they labour under, in their present situation, and have earnestly requested that they may be invested with the Powers, Priviledges & Immunities of a District,

Therefore, Be it enacted by His Excellency the Gov[r] Councill and House of Representatives That the said Neck of Land Beginning where Brunswick Line meets the upper End of said Neck which is four Rods above the Narrows of said Neck commonly called the Carrying Place from thence including the whole of said Neck down to the Sea, Together with the Islands Adjacent, hereafter mentioned, Viz[t] Great Sebasco-degin Island, alias Shapleigh's Island, Little Sebascodegin Island, and Wills Island, lying to the Southeast side of said Neck; Birch Island, White's Island, and two Goose Islands lying on the Northwest side of said Neck, and Damaris Cove Island, lying at the lower End of said Neck, be and hereby are incorporated into a seperate District by the Name of

And the said Inhabitants of said Neck of Land and Islands be and hereby are invested with all the Powers, Priviledges and Immunities, that other Towns in this Province by Law do, or may enjoy, that of sending a Representative only excepted.

And be it further enacted, that John Minott Esqr be and hereby is impowered to Issue his Warrant to some Principal Inhabitant of the said District requiring him in his Majestys Name to warn & notify the said Inhabitants qualifyed to vote in Town Affairs, that they meet together at such Time, and place, in said District, as by said Warrant shall be appointed, to chuse such Officers as the Law directs, & may be necessary to manage the Affairs of said District and the said Inbabitants being so mett, shall be and hereby are impowered to chuse such Officers Accordingly.

In Council Deccm^r 21st 1757 Read a first and second time and pass'd to be Engrossd

Sent down for Concurrence A Oliver Sec^r

In the House of Rep^rs Decr 21. 1757

Read a first Time. 23rd Read a second time. Jan: 4. 1758. Read a third Time, and passed a Concurrence.

T. Hubbard Spk^r

"to bring in a Clause enabling them to join wth Brunswick in ye Choice of a rep^ve."

Message 1757

Gentlemen of the Council & House of Representatives

When I last mett You, it was upon a sudden & alarming Emergency, to provide such Expedients as might remove the Danger that was upon the Country.

I now call upon You, at your usual time of Meeting to Deliberate upon & Form Such a Permanent System of well-grounded Measures as may not leave the Country to the dangerons Risque of Temporary Expedients & shiftings off of Dangers when they are near; but may found its Being & its Well-being on such Wise Steady and Uniform Courses as may keep them farr off.

When You see the Enemy possess'd of every Pass & Post, & Masters of the intire Water-communication thro' out the whole country; You will see how firmly they hold the Command of the Continent: When You consider their Alliance & ascendancy over yᵉ Savages; You will see how firmly they hold yᵉ Command of every Indian on yᵉ Continent: When you Consider this Command (as it is) United and Effective in its Power; & Feel how great that Power is; What it has done, & _ it is prepared to do; If the Facts themselves will not convince You of yᵉ Danger you are in from the Enemy, My Word cannot. When you consider the State of this Country Whether it be not Labouring almost to its utmost Strength under the Weight of Taxes; and whether It be in any Suitable or Effectual State of Defense either in its Frontiers or its Militia; in any state of Defense to Which the Liberties yᵉ Lives yᵉ dear-bought Property of the People can be faithfully entrusted; If Your own Eyes will not convince of the Danger you are in from your own helpless Condition; My words cannot.

If you are convinc'd of these interesting Truths, and it much imports the Safety of the Country that You, Gentlemen, of yᵉ General Court, should be convinc'd, you will then by Law Provide that Your Frontiers may be Effectually coverd That your Militia may be a Real & Actual Defense. The Country has People Spirit & Abilities — An effectual Law adapted to our present circumstances, to Arm & Form them is all that is Wanting: This Remedy lyes, Gentlemen, with You, & whether You will apply it or not is Your Business and not Mine. Under the unhappy & defective State You are in, I can Do my Duty, for I can Do all that is in my Power: And all that is in my Power, however ineffectual that may be, I will do, to maintain & Defend this Country.

But if you will by Law Provide for the Effectual Execution of such Powers, as Your ever valuable Charter gives You to use for your Defense and the Repelling of any Enemy that shall attempt or Enterprize the Destruction or Invasion of the Province: I will then from a Confidence in the Courage and Spirit of the People be Answerable for the Safety & Well being of the Province.

I do not call upon you to go into Expeditions and Offensive Measures, that I know wou'd prove fruitless, that wou'd wast the Treasure, & exhaust ye Strength of ye Province; I do not call upon You to fight for Parts of this Country least Ye loose the Whole: I advise You to save Your strength, to collect your Force, to treasure up your Money 'till God by ye course of his Providence shall call us forth One & All to Wreck his Vengeance on ye Breakers of Peace, the Violaters of Faith, the Enimies of Liberty, the French in Canada. When that Good Time shall come, we know that One & All we are willing, One & All we are able to destroy Them. All that can be hoped at present, & all that I do hope from You, under ye Circumstances to which the Enemy & your Misfortunes have reduced You, is that You will in the mean time Provide for ye Defense of this Country that Your Fathers have left You: And that You will not in ye mean time give up that Good Old Cause for which They have so often bled.

Gentlemen of the House of Representatives.

On these Principles I recommend to You in the First place to Examine into ye State of this Defense, & to take Care, as far as comes within Your Department, that no Monies be applyed to Useless or Wastfull Measures; That ye Service of the People be not fraudulently or causelessly employ'd: Next, as Your Taxes are & must continue (while ye Enimy thus prevails) very great & greivous, that You be notte qui exhausted to examine into ye State of these Resources whence they arise: And that Ye establish the sure & lasting Interest of the Country on that Trade which is founded in Ecconomy, which is founded in ye Profitts that arise from your own Produce Labour and Exports.

To this End I shall lay before You such matters of Information as come to my Knowledge, and shall direct ye Secretary to lay before You all such Papers as may be of Use in your deliberations. I have directed him to lay before You The Earl of Loudouns letters to me proposing as a Plan whereby much may be saved to this Province that I shou'd send him some Companies of Rangers in lieu of Troops now in the pay of ye Province at Fort Edward. And I make no doubt, You will provide accordingly, as by this measure, only Part will be expended of What must have been otherwise necessary to keep ye Regiment up till March, & ye greater Part saved to ye Province: By my letter to his Lordship You will see what Measures I proposed to save the Expence of New Levies.—

T Pownall

New Marblehead, Report Jany 1758.

The Com^tee of both Houses appointed on the Petition, of the Inhabitants of New Marblehead (so called) and the Answer thereto, having attended that Service beg Leave to report.

That the Lands included in the Township of s^d New Marblehead (as the Com^tee were informed by the Agent for the

Proprietors, & the Respondents, were granted (long since) by the gen[l] Court to a Number of Persons on certain Conditions and Forfietures, with which, some of them in Part, and Others not at all.

The Com[tee] are therefore of Opinion That as the Record of the Grant to said Proprietors was consumed when the Town House was burnt the s[d] Proprietors be directed to lay their original Grant before this Court; as also an Acco[t] how far the respective Proprietors have complyed with the Conditions thereof, on or before the second Tuesday of the next Sitting of this Court; without which, the Com[tee] apprehend they cannot proceed, knowingly any further in said Affair—

by order of the Committe

John Hill

In Council Jan[y] 12, 1758 Read and Accepted & accordingly Ordered that the said Proprietors lay their Original Grant before this Court, as also an Account how far the respective Proprietors have complyed with the Condition thereof on or before the second Tuesday of the Next sitting of this Court.

Sent down for Concurrence Tho[s] Clarke Dp[ty] Secry

In the House of Rep[rs] Jan[y] 1758.

Read and Concurred T. Hubbard Spk[r]

Of the Defense of our Inland Frontiers.

[Enclosed in Gov[r] Pownal's Letter to M[r] Pitt.]

For the Eastern Frontiers all that I shall require at present is that the House will make Provision for the usual Establishment for the Forts & Garrisons there till the opening of the Campaign in Spring. When that Time comes it will be necessary to get out into the Field our Scouting Parties.

I do therefore Recommend it to the House to make Provision as I shall place in the Lodgment at the upper Gar-
18 rison in Lebanon 18 men to Scout over the Tract between that and Phillips Town Garrison.

25 Men in the Lodgment in Phillips Town Garrison or Saco Truck House to Scout over the Country between those Posts.

15 Men at a Lodgment in Narragansett No. 1. to Scout between Pierson & Hobbs Town.

15 Men at the Lodgment in Pierson & Hobbs Town to Scout between that & New Marblehead.

8 Men at New Marblehead to Scout between that and New Boston.

12 Men at New Boston to Scout between that and New Glocester.

36 Men at New Glocester to Scout between that and the Falls of Amarescoggin.

Now to continue this Line of Scouts without Interruption It is necessary there shou'd be a Lodgment (a Block house or Picketted House) If the House will make Provision for such a sufficient one here the Fort at Brunswick will become Useless, and I will accordingly Dismantle it to save Expence there being then a Lodgment
20 here I shou'd post 20 Men here to Scout the Country lying between Amarescoggin and the upper part of Topsham on Kennebec.

15 Men at Frankfort to Scout the Country between Kenebeck & Sheepscott River.

6 Men at Sheepscott Town Garrison to Scout the Country lying between that and the head of Damariscotta.

15 Men at the Fort here to Scout the Country between Damariscotta and Broad Bay.

20 Men at the block house here to Scout the Country between this and Georges in all

203

The Officers necessary for these Parties will be as far as the District of Sir William Pepperells Regiment Extends A Captain to take Care of the Duty of the whole. a Lieu^t^ which I shall Post at the Truck House at Saco. the Commanders at the other Posts and Parties need be only Ensigns or Serjeants.

For the District of Brigadier Waldo's Régiment two Captains to take care of the Duty of the whole, one on the Western part of Kennebec, one on the Eastern. A Lieutenant which I shall post at the Falls of Amorescoggin. A Lieutenant over that Party which Scouts towards Georges, and the rest Ensigns or Serjeants. The reason of having Lieutenants in these several Districts is that there may be a proper Officer to command these Parties when by Rendevouz form'd into larger Bodies.

I shall order these lesser Parties at proper Seasons to Rendevouz & Form in Larger Bodies to make Incursions for a few days up into the Country. Willing at all Times of my own free Motion to Explain the principles upon which I act, and at all Times Willing to take the Advice of the People even in matters where the Determination does by the Charter lye wholly with the Governor. I do in this manner lay the State of the Service of our Inland Frontiers before You.

It hath been found necessary to Erect several Forts & Establish several Garrisons towards the Entrance of the Rivers Seawards as a further Defense & Cover to the Inhabitants against the Enemy coming from Penobscott Bay upon our Sealine.

Now the Expence of all these Forts & Garrisons might be saved, and the Defense of the People more Effectually provided for against this Enemy, by one sufficient Fort in Penobscott Bay. If therefore the House will make Provision for the Building such a Fort I will Dismantle those at Pemaquid & Georges & with the Stores of those Furnish & Arm such Fort, and the same, if not a less number of Men than is employ'd in these two Forts will serve for this one. So that no Expence will be incurr'd but in the Erecting it. A Reimbursement of which Expence might surely arise from the Petitioners who pray for a Grant of this Land as they would (if their Petition be Granted) thus receive the Land already Fortified and Defended for them, & so much more Valuable.

A Fort Erected there now in time of War Effectually Secures the Property to the Province from any Pretence of Claim either from French or Indian.

A Fort there would effectually in Time of War Restrain all the Indian Enemies we have left in the Eastern parts, the Noridgwaegs, Penobscot and St John's, and in Time of Peace would be the properest place for a Truck House removed from the Settlements.

Further by Taking Post there we may Form so easy a Communication between that and Fort Halifax on Kennebecke River as totally & absolutely to Possess and Command all that Country. By these two Forts and a much Less number of Scouts than we must continue to keep up without it. These two Forts I say, and the Line between constantly cover'd with a Scout will also Effectually cutt off all communication with the Eastern Indian with Canada Thro' the Territories of New England, it must necessarily turn their Path up thro' St Johns by which means they will soon cease to know the Country & will consequently cease to make War in it, or to hunt in it.

The Nature of the Thing points out this measure: The occasion calls for it: There never was so good an opportunity as the present: While the Enemy must be collecting all their Strength to the Westward to oppose Lord Loudoun: If you loose this opportunity You can never have an other and Remember I do declare you will ever after Repent you did not take this Advise.

I must here on the part of the Eastern Frontiers in the same manner as on the Western add, That if the Particular Circumstances of any Settlement require the assistance of the Government to enable them to Defend themselves & maintain their Possessions against the Enemy. Whenever the House will think it proper to make Provision for such I will take them into Pay according to the Establishment.

T Pownall —

Message.

Gentlemen of the House of Representatives.

I am sensible that you have made provision for the pay & Subsistence of eight men at Fort Halifax but I am at a loss what could be intended by the Expression of adding eight Men.

When I recommended the making provision for the pay of an Officer to have the direction of the Forces on the Western Frontiers I did not intend a General Officer as that term is used to distinguish the Rank of Officers but such an Officer as you have formerly made provision for a Captain or Commander of the whole. If it was necessary last Year it is as much so now and you have answered none of the Reasons contained in my last Message to you on this Subject.

T Pownall

Council Chamber January 21. 1758

Message, Jan. 21, 1758.

Gentlemen of the House of Representatives,

I laid before you a Plan for the Defence of the Frontiers, calculated to ease the Province of part of the Expence it has been at in former Years. In your Establishment for the pay and Subsistance of Officers and Men you have carried Matters to such an Extreme as to expose the Frontiers to the greatest danger, for want of a proper force to defend them: Your Attempt to reduce the Garrison at Fort Halifax to thirty Men, is in effect a dismantling the Fort, for I shall never think it safe to trust that Fort to so small a Number: And your declining to provide for the pay of a Captain, to have a General Command over the Forces on the Western Frontiers, will frustrate the design of raising those Forces and occasion Confusion among the several Scouting Parties; for it is not possible for me, at this distance, seasonably to be acquainted with their Circumstances to give out my Orders, and there is a Necessity that some one Person should have General Instructions from me, and have a discretionary power given him to direct such Parties in all Emergencies, when there is not time to apply to me. I have no further Arguments, Gentlemen, to use with you. It is your own Interest that you neglect; and it is to you, and not to me that the ill Consequences of such measures must be attributed.

T Pownall

Province House January 21st 1758.

Message

Gentn of the Council & House of Representatives

The Secretary has laid before me your Vote of an Establishment of Pay and Subsistence of the Forces on the Frontiers. The Scouting Parties on the Western Frontiers you have confined to certain Stations, which is taking the direction out of my hands, to whom by the Constitution of your Charter it belongs. I cannot but hope that it proceeds from a meer oversight, not from any Intention to exercise any powers that do not belong to you, and that you will very readily make the necessary Amendments or Alterations in your Vote.

T. Pownall

Council Chamber January 24 1758

Message. Jany 25, 1758

Gentlemen of the House of Representatives

Seeing you are resolved to turn Matters to that Extream, that you will leave the Frontiers without any provision of Defence, unless I will sign my Consent to a Vote of your House, wherein you assume a Right to determine the Stations and Destination of a Scouting Body of Troops. Which Vote the Council after divers proposals of amendment, in order to remove the difficulty I was under, have at length agreed to; I will, to prevent the distressed State that the Inhabitants must be reduced to by this your Conduct, sign my Consent to the Establishment of pay and Subsistance that you have provided by that Vote, at the same time declaring to you, that I Protest the Breach you have made upon the Constitution of your Charter, and the Infringment on the Rights of the Crown.—

In the Plan I laid before you I have told you, and given you my reasons for it, that I should employ the Forces in the same Manner, that you Determine in your Vote that they shall be employed; so that there is no difference about _ Service, the only Question is, who shall direct and limit this Service, the House of Representatives or the Kings Governor: But this your Charter leaves no room to make a Question of.

T Pownall

Council Chamber Jany 25, 1758

Letter, Capt. Wm Lithgow to Gov. Pownall Feb. 16, 1758

May it Please Your Excellency —

I am Hon^{rd} with your orders of Decr 24. 57 which Came to Hand the 4th instant Respacting the march of Sundery Millitia officers with their Companyes to the assistance of this Place in Case of an Invasion or attack from the Enemy, and with s^d orders Rec'd also a Coppy of Yo'r Excellency's orders to those Several Captains.— the Particulars of which Instructions I have Carefully Considered and Shall Duely obey — this with Submission I look on as an act Yo'r Excellencys Care & goodness to us of this Place, and think it as good an exp'dient or Precaution as Cou'd be taken for our Preservation, wou'd it answear the good designe Yo'r Excellency Proposes thereby — which I very much doubt.— and with Submission Give my Reason therefor (vizt) Topsham, Frankfort, & Newcastle, are Towns or Districts Situated on the frontiers of this County — and are as much expos'd to the Incursions of the Enemy as any other Parts I know off, George Town is Somthing more Secure then the former,— and as those Inhabitants Live in Dainger them Selves, and arc weak in Numbers, I therefor apprehend 'twill be Difficult for the $Comm^{drs}$ of the Millitia in s^d Towns to bring their Companys from their Habitations to the Defence of this Place if need Shou'd so Requier —

this meathod was put to tryal in y^e year 55 and then I had Instructions to Call on those Inhabitants now under Consideration which Instructions neerly Correspond's with those Rec^d from your Excellency and when I demanded ye assistance of 200 men agreeable to my orders I Cou'd Receive no more then about 30 or 40 of ye above Inhabitants.— upon which Governour Shirley ordred a Detachment out of York & Falmouth Sufficient to Compleat s^d Number.—

those Forces ware then ordered to assist In guarding and Transpoarting Supplyes to this Place as it was judged very hazardous at that Time.— and how those same Inhabitants will answer the next Demand, Time may Determine.—

I have bin (and am) verry apprehensive of an attack from ye Enemy.— especially Since they have taken the Forts Osswagoa & Wm Hennery — and the most likely Time for such an attack (as I apprehend) wou'd be when our forces are in quarters, which the Enemy might do ye laterend of Winter when it's generaly good Travaling on Snow Shoes Ether on ye Rivers or by Land as the Snow falls so deep as Covers the Windfalls or old Trees & small undergroath which other wise wou'd much Perplex their March.—
— but as an Expidition any Time in ye Winter wou'd be attended with Difficulty.—I Rather think it wou'd Suite them best Early in the Spring when first the Rivers opens which generaly hapen ye first of April, at which Time they Cou'd easely Com by Water.—

I thought it not amiss here (but Rather my Duty) to mention the first of these Particulars to you'r Excellency as it Conserns the Saifty of this Place — I shall hold the garrison &. c^a^ in as grate Redness as Possible (if they Com) for their Reception,—

may it please Your Excellency I farther beg leave to acquaint you that the Spring Season being the most Proper Time for us to Transpoart Supplyes to the Fort for the ensueing year and the Summer for Providing Hay for the Cattle belonging to ye Fort all which Business will be attended with Dainger, as we are obliged to Transpoart our Supply's from the vessel that brings them 24 Mills up a narrow River not a Musquet Shott across, and in many Placeses so Rapid as it Runs at least 10 or Twelve Knotts at which Placeses we are oblig'd to warp or Track up the Stream for miles togeather, and as we are obliged at Times to waid to heave the Boats off Rocks &. c^a^ by which we are Constantely wett, and verry unfitt in those Circumstances to defend our

Selves against yᵉ Enemy if thay should attack us at such a Time.

and if the Enemy shou'd think Proper to attempt the distruction of the Fort, I apprehend they Could not take a more Conveniant Time then when we are uppon this Business, as the majority of the garrison is obliged to attend this Duty which weakness the Fort and thereby wou'd the more easilly becom a Conquest to yᵉ Enemy — and as this Business will require a much Stronger Guard then what Can be Spared out of the Fort & Store House — I therefor humbly Intreat there be such a guard ordred to attend on this Duty, as your Excellency may Judge Proper, — I enclose your Excellency one of governour Shirleys orders (not as a Precedent) and would acquaint your Excellency Som Dissputes have arisen on sᵈ orders between those of the garrison, and the officers & soldiers of the marching Companys which was ocasioned by the Refusal of those Scouting Partyes to Man or assist in the Boats, — I tould them it was my opinion as their Pay and Provision was more then ours of the garrison thay ware at least equiely oblig'd with us of the Fort to Do all the Parts of Duty then Required which they denyed and wou'd only act as a guard unless I Could Perswaid their men to assist in the Boats (which is vastely the hardest Service) I then tould them I thought the governours orders Imply'd their being directed by me as well in that Part of the Duty as that of my directing them as a guard, but they Cou'd or wou'd not understand those orders in that light, — by which the grater Part boath of Dainger and fatigue fell on those of the Fort, but to do Justice to the Two Captains Nicholes & Fitch when in the Service ware allway Redy to assist in the Boats, but as others Discoriged it made a Considderable uneasiness amongst the Soldiers of the Fort as they ware obliged to do the grater Par̄ of the fatigue, — and to Remedied this for the future, I would humbly Intreat that it may be Specified in any orders your Excellency Shall See Cause to Send, how far it is the Duty of Such guards to be assisting to those of the garrison in this Particular.—

and as I said before this River Commonly opens the first of April, at which Time (or as soon as the Scouting Companys are in Reddyness (we go about Transpoarting the above s[d] Supply's So that it will be Requisit that your Excellencys orders be here by that Time.——

and with all due Submission I humbly beg leave to Subscribe my selfe your Excellencyes.—

most obedient and most devoted Humble Servant

Will[m] Lithgow

Fort Halifax

Letter, Cha. Apthorp & Son & Tho[s] Hancock, Agents, to Gov. Pownall

Boston March 17th 1758

Sir

We the Subscribers Agents for His Majesty's Province of Nova Scotia, Beg the fav[r] of Your Excellency, That Cap[t] John Doggett of the Sloop Cumberland bound to Chegnecto with Artifficers and Materialls.- And a Sloop Loading at York by Jon[a] Sayward for the same place, both being wholly for Acco[tt] of the Government, may have Liberty to Clear out and proceed to said Place ——

We are Your Excellency's Most Obed hum[l] Serv[t]

Cha. Apthorp & Son
Thomas Hancock

Petition of Cha[s] Apthorp & others. "March 24th 1758."

Province of the Massachusetts Bay

To His Excellency Thomas Pownall Esq[r] Cap[t] Gen[l] and Commander in Chief in & over his Majestys said Province and to the Hon[ble] his Majestys Council & House of Representatives in General Court Assembled

The Petition of sundry persons who have Expended large sums of Money in Advancing the Settlements of the Eastern part of this Province in the County of York Humbly shews —

That said Eastern parts are by their Situation much more exposed to the Incursions of the Enemy than any other part of this province, & less capable of Defence & Releif, as they lie so detach'd from the main Body, that for a Century past, there have been Attempts (tho' fruitless to settle s[d] Country; but at present there Appears, from the great Expence & steady application of your pet[rs] & others, the highest humane probability of surmounting the difficulty, and accomplishing that Undertaking. which must unavoidably be productive of the greatest Benefits to this province, & as that Motive has always been an Inducement to your Exc[y] & Hon[rs] to Give your Attention & Assistance to such as proposed the same: Your Pet[rs] beg Leave in Behalf of themselves & others, to Lay before you the present Situation of the Eastern Country, & the flourishing Condition (considered with former times) it is now in. There are several frontier Towns namely, Lebanon Phillips town, Narragansett, Gorehamtown, New Boston, New Marbleh[d] & New Gloucester, Frankfort, Newcastle, Broadbay, & Georges, which Cover a great number of Towns below on the Sea Shore, which lower Towns in former Wars Used to be broke up, & only for want of Settlements that might prove a Barrier to them in time of Danger. But since this last War said lower Towns have really Increased in Inhabitants. Now your pet[rs] humbly beg Leave to lay before your Ex[y] & Hon[rs] the great Danger & distressing circumstances, those unhappy People will be in, who Inhabit the aforementioned Towns Without the fatherly Interposition of your Ex[y] & Hon[rs], for if they are left destitute of Releif, there is no Doubt but the Enemy next Month, that being the usual time of Attacking will be upon them, & most probable destroy many, & certainly drive off all the others with their familys. which will render the Towns below, frontier Towns, & leave them Exposed to the like Ravages of the Enemy, & finally terminate in the Death of many valuable Subjects, and the total Dispersion of the Inhabitants & breaking up of the Eastern Settlements. both to the entire ruin of many Men & familys, who now are good Livers there, & greatly beneficial to the publick in subduing a Wilderness, & rendering the same (under God) capable of producing the necessarys of Life. and to the great Loss of those who have so vigorously Exerted y^{m}selves, in securing that Country to the Crown of Great Britain, & for the Advancement of this Province, and who have been hitherto heartily & generously Encouraged in their Attempts by the kind Assistance & Countenance of the Goverment.

Now your pet^{rs} would humbly remonstrate to your Ex^{y} & Hon^{rs} a Method, that if agreeable, would prove in all probability effectual to save & protect the Inhabitants of s^{d} frontier Towns & their Settlements, together with those settled below from the crueltys of the Enemy, & from the Horrors of War. which is, that there be one hundred & fifty Men raised out of said frontier Towns, to be formed into ranging Companys, & so stationed & Ordered, where Your Ex^{y} shall think most proper for the preservation of the whole. which Method by the Blessing of God has for some time past had the desired Effect, & raised those Settlements to a flourishing Condition.

there is another thing y^{r} pet^{rs} beg Leave to represent to y^{r} Ex̃y & Hoñ that if immediate Aid be afforded to those frontiers Towns as abovementioned whereby they will become a Defence & Safeguard to the lower ones great Numbers in s^{d} last mentioned Towns will readily Enter into the Goverments Service On the intended Expedition or at least there is great probability it will be so, but if their frontier Towns are not covered & protected it is not likely nay its unreasonable to Imagine that any of them will quit their Settlements, for they must know as the Out Towns are broke up they themselves their Wifes & Children will lye Exposed to like destruction and All the help & Strength they can Muster will we fear prove ineffectual for their preservation because it will be impossible for them to be Scouting & under Arms and at the same time take the due & proper care of their Husbandry on which alone (if not in the Goverment pay) they depend for their Support & this was the Motive that Induced your pet[rs] humbly to reçom̃end to your Ex[y] & Hoñrs the raising the Men out of the within mentioned frontier Towns which Men could be no Ways Serviceable in any other publick Capacity for it is impossible upon due Reflection to Imagine that they would go on any Expedition and Leave their Wifes & Children to the Mercy of the Enemy whose horrid Barbaritys have been so often experienced.

Now as y[r] Ex[y] & Hoñrs have from time to time giving such Convincing proofs of your paternal Care of the province in General & of this part of it in particular & have discovered the highest Satisfaction in Advancing that Settlement well knowing the happy Consequences naturally resulting therefrom to the Crown & this province as well as others. Your Pet[rs] humbly & Earnestly Beg your wise Consideration of the premisses & that you would still persevere in releiving the distressed, in Guarding those who sat down there with a full Assurance of your protection, in Encouraging them to go on in their Settlements with Alacrity & Spirit to reduce a Wilderness formerly the Habitation of Savages & Beast_ only to a fruitfull Country, for should you now in this critical Juncture withdraw your wonted Kindness & Affectionate Care, in vain will those unfortunate people have spent their Labour, in vain will all the generous & hearty Attempts be for the Settlement of that Country, & in fact it will be a lasting Discouragement for the future to make any further Trials, & the Subjecting many well disposed people to the miserys of Death or at least to those of Captivity all which y[r] pet[rs] are well assured therefore not Satisfied Y[r] Ex[y] & Hon[rs] will prevent by doing what shall to you in your known Wisdom & Care for the publick seem most proper & as in Duty &c

Cha Apthorpe	Thomas Hancock	James Pitts
Silv Gardiner	Will[m] Bowdoin	Cudwallador Ford
Nath[l] Thwing	Belcher Noyes	David Jeffries
Benj[a] Hallowell	James Halsey	

" referred to the next Sitting

Petition of W[m] Merritt. 1758.

Province of the Massachusets Bay

To His Excellency Thomas Pownall Esquire Captain General Governor and Commander in Chief in and Over the Province aforesaid Vice Admiral of the Same, And To the Hon[ble] His Majesty's Council, and the House of Representatives of the said Province in General Court Assembled by Adjournment at Boston April 16th 1760

The Petition of William Merritt of Boston, Ship Carpenter Humbly Sheweth

That your petitioner on the 8th of August 1758 Out of a true and Sincere Zeal for the Interest of his King and Country voluntarily Entered himself on board his Maj[tys] Province Ship of War the King George Commanded by Cap[t] Benjamin Hollowell, and proceeded in her to Georges at the Eastern parts of this Province, where on her Arrival your pet[r] with Sundry others were Ordered on board Cap[t] Souther an Armed Smal Vessel to proceed to Penobscot in Quest of the Enemy there Supposed to be in Sundry small crafts Lurking among the Islands — That about four days after your pet[r] arrived at Penobscot he was Ordered to proceed in the Barge with an Officer and nine men more to make a Discovery, Upon which, So it happened, that the whole Barges Company of eleven men were Surprized and taken prisoners by One hundred and twenty one Indians and fifty one Neutral French and carried by them within about eight miles of Georges where the Enemey were. - preparing to make an Attack on the Fort, And there your Pet^r with the rest of the Barges Crew were tied and Staked down to the ground for four days and three nights without any manner of Subsistence except a little Rock Weed—

That the Enemy not proceeding in their intended Attack against the Fort carried your pet^r to Penobscott and from thence to St Johns where your Pet^r was Sold by the Enemy to a Popish Fryer who Some days afterwards Sold your pet^r to a french Neutral who he Served thirteen days, at which time the English with a repeling force, broke up the Settlement, and your pet^rs new Master returned him back again to the Indians, with whom he remained inhumanly treated for nine days, then the Indians travelled your Petitioner fifteen miles further into the Country and there Sold him to another Master who again travelled your Petitioner quite up to Quebeck and there Sold your petitioner again to the Governor who on the fifteenth of November 1758. Ordered your pet^r with Several others into the Common Prison under close Confinement, where he Continued Suffering great hardships until such time as the City was Surrendered to the English on the nineteenth of September last being ten months and four days, and during the time of the Seige was Exposed to the violent fire and Bombardment of the English every moment in danger of loosing his Life, tho' he and his fellow Sufferers Earnestly addressed the Governor to be removed into a Bomb Proff Prison which he refused, And Answered that they should perish in the flames, when at length he was happily delivered by a glorious Victory over the insulting and Cruel Enemy.—

That your petitioner after the Surrender of Quebeck was transported to Halifax and from thence to Boston where he Arrived the 14th of February 1760 in a poor and miserable Condition, being Stripped of every thing he had, and during his Captivity and Imprisonment Suffering great hardships of hunger and thirst and Exposed to the violent inclemencys of the weather for a long time, being One year Six months and Six days from his native home, and the greatest part of that time in the hands of a merciless and cruel Enemey and has not as yet received One penny Wages nor any allowance or Consideration for his long and grievous Sufferings.—

Whereupon your petitioner most humbly prays your Excellency and honours to take his pityful Case and Sufferings into your Wise and Compassionate Consideration, and in regard of his Voluntary Entering into His Majestys Service as aforesaid, and his long Captivity and Sufferings as aforementioned You wou'd in your great goodness Order him to be paid his Wages during the time of his Captivity and until his Arrival at Boston as aforesaid, And also to Afford him such allowance and relieff for his grievous Sufferings as in your great and Conspicuous Wisdom and Justice you shall See meet.

And your petr (as in duty bound) shall ever pray &ca —

William Merritt

In the House of Repves April 24 1760

Read and Ordered that the sum of five pounds be paid out of the publick Treasury to John Merrit for the Use of the Petr in full

Sent up for concurrence S: White Spkr

In Council Aprl 25, 1760

Read and Concurred A Oliver Secr

Consented to T Pownall

Letter, Gov. Pownall to The R[t] Hon. W[m] Pitt

(Copy) Boston Sept. 30. 1758.

Sir,

The Good People of his Majesty's province Massachusetts Bay, animated with a Zeal for his Service and placing their honour and Ambition in their Royal Masters Approbation, Have by an Address from both Houses of Legislature desired me to Represent to his Majesty their Services and the difficult Circumstances under which they thus exert them. They have too high a sense of Gratitude for the favors they are constantly receiving from his Majesty to suppose that any thing can be wanting to excite the Motive of his Goodness, and too just a Confidence in the Wisdom and Zeal of his Administration to think any thing needful to be suggested to them in their behalf. They put intire trust in his Majesty's Gracious Promises, they only beg leave to Lay their Services at his Feet, They only desire if their Services are approved, that they may be enabled to continue them.

This Province for many years has been the Frontier and the Advanced Guard to All the Colonies against the Enemy in Canada. This province has alway stood its own Ground and Defended and preserved his Majesty's Dominions. It was once able to do this. It was once the Channel of all the European Trade to America, and the Mart of all the North American Colonies. But the heavy Burthens Which its Trade and Labour sustained to support this Service and the Consequences of its Taxes has turned the Channel of this Trade to New York, Philadelphia & Rhode Island, All which places it once supplied, and all which from the inequality of their Taxes have rose upon its ruin and are become its Rivals. But even Yet, it would have found Resources for this Service in the Zeal, the Multitude & Industry of its People. But the Weight and Burthen of its Taxes and the hard Services of its People, while it thus exerts itself have had a still more ruinous and destructive Effect upon its very Vitals. Those of the Inhabitants which Border upon the Surrounding Colonies, seeing their Neighbours in ease and unincumbred while themselves were loaded and almost sinking under their heavy burthens and worn out with their severe Services, Have in concurrence with such whose Interest it was to gain them gone into Measures to desert a labouring and Sinking Province, Thus it was that this province Lost all its fine flourishing Towns and numbers of People on Merrimack River, which went over and have been assigned over to the Government of New Hampshire. Thus has this Province lost those fruitful and populous Townships assigned to the Government of Rhode Island. Thus have several large Towns Revolted from Us, and gone over to, and been received by the Government of Connecticut, have ceased for some time to pay Taxes and do Duty to this province and are labouring to get this Desertion and Revolt confirmed by the Crown. Thus have Numbers of Our Inhabitants gone over to New York and rendered our Borders with that province a matter of Mischievous and bloody dispute after it hath been twice Solemnly and finally Settled.

This Province thus Wasted and thus Dismembred in loosing its Trade, hath lost the Sinews, and in being Deprived of its Lands and People, has lost the hands of War, Yet retaining still the same Unwaried and Unremitted Spirit, hath still stood foremost in its Māsters Service

This Remains of a Once Flourishing and Large Province hath in this War as in all others, taken the Lead in the Kings Service. In the year 1755, the Expedition under

General Johnson cost this Province	87,058 - 4 - 1
The Expedition in 1756, under General Winslow	101,613 - 11 - 11

The Expedition in 1757 under Lord Loudoun	48,319 - 16 - 3
Besides Fire Arms and powder bought for and Used and expended in said Expeditions	5,364 - 11 - 11
in All	242,356 - 4 - 2
Of which the Province has been reimbursed by the Crown	70,117 - 1 - 3

So that this Province (besides supporting a number of Forts and Subsisting and paying the Garrisons thereof and keeping up a number of Scouts upon a Frontier of 200 Miles, together with the Support of his majesty's Government which is Annually about 45,000 — Besides Supporting and Maintaining a stout Twenty Gun Ship granted to his Majesty and employed in his Majesty's Service at a large Annual Expence, which this Spring took four of the Enemys Store Ships bound to Louisbourg and Quebeck) had expended in March, 1758 in the General Service 172,239 - 2 - 11

To pay which Sum the Province in March 58 stood Charged with 84,943.8.10 levied and Apportioned in the year 1757. to be paid in June 1758. with 73,000 — to be levied in 1758, to be paid in 1759. with 73,930 — to be levied in 1759, to be paid in 1760. Which Sums so to be levied in those respective Years were exclusive of the Annual Support of Government in each of those Years.

Notwithstanding, the Province thus deprived of Great part of its Trade, Notwithstanding it had been thus deprived of its Lands and people, who should have borne their Share in its Taxes and Services, Notwithstanding the heavy Debt which it already laboured under, and was charged upon the following years, Notwithstanding it had lost so many of its children in the many Unhappy Expeditions, and had at that time 1000, included under Capitulation not to Serve, & great numbers exempt by proclamation for former Services, Notwithstanding the great number in the Province Service, in the Kings Service and Kings Ships, Transports, Batteaumen Carpenters and Rangers under the General Service in all above 2500 Men already employed, Notwithstanding these Difficulties in the Circumstances of the province, notwithstanding these inabilities, Yet such was their Spirit against his Majesty's Enemy's and their Zeal in his Service, Such their Confidence in his Majesty's Measures & his gracious promises, that upon His Majesty's late Call upon them in March last, they Granted pay, Cloathing and Subsistence for 7000 Men for this Years Campaign, and made very strict & severe Acts by which those Men were draughted from amongst the Freeholders of the province, which together with those employed in the other parts of his Majesty's Service is a draught of near 10,000 Men out of Effective fighting men in the province.

To Defray which Expences and the Debts then Outstanding — The General Court in their Session in May. 1758. levied and apportioned upon polls and Estates the sum of 82,190- 6. 8 for the year 1758. and Ordered a further Tax of 103,930 for 1759. A Tax of 100,000 for 1760, and 70,809-13-4 for 1761. so that the province has Contracted a Debt of 356,930 — for which it pays 6 per Cent, The whole of which must be paid by the end of the year 1761. exclusive of any provision made for the Support of the current Charges of Government in 1759, 1760, 1761. Which if estimated by what it has in fact come to in 1755, 1756, 1757 will amount to 132,000. a Sum of 488,930 — equal to £366,698 — Sterling to be raised in this and the three years next ensuing, exclusive of any Expeditions or Offensive Campaigns in those years. That it may be known (for I dare say it will hardly be conceived) how hard this Service presses upon the Inhabitants.— I beg leave Sir, to inform you that most of the Soldiers in the Ranks are Freeholders who pay Taxes that there are the Sons of some of Our Representatives, the Sons of some of Our Militia Colonels and the Sons of many of Our Field Officers and other Officers now doing duty as privates in the number I have this year raised.— And that the Sons of some of Our principal Merchants one who pays £500 Sterling ℘ Annum Taxes were imposed upon the same.

That it may be known how heavy this Debt now contracted lyes upon the Subject, I beg leave Sir, to inform you that every poll within the province pays ℘ Annum two Dollars and 1-5 And that the Tax upon Estates Real and Personal reckoned at six years income arise in the Town of Boston to thirteen shillings and two pence in the pound, and even in most of those Towns which have increased in their people and Cultured Lands since the last Valuation to above four shillings, besides Duties Excise and Impost that raises the European Value of Goods to near 60 per Cent within the province. If this Service be compared with that of any other of the Colonies (except Connecticut) it will be found to exceed.

If then the declining Circumstances (to which this province is reduced by thus exerting itself) be compared with any one of those its Rivals, their Abilities will be found to Exceed.

Thus has this Province exerted itself, And thus have these Repeated Exertions, as Efforts so disproportionate to its natural strength must necessarily do, at length reduced it to that Condition that while they have expended to the utmost Extent of their Annual Income and have charged succeeding years with Debts that are equal to that Income, that very Income decreases, they are therefore totally disabled to proceed with those Efforts which the Service requires and which their Zeal would Exert. They make no Claims upon the Mother Countrey for what they have done, they have done their Duty, they derive no merits from their Services, they seek no Rewards for what is past. They are happy in reflecting that they have been able hitherto to do their duty, they Lament their Inability to proceed with the same Efforts of it, Yet Zealous to continue the same Efforts and the same Services, They hope to be enabled yet to Act, And they found those hopes on his Majesty's gracious intentions of a Recompence in proportion to the Vigour, wherewith they have Acted, And they are Conscious that in that proportion they have alway stood Foremost in their Masters Service.

If the Countrey has been hitherto preserved by the Efforts which this province has made, as is a certain fact, If those Efforts are still required and necessary, as they certainly are, for whatever share the other provinces may have bore this always has and always must be the Main Anchor. The Province must be restored by some recompense or reimbursement to that state wherein it was able thus to exert itself — Without such the province will not only be unable to exert any further such like Efforts at present, But the Government will never more be able to make an Offensive Effort upon any Occasion howsoever pressing. The province has not only exceeded its Resourses but the Faith of the Government is at Stake.

The Assurance of a Recompence is the Fund on which the Money was advanced and if this Fails the Government is Bankrupt. So that not only the preservation of the Countrey by this Province being able to continue its Efforts, but the preservation of the Government of this province itself depends upon that Recompence.

Not only my Duty to the province but my Duty to his Majesty requires me to make this Representation I am sensible how unequal I am to my Duty, I humbly Sir pray Your Candid Acceptance & favourable report of my imperfect Services to his Majesty.

I have the Honor to be with the highest Esteem Sir Your most Obedient & most humble Servant

T. Pownall

P. S. October. 2d.

Since the Writing of the above by a Letter from Our Agent, I am informed of the Grant which the Parliament, At His Majesty's Recommendation have made to this province, as a Reimbursement for provisions supplied by it to the Army in 1756. I meet the General Court the 4th of this Month, and shall represent it to them, and as I know them to be a Grateful as well as a Dutiful people, It will, I may be Answerable, have every good Effect upon them

T. P.

Speech. Oct. 4, 1758.

Gentlemen of the Council & House of Representatives

After our devout and most unfeigned Thanks to Almighty God that he hath given us the Victory, I do most heartily Congratulate You on the Blessings that must be the Consequence of it.

By the Reduction of the Island Cape Breton & its Dependencies, the Key of the Enemies only Port is given to us, We have again the uninterrupted Possession of the North American Seas, and the Powers of Trade are again Restored to his Majestys Subjects.

By the Measures taking in Consequence of this Grand Stroke, the Enemy must be totally shut out from any Possessions on the Coast of Atlantic from Labradore to Florida.

By the Destruction of Fort Frontenac, and the Enemy's whole Naval Force their Stores & Magazines at Cadaraqui The Dominion of the Lakes which sooner or later must be the Dominion of America, is again Restored to the British Empire.

By the Good Work now in hand the very Gates of Canada must We trust in God be put into our hands; We have receiv'd a check which has somewhat delayed matters, and no Wonder that we should at the Post which the Enemy Defends as their very Gates; But we have put our hand again to the Plough, and if we do not look back, it must go over the very foundations of the Enemy's Country.

His Majesty's Most Gracious Promises have been a great Encouragement to You, and the very Foundation that enabled you to make the Efforts You have done.—

His Majesty hath Recommended to Parliament the Services You engaged in the Year 1756, and You will see they have accordingly Granted £27,380 : 19 : 11½ Sterling to Reimburse You the Expences You incurr'd in supplying Provisions to the Troops that Campaign — This Gracious & Paternal Regard in his Majesty, This Kind & Affectionate Attention in the Parliament of Great Britain to the Interest of this Province cannot but Affect us with warmest Gratitude, and be an Earnest, a certain Assurance that We shall never fail of recieving from thence a Compensation for our Services in proportion to the Spirit with which at any time We shall exert them

As it is your Method and what is thought prudent for a Young Country to make a Temporary Provision for the Troops which you pay from time to time as occasion may arise and the Service may require. I must Recommend to your consideration such further Provision as the present State of the Service may require.

For the Troops with General Abercromby; For the Forces on the Frontiers; For the Ship King George.

There have some Expenses arisen by sending such of our Soldiers to the Army as the Officers did not Collect and take with them when they marched; and some by sending back such as they suffered to Return; As the General Court have done so much to Assist & Support the Levies both in their Grants and in the Laws they provided, sure tis but Justice that if there be any by whose Faults these Expences have arisen They should bear them

I cannot here Omit making my publick Acknowledgments to His Honor the Lieutenant Governor for the Labours he took, and the Effects his Labours had in Stopping some Evils that were arising from these Faults.

Having been informed that Numbers of our People who have been dismissed from the Service as Unfit by sickness for farther Duty were lying upon the Road in great Want & Distress brought on by serving the Publick requires I have with the Advice of his Majestys Council sent forward Mr Foye to see that such as are Real Objects of publick Care be taken care of properly, and on proper Terms, and that such as are not, be not suffered to loiter upon the Road but be sent to their respective places, by which I should hope on one hand that none who are in distress will be neglected, and on the other that such Endless Accounts as have been sent in on these occasions may be avoided.

Being also applied to in very pressing Terms that the Sick of our Troops were dying for want of Medicines proper for Camp disorders, I could not suffer the People to dye while I examin'd the Propriety of this fresh Application thô so Much had been already Granted.— Some such Medicines therefore have been sent to our People.

Gentlemen of the Council & House of Representves

Amidst the Blessings that have Attended the General Service, I must Acquaint you that the Enemy unable to Resist, and not daring to withstand these Operations where the General Forces are Collected, Have by several Attempts turned their Arms against the Eastern & Western Frontiers of this

Province by its situation alone uncovered with the General Operations and weakened by the Numbers we have sent off to that Service. I recieved information from Brigadier Monckton Commanding in Nova Scotia that the Enemy in conjunction with the Indians of St Johns & Penobscot were Meditating an Attempt against Georges Fort and the Settlements there. The Attempt was made, But by the measures taken to oppose it, I have the pleasure to Acquaint You that the Attempt was without Effect. I had some Men at the Castle which were intended for the Western Forces, These with Stores & Ammunition were thrown into George's Fort as a Reinforcement. The fitting out the Sloop Massachusetts (already in the Pay of this Government) as a Tender to the King George is all the Expence the Government will incur on this Occasion.

The State and Situation of our Frontiers become every day more & more Critical. I must therefore earnestly Recommend them to Your most Serious Consideration; I shall direct the Secretary to lay before You all Papers relative to the Matters of Your Consideration

T Pownall

Octr 4. 1758.

Copy Examin'd

Letter from James Howard

Fort Western Decr 10, 1758.

May it please Your Excellency Captn William Lithgow Esq told me that Your Excellency gave Orders to him to send up the Mens Names that were Uneasy by Reason of their Being so long Detained in the Service at this Fort all whose Names Your Excellency may See here Signed with their own Hands — and I with all Dutifull Submission pray Your Excellency would be pleased to order them to be Dismissed as soon as the Circumstances will Admit, and with all Submission begg leave to Subscribe myself

Your Excellency's Most Dutiful & most Obedient Humble Serv[t]

James Howard

Morris his X mark Wheeler

William Brooks

John his ɕ mark Gazlin

Province of the Massachusetts Bay

To his Excellency Thomas Pownall Esq Cap[t] General & Commander in chief in and over said Province, the Hon[ble] his Majesty's Council, & House of Representatives in Gen[l] Court assembled December 28th 1758

The Petition of the Inhabitants of a place called New marblehead in the County of York, Humbly Sheweth

That they labour under great Difficulties for Want of having the Gospel preach'd amongst them, having never had a proper Meeting House at all nor a minister these many Years; for what the Proprietors formerly in part built, and called a Meeting House, was nothing more than the Name of one, never answerd the Purpose, and is long since gone to Ruin. Neither have said Inhabitants had any Minister with them for these five years past, excepting one Winter they themselves hired a Gentleman to preach, which they were poorly able to do, being but Twenty Eight in Number, and in low Circumstances. Their distress'd Condition they have often represented to the Proprietors, and begged their Assistance; but they altho' Sixty in Number, are all excepting four, Non-residents; and having given a small Part of a Right to some or Other of the Inhabitants for Setling, own more than three Quarters of the Township yet, and notwithstanding their unimprov'd Lands are daily advanced in Value by the Improvements made by the Inhabitants, yet they are deaf to all their Cries, and refuse to be at any Expence, that they may have a Setled Ministry amongst them, by means whereof they have been Obliged to live like Heathen. To remedy which your Petitioners about two Years ago, apply'd to the Hon[ble] the Gen[l] Court for Relief, and the Matter was then in part inquired into, but for what Reasons your Petitioners cannot tell, never came to an Issue, so that they have remain'd in the same bad Situation ever Since.

Your Petitioners are not only sufferrers in the above Particulars but their Children are also bred up in Ignorance for want of a School, having never had one in the Place since the first Settlement thereof, altho near or quite Twenty Years since. For not having Incouragement from the Proprietors, the Number of Inhabitants, have increas'd but slowly, and now not one half requisite by Law to transact Town Affairs, wherefore it was not possible for them legally to raise Money among themselves for the Support of a School or any other Use that might be for the good of the whole.

These Difficulties your Petitioners have long sufferred and must yet longer, unless relived by this Hon[ble] Court —

Wherefore they humbly pray your Excellency and Honours that a Tax may be laid on the Non resident Proprietors Lands in said Township, in Order to raise a Fund for building a Meeting House, and Supporting a Minister amongst them; And that said Inhabitants may have Power to raise & Collect Money among themselves, for the Support of a School in s[d] Township, or any Other Use that may be Judg'd by the Major part of said Inhabitants for the Benefit of the whole; or that they may Otherwise have Redress, as to your Excellency & Honours known Wisdom & Goodness shall seem meet —

And your Petitioners as in Duty bound will ever pray

Abraham anderson	Samuel Webb	John Manchester
Gli Webb	Caleb Graffam	Thomas Meayberr_
John farrow	Samel Mathes	Hugh Crague
Curtis Chute	Robert Mugford	Ephreaim Winship
William Elder	John Bodge	Zerubebel Hunawel
Joseph Starling	John Stevens Junr	Thos Chute
	William Meayberry	Richard Mayberry

In the House of Rep^rs^ Jan^ry^ 12th 1759.—

Read and Ordered, That the Petitioners notify the non resident proprietors of the Township of New Marblehead of this Pet^n^ by inserting the Substance thereof in one or more of the public prints for three Weeks successively, That they shew Cause (if any they have) on the second Wednesday of the next Sitting of this Court why the Prayer thereof should not be granted.

Sent up for Concurrence T. Hubbard Spk^r^

In Council Jan^ry^ 15. Read & Concurred

A Oliver Sec^r^

In Council March 1st 1759. Read and it appearing that the Time for Notifying the Non Resident Proprietors of the Township of New Marbled of this Petition by inserting the Substance thereof in one or more of the Publick Prints for three Weeks Successively is eslapsed. Therefore Ordered that the Consideration thereof be referred to the second Wednesday of the next May Session and that in the mean Time the Pet^rs^ notify them thereof agreeable to the former Order

Sent down for Concurrence Thos Clarke Dp^ty^ Secry

In the House of Rep^ves^ March 2 1759

Read and Concurd T. Hubbard Spk^r^

In Council June 13. 1759 Read again together with the Answer of the Non resident Proprietors and Ordered that

Samuel Watts and Benj[a] Lincoln Esq[rs] with such as the Hon[ble] House shall appoint be a Committee to take this Petition and Answer under Consideration and report what they Judge proper to be done thereon.

Sent down for Concurrence Tho[s] Clarke Dp[ty] Secry

In the House of Rep[res] June 13, 1759

Read and Concur'd and M[r] Bradbury Col[o] Lawrence and Cap[t] Marcy are Joyned in the Affair.

S. White Spk[r]

Message, Jan[y] 17, 1759.

Gentlemen of the Council and House of Representatives

There are at y[e] Forts Halifax and Western some Men with whom, I should be sorry to say, the Government had broke Faith. They were inlisted or impressed for that Service to continue a Year. It is now the third Year, and they are there still. As no provision hath been made since I came to the Chair to enable me to inlist Others in their room, I have used every just & due method to persuade them to continue. They do now claim their dismission. If I dismiss them the Garrison must be broke up & dismantled: if I detain them we shall continue within Ourselves, which has remained already too long an Example that this Government once grievously complained of, and which may on some future occasion preclude all pretence of reclaiming what this Government would be sorry to be refused. That Justice therefore which we expect from Others towards our own People let us shew to them Ourselves.

The provision of a few dollars will enable to inlist Others, so as to dismiss these. I must therefore recommend it to you

T Pownall

Council Chamber January. 17. 1759

Letter from Wm Lithgow "without Date."

May it Please Your Excellency.

In obedience to Your Excellency's Orders to me in Council Chamber last Octr 1758 I here present Your Excellency the Several Mens Names under their Hands, who are Desirous of their Dismissions, and who have served in this Fort, some three and some Two Years.

The Others that have not signed, I have according to Order gave them Your Excellency's Word and Honour, that any of such, as may be desirous of their Dismissions the first of Novr 1759 will then According to Your Excellency's Word be discharged. This I take to be the Sense of Your Excellency's Instructions to me on this Particular — and as to any other Orders Your Excellency then gave me in Charge as Scouting &c — I have not been regardless thereof.

May it Please Your Excellency — as the within Subscribers are uneasy on account of their having been detained here longer then what they engaged for, which was one Year, and now it is going on Three Years Since their Inlistments, therefore by their earnest desire to me, I would with Submission humbly Intreat Your Excellency in their behalfs, that they may be Released as soon as ye Circumstances of this Affair will Permit, all which I would humbly Recommend & Submitt to Your Excellency's most Wise Consideration, and with due Submission, beg leave to Subscribe my self Your Excellency's most Obedient & Most humble Servant

William Lithgow

John Blake	James McPhetres	John Wharton
Joseph Woods	John Limercy	James McKibb
James his ∞ mark McManus	Timothy Bryan	John Pumorey
Bennet Woods	Michael his X mark Odriscal	Edward his X mark Cumerford
William Martin	Henery Hassett	Alex^{d} Grindley

Message. Feb. 1, 1759

Gentlemen of the Council & House of Representatives —

When in my General Considerations of the Frontiers I suggested to y[e] Gen[l] Court the Measure of Building a Fort at Penobscot, altho I was fully possess'd of the Necessity of its being done before Peace. Altho I saw that the General Court was of y[e] same Opinion & truely represented the Sense of y[e] Country which also was the same: Yet seing the Difficulties under which y[e] Country labour'd to make Supplies for y[e] many unavoidable Expences that were coming upon them I was unwilling at that Time or at any other Time by Urging the Matter further to reduce the General Court to that Disadvantageous Alternative either of Refusing to Take Possession of & Fortifye their Territory as by Charter granted, or of engaging in an Expence they knew not the End of & were very unable to engage in: Yet as I endeavor never to loose sight of the Interest of the Country; So in this particular I never lost sight of this Measure. I laid it before his Majesty's Ministers, I proposed it to the late General who refer'd it to his Majesty's Ministers; When Major Gen[l] Amherst was Appointed General I proposed it also to him, least by waiting for Orders from England the Opportunity shou'd be lost. His Excellency is sensible not only of y[e] Importance but Necessity of – Measure & also of y[e] Necessity of its being done immediately & has engaged to reimburse me the Expence of Building such in whatever manner is most agreeable to Me, Neither will any expence Arise to the Province in Furnishing such Fort with Gunns & Ordenance Stores or other Necessaries as I have all such, belonging to y[e] Province now ready, All therefore that on this Occasion I apply to You for is that you will make Provision for such a Force as shall enable me to Take Possession of this Country & carry the Measure of Fortifyeing it into Execution, & also make Provision for the Pay & Subsistance of such Garrison as must be left there. To make which Matter also very easy to ye Country Ways & Means may be found.

As the Crown has taken Possession of & Fortifyed St John's River, The Enimy have now no Outlet to ye sea but thro this River Penobscot; The Door being Shutt upon them in every other Part, & that only left open which leads to this Province, You must be in a worse Situation than You were before If You will not do Your Part, by yourselves taking Possession of these Lands. You know that as long as an Indian has any Claim to these Lands, the French will maintain a Title to them: And thus notwithstanding all that has been done elsewhere, a Thorn will be left in the Side of this Province and whatever Peace may be made & however the Other Provinces may enjoy it, This Province must labour on still under ye Miseries of Warr even in the time of Peace. All this may be prevented by Taking Possession of this Country now in Time of Warr: By doing this You will have ye Honor of Compleating His Majesty's Dominions on the Atlantic: You will root up the seeds of another Warr and secure the Title of these Lands to the Subjects of this Province. Had You no immediat Assistance in Doing this You cou'd not in Duty to his Majesty who has Done & is Doing so much for You; You coud not in Duty to Your fellow subjects of this Province, refuse to engage in this Service But now General Amherst has Offer'd to reimburse the Expences of Building this Fort & fortifyeing What You thus Take Possession of If You Refuse it, You are without Excuse.

T Pownall

Province House 1 Feb^{r} 1759.

Letter, John McKechnie to Gov Pownall 12 Feb. 1759

May it Please your Excellency

About five o Clock P. M. Saturday last Three Indians at a Small distance from the fort with a flagg, was at I much a loss what to do in such a Critical Circumstance having no Instructions relative thereto, My Capt not being at home made it the more Difficult, for he Set out the tuesday preceeding with Seven men and a pillot for the head of St Georges river in Order to find out the Carrying places between penobscut Bay and the Same

I ordered a flagg to be put up at the fort, took with me the Armourer who understands the best of any in this place/ the Indian Language went to near where they were the three Indians came to us. I asked them what they came here for, they ansrd they had good News to tell but could not do it that Night being weary travelling, I took their arms from y^m which Consisted of two guns one pistol & one hatchet & sent them to the fort. Told the Ind^s that they could Not be admitted into the fort till I knew what they had to say. they urged it very Much Saying that the English men would kill them if we did not take Care of them. I took them to a small house about forty rods from our walls where they could Not get out, Nor None other Ind's to them, without being Discovered by our Centry's, gave them Strict charge Not to come out, for our guards would certainly fire upon them if they did, they said they would not come out till I came to them in the Morning, which I did and they delivered themselves as in their letter herewith sent, I insisted on One of them staying as a pledge of their fidelity, which altho' at first they Seemed backward at last Consented. I gave the two that went away a little eatible provisions to carry them along, took the other in to the Guard room put a Centry over him; which I intend to take care of till my Capt come home. Now I have given your Excellency a full Acc^t of my proceedings, as also of what the Ind^s said according as the arm^r told me and if I have committed any Indiscrations in the affair I hope your Exc^{ly} will impute it to my Ignorance & want of instructions, which

I believe would be very Acceptible to Cap[t] North, before those twelve come in again No more but am

May it please your Excellency your Excellency's Most humble & obed[t] Serv[t]

John M[c]kechnie

S[t] Georges 12th Feb[r] 1759

Letter to Mr. McKetchie

Boston 24 February 1759.

M[r] M[c]Kechnie

You have acted very prudently and well and You have My approbation, Continue to do so, Use kindly and well, but also well guard and watch the Hostage Indian. Lett him have no Opportunity of Escaping.

Stand firmly on Your Guard and Keep a Good look out for fear these Indians should have been sent only as Spies previous to an Attempt upon the Fort. Warn the People at the Blockhouse and on the River to be on their Guard. If You think there be any Suspicion of Danger of an Attack Take into the Garrison twenty or thirty of the Block house People and Allow them provisions. Have every thing ready and in Order as thô You expected an Attack every Morning. And see that Your Centries and guard be particularly Alert and Watchful in the Morning just before day break especially Keep out constant Scout — and especially lett them often go out just after dark —. And when You have taken every precaution against Danger, and are as secure as Your Situation will Allow, then Lett the Indians know, that You despise all their Cunning and all their Force. But that if they be True in their Offers — There is my letter which Deliver to them.

Thomas Pownall

Letter, "Gov. Pownall to Col. Preble"

Sir

I received your Letter with pleasure. Your caution against any Lurking designs which the Indians might be supposed to have in coming in, was extreamly proper & prudent — Your Treatment of them also & your Refusing them any means of Trade, & rejecting their offers to it much to your Honor.— If there were any Error in your conduct twas on ye right side & that being small may easily be remedied. Be Steady with ye Indians but not harsh — Treat them with Truth & with plain Truth be they never so disagreable, but at ye same time with benevolence. For the Spirit of my Conduct towards them is to bring them to a Sense of their Duty & proper Connections with us but to do this in order to use them well I make this Observation because I think You was rather too harsh. however thô I wou'd have you abate a little of y^r^ harshness yet I woud not have you abate one Ace of Your Steadiness in letting them know that We now know how to Use our own Strength & their weakness, And tho' we wish to do them Good if by Proper Conduct they will putt it in our power we do it not from any fear of them but from pure motives of Pity & Benevolence.

As I imagine you have had no opportunity of writing since your last of ye 27th so I did not expect to hear from You, & as I cannot know how you circumstanced so I cannot give You any immediate directions as to particulars. By the enclosed Copy of the Establishment You'll see I have gott the Provision for ye Pay & Subsistence of ye 400 men lengthen'd out a month longer You will see also the Establishment for the Garrison as I shall at present dispose of ye Forces provided for.

As to ye Works I write to ye Engineer Mr Burbank & direct him to show You his letter in which You will see his Orders to Obey & Execute all Your Commands.

As to the Indians I do verily believe they mean to come in, but what they want to treat for & Obtain is — first to try to delay the time till the fall that they may see how ye Campaign between ye French; & English turns out.

Secondly to obtain some thing different terms than those I have offered of living near ye Fort. The First You must prevent if possible, & as to ye second there can be no trust in any Treaty they make, if the terms I have proposed be not complied with viz of their living with their Wives & Children under ye Protection of ye Fort nor cou'd I undertake (as I do in my offers) to be answerable for their Protection any where else. As I think they are in Earnest about coming in and as we have gone some Stepps to which they have acceeded of Treating on the terms so I think we cannot use any Hostilities against them & their planting Ground while things remain as they are. Yet I cou'd still wish that a Strong body of our People might go up to their Planting Ground, which possibly may be brought about as follows. If they give you hopes of their coming in You must offer to fetch their Wives & Children & what Goods they may have &c in our Whale boats & to Escort them safe. Push this piece of Kindness upon them that you may have a proper pretence for sending a Strong body so farr as their Dwelling & Planting ground, but with strict Orders under the Severest Penalties to do them no violence, to seek no quarrels nor even to revenge any, unless absolutely drove to it for safety. This is what I wou'd wish to have done without delay, but how to give You Orders is absolutely impracticable for me as I know nothing of ye State & Situation in which You & ye Indians may stand at present. If they have broke off all treaty & you have discover'd their design to deceive I wou'd have You send as Strong a body as You can Spare to burn & Destroy their Corn & Means of Subsistance & to destroy the Indians too if they can catch them. But as Matters now stand, No Risques are to be runn. You must have it executed in such Manner & to make ye Matter sure, or not do it att all. For it is much better never to attempt it, than to miscarry. If therefore You cannot do it so as in all human probability to secure y^r Success Lett it not be done at all.— Remember not only ye Indians but their Allies ye Renegadoes Neutrals are also to be taken into ye Account. When the time draws near for dismissing the men You must then think of the Scout I mention'd to You before namely that of sending by Land a Hundred Men from Penobscot to Fort Halifax on Kenebeck. first up ye little River which comes into Penobscot R^r on ye West side about 12 miles above You. thence over ye Indian carrying Place & down Sebestoocook to F^t Halifax thence to Cushooc, thence to Amescoggin & Pesumpscot, to Falmouth. I have Orderd Provisions (marching allowance) for 100 Men, for seven daies to be lodged at Cushoc.

As I have found out that Fort Halifax is not above 30 miles from You in a N & by W course & that ye Swamp or Meadow at ye Head of ye West branch of Georges River is not above 8 or 10 miles from F^t Halifax & the great Pond at ye head of ye East branch of Georges from whence they carry into Pausegusawackeag is about, if not exactly, half Way between You & Fort Halifax. I must by all means have a Scout that Way & have it thoroughly reconnoitred. Give Orders to ye Scout that goes by Sebastoocook to build a Logg house at ye Carrying Place & Order the Scout that goes by ye heads of Georges River to build a Logg house either at the East or West head as they may be most Convenient. A hundred may do for both these Scouts as that which goes by Georges River need be but a Small one of ten twelve or fifteen & I should apprehend between 80 or 90 enough for the other. However I must leave you to judge of that, according to the Circumstances you are in, & according to the Accounts You have of the Enemy. I had promised Cap[t] Herrick that if it was in my Power He shou'd have y[e] Lieutenancy under You but it happens there is no Lieutenant allow'd You at Present. Nor is there allowance for a Gunner or Interpreter. You cannot do without y[e] Latter And as Macfarlin ask'd me to make some provision for _ I think if You make him a Serjeant with Ensign's or Lieutenant's Rank he will be very well off & the End will be answerd & I make no doubt of his Accepting it, & being thankfull for it. The Reason of my giving him the Rank is that he may appear with proper Character to y[e] Indians & also as he has had it already. And as to y[e] pay tis more than he has ever had before or cou'd have expected except on this Expedition. You dismiss M[r] Burbank as soon as the Establishment is over. You will detain six of y[e] Best of y[e] Whale Boats.

T Pownall

To His Excellency Thomas Pownall Esq[r], The Honourable his Majesties Council and House of Representatives in General Court assembled, Feb. 28th 1759

The memorial of the Subscribers, who usually follow the Fishing Business, on the Eastern Coasts of this Province, Humbly Sheweth.

That in Order to take the Cod Fish about Damarels Cove and those parts in the Months of April and May, it has been found necessary to Catch Shadd and Alewives for Bait, other Bait not at all answering in those Seasons,

That for many years it has been a constant and till last year an Uninterrupted practice to take the said Bait for the most of those two months, in a Small Crick called Mill Crick, that lyes in the Island of Arowsick, upon the Easterly Side of Kenebeck River, the only place we can be Supplyed, with safety and in Season.

But so it is may it please your Excellency and Honours that the Inhabitants of the Town wherein the said Island of Arowsick lyes, whether Legally, or from any misapprehension of the Law, we cant say, Did the last year appoint a Person to inspect the taking Said Bait; who would not suffer us to take any unless we bought them of him, or unless we would give him so much for them – a venture, before we took them our Selves, which proceedings did greatly obstruct and hinder our fishing business, and if continued it must discourage and Break it up, this we believe will be plain, if it is considered that we go more than Twenty Miles from our fishing ground to get this Bait; that we fetch it by Turnes, among all the Boats, that fish at said Cove, So that the hindrance of those that fetch it, is the hindrance of the whole, which must oft happen if a bargain must always be made with Some person, and perhaps one of no very good Condition neither, beside the cost of buying at their own price.

Wherefore your Petitioners most humbly Pray that if the Law does now Justify the said Inhabitants in this proceeding that the Same may be altered or otherwise Relieve your memorialists lest this Branch of the Fishing business where a great Deal of fish is yearly taken be Lost

And as in Duty Bound Shall Pray

Moses Foster	Stephen Burnum	James Eveleth Junr
Stephen Choate	John Caires	Jeremiah Choate
Thomas Choate	David Low Junr	Solomon Burnam
Amos Burnam	Humphrey Choate	Humphry Willems
Jonathan Smith	John Foster	David Burnum
Thomas Lufken Jur	Joshua Martin	Nehemiah Story
Ammi Burnam	Simeon Burnam	Joseph Wells
frances Cogswell	Ebnezer Low	Thomas Burnam
Thomas Giddinge		

In the House of Rep^{ves} March 17 1759

Read and Ordered that the Prayer of this Pet^{n} be so far granted as that the Pet[rs] or any others who may have occasion to take the Fish called Alewives in the Creek called Mill Creek for bait for fishing, shall have liberty to take the said Fish in said Creek for the Use aforesaid; They not to Obstruct or molest the People from taking the said Fish at the same place.

Sent up for concurrence T. Hubbard Spk[r]

In Council March 17, 1759

Read and Nonconcurred A Oliver Sec[r]

New Marblehead Meeting House.

Falmouth May 28th 1759.

We the Subscribers being well acquainted with the House the Proprietors of New Marblehead, built there, design'd for a Meeting House, at y[e] Request of M[r] Abraham Anderson, one of the Inhabitants of New Marblehead, to give our Judgment of s[d] Building, do declare that the said House never was finish'd nor was y[e] work done in a Workmanlike Manner, so far as was done, no Floor ever laid, nor Windows to said House Neither was y[e] House ever under pin'd, nor fit for y[e] People to meet in. —

Nathan Winslow Isaac Ilsley Thomas Haskell
Caleb Graffum Aron Stevens

Province of the Massachusetts Bay —

To His Excellency Thomas Pownall Esq[r] Commander in Chief, and to the Honourable His Majesty's Council, and

House of Representatives of said Province in General Court Assembled the Sixth Day of June 1759. The Subscribers a Comittee of the Proprietors of the Common & undivided Lands in a place call'd New-Marblehead in the County of York: Humbly Shew, in their behalf —

That in Obedience to the Order of this Honourable Court of the 12th and 13th of Jan^ry A. D. 1758 appointed a Committee with Orders to repair to the said place, and take an exact Account of the Condition of that Settlement, in order to its being laid before this Honourable Court, which Comittee not attending that Service, the said Proprietors at their Meeting in March last appointed Messrs John Wight & Samuel Turner to do it, who have accordingly been on the Spot; whose Report together with a true Copy of the Original Grant of the s^d Township with a List of the Original Grantees, we now beg leave to lay before you.

And in Answer to the Petitions of the Inhabitants of that place now depending before your Excellency and this Honble Court we beg leave to say, That A. D. 1737. the Grantees of said Township at their own Expence erected a Meeting House there 38 feet long, 28 feet wide & 14 feet Stud, That A. D. 1743 they settled the Revd Mr John Wight in the Work of the Ministry there, who was Ordain'd and continued there during his Life vizt till 1752, during which Time he was Supported wholly by the Grantees, to which the Settlers, as such, contributed nothing, That Mr Wight made use of the said Meeting House and preach'd in it till the Year 1746 when the Inhabitants pull'd it down, and afterward met in the Fort, or Block-House, built there by the Government. That upon the Death of Mr Wight, the Grantees Apprehended, That it was high Time that the Settlement of the Sixty Families enjoin'd by the Grant should be compleated, and that then it would be most fit that the Inhabitants should by themselves choose and contract with a Minister: And the

Grantees as such should assist them in his Support, This the Proprietors have been always ready to do; And had the Settlement been compleated according to the Terms of the Grant, or in Many Years after, the Inconvenience complained of would not have hapned; As to a Meeting House, the Block House which they have used for that purpose ever since the Meeting House was pull'd down will we hope, be sufficient to accomodate the Families there, till the number of Setlers shall be compleated, And the Inhabitants Incorporated; which we hope by the Order of your Excellency and this Honourable Court, will soon be effected; and in the mean Time the Proprietors have at their last March Meeting ordered the payment of 60 Dollars out of their Treasury to assist the Inhahitants in procuring preaching there, and there is no Reason to doubt, but that the said Proprietors will from Time to Time as there may be occation, make further Grants for that purpose, which we apprehend will be the most Salutary Method of Supporting the preaching the Gospel there, until the said Settlement be compleated, and the Inhabitants Incorporated as aforesaid, and then the Proprietors will readily contribute to assist the Inhabitants in Rebuilding the Meeting House and Resettling a Minister there; and if they fail may be compelled to it — And as a Number of Defective Grantees are in large Arrears of the several Tax's that have been laid on them (& duly Notefied) for bringing forward the Settlement, and the Creditors of the said Township by that Means remaining unpaid, We pray that the present Assessors, vizt Nathan Bowen, John Wight & Samuel Turner or a Quorum of them, may be authorized to Sell and Legally convey so much of the Delinquents Rights through the Township will pay said Arrears. And as the Boundary Lines betwixt this Township, and the Towns of Falmouth & North Yarmouth have never yet been settled, the ascertaining of which is of great Importance to this Township; We pray that your Excellency and Honours will please to Order some proper Methods for effecting the same —

All which is submitted by

Your Excellency's and Honour's Most Obedient,
Hum^{ll} Serv^{ts}

Nathan Bowen   Willm Goodwin
John Wight   Samuel Turner

"New Marblehead Petition &c June 6 1759 To Lie."

A List of 29 Lotts in New Marblehead that were setled April 26th 1759, with the Names of the Origenal Grantees to whome they belong'd

N^{o} By whome drawn.

3, Robert Paramore, 5, Michael Bowden, 6, Samuel Stacey 3^{d}, 7, Ebenez^{r} Hawkes Junr, 10, Thomas Wood, 12, Thomas Chute, 16, James Sharer, 19, Joseph Majory, 21, John Stacey, 22, Richard Reed, 23, John Bayly, 26, James Perryman, 27, Moses Calley, 30, Nathan Bowen, 32, Abrah^{m} Howard Esq, 38, Benjamin James Ju^{r}, 42, Isaac Mansfield, 44, Joseph Howard, 46, Samuel Brimblecomb, 47, Joseph Griffin, 48, Joseph Smethurst, 49, Will.~ Ingalls, 51, John Felton, 52, Joseph Blany Esq, 53, Andrew Tucker, 55, Nathani^{l} Evans, 57, William Meberry, 58, William Goodwin, 61, Giles Ivimy.

An Account of the Settlement att N Marblehead And by who made this 26 April A D 1759 —

No 1 — School Lot unsetled
2 — 8 Acres Land Cleared } Duble house Settl^{d}
3 — Ditto } by Maxwel Maybury 1755
4 — unsetl^{ed} under ye Care Esqr T
5 — 9 Acers Cleard with a house as setled by Epharam Winship 1750

6 — 9 Ditto with a Barn setl^{d} by Epharam Winship 1750
7 — 8 Ditto with a house Setl^{d} by Joseph Sterling 1751
8 — 9 Ditto with the Remains of a house Setl^{ed} by Joseph Sterling 1750
9 — 10 Ditto the house Rotten Down Setled _ John Bodge 1744
10 — 10 Ditto with a house Setl^{ed} — John Bodge 1752
11 — 8 Ditto the house Rotten Down Setl^{ed} Willm Maybery 1740
12 — 7 Ditto the house Rotten Down Setl^{d} Curtis Chute
13 — 7 Ditto } no houses Improved by Cp^{t} Thom^{s}
14 — 7 Ditto } Chute
15 — 8 Ditto ye house Rotten Down Sett^{d} Gershum Mansheter Deceas^{d} 1740
Oulton: 16 — 9 Ditto with a house Setl^{ed} by John Mansheter 1752

17 — 13 Ditto }
18 — 13 Ditto } These Four Belong to Thomas
19 — 13 Ditto } Maybery with a Garrison house
20 — 11 Ditto } on N° 19

21 — 10 Ditto with a house Setl^{ed} by Sam^{ll} Webb 1752
22 — 7 Ditto with a house Setl^{ed} by Saml Mathews Deceased 1751
23 — 8 Ditto with a house Setl^{ed} by Seth Webb }
24 — 8 Ditto the house Rotten Down Own^{d} by s^{d} Webb } 1744
25 — 15 Ditto with a house but N^{o} family }
26 — 15 Ditto Setl^{d} by W Maybery } 1750
27 — 15 Ditto no house, Belongs to Richd Maybery w^{o} Dwelt with his father
28 — 9 Ditto the house Rotten Down Setl^{d} by Nathl Starbord deces^{d} 1745

29 — 12 Ditto the house Rotten Down Setl^{d} by John Farrow Deces^{d} 1740
30 — 12 Ditto a Garrison^{d} house Setl^{d} by John Farrow Deces^{d} 1752
31 — 12 Ditto the house Rotten Down Belonging _ s^{d} Farrow 1743
32 — 12 Ditto with a house Setl^{d} by Stephen Mansheter 1742
33 — 2 Ditto Ministeri^{ll} Lott
34 — 7 Ditto upon which stands Province Fort
35 — 7 Ditto the house Rotten Down Setl^{d} by Rev^{r} Mr Wight
36 — 15 Ditto a Rotten Down house Buil^{t} by Abraham Anderson 1740
37 — 15 Ditto a Rotten Down house Buil^{t} by s^{d} Anderson 1740
38 — 14 Ditto a house now Standing Buil^{t} by s^{d} Anderson 1750
39 — 7 Ditto a house Built & Setl^{d} _ Thom^{s} Humphrys Deces^{d} 1742
40 — 7 Ditto the house Rotten Down Setl^{d} Sam^{ll} Elder Deces^{d} 1743
Oulton 41 — 7 Ditto the house Rotten Down Setl^{d} – Jonas Noys Deces^{d} 1748
42 — 5 Ditto a house Belonging Cp^{t} Chute 1752
43 — 4 Ditto with a house but no family
44 — 7 Ditto with a house Setl^{d} by Zub^{ll} Hunniw^{ll} 1756
45 — 7 Ditto } a Duble house setl^{d} by Willm Elder 1753
46 — 8 Ditto }
47 — 14 Ditto a house now improved by John Steven Deces^{t}
48 — 14 Ditto a house now improv^{d} by John Stevens Seno^{r}
49 — 7 Ditto by Mich^{ll} Walker who is Setl^{d} on the Hundred Acers

50	— 12 Ditto with a Barn belonging Hugh Crage	1751
51	— 12 Ditto with a house belonging s^{d} Crage	
52	— 14 Ditto the house Rotten Down Setl^{d} by Tho Bolton	1741
53	— 14 Ditto a Garrisond house Belonging Willm Bolton	1744
54	— 13 Ditto house Rotten Down Setl^{d} Tho Bolton	1742
55	— 12 Ditto a house Belonging Robert Muckford	1755
56	— 10 Acres with a house Belonging John Maybery	1751
57	— 10 Ditto with a house where s^{d} Maybery now dwells	
58	— 9 Ditto with a house setl^{d} by Eleazer Chase	1751
59	— 9 Ditto the house Rotten Down Setl^{d} by Brown Deces^{d}	1750
60	— 7 Ditto the house standing but no family	1749
61	— 9 Ditto a Garrison^{d} hous Belong^{in} Caleb Grafton	
62	— 2 Ditto no house nor family Belonging Wi^{ll} Knights	
63	— 9 Ditto the house Rotten Down Setl^{d} by Caleb Grafton	1743

Quantity Acers Land Clear^{d} in s^{d} Town 594

p̱ Sam^{ll} Turner
John Wight

The Names of the Familys now Sett^{d} at N Marblehead taken by John Wight & Saml Turner

Setled

No 3	Max^{ll} Maybery	30	John Farrow
5	Chas Winship	32	Stephen Mansheter
6	Gershum Winship	35	Abr^{m} Anderson
7	Joseph Sterling	44	Zub^{l} Hunniwell

10 John Bodge
12 C Chute
42 Tho Chute
16 John Mansheter
19 Tho Maybery
21 Saml Webb
22 Saml Mathews
23 Seth Webb
26 Willm Maybery
27 Richd Maybery

46 Willm Elder
47 John Stevens Junr
48 John Stevens Senr
49 Mich^{l} Walker
51 Hugh Crage
52 Thos Bolton
53 Willm Bolton
55 Robt Muckford
57 John Maybery
58 Eleaz^{r} Chase
61 Caleb Grafton

29

Petition of Proprietors of Neguassett. 1759.

Province of Massachusetts Bay

To His Excellency Thomas Pownall Esquire Captain General Governor and Commander in Chief in and Over the Province aforesaid and Vice Admiral of the Same, and to the Honble His Majestys Council and the House of Representatives of the said Province in General Court Assembled at Boston May 30th 1759.

The Petition of Us the Subscribers the present Proprietors and Planters of a Certain Tract of Land commonly called Neguassett in the County of York holding in the Right of Messrs Lake and Clarke deceased Humbly Shews

That your Petitioners are the Proprietors and Planters of a certain Tract of Land called Neguasset lying in the County of York aforesaid which Tract of Land is bounded & described as follows Beginning at Towessick gutt at the head of Arrowsick Island or George Town so called and running Northerly on Sagadahoc or Kennebeck River to a certain Pine Tree marked which is the first marked tree in ye boundary Line between the said Province and the Plimouth Company from thence Easterly on said Line to Mountsweeg River as the Line is now established, and from thence Southerly down said River and Mountsweeg Bay including an Island called Oak Island and from thence again Southerly Round a point of Land called Phips's point and from thence Westerly to a point called Hawkomoka Point, and from thence Northerly running through Hells-gate so Called into Towessick or Neguassett Bay to the bounds first mentioned as by an Authentick Plan of the said Tract of Land hereunto Annexed and presented wherein the Same is more particularly delineated and described will more fully appear —

That your pet[rs] by reason of their not being incorporated Labour under many and great difficulties and disadvantages with respect to the preaching of the Gospel among them, and having no Settled Minster, but are obliged to Embrace any Opportunity when they can procure it, to have the Gospel preached among them gladly paying for it, and that hitherto has been but very Seldom, untill Since the Month of January last —

That your pet[rs] among themselves by a voluntary private Subscription have Sett up and are Erecting a very Convenient House for the public Worship of God, and with his blessing they intend to finish it in a Commodious and Suitable manner —

That your pet[rs] notwithstanding this, are under many other difficulties by reason of their not being incoraged, as they can carry on no regular Religious Order among themselves and their respective familys [Wch] they greatly Lament and bewail —

Wherefore your petitioners most humbly pray this Hon[ble] Court to take their Unhappy Circumstances into your paternal Consideration and out of your known Wisdom and goodness for the regular Order and promotion of Religion in the Province, to Incorporate your petitioners and the Lands aforementioned into a Township or District by the Name of Woolwich, or such other Name as your Excellency and Honours shall think fitt and to Vest them with such priveledges and immunities as other Towns or Districts within this Province by Law are invested with and Enjoy, and under such Regulations, and Limitations, as this Honble Court shall Judge fitting and proper for their Circumstances —

And your Petitioners (as in duty bound) shall ever pray &ca —

James Grant	Thomas Stinson	Solomon Walker
Samll Harnden	James Savage	Samuel Bauchard
Elijah Grant	Daniel Lankester	Joseph Ḡ
David Gilmor	John Curtis	Joshua Farnham
Elihu Lankester	Jonathan Carlton	Ebnr Smith
Joseph Paine	Richard Greenleaf	Isaac Savage
Michl Card	Joshua Bayley	Andrew Grant
Edward Savage	Aaron Abbit	Nathanael Webb
Simon Cross	Samuel Lemon	Simon Sloman
Joseph Lankeste	James Blanchard	Ebenezer Brookens
Robert Stinson	William Gilmor	John Carlton
Samll Harnden Jur	Daniel Savage	John Pain
S G	Samuel Greenleaf	

In the House of Repves June 9 1759 Read and Ordered that the Petrs serve the Town of George Town (so called) as also the first Parish in said Town with copys of their Petn by leaving an attested copy thereof with their respective Clerks that they may shew cause if any they have on the Second tuesday of the next Sitting of the Court why the Prayer thereof should not be granted.

Sent up for concurrence S: White Spkr

In Council June 9. 1759 Read and Concurd

Thos Clarke Dpty Secry

In Council Octr 11, 1759

Read again together with a Vote of the Town of George

Town relative to the Affair: and Resolved That the Prayer of the Petition be so far granted as that the Petitioners have liberty to bring in a Bill for erecting the Lands prayed for into a District with power to join with the Town of George Town in the Choice of Representatives.

Sent down for Concurrence A Oliver Sec[r]

In the House of Rep[ves] Oct[r] 11. 1759

Read and Concurd S: White Spk[r]

Speech. June 1, 1759

Gentlemen of the Council & House of Representatives

Since the Dissolution of the Late Assembly I have been to the Penobscot Country a Larg & Fine Tract of Land in the Dominions of the British Crown belonging to this Province, but for many Years a Den for Savages & a lurking Place for some Renegadoe French: By the Blessing of God I have succeeded in taking Possession thereof, & have I hope establish'd that Possession by Fixing a Fort on y[e] Penobscot River in such situation as to be very respectable for its own defense being no where commanded, but more so for y[e] Command it holds of both Branches of y[e] River & of the Carrying Place therefrom; of Edgemoggin Reach y[e] Outlett, & of Pentagoet the Rendevouz, of the Eastern Indians when they come against our Frontiers.— This River was y[e] last & only door That the Enimy had left to y[e] Atlantic & I hope this is now fairly shutt upon them, What is Necessary to inform Your Judgment Provision for Carrying y[e] Measure to its Utmost Effect I will order to be laied before You with – Plans & Surveys.

Before my departure I issued out beating Orders for the raising the Second Levy of 1500 Men for which the late House had made Provision: I entrusted the care of Forming & Sending them Off to His Honor the L[t] Gov[r], the very proper Dispositions & Dispatch which He has made deserve my thanks I will lay before You, what has been done as to the Success & Disposal of the Levies, by the Report which the Lt Govr makes to me

T Pownall

Council Chamber June 1st 1759

Message. "6 June 1759."

Memorandums

As the Service that must Arise to this Country from takeing Post & building a Fort at Penobscot – can never arise from a Garrison lying idle in & about ye Fort – I propose to Consider ye Fort rather as a Lodgment for a Body of Men – from whence I will keep out constant Scouts & Ambushes at all ye Passes that lead to our Settlements, so as to Check ye Indians from coming in small lurking Parties —

For this Six Whale-boats will be necessary

As the only Way to Curb & Restrain ye Indians is by offensive measures, such as shall render it impracticable for them to subsist. I propose, if they do not come in by Fair Means, to send a Body of Men to find out their Planting Ground & Settlements & Destroy them, as they do ours. So that in Winter they must be either starv'd (for ye French cannot support them) or come into us & depend upon us for their bread —

As ye best Defense for our Frontiers is a Knowledge & Practical Use of that Knowledge, of the Country — I wou'd propose to send Home by Land (instead of in Sloops) a hundred or 150 Men across from Penobscot to Fort Halifax two ways to which I have found out — & from thence by Amescoggin & Pesumpscot to Falmouth —

I woud also know all ye Passes about Penobscot.

For these services and lengthening out ye Establishment for ye Forces there two months is necessary. If ye Court will do that — I will dismiss them in a shorter time if it can be done sooner

T Pownall

Petition of the Brethren of the Second Church and Parish in Falmouth.

Province of the Massachusetts Bay June 1759

To his Excellency Thomas Pownall Esqr Capt General and Governour in and over his Majestys s^{d} Province the Honourable his Majestys Council and House of Representatives in General Court Assembled

We the Subscribers Inhabitants & Brethren of the Second Church and Parish in Falmouth in the County of York apprehending ourselves greatly aggrieved at the pretended Settlement of one Epraim Clark, in the Ministerial Office over the Church and Congregation in said Parish, in the following very Extraordinary and violent Manner, vizt after a great and Solemn Council of Fifteen Churches mutually chosen and agreed on by both Parties held in said Parish in July 1755. which Council spent three Days in Examining and considering the Objections that were offered against his being settled here as a Minister, and on mature Consideration of the Debates and Arguments us'd on both Sides, the Vote was put, whether it was thought proper for Mr Ephraim Clark to be Settled in said Parish, in the work of the ministry, and it pass'd in the negative; and as the Parties had agreed, that their Result shou'd be desisive, we apprehended the Dispute and Difference, relative to said Mr Clark, was at an end, yet notwithstanding, the said Mr Clark and his Adherents have diverse times since, in vain, sent out Letters to such Churches in the Country, as they thought they cou'd prevail with, to come and Install him; but at last have procur'd Mr John Rogers of Kittery, Mr Cleaveland of Jabacco, and Mr Cleaveland of Glocester, with their Delegates, as we Suppose, who did on the twentieth of May Seventeen Hundred and Fifty-six meet in said Parish, to whom we sent our Remonstrance and desired to be heard, which we cou'd not obtain; whereupon they went to the Meeting-House; where we made a second Demand to be heard, and Instead of making us an answer, they Quitted the Meeting-House, and in a riotous and Tumultuous Manner, went to one Mr Simontons Orchard, and there they performed Some Ceremonies which they call'd and the people Understood to be, an Installment of the said Clark, which proceedings of the said Clark and his adherents and those three Gentlemen; we can't but look upon to be contrary to Law, contrary to the Platform and contrary to the order of the Churches of this Land. Whereupon as Disorders of this nature in Settling of Laymen are continually repeated and the prevail'^g Disposition of the Multitude in many Towns in the Province, is toward them, and as ever since the s^d Installment we have been harrass'd, persecuted and imprisond for Rates and Taxes, to support the s^d Clark in the ministry here, whom we can't but look upon unquallify'd, and unfit for said Office, neither have we hitherto, nor can we in Reason or consience attend his ministry. — – Whefore your aggrieved, afflicted and Persecuted Petitioners most humbly and Earnestly pray, this Great and General Court, wou'd be Graciously pleas'd to take their distressed Circumstances under their wise Consideration and grant that we and our neighbours, who are in like manner oppress'd, may be Exempt from paying Taxes towards the support of the said Clark; and have Liberty to join with the first Parish in said Falmouth or any other way grant such relief to your unhappy Petitioners as your Excellency and Honours shall see meet and your Petitioners as in Duty Bound shall ever pray &c ::

Willm Wescot	Ezekiel Cushing	Ebenezer Doane Ju^{r}
Robert Thorndike	William Wescot Ju^{r}	Robert Mitchell
Josiah Skillin	Jonathan Loveitt	Samuel York
Thos Ficket	Josiah Wastcot	Eben^{r} Thorndike
George Haslem	David Strout	Richard Wescot
Loring Cushing	Joseph Sawyer	Jonathan Mitchell
Willm Strout	Sephen Randell	tho delono
Robart Mayo .	Daniel Strout	John Small
Humphery Richards	John Small Juner	James Small
John Delano	Josiah Stanford	Antony Strout
Joshua Eldridge	Timothy Eldrege	Eze Cushing Junr
Joseph Stanford	Josiah Stanford iuner	Robert Stanford
Christo Strout	Thos Wimbly	Whiteford Mayoo
Isaac Small	Jedediah Lombard	James Wimble
Jere Cushing	Robert Thorndike Juner	Isaac Loveitt
		30

In the House of Rep^{ives} June 7. 1759

Read and Ordered that the Pet^{rs} serve the Clerk of the second Parish in Falmouth with a copy of this Pet^{n} that they shew cause (if any they have) on the second fryday of the next sitting of this Court why the Prayer thereof should not be granted.

Sent up for concurrence

S. White Spk^{r}

In Council 7 June 1759.

Read and Concurred

A Oliver Sec^{r}

In Council Jan^{r} 12: 1760. Read again together with the Answer of the 2^{d} Parish in Falmouth and

Ordered That Samuel Watts & Willm Brattle Esqr wth such as the Honourable House shall join be a Committee to take the Same under consideration and report what they judge proper for this Court to do thereon — Sent down for Concurrence.

A Oliver Sec^r

In the House of Rep^ives Jany 15, 1760.

Read and Concurd and Col^o Gerrish Col^o Sparhawk and Mr Hearsey are Joyned in the Affair.

S: White Spk^r

Report & Order thereon. June 15, 1759.

The Comtee on the Petition of the Inhabitants of the Town Called New Marblehead have Considered the Same, and are humbly of Opinion, that the said Inhabitants be Impowered by this Honble Court to Levey a Tax on all the Lands in s^d Township of one peney half peney ꝑ acre for three Years the s^d Tax to be applyd towards Building a Meeting House & settling a Minister and building a School House & hireing a School Master and other things for the Benifit of s^d Township and that they also be Impower'd to settle the Bounds of s^d Township with the Town of Falmouth. Which is Humbly Submitted

ꝑ Saml Watts

June 15th 1759. ꝑ ord^r

In Council June 15, 1759 Read and Accepted. And Ordered That the Petitioners have liberty to bring in a Bill accordingly,

Sent down for Concurrence A Oliver Sec^r

In the House of Rep^ves June 15 1759

Read and Concur'd S: White Spk^r

Consented to T Pownall

Petition of the Inhabitants of the Second Parish in Falmouth.

Province of the Massachusetts Bay July 1759

To His Excellency Thomas Pownall Esq[r] Cap[t] General & Governour in and Over his Majestys Province of the Massachusetts Bay in New-England &c and Hon[ll] his Majestys Council & House of Representatives in General Court Assembled —

Humbly Shew, we the Subscribers Inhabitants of the Second Parish in the Town of Falmouth in y[e] County of York & Province aforesaid, that whereas a Number of the Church & Inhabitants of the Parish afores[d] Exhibited a Petition to the Gen[l] Court in their Last Sessions praying to be Exempted from paying Taxes towards the Support of one M[r] Ephraim Clark in s[d] Parish; & we not having an Oppertunity of Signing the s[d] Petition then & joining with the Petitioners — We pray that Your Excellency & Honours will grant that we may now join the said Petitioners, & that you will look upon us as Such & Exempt us also from paying Taxes towards the Support of the said Clark & Your Petitioners as in Duty Bound shall ever pray &c.

John Horton — Joshua Strout
Nathaniel Jordan — Josiah Stanford Ju
Ebenezer his X mark Cobb

York ss at a town meeting held at Georgetown August 23 A. D. 1759 by virtue of a warrant for that purpos

Secondly Voted that the town do not incline to make any objections upon the granting the petition of the proprietors and planters comonly called nequaset their being made a town or otherways as the Legislature may think proper humbly hoping that the government will tak_ off from said town and lay on the petitioners a fitt proportion of publick charges to the province and county.

Samuell Denny moderat^{r}

a trew copy as appears of record as

attest Samuell Denny town clark

Letter from Saml Harnden

Georgetown September ye 3^{d} 1759

S^{r}

Pursuant to Your &c Report to the Honourable house I have Notified the town of Georgetown and the first Parrish in said town and inclosed is A Copy of the towns Proceedings in the Affair and the Parrish on Seeing What the town had Done Declined Doing Any thing I Should Gladly have Wated on the Court on this Important Affear But God Was Pleased to Send the Measseals into my family Just as I Was a Prepearing for the Voige five are Now Sick three of Which is Very ill Indeed.

As there is no Opposision I trust the Afair May Be Ishshued Although I am Not there We Indeed With Sumision ask the Power and Privelidge of A town But Being Informed that that Could Not Be Granted – Petetioners Chuse Reither to Be A Districk then a Parrish and the Privelidge of A Vote With Georgetown in the Chose of A Representive I send this By Major Denny Who if You or the Court Want to be Informed in Any Point Can and I trust Will Give A Impershall Account. My Duty to the other Gentlemen of the Commity Except the Same Your Self from

Sr Your humble Sarvant

Sam^{ll} Harnden

P. S S^{r} if I am Under a Mistake in Writing to You I Relie on You to Communicate itt to home itt Should be Sent Cornel Clap

Speech. Oct. 3, 1759.

Gentlemen of the Council and House of Representatives –

By the very Interesting and Important Events with which it hath pleased God to succeed His Majesty's Arms we see the British Empire again rising in America and by wise and prudent Conduct under which they still continue to act we may hope, if we persevere to the End for which we took up Arms, to see it so established as that we may no more Fear the Power or Treachery of the Enemy in Canada. As I most heartily congratulate you on these Events So I would encourage You to remain stedfast in these hopes and to act under this Spirit and Resolution in all that may be required of you for this End. By Gen[l] Amhesrts Letters to me You will see what the immediate Service requires of You. It is with great pleasure I can acquaint You that the Parliament of Great Britain have enabled His Majesty to recompence his Colonies for their Services according as the Active Vigour & Strenuous Efforts of the Respective Provinces shall appear to Merit.

Amongst the many happy Events of this Year there are none in which the People of this Province will partake with more sincere satisfaction than in seeing the Royal Heir to the Protestant Succession arrived to full Age and upon this I do most heartily congratulate You —

Gentlemen of the House of Representatives.

The Estimate of the Current Services lye before You, and I have directed the Treasurer to lay before you the State of the Supplies for these Current services and for the payment of the Troops in the general Service As Your own sense of the service has alway induced you to make Suitable Provision for these I am sure Your Sense of the Benefit as well as Honor that the Province derives from the very high Credit of the Treasury will lead you to make good any Fund that may require your present consideration.—

Upon my Building the Fort at Penobscot I did at your request dismiss the Garrison at Brunswick. I have now also Directed the Dismission of the Garrison at Pemaquid from the same Desire of saving every thing I can to the People amidst their many heavy burthens — I have directed the Scouting Parties at the Lodgments on the Western Frontiers to be dismissed as that part of the Country is now intirely cover'd by the Operations of the Army in those Parts. And I should hope as Measures taken in the Eastern Part shall Produce their Effect, I may be able to Dismiss still more in that Quarter But in the mean while you will remember that as the Enemy's Home is destroyed they must seek their Sustinence abroad; And that Winter is the Season in which they have made the most destructive inroads both on our Eastern and Western Frontiers from Canada.

Gentlemen of the Council & House of Representatives.

I have directed the Secretary to lay before You all such Papers as will require your Consideration.

The State in which insolvent Debtors find themselves after having surrendered their Persons and Discovered their Effects to their Creditors upon the late Act for the relief of Debtors and their Creditors deserves Your Attention And You may depend upon my Assistance in any Remedy which You can apply for their relief consistant with equal justice to all their Creditors both in England and Here and Consistant with His Majesty's declared Will in the disallowance already made.

The Act for providing Quarters for His Majesty's Troops and Recruiting Parties within this Province being temporary is Expired and will, as You will observe from some of the Papers laied before you, require your Consideration.

T Pownall

Octr 3^d^ 1759

Act.

Anno Regni Regis Georgii Secundi Tricesimo Tertio.

An Act for incorporating the Inhabitants of a Tract of Land called Neguasset in the County of York into a District by the Name of

Whereas the Inhabitants of a Tract of Land called Neguassett in the County of York, have represented to this Court the great Difficulties and Inconveniences they labour under in their present Situation, and have earnestly requested that they may be incorporated into a District.

Be it therefore enacted by the Governour, Council and House of Representatives, That the whole of that Tract of Land in the County of York called Neguassett, bounded as follows, Viz[t] Beginning at Towessick Gut at the Head of Arrowsick Island or George-Town so called, and running Northerly on Sagadahoc or Kennebeck River to a certain Pine Tree marked, which is the first marked Tree in the Boundary Line between the Proprietors of said Land and the Plymouth Company, from thence Easterly on said Line to Mountsweeg River as the Line is now established, and from thence Southerly down said River and Mountsweeg Bay including an Island called Oak Island from thence again Southerly round a Point of Land called Phipps's Point, and from thence Westerly to a Point called Hawkomoka Point, and from thence Northerly running through Hells gate so called into Towessick or Neguassett Bay to the Bounds first mentioned, be and hereby is incorporated into a District by the Name of

and that the Inhabitants thereof do the Duties that are required, and be invested with the Powers, Priviledges and Immunities which the Inhabitants of any Town within this Province do or by Law ought to enjoy; excepting only the Priviledge of chusing a Representative to represent them in the General Assembly, and that the Inhabitants of said District shall have full Power, and Right from Time to Time to join with the Town of George Town in the Choice of a Representative or Representatives, in which Choice they shall enjoy all the Priviledges which A by Law they would have been intitled to if this act had not been made.

Provided nevertheless, and be it further enacted, That the said District shall pay their Proportion of all Town, County and Province Taxes already set on or granted to be raised by said Town of George-Town as if this act had not been made.

And be it further enacted That Samuel Denny Esqr be and hereby is impowered to issue his Warrant directed to some principal Inhabitant in said District, requiring him to notify and warn the Inhabitants of said District qualified by Law to vote in Town Affairs to meet at such Time and Place as shall be therein set forth, to chuse all such officers as shall be necessary to manage the Affairs of said District.

In the House of Rep^ves Octr 17 1759

Read three several times and passd to be Engross'd

Sent up for concurrence

Att^r Roland Cotton Cler Dom Rep

In Council Octr 17, 1758 Read a first time —

P. M. Read a second time and passed a Concurrence to be engrossed with the Amendment at **A.**

Sent down for concurrence A Oliver Sec^r

In the House of Rep^ves Octr 17 1759

Read and Concurr'd S White Spk^r

A. Dele and Insert.

the Inhabitants of the several Towns within this Province are intitled to

Petition of Wait Wadsworth & others. 1759

The Province of the Massachusetts Bay

To his Excellency Thomas Pownall Esqr Capt General and Governer and Commander In Chief in and over his Majestys Province of the Masseschusetts Bay in New England and the Honorable his majestys Council and house of Representatives in General Court Assembled Novr the First 1759

The Petition of us the Subscribers Inhabitants of the Towns of Duxborough, Pembrook, Kingston and Plympton most Humbly Sheweth.

That your Petitioners having small and very poor farms or Tenements whereon they now Dwell and some of us not one foot of Land in the world. and Being Desireous of Setling all together In some Convenient place within this Goverment Rather than in Nova-Scotia, where they have offers of Settlements. and Understanding that there is a Large Quantity of unimproved and uncultivated Lands Lying at the Eastward and most Extream parts of this Goverment, at a place called Penobscot River or Bay which may in time be a Benefit to this Goverment, if properly cultivated and Brought under Improvements, Not only of paying of Publick Taxes, for the Support of the Goverment. But also to the Inlarging of its Borders. Your Petitioners Therefore Humbly pray. that your Excellency and Honours would be pleased to grant us a Sutable Tract of Land on said River (or Bay) for a Town Ship under such Rules and Regulations. as you in your Wisdom shall think most proper. and your Petitioners as In Duty bound shall ever pray.

Wait Wadsworth	Blaney Phillips iuner	Nath^ll Simmons
Joshu Thomas	Joseph Foreman Juner	Ebenezer Dawes
Jethro Sprague	Ambros Dawes	Samuel Bradford
Zebedee Chandler	Ezekiel Bradford	John Maclaghlin
Bezaleel	Pelg Chandler	Silvenus Prior
Micah Simmons	Seth Weston	John Phillips
Eliphaz Prior	Simeon Bradford	Thomas Drew
Joshua Stanford	Zenas Drew	Paul Sampson
James Cobb Ju^r	Abner Weston	Sam^el Additon

Benjamin Prior Juner	Peabody Bradford	Joseph Russel
Constant Southworth	Peres Lo	EBenezer Moten
Ebenezer Soule	John Fauce	Micah Soule
Nathaniel Cushing	Elnathan Weston	Seth Bradford
Jacob Weston	Phinehas Sprague	John Hunt Ju^{r}
Robert Stanford	Blany Phillips	Levi Loring
Json Brewster	Joseph Holmes	Edward Tinkham
Wil^{m} Drew	Jabesh Washburn	Wreastling Alden
Nath Loring	William Sprague	Judah Delano
Jedidiah Simmons	Enoch Freeman	Zebulon Drew
George Uffel	Joseph Brewster Juner	Amos Lamson
Peleg Wadsworth	Nath^{ll} Silvester	Sam^{ll} Brewster
William C 56	Joseph Freeman	

Gentlemen of ye Council & House of Representatives

Upon occasion of this Petition I wou'd recommend it to You to consider what Lands We have to Grant

T Pownall

In the House of Rep^{ves} Novr 6, 1759.

Read and Ordered that the consideration of this Pet^{n} be refer'd till the next Session of this Court. And that all Persons Who have any Claims for lands at or near Penobscot give them into the Secretary's Office before _ first day of February next A That this Court may know what lands are belonging to this Province in those parts A

And that Notice be given of this Order in the Boston Newspapers accordingly

Sent up for concurrence S: White Spk^{r}

In Council Novr 6, 1759. Read and Non Concurred, And Voted that Benj^{a} Lynde, John Cushing & William Brattle Esq^{rs} with such as the House shall appoint be a Committee to consider what Lands belong to the province in the Eastern Country at and Near Penobscut and are convenient for settlements & to make report. And the Committee are to give publick notice of the time of Meeting that so such persons as have any Claims to Lands in that part of the Province may exhibit such Claims if they see cause, and that the consideration of this Petition be referred in the mean time.

Sent down for Concurrence A Oliver Sec^r

In the House of Rep^ves Novr 7, 1759

Read and Non concur'd and the House adhere to their own Vote.

Sent up for concurrence S: White Spk^r

In Council Novem^r 9. 1759 Read and Concur'd with the Amendm^t **A**

Sent down for Concurrence Thos Clarke Dp^ty Secry

Dele from **A** to **A**

In the House of Rep^ves Novr 10 1759

Read and Concur'd Att^r Roland Cotton Cler Dom Rep

Consented to T Pownall

Message. Nov. 6, 1759.

Gentlemen of the House of Representatives —

In the same Manner as I did last Year I shall now acquaint You of the State of the several Matters in the General Service, for which You have made Provision, as far as lyes within my own Department.—

The Regulations as to the Bounty Money, The Arms, Accoutrements & Camp Necessaries, being found to be the best calculated for the Security of the Province Interest & of ye Dues of ye Men, are the same this Year as the last. There having been some complaints of undue practices as to ye Billetting Money, The General at my desire sent an officer to Worcester to pay the Billetting money himself, which was an adequate remedy to ye matters complaind of the Improvements also in the regulations as to Sutlers will have a good Effect.

I have seen with great Uneasiness the Extravagant & ill-regulated Expences arising from ye Manner of our Men billetting themselves upon ye Taverns in their way home; I beleive ye summs paied on this account wou'd exceed what You cou'd imagine: The Remedies which I endeavourd to apply had no effect: This Year by a Vote of the General Court it was left to me with ye Advice of Council to make Provision for our Troops on their Return from the Westward. I seiz'd this Opportunity to Desire that the General wou'd provide Magazines for their March Home in the same Manner as was done for their March out or to pay them ye Fourpences in lieu thereof; Tho' this was a thing never done before Yet the General, from a most kind Disposition to do every thing in his power not only to serve but to oblige the Province, has at my Request agreed to the Measure, as you see by the following extract of His Letter to me of Octr 25, 1759 — "at the same time that I return You my particular "thanks for your Favor of _ 15th Inst I shall likewise repeat "those made You by my Secretary in my Name for Your "other Favors of the 9th & 12th of ye same Month together "with ye Answer he has laied before me by which You will "have seen that I have orderd Magazines of Provisions to be "laid up at No 4 where on the return of the Massachusetts "Forces I shall send a Regular officer to see Provisions issued "out to them sufficient to carry them to the Inhabited Coun-"try &, if they choose it, beyond that they shall likewise "have it, but as I apprehend they will not be desirous of "overburthening themselves, & that the Fourpences will be "more agreable to them, That some officer shall be provided "with Money & Directions to pay Every Souldier so many "Fourpences as it will take them Daies to reach their respect-"ive Homes at a moderate March. That their March from "hence to N° 4 may meet with no Difficulties & Delays I "have now a Party of 250 Men ready to clear the road & "make it good." This which I have obtained for you will be a saving of some thousand pounds.—

You will see by the Following Account that the Expedition to Penobscot Cost 5089:17:2 but that if the 400 Men who were employ'd in that Expedition had been sent to join the General Service their pay wou'd have come to 6773:7:6 So that the taking Possession of Penobscot & the Building a Fort here has not only not Cost You one Farthing but that it was formd on such grounds as has saved to the Province £1683.10.4 as must otherwise have been spent had there been no such Expedition & had there been no such Fort. I may therefore Venture to say that Fort Pownall, as it is the best, so it is the Cheapest Fort You have ever had built in this Province.

Account of the Penobscot Expedition under the Command of the Governor

Support of 400 Men from the 31st of March to ye 28th of July	3290.18.6
446l Wt of bread	490.12.0
250lb of Pork	825.0.0
390 Busl of Peas	130.0.0
1750 Gall Mellasses	233.6.8
	5089.17.2
Charge of saied 400 Men had they been as was intended with Genl Amherst from March 31 to Decr 1st	6773.7.6
Saving to the Province	1683.10.4

You had at my Recommendation made very proper provision for the forwarding to their respective Homes those of the Province Forces which were expected from the Eastward. From the Necessity of securing the important acquisition of Quebec & that That Conquest may hold the rest of Canada in Subjection, It became necessary to leave There the whole of the Little Army which took it. These were the Troops that were destined to releive this Province Troops in the several Garrisons & Forts of Cape Breton & Nova Scotia; Others must be now Destined for that Service — But from the Time to which it is most likely the Campaign will continue at the Westward, & from ye Time that an army of such Troops as may be destined to releive ours will take; togather with the length & incertainty of the Voyage of those Troops to ye several Posts, & of Ours Home, it must be certainly between two & three months before we can expect to see our People here. I must therefore most earnestly recommend to You to make Provision that our People may not suffer in the mean while. You will therefore not only make further provision for their Pay, but take Care that They may have what is Comfortable & Necessary for their Health Cloathing & Lodging during these cold winter months. And that the Families of these poor Souldiers may not be deprived of the Benefit which they wou'd have received from ye Pay as well as of ye Comfort of seeing their Freinds return in ye beginning of Winter I must recommend to Your Charitable Consideration the Condition of Many of these Poor Families.

From the punctuall manner in which the Admiral sent home a Number of our Seamen by the first Opportunity I do every day expect ye Return of the whole.

T Pownall

Province House Novr 6, 1759 —

Frankfort, Petition, June 6, 1759.

To His Excellency Thomas Pownal Esqr Governour and Commander in Cheiff in and over his majesties Province of the Massachusetts Bay and Vice Admiral of the Same and the Honourable the Council and Honourable House of Repersentatives Humbly Sheweth

That wee the Subscribers &c are a number of Inhabitants in the Plantation of Frankfort Laying betwen Kennebeck and Sheepscut Rivers, and within the Bounds of the Kennbek Purchas from the Late Colony of New Plymouth of the lands fifteen miles on Each side of Kennebeck River to the Number of about one hundred famelys and hath been for a number of years bringing forward a Settlement there; and, whereas wee find by Experance that in the Curcomstances wee are in and for want of our being Errected into a town and being invested with the Powers and Priviledges that others of his Majesties Good Subjects do Injoy it Prevents Our orderly Proceeding to the Calling, Settleing and Supporting a Gospel Minister; Imploying and Maintaining a School master for the teaching Our Children and many Other Inconvenances not neaceassary to be mentiond to your Excellency and Honours you well Knowing what People meet with where Order and Government is wanting – Wee therefore most Humbly Pray your Excellency and Honours to Take the Primisses and our Curcomstances into your Wise Consideration and Errect us into a town and Invest us with all the Powers and Priveledges as other of his Majesties Good Subjects do Injoy in any Town in said Province by the Name of Frankfort or any other Name as your Excellency in your Great Wisdom Shall think Proper with the following butts and Bounds Viz[tt] begining on the Est side of Kennebeck River at a Pine tree marked Standing on said River and on the North West Corner of a Tract of land belonging to the Proprietors holding under Clark and Lake which North West Corner is a little above merremeeting Bay and is the North line of nequassett Township So Called; from thence Runing an East Southeast Course on said North Line over to Mounsweeg Bay then Down said Bay and Round to Sheepscut

River; then Northely up said River tell it meets with the South Line of a thirty two Hundreed acre Lott; then Runing Southerly down Said River Keeping on the west Side of Swan Island to the first mentiond Bounds which includs Swan Island in said township all which by the Plan anext will more fully appear —

And May it Please your Excellency and Honours if you will be Pleased to Grant Our Request you will Greatly Contribet to the Happiness of his Majesties Faithfull Subjects and your Most Dutefull and Very Humble Sarvants in this Place And as in Duty Bound Shall Every Pray —

Dated at Frankfort Nov[r] 6: 1759 —

Samuel Schuyler Sheepscut River Job Averell Sheepscot River
Abram Nicodemus Place Ditto Samuel Goodwin Goodwin
Thomas Parker Do James Stewart Ditto Philip Call

Michall S	Joseph $\overset{mark}{A}$ Hitching	James Whielden
Robort	Moses $\overset{his}{\ }$Gray	Timothy Whielden
Mathew Hastings	Samuel	Sam[ll] Oldham
James Cooper	Samuel	John peter Coul
John Andrews	Bartholmey $\overset{his}{X}$ Fowler	John
David Joy	James Clark $\overset{mark}{\ }$junr	Abram Pochard
William $\overset{his}{X}$ Moore	Thomas $\overset{his}{J}$ Murfe	John $\overset{his}{X}$
J $\overset{mark}{\ }$	Robert $\overset{his}{X}$ $\overset{mark}{\ }$Lambert	$\overset{mark}{M}$ $\overset{his}{X}$ W
Jon[r] Bryant	$\overset{mark}{\ }$Benjamin Averell	Abiathar $\overset{mark}{\ }$Kendall
William Story	William Clark	Abner Marson
John	Joshua Chamberlain	Caleb Goodwin
Joshua	John $\overset{his}{II}$ Blagdon	Michel Stiffin
Jaques Bagnon	Joshua $\overset{mark}{\ }$Bickford	Nathanel Rundlet
Charles Estienne Houdlette		Sherebiah $\overset{his}{O}$ Lambert
Thomas Low	J	David $\overset{mark}{\ }$Clancy

Message to His Excellency, Nov. 9, 1759.

May it please your Excellency

The House having taken into consideration your Excellencys Message of the 6th Inst beg leave to make our Acknowledgements for those wise and saving Measures which your Excellency has pursued in carrying into Effect the important design of securing the Country of Penobscott and with due Gratitude we perceive that Fort Pownall thro' your Excellencys Wisdom and Care may justly be esteemed the best and least expensive Fortress of any that have been erected in the Province.

We cannot be insensible how highly we are oblig'd to your Excellency for the other Instances of your attention for the Interest of the Province and your concern to prevent those undue Practices particularly relating to the Billeting of our men which your Excellencys vigilence has discover'd Nor can we forbear to acknowledge how greatly we are indebted to General Amherst who has allways discover'd an inclination to serve and oblige this Province for so readily applying the adequate and seasonable Remedy to those abuses which your Excellency had pointed out and which must prove so great a saving to the Province.

It is with peculiar Pleasure we observe your Excellency's paternal Care and Tenderness for our men in the Eastern Service for whom the House have most readily made what they apprehend a proper and ample Provision.

In the House of Repves Novr 9 1759

Read and Voted that this Message be Sent to His Excellency And Mr Flucker Capt Stevens Colo Lawrence Mr Tyler and Colo Bourn wait upon His Excellency and Present the Same to him accordingly

S: White Spkr

Govr Pownall to Mr Secretary Pitt

Boston Nov. 20. 1759

Sir

I have this day receiv^{d} from Lt Col Arbuthnot one of my officers commanding 250 of ye Province Troops at St Johns R^{r} in N Scotia, an account that the Inhabitants of that River hearing of the Reduction of Quebec have surrender'd themselves to him Prisoners at Discretion — Col Arbuthnot had this Summer buru'd five of their Villages and taken several Vessels However they desired to continue on their Lands But as His Prudence did not permitt him to trust them he went up with two Schooners & has brought off about 200 of them, more are coming in. On ye 3^{d} of Novr He receiv'd a Letter from ye Jesuit Missionaire there Surrendring himself & desiring if he may be permitted to remain there & Save his Cure that He may be admitted to take ye Oaths of Fidelity This Priest attempts likewise to mediate for ye Indians to whom also He was Missionaire.

I did not think it material, as I do not presume to make any merit of it, to trouble you, amid so many greater affairs, with my little excursion to Penobscot Country, Genl Amherst having, as I suppose, acquainted you of the Success of it my Establising ye Possession there by Building a Fort: But on this occasion permitt me Sir, to observe one good effect of it — As every other River on ye Atlantic was possess'd by ye King's Arms, Had this, a large River navigable to the largest Ship for near sixty miles from ye Sea, been left open, This in ye very Frontiers of this Province wou'd have been ye Rendevous of all those Canadians & Indians who have now no remedy left for subsistance but to Surrender.

As I have applications from a great many Families for Grants of land at Penobscot Which Families are ready to go down there next spring, I am taking Measure to settle it

Forthwith — And I hope this will not prove the least advantageous amongst the Acquisitions of this Year.

I have y[e] honor to be Sir Your most obed[t] & most humble Servant T Pownall

Petition of Rain Curtis, 1759.

To his Excellency Thomas Pownal Esq[r] Captain General Governour and Commander in Chief in and over his Majestys Province of the Massachusetts Bay, and To the Honourable his Majestys Council & House of Representatives, for said Province in General Court Assembled the Day of December A Dom 1759 Humbly Sheweth

Rain Curtis of Marblehead in said Province mariner That in July A D 1756 he enlisted himself on Board the Province Ship King George @ 40/ ℘ Month and Continued in the service of this Province till the Twentieth day of August in the same year when he with divers others were taken in the Boat belonging to the Province Sloop near Mount Desart by the S[t] Johns Indians & by them carried to S[t] John from whence about the last of October following He was carried to Quebec and there immediately imprisoned & kept in Prison in a Cold Suffering Starving Condition from that time till the surrender of Quebec to his Majestys Forces That your Petitioner is poor and needy & therefore Humbly prays That your Excellency and Honours will be pleasd to Grant him somewhat in Consideration of his Captivity and Sufferings or at least order him to be paid the same wages ℘ month from the time of his being taken as aforesaid untill his return Home to Marblehead (which was on the Fourteenth day of November last) as your petitioner would have been entituled to had he Continued in pay on board the province Ship during that Time And Your Petitioner as in Duty bound shall ever pray

Rain Cortes

Essex ss.. Decemb^{r} 27th 1759

Then personally Appeared Rain Curtis abovementiond & made Oath y^{t} the Facts contained in ye forgoing Petition were true

Coram Wm Bourn J. Pacis

In the House of Rep^{ves} Jany 26 1760

Read and Ordered that the Sum of Six pounds be allowed and paid out of the publick Treasury to the Pet^{r} in full consideration for his services and sufferings within mentioned.

Sent up for concurrence S White Spk^{r}

In Council Jan^{r} 21. Read & concurred

A Oliver Sec^{r}

Consented to T Pownall

Gorhamtown, Petition. 1759

Province of the Masachusets Bay

To his Excellency Thomas Pownall Esqr Governour in Cheif in and over his Majesties Province of the Masachusets Bay in New England and Vice admiral of the Same ~ and the honou^{ble} his Majestys Council & house of representatives in General Court assembled December 3 1759

The Petition of a number of the Inhabitants of Naraganset Township Numb^{r} 7 alias Gorhamtown in the County of York Humbly Sheweth

That we have with great Difficulty and Hardship for many Years past lived in s^{d} Exposed Frontier Township and in Jeopardy of our Lives and indeed with the Loss of Several Lives have we indeavored to maintain our ground to this Time which we could not have done had it not been for The assistance of this Government Heretofore _ That through the

Good hand of Providence our Numbers are now increased to Sixty families in s[d] Township Since which the Proprietors of s[d] Township, who before were very helpfull and generous have neglected us by means whereof and for want of Proper athority among our selves we are in a suffering Condition. Particularly as we have no meeting house nor School our Highways are Neglected and in many Places unpassable our Cattle and Fences without Regulation Some Disorderly poor Persons are rushing in among us and many other things too many to be here related insomuch that Every Thing Seems to tend to Disorder & Confusion, In order of the remidying and preventind of which your Petitioners Humbly Beseech your Excellency and Honours we may be imbodied into a Town bounded on the back Lines of Scarborough & falmouth and from s[d] Lines to extend into the Country adjoining Naraganset No[br] 1 according to the Grant Given by this Honourable Court and that we May be Invested with all the authority and Priviledges of any other Town: Notwithstanding which your Petitioners humbly Pray Your Excellency & Honours that as we are mostly very Poor and on an Exposed Frontier we may not as yet be Subject to any Part of the pucblict Tax; But Pray your Excellency with your Honours that we may be Impowered from this Honourable Court to tax the Nonresident in Conjunction with the Resident Proprietors Lands at Such a Sum pr acre & for Such a term of time as Your Excellency & honours Shall think Proper In Order to Defray the Nessasary Charges that may from Time to Time arise amnogst our Selves: and your Petitioners as in Duty Bound will Ever Pray

Edmund Phinney	John Phinney	Stephen Phiney
Nathaniel Whitney	Briant Morton	Moses
John Williams	John Whitmore	Jeames Mosher
Saimuel Crocket	Nethaniel frost	Joseph Cate
Seth Harding	John Sawyer	A

John Cresy Nathan Whitney John Irish
James Gilkey

In the House of Rep^{ves} Jany 9, 1760

Read and Ordered that the Pet^{rs} serve the Non resident Prop^{rs} of Gorham Town (so called) with a copy of this Pet^{n} by inserting the Substance thereof in one of the Boston News Papers three Weeks successively. That so they shew cause if any they have on the Second fryday of the next Sitting of this Court why the Prayer thereof should not be granted

Sent up for concurrence

Att^{r} Roland Cotton Cler Dom Rep

In Council Jany 9. 1760 —

Read and Concurred A Oliver Sec^{r}

In Council March 27. 1760 Read and Sent down

In the House of Rep^{ves} June 5 1760

Read again and Ordered that Col^{o} Williams Maj^{r} Cushing and Dr Sayer with such as the Honble Board shall appoint be a Comm^{ee} to take this Petition and the Answers under consideration and make report.

Sent up for concurrence James Otis Speaker

In Council June 5th 1760

Read & Concurr'd & Judge Oliver & Co^{l} Sparhawk are Joyned in the affaire

A Oliver Sec^{r}

The State of the Case between the first parish in Falmouth & Cape Elizabeth now pending at the General Court.

1760 Jany 18. A number of the Inhabitants of Cape Elizabeth it being then the second parish in Falmouth, being aggrieved at the Instalment of the Revd Mr Clark petitioned the General Court & by order of said Court at their own earnest request were set of to the first Parish — "there to do Duty & receive Priviledge till the further order of said Court" — For this favour they then expressed their Gratitude.

The first Parish apprehend that there never has been any "further Order of Court," since to set them back & as the same Religious Reasons, for their Request to be set of to the first parish cotinue in full force, they have continued to rate them to ministerial Charges to the year 1769 inclusive — they have not done it in 1770 Out of Obedience to a Resolve of the Court in March 1770. tho they apprehend Cape Elizabeth obtained that Resolve unfairly.

Cape Elizabeth say that the Act of Incorporation passed in Sepr 1765 — set those persons back — & that the matter was then laid before the Court, & that it was the Design of said Act in part to set them back.

As to the matters then being laid before the Court, or their expressly designing to set them back by said Act. we absolutely deny it.— this does not appear from the Act itself — & we call on Cape Elizabeth to prove it.— the contrary appears by Wm Simonton Esq^rs Deposition.

Tis true, some of those persons, the year before s^d Act of Incorporation was passed, petitioned to be set back to ye second parish,— (viz Ezekiel Cushing Esq. & others)

the first Parish was notified, & expressed their willingness to have it done, and if those petitioners had prosecuted the Matter to Effect it probably would have been done, but they never obtained any Order of Court about it. the petition died.— nor was it revived & reconsidered the year after when the District was incorporated as is now pretended. as plainly appears by William Simonton Esq^rs Deposition.

Tis true the Town of Falmouth, (not the first parish,) in answer to the petition of the Second parish to be incorporated, requested that those persons who were set of to the first parish as afores^d, might not be set back again, by the

Act of Incorporation.— & they are not, as y[e] first parish apprehends, for they are not mentioned in the Act at all. Cape Elizabeth supposes they are set back because they are not excepted out of the act. But this, we think, is a very strange Construction of said Act — The Resolve passed in Jan[y] 1760 granted said Petitioners a peculiar ecclesiastical or parochial Privilege. nothing short of an Express Resolve of y[e] same Authority can take away that priviledge nor can such persons be exempt from the Duty annexed to that priviledge, any more than be deprived of the priviledge itself, without an express Order of Court for that purpose. The Act of Incorporation certainly is no such Order it was passed for a purpose totally different. viz to vest that parish (which enjoyd parish priviledges before) with Town priviledges only. The Ideas of a Town & parish are entirely & totally distinct a parish may be made up of persons out of Twenty Towns.

The above is not the Reasoning of the first parish only it was also the Reasoning & Opinion of this hon[d] Court in the Year 1767. & indeed the suspicion of Cape Elizabeth too. at least of their Select men.

For Jan[y] 22. 1767. said Select men Petitioned this Court, setting forth that those persons who were set of to first parish in 1760 were not to their knowledge set back by any particular Act of Court — that they indeed apprehended the Incorporation Act set them back & therefore they had Rated them, & praying the Opinion & Resolve of the Court respecting that point. after Notice given & answer made by the first parish, a Committee of Both Houses in June 1767, reported among other Things, "that for the present all those "persons who were set of to the first parish as afores[d] be held "to pay Taxes to the first Parish, unless they or any of them "shall signify to the Assessors of each Parish by writing "under their hands their Desire of being taxed to the second "parish in which case they shall pay Taxes to the second parish and to that only."

This Report was accepted and resolved by both Houses; and that it was not signed by the Governor was the fault of Cape Elizabeth, (the first Parish having no person then at Court on their Behalf) Thus having the Opinion of both houses on their side and no person leav' their names as afores[d] no wonder the first parish still proceeded to rate those persons as usual — and the Parish Treasurer issued his Warrant of Distress against a Defective Collector, (Joseph Sawyer) for neglecting to collect the Rates of those persons for 1766. He was imprisoned, commenced an Action ag[t] the Treasurer. demand[d] Three thousand pounds — Damages for false Imprisonment.— another Collector distraind for Rates of Jon[a] Loveit one of those persons. & the assessors were thereupon sued, by him, for Ten pounds Damage — while things were in this Scituation, and while the parish had a Demand of more thān a hundred & thirty pounds against those persons for Rates — it was represented to this honorable Court in March 1770, that the first parish had no Objection to those persons being declared to be set back to Cape Elizabeth by the Act of Incorporation — and that they wanted to have it settled so (which was a misrepresentation) The Court being thus misinformed passd a Resolve that they were set back by said Act of Incorporation & ought from that Time to pay parish taxes in s[d] District, and no where else.—the first parish not notified nor heard.— At this the first parish when they heard of it & observed the great Exultations of Cape Elizabeth who could not conceal their Joy at having thus over reached them, were greatly surprised and aggrieved. immediately petitioned this hon. Court. for Redress, obtained an Order, to suspend that Resolve till the first parish could be heard.— they never could since obtain such an hearing.— and at this sessions April 1771, the persons appointed by the first parish to attend being necessarily detained at home by ye approaching Court in Falmouth, & expecting a short sessions only of the General Court concluded to defer it till Election. and accordingly notified the Cape Elizabeth Agent of it — who notwithstanding his word & promise not to go without giving Notice, nor could we appoint another person to be sent after him till a week after.

It is entirely the fault of Cape Elizabeth that the General Court is put to so much trouble about this affair.— had they prosecuted the petition Ezekiel Cushing Esq. & others to effect in 1764, they might have obtained an Order to set those persons back then — had they got the Resolve signed by the Governor in 1767; & taken the Advantage of it. they might have obtained their Request then — had they notified the first parish, as they were ordered to do by the Genl Court, when they again Petitioned in 1768, it might have been done then.— As was before observed, it was the request. the earnest Request, for Reasons of Conscience which yet remain of these persons to be set of to us. we never desird it.—We are brought into great Difficulty by it for doing them an Act of Kindness.— our Ministers salcrys are greatly in arrear; we are prosecuted at Law. & have expended considerable sums to defend ourselves; we have twice already & now the third time been at ye Expence of send^{g} 130 miles to the General Court. to obtain Relief from a Resolve which passed against us without being heard — entirely through a misrepresentation of the matter.

We now therefore humbly pray

That said Resolve passed against the first Parish March 1770, may be wholly set aside — and that instead thereof it may be now Resolved —

That those persons who in the Year 1760 were set of to the first Parish in Falmouth from the second be held to pay parish Taxes in said first parish from that Time to the Year 1769. inclusive of said year 1769. that from and after the year 1769. they be set back to the District of Cape Elizabeth to pay Parish Taxes there & no where else.

And if it should be further resolved that neither they nor any others in Cape Elizabeth should ever be set back to us again nor have any Connexion with us.— the Vexation & Trouble they have already given us will make us heartily to acquiesce in such a Resolve —

The Dispute is really with Cape Elizabeth, they have rated & collected taxes of y[e] same persons, and must therefore indemnify those persons, which can be done only by paying out of their Treasury to the first parish such sum as is due from those persons — and as s[d] Cape Elizabeth has chosen an agent (as is supposed) to conduct this matter; they have thereby taken it on themselves.

In Justice Equity & good Conscience Cape Elizabeth ought to pay all the Cost & Expence they have unnecessarily caused us to be at.

Speech. Jan[y] 2, 1760

Gentlemen of the Council & House of Representatives —

I call you together at this Season that having closed the Business of the Year last past and all matters relating to the General Service thereof — You may consider your Circumstances with a View to that which is approaching — For as You cannot entertain an Idea of leaving incompleat the Work of this War already so greatly and gloriously advanced, or of resigning the good Effects and good Hopes which the many Conquests made by his Majesty's Arms lead to; You must expect to be called upon, for Your Aid of Troops, in the same manner as You have been hitherto: — Having therefore taken into Consideration the Circumstances of those Troops belonging to, and in the Pay of, this Province which are doing Duty at Louisbourgh, Halifax and Lunenburgh and do intirely Garrison Anapolis, Fort Cumberland at Chicnecto and Fort Frederick at S[t] Johns.— You will consider of making the Earliest Provision for those which may be further wanted for the Operations of the ensuing Campaign so that they may be ready at the First Call.—

Gentlemen of the House of Representatives.

By the State of the Treasury which the Treasurer will lay before You, You will see that the Treasury is already supplyed to carry Us to May next upon the present Appropriations, if you make some Transfers — And there is unappropriated in the Treasury the Sum of £20,688–17[s]–6[d] Sterling remitted to the Treasurer by M[r] Agent Bollan which Sum will so far as it goes prevent the necessity of Borrowing. Upon this Veiw I cannot but with Pleasure observe the exact Economy and high Credit of the Treasury and also the good Faith with which the Government has, by the Assistance of the Crown, maintained this Credit.

Gentlemen of the Council & House of Representatives.

There are a Great many Families stand ready to go down to Penobscot — I must therefore recommend it to your very serious Consideration that now every other obstacle is removed You will take Care that no Incertainty in the Titles of the Grants they may have, may be any Obstruction to Settlements which will be greatly beneficial to the Strength and Interest of the Province.

I shall by Message lay before You such further Matters as arise and require your Consideration.

T Pownall

Council Chamber Jan 2[d] 1760

Petition of Robt Carver. 1760

Province of the Massachusetts Bay

To his Excellency Thomas Pownall Esqr Governour & Commander in Chief, The Honble his Majestys Council & Honble House of Representatives in General Court assembled

The Petition of Robert Carver in Behalf of himself & neighbours living at Madamcook in the County of York Humbly Shews,

That during the present War the Inhabitants living at Madamcook have been greatly Exposed to the Ravages of – Indian, seven have been Killed & several Captivated & from the frequent Alarms of the approach of Indians have been drove into Garrison & prevented doing their Husbandry Busness, which has greatly impoverished & Reduced the said Inhabitants.

That the General Court for several Years past having a Regard to the Exposed situation & Distress of the said Inhabitants made an Establishment for the Raising & Pay of a Sergeant & nine privates for their Protection, but in the last Establishm^t for the Defence of the Eastern Frontiers the said Relief was omitted, and the said Inhabitants now lye naked & Exposed to the Ravages & cruelty of the Indian Enemy.

Your Pet^r therefore humbly Prays that your Excellency & Honors would be pleased to Compassionate the Case of said Inhabitants & Grant them such Relief herein as in your great Goodness shall seem meet, and as in Duty Bound your Pet^r will Ever Pray &c

Robt Carver

Jan 3 1760 Ordered to lie on the Table.

Report.

The Committee upon the Petition of Ezekiel Cushing and Others of the second Parish in Falmouth have maturely considered it, with the answer thereto, the Papers put in by the said Ezekiel in favour of the Petitioners as also Col° Waldo in favour of the Respondents And upon the whole beg Leave first to report Facts, and then our Opinion upon the same: First, That on the thirtieth Day of July 1755. an Ecclesiastical Council was convened at the second Parish in said Falmouth, consisting of fifteen Churches; unto which Council the Difference mentioned in said Petition was submitted and by the Committees of the contending Parties, the Result of the said Council was to be decisive and final.—— The Charges exhibited to said Council against Mr Clark were as follows:

(1) His Want of a liberal and learned Education.

(2) His separating Principles, which he set out upon when Ordained over a Separation in Boston.

(3) His immoral Conduct.

(4) The Divisions, Contentions and Mischiefs that will attend said Parish if Mr Clark should he be Installed over the Church there.

— Said venerable Council having considered the same put the following Question —

Question, Whether the venerable Council, considering all Things which have been offered;— think it expedient to proceed to the Instalment of Mr Ephraim Clark in the Work of the Ministry in this Place —

Voted in the Negative.

And accordingly this was Part of their Result, that they advis'd that he should not be instal'd over said Church. At the same Time adding therein. that they find nothing in the Objections made against Mr Clarks moral character sufficient to influence them to such a Conclusion

They go on in their Result to advise said Church to take every prudent Step in Order to such a settlement, as may be, if possible, unexceptionable to those of their Brethren who have differ'd from them.

The above Facts were taken from the Minutes and Result of Council, and sworn to by the Revd Mr Langdon of Portsmouth, their Scribe.

Soon after this Result said Church in Falmouth sent to the following Churches to instal Mr Clark over them, vizt The second Church in Kittery; the first and second Churches in Berwick; the second Church in York; and two Churches more, to wit, one in Ipswich and another in Glocester. How many of the Churches were present the Committee can't determine. Three only of their reverend Pastors were present, to wit, Mr John Rogers and Messieurs Cleavelands, who in direct Opposition to the Result aforesaid, and without any Renewal of the Call of Mr Clark, either by Church or Parish install'd him.—Which very extraordinary Doings of theirs were laid before the Convention of Ministers at their Annual Meeting May the 27th 1756, who thereupon voted (nemine Contradicente) that in the Opinion of this Convention, all such Proceedings are very irregular. Against which they think themselves obliged to bear their Testimony as having a manifest Tendency to destroy these Churches if not seasonably discountenanced.

The Committee can't but in Justice to the said Ezekiel observe that the several Charges in the Respondents' Answer against him are without Ground and injurious.

Upon the whole the Committee apprehend the Interest of Religion, the Order and Peace of the Churches of this Land in General, and in the second Parish in Falmouth and their Vicinity in special, make it reasonable and necessary that such of said second Parish as are aggrieved at the Settlement of said Mr Clark in Manner aforesaid, be with their Estates exempt from paying Taxes to his Support and Maintainance: and therefore humbly propose the following Order may pass:

Saml Watts ꝑ order

That such of the Inhabitants of the second Parish in Falmouth who are aggrieved at the Instalment of Mr Clark, and are desirous not to set under his Ministry (Upon their transmitting their Names together with their Desires to be set to the first Parish in Falmouth) into the Secretary's Office in Boston on or before the last Day of May next, be and hereby are with their Estates set off to said first Parish in Falmouth, there to do Duty and recieve Priviledges till the further Order of this Court.

In Council Jany 18. 1760. Read and Accepted, And

Resolved That such of the Inhabitants of the Second Parish in Falmouth who are aggrieved at the Instalment of Mr Clark, and are desirous not to sit under his Ministry (upon their transmitting their Names together with their desires to be sett to the first Parish in Falmouth) into the Secretarys Office in Boston on or before the last day of May next, be and hereby are with their Estates sett off to said first Parish in Falmouth, there to do duty and receive Priviledge till the further Order of this Court

Sent down for Concurrence

A Oliver Sec^y

In the House of Rep^ves Jany 18. 1760

Read and Concur'd S: White Spk^r

Consented to T. Pownall

Charter.

Anno Regni Regis Georgii secundi tricesimo tertio

An Act for Erecting the New plantation called Francfort lying upon the East Side of the River Kennebeck in the County of York into a Township by the Name of

Whereas it hath been represented to this Court by the proprietors of the Kennebeck purchase from the late Colony of New plymouth that the Erecting the New plantation called

Francfort lying upon the East Side of the River Kennebeck in the County of York into a Township will greatly contribute to the Growth thereof

Be it Enacted by the Governour, Council & House of Representatives that the plantation aforesaid bounded as follows, viz[t]: beginning upon Kennebeck river two Miles and one hundred Rods to the Northward of the Block house within s[d] plantation and from thence running an East South East Course over to Sheepscott River; thence to run Southerly down s[d] Sheepscot River to the mouth of Monsweag River then Northerly up said Monsweag River to the Northern boundary Line of the District of Woolwich; then to run a West North West Course along said Northern boundary Line of Woolwich to the River Kennebeck, thence Northerly up said river Kennebeck to the bounds first mentioned & to include Swan Island and all other Islands in s[d] River Kennebeck lying within the Northern & Southern Boundary Lines of said plantation, be and hereby is Erected into a Township by the Name of

And that the Inhabitants thereof be and hereby are invested with all the powers, priviledges and Immunities which the Inhabitants of the Towns within this Province do, or by Law ought to enjoy; that of sending a Representative to the General Assembly only excepted —

And be it further Enacted that Samuel Denney Esq[r] be and hereby is empowered to issue his Warrant directed to some principal Inhabitant in said Township A. qualified by Law to vote in Town affairs to meet at such time and place as shall be therein set forth, to chuse all such Officers as shall be necessary to manage the Affairs of said Township —

In Council Jan[y] 30. 1760 Read a first time —

Jan[y] 31 Read a second time and passed to be engrossed
Sent up for Concurrence A Oliver Sec[r]

In the House of Rep^{ves} Feby 1 1760

A M. Read a first time

P M. Read a Second and third time and the Question was put Whether the Bill pass to be Engross'd

It pass'd in the Negative

In the House of Rep^{ves} Feby 12 1760

Read again and on A Motion made and Seconded Ordered that the Vote of Non concurrence upon the Vote of the Honble Board be reconsidered And the Bill being read three several times passed a Concurrence to be Engross'd

S. White Spk^{r}

A — to notify & warn the Inhabitants in s^{d} Township —

Letter, Col. Jed^{h} Preble to Gov. Pownall

Fort Pownall ye 4th March 1760

May it Please your Excellency

I arrived here with my Family ye 24 of Last month found the Garrison in good Health the Soldiers ware employed in my Absence in Scouting but made no discovery of the Eenemy.

Last Sunday ten oclock I was informed the Centry had discovered A Flagg of Truce on the other Side of the River, I immediately sent Macfarling with A Flagg, he found Five Indians there, two of which he brought over, I ordered them to his House, where I had a Confernce with them, the particulars of which have enclosed to your Excellency, as allso A number of French Papers which the Indians freely gave me that they said they had taken out of A House at Quebeck all which wish safe to your Excellencys Hand

I realy believe they are now in Good earnest and intend to bring in their Familys they have given me all the assureance, Could be expected from Indians that they will.

they ware ready & willing to Leave one of their men with me as A proof of their fidelity & have promised to return in three weeks or Sooner.

I shall Want your Excellencys orders by the return of my Sloop which I have sent for the sake of Grater dispatch, that I may know in what manner I am to Conduct if they bring in their Familyes

I am may it please your Excellency your Excellencys most obedient Humble Serv[t] Jedidiah Preble

Message. March 21, 1760

Gentlemen of the Council & House of Representatives.—

Since I met You last I have received the King's Command, signified by His Secretary of State the Right Honourable M[r] Pitt, to acquaint You "that His Majesty, having nothing so much at heart as to improve the great and Important Advantages gain'd the last Campaign in North America; and not doubting but that, in this promising and decisive Crisis, all his Faithful and brave Subjects here will continue most chearfully to cooperate with and second to the Utmost the large expence and extraordinary Succours, supplied by Great Britain for their Preservation, and future Security, By Compleating the Reduction of Canada; Expects that You will make Provision for the Levy, Pay, and Cloathing of at least as large a Body of Men as You did for the last Campaign and even as many more as the Number of its Inhabitants may allow, and that no Encouragement may be wanting to this great and salutary Attempt His Majesty is further most graciously pleased to permit his Secretary of State to acquaint me that strong Recommendations will be made to Parliament in their Sessions of next Year to grant a Proper Compensation for such Expences according as the Active Vigour and

Strenuous Efforts of the respective Provinces shall justly appear to merit"

Nothing can give a higher Satisfaction to a faithful and spirited People upon knowing that His Majesty's Pleasure than to reflect that, from an invaried Sense of the Public Interest, from an unremitted Zeal for his Majesty's Service, You have, even previous to His Majesty's Commands, already done these things, by the ample Provision which you have made for the same in Your last Sessions: Nor do I know any thing that has given me so much satisfaction, since I have had the Honor to Command in this Province, as to have been able to lay before His Majesty's Ministers the great Merit of this Your Active Vigour in the Strenuous Efforts You have made.

You will not therefore let this happy conjuncture of Circumstances suffer by the want of any thing which may be requisite to give a full Operation to the Provision you have made, so that the whole may be compleat for Service by the time they shall be called upon. I hear from many Parts of the Province that the Levies go on with Dispatch and Success, and I have the same promising Accounts from our Troops in Garrison at Cape Breton & Nova Scotia; The Spirit of enlisting is in some parts somewhat suspended from some undue expectations of the People who have usually been ready to enlist — I shall order the Adjutant General to lay before you the state of the Levies as soon as it can be compleated & You will then judge what further provision may be necessary.—

I have received an Account from Brig[a] Pribble that the Penobscot Indians have again desired Peace, and that they have given him all the Assurance that could be expected from Indians, that they are in good Earnest,— and do now intend to bring in their Families — I do still remain of opinion that Unless these Indians do, as a previous Measure, Fix their Residence somewhere near the Frontier, and become Domiciliate with us, as most of the Indian Tribes have long been with the French in Canada, so as to be responsible in their Tribe for the faithful Execution of their Treaties — There can no Treaty nor Peace held with them, nor can I answer it to our Eastern Setlers to put their Lives and safety in a situation that must be subject to the Faith of Indians — While I think our Frontiers are much safer under those Precautions which We have taken in a state of Wàr — But if the Indians will Do this, which I have required, I am ready to make Peace with them, and have Ordered Brigadier Pribble to send to me here such Deputation of their People as they shall appoint to Ratifye and Confirm the same.

From Accounts I have received of the number of Indians which the French have Posted on the upper Parts of the River Chaudiere I must recommend to You the making Provision for such Scouts and Garrisons as may be sufficient to put us out of Danger of a Surprize from that Quarter.

His Majesty Having been pleased as a Mark of his Royal Favour to appoint me to the Government of South Carolina and having favoured me with leave to go to England to receive His further Commands, The Right Honble Lords Commissioners for Trade and Plantations think it Expedient for his Majesty's Service that I should return thither as soon as conveniently may be. I am therefore this Session to take my leave of You and of the Province, which I do under the most greatfull Sense of the Honor and Happiness I have enjoyed Therein and Tho' this Parting with Freinds be an unpleasant Task,— Yet I cannot, upon this Occasion, but Congratulate you on the Appointment His Majesty has been pleased to make of Govr Bernard to the Command of this Province, a Gentleman whose Abilities and Good Inclinations to the Public Weal must render any Province happy that He Governs — You will therefore consider of such Provision for his reception as may be not only suitable to the Honor & Dignity of the Commission which He bears, but also to the Good Hopes which the Province may Assure itself of in his Administration.

I had nothing further to recommend to You, but the Calamity which has fallen upon this Town by Fire gives melancholly occasion for me to Call upon You, that while, Eye-witnesses of the Dreadfull Devastation You view the Ruinous Condition of a Town that has long bore so large a Share in the public Burthens, You may consider in what manner the Country can most Effectually Releive it.

T Pownall

March 21, 1760.—

Petition, March 24, 1760.

To his Excellency Thomas Pownall Esq[r] Cap[t] General & Governour in Chief in and over his Majesty[s] Province of y[e] Massachusetts Bay in New England The Hon[ble] his Majestys Councel & house of Representitives in General Court Assembled The Petetion of Jacob Hamblen & Hugh Mclellan a Committee of the well Affected Resedent Proprietors, & well Affected Inhabitants of Narraganset Township N[o] 7 Alias Gorham Town Humbly Sheweth that whereas we have heard that John Phinney, Briant Morton and others have Prefer[d] a Petition to the great and Gen[l] Court of this Province Praying that the Inhabitants be invested with y[e] Power and prevaledge as propper to an Incorporate State Equal with Other Towns &c.

We your Humble Petitioners in y[e] Name & behalfe of all y[e] well Affected who are hearty well wishers to government & fully Attached to y[e] Constitution of our Churches & bare a true Affection to a Learned Ministry, and have not the least Inclination to prove prejuditial to any Publick Intrest nor prevent the exersise of any power that may be for the Real benefit and Peace of Society, nor prevent any Power Lodg[d] in any hands that may Answer y[e] end of Government (viz) God[s] Glory & the Good of men — we therefore would lay before your Excellency & Hon[rs] the Reasons We think why no good end Can possobly be Served by Granting y[e] prayer of s[d] Petition — And they are as follows —

1st Because they who are Petitioners as well as y[e] Rest of the Inhabitants are Sufficiently Poor without y[e] Additional burden of Province County and Town Tax to make them more so.

2[ndly] Because of that Temper which has appear[d] in the Petitioners for a Number of years Forebods no good to y[e] well Affected nor Proprietors.

3[dly] Because it will give Rise to many Law Suits att y[e] Common Cost as they seem to threaten. And thereby gratify Letigious Minds.

4[thly] Because the well Affected — as well as y[e] Disaffected must all have Part in Building a meeting House for the Town over and above the Meeting House Built by the Proprietors if a Major Vote Can be obtain[d]. And this will Answer a Grand end to them (viz) Make us Assist in building a House.

Your Humble Petitioners therefore for the Reasons offerd. with more that might be offerd. Pray your Excellency and Honours to Dismiss the said Petition of Phinney, Morton and others. And your Petitioners as in Duty Bound Shall ever Pray —

March 24th 1760 Jacob Hamblen
Hugh M[c]lellan

The well Affected Resident Proprietors own Sixteen Rights the Disaffected Resedent Proprietors own Ten Rights. Certain. & four more Uncertain.

Gorhamtown, Petition, 1760.

Province of the Massachusetts Bay

To His Excellency Thomas Pownall Esq[r] Cap[t] Gen[l] & Comander in Cheif in & over said Province the Hon[ble] his Majestys Council &. House of Representatives in Gen[l] Court assembled 1760 —

The Petition of a Number of The Non Residents Proprietors of Nareagansett No 7 alias Gorhamtown in the County of York Humbly Sheweth That having herd a Petition of a Number of the Inhabitants of said Gorhamtown praying that they might be Incorporated into a Town & that the Resident and non Resident Proprietors Lands in s[d] Township may be Taxed for a Number of years as the Hon[ble] Court shall order we are humbly of Opinion that Their Request is very Reasonable & with Regard to the Lands being Taxed in Perticular & for that the said Propiety were obliged to Build a Meeting House and Settle a School and that altho some money was Voted about Sixteen years ago for that End yet it was otherwise appropriated & they have not nor ever had any meeting House Built nor School Setled by the s[d] Proprietors among them Wherefore we Humbly Pray that said Petition may be Granted and as in Duty Bound shall ever Pray —

James Bryant	John Bayley	W Riggs
Geor:	Solomon Haskell	Benj[n] Haskell
John Johnson	Joseph Weston	Joseph Parker

Gorhamtown, Petition

To his Excellency Thomas Pownall Esq[r] Cap[t] General and governour In Chief In & over, his Majestys Province of the Massechuseets Bay In New England the honrable his Majestyes Councel & house of Representatives In General Court assembled John Waite William Cotton and Joshua Bangs In the name and Behalfe of the Nonresident Proprietors of the Narreganset township N° 7 alias Gorehamtown humbly Begg leave to shew that said Proprietors have transiently heard that Messrs John Phinney Bryant-Morton & others have Petitioned your Excelency and Honours to be Incorperated & Vested with the Power & Priviledges of other Towns within s^d^ Province; Be Exempt from Publick tax, and be Enabled to tax the Non-resident proprietors land: with the lands of the Resident Proprietors to defray their Necessary Charges—

To which Petition said Proprietors, have heard your Exclency and Honours Orderd said Proprietors should be Sarved with a Copy that they Shew Cause if any they have why there prayer should not be granted on which transient Report s^d^ Proprietors being Notified & Meet,— Choose Moses Pearson Esqr there Agent to Attend this Honour^le^ Court with there Reasons why the Prayer of s^d^ Petition should Not be granted and we the Subscribers to draw up the Reasons to Prefar the next sitting of the great & general Court, beaing thus far Oblig'd to act In the dark haveing seen no Publick Print Intimateing the order of Court thereupon & beaing Refus'd a Copy of s^d^ Phinney, Morton & others Petition, Your humble Petitioners therefore Pray your Exceelency & Honours to Accept of Our Reasons why we Cannot be Content that the Prayer be Granted; which are as follows: for that the Proprietors have Settled a gospel Minister within the Meaning of the law & at their own Charge have for Near teen years supported and are ready to Support still, & the Money Raised for highways & other Accidental Charges to the amount In the whole Near teen thousand Pounds old tenner is an act of liberallity Perhaps Not to be Equald In the like Case though-out North: America: Notwithstanding which some uneasy tempers which had crept Into town that ware neaver Easy any wheare; began to be troublesom to the

Proprietors, & failing in many attempts turned their Plan of operation against the Proprietors, Minister, & Ran such lengths as Prehaps were Never before heard of In all Christendon & which the Proprietors agent will lay before his Excelency & Honours if Expedient, & soon Sepperated themselves from his Communion, on which A councel was Called & upon the whole that it Might be for the best to dissolve the Union between their Pastor & them leaveing the Pastor & those attached to his Interest In full Possession of his & their former Privilidges; thinking that the disaffected after a little while would cool & Return to there deuty Insted of which they soon look out for one to lead them as a Minister & found one Namely a layman who for his Misconduct has been & still is In bad standing In the Church whereof he is a Member Contrary to all advice given by thire best friends: & affter some faint attempts to get Ministers to assist In the ordination of their New Choosen Minister which No Authority on Earth Could assist in the like Case four of the boldest of them: to wit — two Captains one lieutenants & one who Never had the favour of a Commission: And this May it Please your Exelency & Honours is the true state of the case with them who are Petitioners In order to their beaing Incorporate: which Necessity Reather then Inclination has forced us to Expose to light: & with Regard to the Meeting-house have been & still are Ready to build the same when Ever we think it May be done In Safety; & In order thereto have Raised £800 Old Tenner towards the same over & above the Money laid out on the flanker as a Place of Worship which has hitherto sarvd for that Purpose: & Moreover it is the Oppinion of the Proprietors that y[e] dissign of the Petitioners Namely Phinny & his Petitioners Is to burden the Proprietors with an Additional tax for the Support of their own Minister over & above y[e] tax Raised & to be Raised for the Proprietors Minister which they are under obligation to

Perform Pursuant to the Covenant made betwen the Parties which still is In force, & ye Proprietors are humbly of Oppenion that ye Petitioners themselves Cannot Receive any benefit by beaing Incorporate, and if Not to them it must Necessarily be Intollerable to such of their Neighbours as they are Not well affected to, to the Proprietors who have been so bountifull towards them by Cutting as Many ways thro' the proprietors land as their displeasure shall dispose them, & Many other Inconveniances to_ many to be Mentioned will follow upon haveing Power In such Hands. Upon the whole your humble Petitioners Pray that the Petition of John Phinney, Bryant Morten & Others be dismissed: and your Petitioners as in duety bound shall Ever Pray

Jn° Waite
William Cotton } Committe_
Joshua Bangs

*Petition of Richard Cutt J^r^*

To the Honble Spencer Phipps Esqr Lieu^t^ Governour & Commander in Chief in & over the Province of the Massachusetts Bay to the hon^ble^ his Majestys Council and to the hon^ble^ house of Representatives in Great and Genl Court on the 30th day of May A. D. 1760. Assembled.

The Petition of Richard Cutt Junr of Kittery in ye County of York Esqr Humbly Shews that at a legal Parish meeting held In the lower parish in the town of Kittery on ye 11th day of December last it was among other things Voted that the Whole Soil of said Parish Should be divided into two Separate Parishes in Equal halves for Quantity & Quality and Chose a Comittee & proper Attendants to divide ye same and Voted y^t^ ye Reverend John Newmarch should be Supported by ye whole Parish aforesaid as to maintainance notwithstanding a Division of s[d] Parish. Which Committee have since Divided s[d] Lower Parish & made Report thereof, and at s[d] Parish meeting your Petitioner was Chosen & Appointed by said Parish to Apply to this great & Gen[l] Court for a Confirmation of the Division of s[d] Parish Wherefore your Petitioner humbly Prays your Excellency & hon[s] to Confirm y[e] Proceedings of s[d] Parish & the Division thereof as by s[d] Committee Reported & your Petitioner as in Duty Bound shall Ever pray &c

Rich[d] Cutt J[r]

New Marblehead

We hereby Certifie that the Proprietors of New Marblehead At their Meeting yesterday Granted £120 to be paid out of the Proprietors Treasury and applied to the Assisting the Inhabitants of the Township to settle A Minister there, And toward his Support for One year to Commence and be Accounted from the Ordination of such Minister; And sixty pounds per year more for the two years next Coming after that Time, toward Support of s[d] Minister. Provided the Greate & Gene[l] Court do not lay Any Tax's on s[d] Proprietors or Order Any Tax's to be laid on them during that Time —

Which grant is to the Mutual Sattisfaction of the Proprietors & Inhabitants, Who have agreed that the Petition of the Inhabitants Now depending before the Greate & General Court do Cease & be no further prosecuted.

Nathan Bowen for & in behalf
Marblehead June 6, 1760 of s[d] Proprietors
Abraham Anderson for & in
behalf of the Inhabitants

Superscribed — To Jacob Fowle Esq[r] In the House of Representatives In Boston

Order on Gorham Town Petition, 1760.

In Council June 10, 1760 —

A Petition of Edm[d] Phinney & Others Inhabitants of Narraganset N° 7. alias Gorham Town — Praying that they may be incorporated into a Township, but that in consideration of their Poverty they may be freed from the Public Tax, and that the Lands of the Non resident proprietors in conjunction with the Lands of the resident Proprietors may be taxed for defreying necessary Charges — having been together with the answer on the 5 Instant committed to a Committee of both Houses, the Committee on the part of the Board reported That they had heard the Parties and fully considered the matter, and were of Opinion that said Petition be dismissed. Ordered that said Petition be dismissed accordingly —

Sent down for Concurrence A Oliver Sec[r]

In the House of Rep[ves] June 10 1760

Read and Concur'd James Otis Speaker

County of Cumberland incorporated 19 June 1760.

Scarboro 19 Oct. 1658 Black point, blue point, &c.

North Yarmouth 31 Oct. 1713

Falmouth 12 Nov. 1718 Spurwinck & Casco bay/ Ancient town made a town 19 Oct. 1658/

Brunswick 26 June 1738

Harpswell 25 Jan[y] 1738 Merriconeag Neck

Windham 12 June 1762 New Marblehead

Gorham 30 Oct. 1764 Gorhamtown

Cape Elizabeth 1 Nov. 1765 2[d] Parish of Falmouth

New Gloucester 8 Mar. 1774 New Gloucester

Gray 19 June 1778 New Boston

Standish 30 Nov. 1785 Plant. Pearsontown

Portland 4 July 1786 Falmouth Neck

Turner 7 July 1786 Plant. Sylvester

Freeport 14 Feb. 1789 N. E. part of North Yarmouth & Prouts Gore

Durham 16 Feb. 1789 Royalsboro

Hebron 6 Mar. 1792 Shepardsfield — Additional Act June 21, 1804 — bounds —

Buckfield 16 March 1793 Bucktown or N° 5

Paris 20 June 1793 N° 4

Bridgeton 7 Feb. 1794 Plant. Bridgeton

Poland 17 Feb. 1795 a tract of land bounded by several towns

Jay 26 D° Phipps Canada

Livermore 28 D° Plant. Livermore, lying on both sides Androscoggin River

Plant. Raymondstown

Plant. Bakerstown

Norway 9 March 1797 several tracts & grants

Otisfield 19 Feb. 1798 Plant. Otisfield, Phillips gore annexed Feby 9th 1803

Hartford 13 June 98 Plant. East Butterfield

Sumner " " West Butterfield

Rumford 21 Feb. 1800 New Pennicook

Minot 18 Feb. 1802 N. part of Poland

Pejepscot 6 Mar. 1802 Pejepscot Claim & Little's gore

Baldwin 23 June 1802 Plant. Flintstown

Raymond 21st June 1803 " Raymond

Dixfield 21 June 1803 part of land granted to Jonathan Holman & o^rs north side of Androscoggin River

Harrison 8th March 1805 part of Otisfield & Bridgetown

Pownal 3 March 1808 part of Freeport & North Yarmouth

Stroudwater 14 Feby 1814 part of Falmouth (named changed to Westbrook 9th June 1814)

Minot 1 March 1815 Northerly part of Poland

Danville 1st Feby 1819 formerly Pejepscot

County of Lincoln incorporated 21. June 1760 —— divided into 3 Counties 25 June 1789 Divided again 20th Feb. 1799

Georgetown 13 June 1716 Arowsick island
Newcastle 19 June 1753 Sheepscot
Woolwich 20 Oct. 1759 Nequaset
Wiscasset June 10, 1802 Frankfort
Bowdoinham 18 Sept. 1762
Topsham 31 Jany 1764 Topsham
Boothbay 3 Nov. 1764 Townsend
Bristol 18 June 1765 Walpole, Harrington & Pemaquid
K Hallowell 26 April 1771
K Vassallboro D°
K Winthrop D° Pond Town
K Winslow D°
Waldoboro 29 June 1773 Broad Bay
Edgecumbe 5 Mar. 1774 Freetown & Jeremy Squam island
Warren 7 Nov. 1776 St. Georges
Thomastown 20 Mar. 1777 E. part of Warren
K Pittston 4 Feb. 1779 Gardinerstown & E. part of St. Georges
Bath 17 Feb. 1781 2d Parish Georgetown
Union 20 Oct. 1786 Plant. Sterlington
Bowdoin 21 Mar. 1788 Plant. West Bodoinham
K Canaan 18 June 1788
K Fairfield D° Plant. Fairfield
K Green D° Plant. Lewiston
K Norridgewock D° Plant. Norridgewock
Nobleboro 20 Nov. 1788 Plant. Walpole
Cushing 28 Jany 1789 Plant. St Georges
Cambden 17 Feb. 1791

K Readfield 11 Mar. 1791 N. part of Winthrop
K Monmouth 20 Jany 1792 Plant. of Wales
K Sidney 30 Jany 1792 W. part of Vassalboro'
K Mount Vernon 27 June 1792 Plan. Washington
K Farmington 1 Feb. 1794 Sandy River N° 1
K New Sharon 20 June 1794 Plant. Unity
X New Milford 25 June 1794 N. precinct of Pownalboro Alna
Dresden D° W. precinct of D°
Lewiston 18 Feb 1795 Plant. Lewiston & Gore
Litchfield D° — Plant. Smithfield
K Clinton 28 D° — Plant. Hancock E. side Kennebeck River
K Fayette — D° — Plant. Sterling
K Starks — D° — Plant. Lower Sandy River
Plan. Medumcook
D° Ballstown made a town by the name of Whitfield 19 June 1809
K Belgrade 3 Feb. 1796
K Harlem 8 D° —
K Augusta 20th Feby 1797 / 9 June 1797 } Northerly part of Hallowell
K Wayne 12 Feb. 1798
K Cornville 24 D° " N° 2 First Range of Townships & adjoining Plymouth patent E. side Kennebec River
K Anson 1 March 98 N° 1 D° W. side D°
K Leeds 16 Feb. 1801 Plantation Littleboro
K Sandy River N° 3
K New Vineyard Plant.
Thompsonborough 22^{d} June 99 Westerly part of Bowdoin called 20 Feb 1802 Lisbon 20 Feb. 1802 Little River annexed 4th Mar 180–
K Strong 31 Jan. 1801 N° 3 or Reedstown W. side Kennebec River

K Vienna 20 Feb. 1802 Plant. Goshen or Wymans

Chesterville Feb. 20, 1802 Plant. of Chester — lying on both sides of Sandy River

Avon Feb. 22, 1802 Plant. N° 2 in Abbots purchase lying on both sides of Sandy River 1st range Townships N. great Ammariscoggin River.

New Vineyard D° — Plant. N° 2 1st range Townships lying on W. side of Kennebec River & N. of Plymouth Claim.

St George Feb. 7, 1803 E. part of Cushing

Palermo June 23, 1804 Great pond settlement plantation

Hope June 23d 1804 Barrelstown plantation

Jefferson Feby 24th 1807 Balltown D° easterly part

Friendship Feby 25 1807 Meduncook D°

Montville Feby 18th 1807 2d grand Division of the 20y associates plantation of Davistown

Whitfield Balltown plantation.

Putnam 27 Feby 1811 Several tracts

X Alna 28 Feby 1811 formerly New Milford

Phipsburgh 26 Jany 1814 formerly part of the town of Georgetown

Wales Feby 1st 1816 Wales plantation —

Wells, Petition.

To His Excellency Francis Bernard Esqr Captain General & Governor in Chief in & Over His Majesty's Province of the Massachusetts Bay — The Honble His Majestys Council & House of Representatives for said Province in General Court Convened the 13th Day of Augt 1760

The Humble Petition of Sundry of the Inhabitants and Freeholders of the Town of Wells in the County of York Shews

That upwards of Sixty Years ago a Number of Lots of Land were laid out in said Town (from the High Way leading from Ogunquet River to Little River so calld) runing on a West North West Course as then Returnd & Markd upon which the Owners Enterd Fenced & Improvd and on the North Easterly Side of a Place calld the Gore the lots were laid out on a North West Course as was then Returnd & have been so Improved ever Since —

That one James Boston having Purchased one of the Lots first mentioned Lately run out the same without regarding the Old boundaries being Directed only by the Compass as it now stands whereby the Lines of said Lots are made very Different from the old Lines and if all the said Lots should be so run they being two Miles & an half in Length many of them Run quite across other lots at the upper End as they were formerly laid out & the owner of One lot take away anothers Orchard house Barn & other Improvements and Introduce a General Contention & Confusion in the Town as may appear by Inspection of a Plan herewith Presented.

That the said Boston taking advantage of this Variation bro't an Action of Trespass against One Stevens who Owned a Lot Contiguous and as the Dispute arose about Boundaries it was Judgd best to Issue it by a Reference that the Disputed Limits might be viewd &c and tho' the Referrees coud not but See the Consequence of Departing from the old Boundaries in this Instance (for Stevens woud have the same Right to run in upon the next Lot that Boston had upon his & so thrô-out) yet they settled the Late running by their Report and have Opend a Door for a General Mutation, which cant be Equitable because the Improvements are not Equal —

That upon Motion made to the Court Judgment on said Report is at Present Suspended — and as this matter Affects the Peace of Said Town for if Judgment should be Enterd on this Report (the Rule being to make a finall Settlem^{t} of the Line) Stevens must run so far on the next as Boston does on his & so on or some be without Redress which does not Seem to be Just as the Right to this Land is Derived from the Town & the title of One Lot as good as another And as this Variation of Lines is Occasiond by the Variation of the Compass (which as Your Petitioners are informed is more than two Degrees more Northerly than it was forty Years ago) They most Humbly Pray this Hou^{ble} Court would take Cognizançe of & Consider the Premises Set aside the said Report or order that no Judgment be Enterd thereon and Establish the old Boundaries of said Lots to Prevent a Multiplicity of Law Suits or Grant such other Relief or take such other Method to Prevent the Mischief & Inconvenience feared as in Your Great Wisdom & Goodness you shall judge proper and Your Petition^{r}s as in Duty Bound shall ever pray &c

Nathaniel Hill	Sarah Jefferds	John Storer
Joseph Storer	John Storer Junr	John Gendale
John Gooch	Zachariah his Z mark Goodale	John Wheelwright
Sayer	Nathel Clark J^{r}	Nathan
Snell Wheelwright	Samuell Davies	Joshua Clark
John Cusens	Sam^{ll} Clark	Daniel Clark
Samuel Jefferds	Sam̃ Wheelwright	Nath Wells
Hanry Boothby	John Cole	John Clark
Nath: Wheelwright	Jeramiah Littlefield	William Sayer
Joseph Hill	John H–d Hubbard	John
Joseph	Joseph Littlefield	Samuel
Nehemiah Littlefield	Samuel Treadwell	Moses Stevens
Jeremy Stevens	James Davis	Benj Kimball
John Brown	Hans Patten	

Petition of Committee of Harpswell 1760

Province of the Mass[a] Bay.

To His Excellency Francis Barnard Esq; Governour & Commander in Chief; The Honourable His Majestys Councill and House of Representatives in General Court assembled Sep[r] 16, 1760

The Petition of the Committee for the District of Harpswell humbly sheweth.—

That there are settled in said District, to the Number of sixty Families & upwards, who are embodyed in a Church State, and have regularly ordained a Minister of the Gospell, to their general Satisfaction; under this hopefull Prospect, that they expect the inhabitants in said District, will be greatly increased, if this Honoured Court would please to encourage said Infant Settlement, For which Purpose, they humbly ask Leave to represent their present Difficulties, that they may be remedied as in their great Wisdom shall seem meet. A Constable for the District of Harpswell, was chosen in March 1759 The Rates were made by the Select Men of said District. The Ministerial Tax, together with Ten Pounds, voted to defray Parish Charges, were made into a Rate. We being in our Infant State, not perfectly acquainted with the Rules which the Law describes the same was not executed in that Manner the Bill not being offered nor committed to the said Constable, in his Steed was chosen a Collector to collect the proportionable Part of s[d] Tax, assest upon the Inhabitants of the said District, except of those upon an Island adjacent, belonging to the District of Harpswell commonly called by the Name of great Sebascodegin, for which Place a Collector was chosen to collect the proprietors Part of said Tax assest upon the Inhabitants thereof which should have been committed to the former Constable of said Island but was neglected. Neither of which Collectors being lawfully chosen, are vested with lawfull Power & Authority to collect the same. The want of which, a great Part of ye aforesaid Tax cannot be collected, which renders the said District under very distressing Circumstances. Wherefore your humble Petitioners, being incumbered with these Difficulties, most humbly address this Hon[d] Court, for the Remedy thereof, and for the Encouragement of the Gospell settled amongst us, that Nehemiah Curtis & Jn[o] Snow Collectors, the latter of which is for Sebascodegin aforesaid, may be vested with sufficient Power & Authority to Collect y[e] Whole of those Taxes not collected, leavelled against the several Persons in their respective Bills. All which is humbly submitted to the Wisdom & Justice of this Hon[d] Court, and we, your humble Petitioners, as in Duty bound, shall ever pray &

Timothy Bailey } Committee chosen by
L T } y[e] District to act in
Alx[dr] Willson } this Affair.

In the House of Rep[ves] Dec[r] 31 1760

Read and Voted that the within named Nehemiah Curtis – John Snow be required and they are hereby impowered to proceed and perfect the collecting the Taxes within mentioned according to Law, any failure with respect to their qualifications hitherto notwithstanding.

Sent up for concurrence James Otis Speaker

In Council 31 Decr 1760 ~

Read and Concurred A Oliver Sec[r]

Consented to Fra Bernard

Petition of Moses Twitchel & others, 1760.

Province of the Massachusetts Bay

To His Excellency Francis Bernard Esqr Goverñ in and over said Province, the Honble his Majestys Council, &

House of Representatives in Genl Court assembled Nov 1760 Humbly Sheweth

The Petition of a Number of Inhabitants of Casco Bay in said Province

That the Devastation made by the Indian Wars Loss of Records & C[a] in Times past Titles are very precarious here; some of your Petitioners many Years ago have with great Care and Circumspection made Purchases; and large Improvements on the Same, notwithstanding which some old Claim frequently appears and they have been from Time to Time ousted. Others seeing their Fate have refrained purchasing, so that at present most of your Petitioners have but very little Land, & some none at all. Your Petitioners have many, yea most of them a Number of Sons, who are innured to Labour and would be very glad to cultivate and improve Land provided they might have a Grant on a sure footing and as your Petitioners are well knowing that there is a large Quantity of Good Land uncultivated and unimproved on the Northern and Western Side of the Island of Mount Desert and next adjoining the same on the main they humbly beseech your Excellency and Honours that they may have a Township or Townships granted to them their Heirs & Assigns at that Place together with the Islands that may lay between said Township or Townships and the Sea and your Petitioners are willing to give Bond to Settle there with their Families in any convenient Time allow'd by the Court, and will as in Duty bound ever pray

Sam[l] Webb Jonathan Carter
Abraham Clark Solomon Jackson

Petition of Wait Wadsworth & others, Com[ee] 1760

Province of the Massachusetts Bay

To his Exellency Francis Bernard Esq[r] Cap[t] General and Governor and Commander in Chief in and over the

Province afores[d] the Hon[ble] his Majestys Council and House of Representatives in General Court Assembled December the 17th 1760

The Memorial of Blaney Philips and Wait Wadsworth of Duxborough in the County of Plymouth Humbly sheweth that whereas we with a Number of the inhabitants of Duxborough Plymton and Pembrook Did Petition this Hou[ble] Court the Last year that s[d] Court woold Make them a Grant of a Suteable tract of Land for a Township on pornopscott River or Bay for Reasons mentioned in s[d] Petition and as we understand has not as yet ben pas[d] upon by the Hon[ble] Court your memorilest therefore Most Humbly Pray that s[d] Petition may be Revived and a Grant made of s[d] land if your Exellency and Honnours shall think fit and your Memorilest as in duty Bound shall ever pray

Wait Wadsworth }
Blany Philips } Committee for s[d] Petitioners
Briggs Alden }

Provision to be made for Phillipstown 1761

York ss Anno Regni Regis Georgÿ Tertio Magna Britannia, Francia, et Hibernia &[c] Primo

At His Majestys Court of General Sessions of the peace begun and held at York within and for the County of York on the first Tuesday of January being the sixth Day of said Month Annoque Domini 1761 —

Whereas Information is brought to this Court that Divers Inhabitants of the Plaintation called Phillips Town, are now Visited with the Contagious and Mortal Distemper of the Small Pox which Persons are Very Poor and unable to Provide the Necessaries for Support of Life, Nurses & Phisicians Needfull in Such Cases and the said Plantation not being

Incorporated into a Township are not Impowered to Provide for their sick & poor as other Towns are,

These are Therefore to recommend the Distressed Circumstances of the said Inhabitants to the Consideration of Foxwell Curtis Cutt Benjamin Chadbourn Esq^rs & Capt John Lord and to Desire them to order such Provision to be made of Phisicians Nurses & Necessaries for the Sickness of the Said Persons & others in the said Plantation as may be in the Like Distress as they think Convenient the said Gentlemen to keep Acco^ts of what they may advance for the above Perposes and what Families & Persons receive such suplys that so the Suplys made to such as may be Poor and not able to Discharge the acco^ts may be recommended to this Great and General Court for Payment for as much as the Distemper was brought amongst said Inhabitants by Soldiers Imployed by this Government in the Present Expedition for the reduction of Canada

by order Court Attest Jno ffrost Cler.

Copy of record Exam^d p

Jno ffrost Cler.

Dr Fox. Cur. Cutt To Dorcas Goodridge —
Jany To 23 Days attend^g upon the People sick
w^t ye Small Pox at Philipstown @ 4/4.12.0
Berwick Ap. 10th 1761 Errors Excepted p

Dorcas her G mark

York ss/ April 20th 1761

Dorcas Goodridge above named made Solemn Oath to the Truth of the foregoing acco^t

Before Benj^a Chadbourn J. Peace

N. B. The above persons were Soldiers.

Dr The County of York to supplies to the sick
wth ye Small Pox at Phillipstown by Foxwell Curtis Cutt

Jany To 23 Days nursing of Dorcas Goodridge as ℘ her acc^t attested @ 4/ — 4-12 —
T 26^lb Beaf & Pork for the use of nurses &c @6^d — 0- 8- 8

£5- 0 8

Berwick April 27th 1761 Errors Excepted

℘ Fox. C. Cutt —

The above persons were Soldiers —

New Marblehead, Petition

Province of the Massachusetts Bay in New England

To His Excellency Francis Barnard Esq Governour in Chief, To the Honble His Majestys Council and House of Representatives of s^d Province

Humbly Shew the Grantees of a Township call'd New Marblehead in the County of Cumberland; That in Obedience to the Order of this Hou^ble Court in October A D 1758, they sent to the s^d Township Messrs John Wight & Samuel Turner With orders to take an exact Account of the state of the Township, And the progress made by each Grantee toward a Settlement; Who Made Report upon Oath, Which was laid before this Honble Court, Whereby it appears that Twenty nine of the Grantees had setled Families there, (A List whereof are hereunto Annex'd) The other Grantees tho' all of them (but N° 4 drawn by George Pigot) have Cleared Lands on their respective Lotts, they have not Settled Families, there, By which neglect the few Families there have been exposed to greate Difficulties. That this Small Settlement have for many years past dwelt there, without any Gospell Ministry or Any Civil Government Among them. That the Grantees find it necessary that a further division
if 100 Acre Lotts be laid out there, Which can't be Effected

with any Certainty until they Obtain a Settlement of the Boundary Lines betwixt the s^{d} Grant, & the Towns of Falmouth and North Yarmouth on Which they Joyn, Which They Apprehend cannot be effected but by the Aid of this Honble Court.

Wherefore the s^{d} Grantees humbly Pray your Excellency and this Honourable Court

1 That The Twenty Nine setled Numbers be Confirmd to the Respective Grantees & their Heirs. And the non setlers be Compeld as Soon as May be, to compleat their Settlements.

2 That the settlement of the s^{d} Boundary lines May be ordered. And

3 That the Inhabitants there may be Incorporated into some order of Government. And as the Original home Lotts were laid out but 10 acres (to make the settlement compact & Defenceable,) Which has greatly hurt and Discouraged the s^{d} Settlement, your Petitioners now pray that the non setlers may not be compell'd to settle on s^{d} 10 Acre Lotts, Each of them having An 100 Acre Lott Adjoining to the s^{d} home Lotts Already laid out, which will better Suit them and Serve the Township in General. All which is Submitted by your Excell^{ys} & Hon^{rs} Most Hum^{l} Serv^{ts}

Nathan Bowen
John Wight
John Ingalls } Comm^{ttee} for s^{d} Prop^{rs} in this Behalfe

And the s^{d} Com^{tee} further beg leave to inform your Exc^{y} & Hon^{r}s That in the Origenal Grant of the Township, A Right thro' the Township was Reservd for the first Minister, Another for the Ministry, And a third for the school; The first became the property of the Revd Mr Wight dec^{d} as first Minister, The second in its present Rough & uncultivated State can be of little use to the next Minister at least for Some time as the property will not be his, That The sch

Lott N° 44, in the Body of 100 Acre Lotts already laid out lays near the Centre of the s[d] Lotts and where the Settlements are most likely to be made, and therefore Most Sutable for the Meeting house & Commodious for the next Minister if it may be had for that purpose. Wherefore they pray that the s[d] Grantees or your Petitions their Com[tee] may be Impower'd to transfer the s[d] 100 Acre Lott N° 44. To the use afores[d] Saving four Acres to lay in Common for a Meeting House, School House, Burying place & other Public uses, And if your Exc[y] & Honours Should think the Residue of the s[d] School Right, Which will be near 300 Acres should be insufficient for the purpose, your s[d] Petitioners will take Care that in their Laying Out the next Division a like quantity of Land shall be laid Out and Assignd to s[d] School Right, as equivalent thereto, which is also Humbly Submitted

Nathan Bowen
John Wight
John Ingalls

In Council Jan[y] 8, 1761 Read and Ordered That John Chandler Esq[r] with such as the Hon[le] House shall join be a Committee to take this Petition under Consideration & report what they judge proper for this Court to do thereon

Sent down for Concurrence A Oliver Sec[r]

Read and Col° Clap and Major Cushing are joined in the Affair.

James Otis Speaker

Report of Committee.

The Com[tee] to whom was Referred the within Petition humbly report as their Opinion that the Right belonging to the Twenty Nine persons contained in the Annexed List be confirmed to them their heirs and assigns forever, & that the plantation be Erected into a District —

That the other Originall Admitted settlers or those who hold under them being thirty one, be allowed one year from this time to Comply with the Conditions of ye Grant, and such of them as do not; their Supposed Shares or Rights Revert to the province & be disposed of as this Court shall order. That a Comittee be Appointed, at the Charge of petitioners to fix and ascertain the bounds of ye plantation adjoyning to the Towns of Falmouth & North Yarmouth they giving proper notice of the time of their meeting for that purposs — And that the School Lott N° 44 be appropriated for the encouragement of the Next Ordain_ Minister amongst them reserving four Acres thereof for Erecting a Meeting house on & for other publick uses and that previous to the laying out any Further Division a hundred Acres of good land be laid out for the use of the School in Lieu of s^d^ Lott N° 44

p order of ye Com^te^ John Chandler

In Council Jany 20, 1761. Read and Accepted, and Ordered That Richd Cutt Esq with such as the honourable House shall join be a Committee to run the Lines mentioned in said Report

Sent down for Concurrence A Oliver Sec^r^

In the House of Rep^ves^ Jany 20 1761

Read and Concur'd and Mr Bradbury and Dr Sayer are Joyned in the Affair

James Otis Speaker

Consented to Fra Bernard

Petition for Township 1761

To His Excellency Francis Barnard Esq Captng general and Commander in Cheif in and over His Majestys Province of the Massachusets Bay in New England and to the Honble His Majestys Council and the House of Representatives of the said Province February **21th 1761** —

The petition of us Whose Names are hear unto Subscribed Humbly Shews

That your petitioners Having been Imployd in the Late wars by the Massachusetts Government and We hearing that Land was to be Disposed of by the Government for the incouregment of Settlers and their fore most Humbley pry y^{r} Excellency and Hon^{rs} in Considderation of our past Scariveases to Graint us a town ship at or about mount Deseart and your petitioners as in duty bound shall ever pray &c

David Bean	James Bean	Thaddeus Trafton
Thomas Lindsey	Charls Trafton	Joseph Main
Joseph Allen	Moses Welch	Hezekiah Elwell
Martin his **X** mark Grant	Timothy C	Joseph his **X** mark Dill
James Grover	Nathanael Abbot	Simon Grover
Joshua Trafton	Itham Trafton	Webster Simpson
James Gowen	J Allen	Peter Grant
Daniel Grant	Mathew Austin	John Bane
Josiah Black Junr	Benj^{a} Donnell	Nathaniel Harmon
Nathaniel Preble	Benjamin Prebel	John Bradbury J^{r}
Matthias Whiteny	William Babb	Jonathan Farnam
Joseph Carlile	Joshua his **X** mark Gray	Joseph Bradbury
Ebenezer Grant	Josiah Black	William beal
Joseph Horn	Jonathan Clay	Abr^{m} Lunt
Thos Moody	Thomas Hains	Samuel Cook
James Sayward	John Norman	Richard B
John Harmon	Abraham Linscut	Jonathan Mellen
Joseph Moody	Joseph Shaw	Joshua McLeary
James Horne	William Grow	Elisha Horne
Joshua Simpson	Jonathan Nowell	Dummer Sewall
Samuel Adams ju^{r}	Matthew Bright	Jonathan Bean

Alex[r] McIntire Jun[r]	Henry Simpson	Partick his F mark fishgearile
Jeremiah Bragdon	Ebennezzar his ꝏ mark Smith	Charles Bane
Samuel Adams	W[m] Ball	Joseph Baker
Thomas Adams	petiah	Nathaneil Adams
Jn[o] Frost Jun[r]	Daniel Blasdell	Timothy Frost
Ebenezer Blasdell	Silas Nowell Juner	John Grover
Abraham Chapman		

Indorsed Petition of a Number of Soldiers for a Townsh[p]
April 1 1761 James Bean

Col E Jones M[r] Witt Col Dwight Y[e] Com[te] report That This Petit[n] be refer[d] to next May Session.

Petition of Sam[l] Adams. 1761.

To His Excellency Francis Bernard Esq[r] Captain General & Comander in Cheife in & over His Majestys Province of the Massachusetts Bay — the Hon[bl] the Council & House of Representatives in General Court assembled June 3[d] 1761

The Petition of Samuel Adams Clerk to the Proprietors of a certain Tract of undivided Land containing Nineteen thousand Acres, lying on the Western side of Kennebunk River in the County of York, called Phillipstown Humbly Shews

That the said Proprietors at their Meeting legally called & held the first Ins[t] did unanimously agree, that in order to the effectual Settlement of said Land, it was necessary to make division of the whole that so Each may know & possess their respective Rights in severalty — But so it hath happen'd as appears by their Votes, that in the year 1730 a Division was made of Two thousand Acres thereof into forty Lotts of fifty Acres Each, & the Proprietors severally drew their Lotts, but no Possession was ever taken of any of said Lotts, nor is the Plan of said Division (if in being) any where to be found; so that the Proprietors are utterly at a Loss to know where said divided part lies, & of Consequence are prevented from making Division of the whole (as they are desirous of doing) or even any part of it.

Wherefore Your Petitioner in Behalf & at the Request of said Proprietors humbly prays, that Your Excellency & Honours would in your known Goodness remove this Difficulty in the way of their Settlement by an Order that the said former Division may be null and void.

As in all duty bound your Pet^{r} ever prays

Samuel Adams

In Council June 4, 1761. Read and ordered That the Prayer of the Petition be granted. And that the Petitioner have leave to bring in a Bill accordingly

Sent down for concurrence. A Oliver Sec^{r}

In the House of Rep^{ves} June 13 1761

Read and Concurr'd James Otis Speaker

June 1 1761 met by Adjournm^{t}

Present Jos Moulton jun^{r} Esqr James Bowdoin Esq$_{s}$ James Pitts Esq Mr Henry Bromfield Mr Wm Gray Mr Wm Andrews Mr John Andrews Saml Adams

Coll^{o} Moulton desird to be excusd being Moderator & James Bowdoin Esqr was chosen in his room —

Voted that the Clerk be desird to prefer a petition to the Genl Court setting forth that —

---

voted that this meeting be adjourned to the first thursday in August next at five o'Clock afternoon.

Survey of the Country.

In the House of Representatives June 11, 1761

Voted that a Survey of y[e] Country from Kennebeck to y[e] River of S[t] Lawrence is Necessary & Practicable,

& that to answer y[e] purposes thereof One Scouting party, Consisting of one Captain, Two Surveyors, & Nine privates, be Established in y[e] pay of this Government in y[e] following Manner

One Captain, at Eleven pounds ℘ Month the first Surveyor, Eight pounds the Second Surveyor, Six pounds the Privates at three pounds twelve shillings each the service to commence y[e] first of August. & to end y[e] middle of October next.

& that if s[d] Privates should be taken out of any of y[e] forts where they are in y[e] pay of this Government that Pay shall be considerd as a part of y[e] above Establishment.

Sent up for concurrence, James Otis, Speaker

In Council July 11, 1761. Read and Concurred

A Oliver Sec[y]

Consented to Fra. Bernard

Scarborough, Petition. 1761.

To His Excellency Francis Barnard Esquire Captain General and Governor in Chief in and over His Majestys Province of the Massachusetts Bay The Honourable his Majestys Council and House of Representives in General Court assembled at Boston May 1761 —

The Freeholders & other Inhabitants of the Town of Scarborough Qualify'd by Law to Vote agreeable to Charter Humbly Shews —

That in the Month of February last past Enoch Freeman

Esqr Requested of your Petitioners (by Posting up Papers at the different Publick Places at said — That we would give him our Votes at our March meeting for being County Register When the time for puting up the Annual warning for March meeting came the Select men put an Article in the warning to Chuse a Register, Mr Small Town Clerk said it had better be in the following words, vizt "And also to Act on any thing that may be found Necessary," a Practice which we have offten used and never found it disputed befor_, and at the time of said March meeting last past Edward Milliken Esqr Being Chosen Moderator (on purpose that we might Act wisely & Safely) he having the direction of the Meeting &c Order'd all Persons Qualify'd by Law to Vote to bring in their Votes for a Register of Deeds which was then don agreeable to Law and Coustome as we then and do still Think at least with all Humble submission to your Excellency your Honours & Gentlemen we think was Consistant with the Honest intent and meaning of the Law, Especialy as Enoch Freeman Esqr aff^{d} was at the meeting with a Number of his Friends from Falmouth making Interest for him before and at the very Time of the Meeting Mr Nathaniel Green was allso There So that The whole Town was as well Acquainted with the Choice of a Register and allso of the Candidates as they Ever can be of any Vote Notwithstanding of which the Justices of – Inferiour Court held at Falmouth this Instant May has Sett our Votes aside. We have Much more to say if Occasion Require But wont intrude on your Excellency & Your Honour's &cc Goodness hoping the Honesty of our Request will be sufficient Wherefore your Petitioners Humbly Prays That Your Excellency Your Honours and Gentlemen would Take our Case into your wise Consideration and Grant us the Privilege of our Votes as they were Honestly and Truely Voted last March or otherways The Privilege of Voting again Before the May Sessions at Falmouth are over

Being Adjourned to next July and Your Petitioners as in Duty Bound Shall Ever Pray —

Joseph Waterhouse	Willm his O mark Mitchell	William Harmon
Elisha Bragdon	John Berry	Samuel Davis
Benja his X mark Blake	Benj	than Tilliken
Robert mcLaughlin	John Hodgden	Thomas his X mark
John Milliken	Nathll Milliken	Samull Boothby
Morris Obrian	Jonathan Wingett	Daniel Marston
ll Boothby Junr	Nathaniel Seavey	Samll Carll Junr
David Libby Jur	John ball	Benjamin Carter
Lemuel Smith	Abraham Tbr	James Boothby
Josua Moonenday	John Inaes	John Libby
Samson Plumer	Josiah Ring	Samll Small
Andrew Libby	Edmd Hagens	Joseph Stephens
Samuel Libbee	Samll Fogg	Joseph Fogg
Daniel Fogg	Joshua Brown	

In the House of Representatives June 19, 1761

Whereas it appears to this Court that in the Choice of a County Register, for the County of Cumberland last spring, the Inhabitants of the Town of Scarborough had not any voice, Therefore Resolved, That the proceeding of the Justices of the General Sessions for said County, at their Meeting in May last, be sett asside & that the severall Towns in said County be impower'd & they are hereby impower'd to vote anew for a County Register & to make return of their votes at ye Generall Sessions of said County to be held in September next and the selectmen in the severall Towns in sd County are hereby directed to notify them accordingly and all Records & proceedings done & performed by Enoch Freeman Esqr as county Register by virtue of his appointment by the Justices at their meeting in Novr last or in consequence of the choice in May last, (said proceedings being otherways regular) are hereby confirmed & are to be held good & valid to all Intents & purposes & ye said Enoch Freeman is hereby Impowered to continue to act as county register for ye County of Cumberland aforesaid untill the Generall Sessions of ye Justices of s^d^ County to be held in September next—

Sent up for concurrence

Att^r^ R Cotton Cler Dom Rep

In Council June 20. 1761. Read and Non concurred And Ordered That this Petition be dismissed

Sent down for concurrence A Oliver Sec^r^

In the House of Rep^ves^ June 23 1761

Read and Nonconcurred and the House adhere to their own Vote as taken into a new Draft

Sent up for concurrence

Att^r^ R Cotton Cler Dom Rep

In Council July 1, 1761. Read and Nonconcurred

A Oliver Sec^r^

In the House of Representatives June 23 1761

Whereas it appears to this Court that in the Choice of a County Register, for ye County of Cumberland, last Spring, the Inhabitants of the Town of Scarborough had not any voice, Therefore resolved, that the Proceedings of the Justices of the Generall Sessions for said County, at their Meeting in May last, be sett asside so far as they relate to this Matter, and that the severall Towns in said County be Impowered & they are hereby Impower'd to vote anew for a County register at their next March Meeting & to make return of their votes at ye Generall Sessions of said County to be held in May next and the selectmen of the several Towns in s^d^ County are hereby directed to notifie them accordingly and all Records & Proceedings done & performed by Enock Freeman Esqr as county register by virtue of his appointment by the Justices at their Meeting in Novr last, or in Consequence of the Choice in May last (said Proceedings being otherways regular) are hereby confirmed & are to be held good & valid to all Intents & Purposes & the said Enock Freeman is hereby Impower'd to Continue to act as County register for ye County of Cumberland aforesaid untill the Generall Sessions of ye Justices of said County in May next.

Anno regni regis Georgÿ tertÿ Secundo

An act to annull a division heretofore made by the proprietors of common & undivided lands in a place called Philips town in the county of York.

Whereas the proprietors of the common and undivided lands in a place called Philips town in the county of York have petitioned this court setting forth that in order to an effectual settlement of the said lands it is needfull that a division be made thereof that so each proprietor may know & settle his part in severalty, and that it appears by the records of said proprietors that in the year 1730 a division was made of two thousand acres part of the said land into forty lots of fifty acres each and that the proprietors drew their several lots in the said division, but that it no way appears A where the land so divided is, nor any plan of the division being to be found, the petitioners did thereupon pray that the said ancient division may by the authority of this court be annulled & vacated to the end they may proceed regularly to a new division.

Be it therefore enacted by the governor council and house of representatives that the said division made in the said year 1730 be and hereby is annulled & made void – that the said proprietors be and hereby are enabled to proceed to a division of the whole or any part of the lands by them held in common as afores[d] as they might have done if the division afores[d] in the year 1730 had never been made Provided always That nothing in this Act shall be understood or construed to affect the Right or Title of any person actually settled upon lands in any part of Phillips Town; **B** but such Right and Title shall be and remain as if this Act had never passed—

In Council July 7, 1761. Read a first and second time and passed to be engrossed—

Sent down for concurrence A Oliver Sec[r]

In the House of Rep[ves] July 9, 1761

Read and Ordered that the consideration of this Bill be refer'd to the next sitting of this Court. and that in the mean time Samuel Adams Clerk to the Prop[rs] of Phillips Town Insert the Substance of this Bill in one of the Boston News-papers three Weeks successively; as also Post the same up in some publick place in said Plantation of Phillips Town, That so any Persons concerned may shew cause (if any they have) at the next sitting of this Court why the said Bill should not pass into a Law.

Sent up for concurrence James Otis Speaker

In Council July 9, 1761 Read & Concurred

A Oliver Sec[r]

In Council Nov[r] 25, 1761

The Board resuming the Consideration of this Bill, and it appearing that publick notice of the Substance thereof had been – agreeable to the foregoing Order, and no objections being offer'd thereto – It is thereupon Order'd that the same do pass to be Engross'd with the following Amendments viz

at **A** – dele where the Land so divided is

insert where & in what manner the said Lotts were laid & bounded.

at **B** insert assign'd or allotted to him – before the making of the Division aforementioned.

Sent down for Concurrence A Oliver Sec[r]

In the House of Rep[ves] Nov[r] 26 1761

Read three several times and concur'd

James Otis Speaker

At a Parish Meeting held in the first Parish in Scarborough August the 27th 1761 —

Voted and Concured (at sd Meeting) with the Churches Vote to Give Mr Phinehas Whitney a Call to Setle in the Ministery in said Parish

Attest Samll Fogg Parish Clark

At a Parish Meeting held in the first Parish in Scarborough March ye 16th 1762 —

Unanimously Voted and Concured with the Churches Vote to Give Mr Samuel Foxcraft a Call to Setle in the Work of the Ministery in this Parish

Attest Samll Fogg Parish Clark

Letter, Ichabod Goodwin to Hon. Thos Hutchinson

Berwick 16 Novbr 1761

Sir

I Reseved yor Leter Confirmen the mestack in the Roll as your Leter to mee that I never Reseved.

You say or Sir Willam Pepprell that I have spock to Cornel Sparock and hee Told me that hee wod Luck mongest his papers But hee hant Let mee now whar he Has found it if your honon Cant help mee I dont now whot I shall dow I left my papers in the in gagment bot whot Your Onorer noues a bout it you had the Copey and the som was 11–9–0 & som penc I think at the best of my Judment and if your honer Can dow Aney thing for mee pray Lett Mager Cutt now and you will a blige your

frend & verey Hombill Servent

Ichabod Goodwin

Petition of Saml Adams

To His Excellency Francis Bernard Esqr Captain General & Commander in Cheife in & over the Province of the Massachusetts Bay; The Honourable the Councill & House of Representatives in General Court assembled the 20th of November 1761

Samuel Adams of Boston Clerk to the Proprietors of a Tract of Land in the County of York called Phillipstown, begs leave humbly to make known to – Hon[bl] Court, that in obedience to their order he hath notifyd the Resident Proprietors of said Land of the Substance of a Bill now pending in said Court for setting aside an ancient division of said Land for Reasons offerd, by inserting an Advertisement in one of the Boston News papers, & also by causing the same to be posted in a publick place in said Phillipstown, which last he is informd by a Letter from Jeremiah Moulton Esq of York, is done to all which he is ready to give his Affidavit —

Wherefore he humbly prays that said Bill may be passd into a Law, no persons appearing to object thereto.

Sam[l] Adams

Petition of Eben[r] Thorndike & others 1762

Province of the Massachusetts Bay Jan[ry] 3[d] 1762

To his Excellency Francis Bernard Esq[r] Captain General and Governour in and over his Majesty's Province afores'd the Honourable His Majesty's Council and House of Representatives, in General Court Assembled

We the Subscribers having been Soldiers at Fort Pownall and now Settled at a Place called Magebaggadeuse on the Eastern Side of Penobscott Bay, and others desirous of settling there themselves, or Settling other good Families in their Room; for the Accommodation of Numbers that want Land, and to carry on the Fishery, Humbly request,

Your Excellency and Honours wou'd Please to grant Your Petitioners and their Heirs, a Township to be bounded as follows, beginning about three miles above Casteens River, at a Place called Sandy Point and to run East North East Eight Miles, then South South East to the Ocean and then West South West Eight Miles, and then to the first Bounds mentioned, a Neck of Land Water and Islands, And Your Petitioners as in Duty bound shall ever pray &c —

Edward Milliken	Eben^{r} Thorndike	Nath^{ll} Milliken
Samuel Freeman	Joseph Brown	Eze Cushing
John Bicknell Junr	Ezekiel Cushing Ju^{r}	Mark Haskell
Jeremiah Cushing	Benj^{a} Milliken	Joseph Milliken
Lemuel Smith	Sam^{ll} Cate	David Elwill
Nathan^{ell} Harmon	Dan^{ll} Mackey	John Trott
Willm Masury	Samuel Trott	Henry Herrick
John Trott	William Morgan	Thomas Trott
William Bartlett	Stephen Huchinson	John Roundey
Samuel Osborn	Nicolas Thorndike	John Melbery Milliken
Andrew Thorndike	Thomas Milliken	Joseph Wood
William Haskell	Anthony Dyer	Thomas Stroute
Samuel Wood	Benjamin Robbins	Samll Trask
Benjamin Robbins	Joshua Silvester juner	ArChebaild Hency
Samuel Silvester	Josiah heney	David Silvester
Daniel Noyes	Samuel Silvester	Stephen Combes
Samuel Trask	Joshua Combes	Joseph Trask
Andrew Simonton	David Trask	William Dyer
Spencer Bret	George Dyer	Rougles Colbe
Bengman Thorndike	Thomas Trask	David Alden
Thomas Williamson	John Thorndike	Bengman frizzel
Joshua Woodbery	Adam Silvester	Samuell Clark
Paul Thorndike	John Robinson Ju^{r}	Nath^{ll} Ingersoll
Nathaniel Jordan ju	Joseph Wilson	Edward Milliken Ju^{r}

Petition of David Marsh & others 1762

Haverhill Jan^{ry} 6th 1762

To Messrs David Marsh, Enoch Bartlet, James McHard

Esqr, James Duncan, Cpt Edmond Moors, Cpt Peter Parker, Dudly Calton & Benj Harrod

We the Subscribers being desirous of setling some of the Land upon the Sea Coasts or Rivers between the Lands belonging to the Heirs of the Late Honourable Brigadier General Waldo and the River Passamaquade or St Croix desier our Names may be carryed to the great and General Court at their next Session with a Petition which we desier you'll please to draw and Lay before the same for Lands within s^d Limmits for the purposes aforesaid —

William Fairfield	John Dow Junr	James Duncan Junr
Isaac Bradley	Jonathan Buck	John Dow tersus
David Remmick	Nathaniell Rolf	David Marsh Junr
Nathaniell Jonston	John Jonston	Moses Marsh
Jesse Jonston	William Lampson	Thomas Jonston
Daniel Jonston	Caleb Jonston	William Townsend
Olliver Knight	Charles Haddock	Tristram Knight
Josiah Fulsom	John Knight Junr	Edmond Herriman
Enoch Noyes	Benjamin Moores	Samuell Little
Samuell Clements	Joshua Sawyer	James McHard Juner
James Sawyer	William McHard	Peter Clements
Daniel Hills	Jonathan Kimball	Benj^a Kimball
Philip Clements	Jonathan Kimball Junr	Jeremiah Pecker
Benjn Pettingall	Benjamin Clements	Cutten Marsh
Isaac Snow	Jacob Sayer	Enoch Badger
Peter Morse Junr	Amiruhamah Moores	Ebenezer Mudget
John Moody	Joshua Howard	John Eaton
Moses Mudgit	Elias Jonston	Hanes Johnston
John Ayers	Edmond Sayer	John Woodman
Joseph Sayer	Moses Swasey	Simeon Goodwin
Daniel Poor	John Goodwin	Jonathan Poor
Joseph Pilsbury	Daniel Poor Junr	Benjn Pilsbury
Moses Kelly	Ben^n Morse	Stephen Coffin
James Woodward	Thomas West	Asa Heath

William Page	Moses Little	Asael Herriman
Stephen Little	Peter Herriman	John Bayley
Moses Bartlet	Ephraim Noyes	Lewis Page
John Hazen Junr	Willam Page	James Bricket
Samuell Robie	Samuell Bayley	Nathaniel Bartlet
James Cook	Thomas Whitacer	William Cook
Daniel Bartlet	Jonathan Webster Junr	Jacob Bayley
Samuell Ayers	Ephram Baley	James Pecker
Joshua Baley	Samuell Morrison	Edmond Morse
Samuell Ayers ters	Jacob Morse	Ezekiel Wilson
Theophilus Eaton	Mark Emerson	Ezekiel Eaton
Joseph Johnston	Joseph Hadley	Jacob Ayers
John Mills	John Farnam	Moses Morse
Asa Herriman	Maxey Hesseltine	John Mulliakin
John Hesseltine	Joseph Jillings	William Marshal
Wilks West	John Hazen	David Pettangal
Moses Hazen	Nathaniel Burpey	Ebenezer Hale
Joseph Swaysey	Robert Hale	Ezra Chase
James Winn	David George	Alpheus Godwin
Israel Morrill	Samuel Plummer	Timothy George
Kelly Plummer	Eliphalet Martin	Jasial Herriman
Samuel Johnston	Peter Johnston	Ebenezar Kimball
Josiah Brown	Samuell Kimball	Jacob Buck
Ebenezar Day	Jonathan Buck Junr	Daniell Jaques
John Whiting	Bezeliel Calton	Nathan Baker
Dudley Carlton Junr	Joshua Springer	William Kimball
Nathaniel Marsh	Stephen Knight	Moses Chase
John Duncan	James Simonds	George Duncan Junr
Joel Herriman	William Duncan	Samuel Souther
William Duncan Junr	Benjn Eaton	George Duncan ters
Jonathan Eaton	Abraham Duncan	Andrew Frink
John Duncan ters	Ezekiel Belknap	John Humphrey
James Clemans	Samuell Bell	Peter Page
Alexander Wilson	James King	James Wilson

Ebenezar Eaton	John Otterson	Ammy Hanes
Samuell Fisher	Samuell George	John Duncan
Timothy Smith	David Slorow	John Pell
George Duncan ye fath	Samuel Trask	John Bell
Barnard Kimball	Adam Dickey	Joseph Hanes
John Barnet	Evan Jones	Samuel Hides
Richard Ayer	Mathew Slorow	Ebenezar Kimball
Thomas Berverly	Richard Emarson Junr	David Berverly
David Hanes	James Tood	Jonathan Nelson
Isaac Bruester	Dudley Lad	James Patterson
Samuel Moores	Mathew Patten	Enoch Marsh
Joseph Bell	Ebenezar Portar	Peter Ewons
Samuell Duncan	James Aiken	Samuell Foster
Adam Wier	Ephraim Chandler	John Wier
Sammuel Johnston	David Stell	Ruben Mills
Samuell Cockran	Benjn Gage Junr	John Gilman
Nathaniell Gage Junr	Robert Stewart	Amos Mulliakim
John Cockran	Moses Day	Jonathan Stevens ju^{r}
Benjn Day	Robt Parker	William Easman
Joseph Frey ju^{r}	Jacob Kimball	Saml Chickering
Benj^{a} Cudworth	John Chickering ju^{r}	William Cockran
David Nevens	Nathaniell Cockran	Benj^{a} Stevens
Mathew Thornton	Nicholas Holt	William Wallis
Samuel Foster	John McLaughlin	Ward Noice
James Cockran	Abiel Freye	Joseph McCartney
Samuel Blodget	Jonathan Gilmore	James Lister
William Blair	John Stinson	Sammuel Allison
William Gooch	Timothy Walker	Simon Elliot
Hugh Ramsey	Nathan Jóans	John Hogg
Ephraim Peerce	Daniel Spauldin	Nathl Allen
William Hopkins	Elies Joans	James Gregg
Jon^{a} Bates	Joseph Boyes	James fowls Junr
Jeremiah Hesseltine	Nathl frye Ju^{r}	William Bradley
John Swa	Daniel Page	George Duncan

Jabez Fisher	Jo^{s} Hall	Jeremiah Fisher
Jno Baker	Samuel Fisher	James Harrod
James Pecker Ju^{r}	Jno Prince	Ebinezer Herrick
Josiah Snelling	Isaac Osgood	Benj^{a} Hammatt
Baley Bartlet	Jo^{s} Mullikin Ju^{r}	William Greenleaf
Benj^{a} Cushing	William Maxwell	Saml Hogg
Simeon Parker	John Truman	John Varnum
James Richardson	Wm Frye	Rufus Clap
Joseph Stevens	George Duncan Junr	Nathan Parker
John Duncan Junr	Peter Parker ju^{r}	John Dummer
John Farnum ju^{r}	Jno Cogswell Ju^{r}	Benjn Harrod Junr
Jonathin Begley	Ephraim Bound	David Dixon
John Indicott	William McHard Juiner	Nath^{ll} Brown
Samuel Glover	Nath^{ll} Brown Ju^{r}	John Hall
Samson Stoddard	Theophilus Mansfield	John Warren Ju^{r}
Benj^{a} Bond	Benj^{a} Ingals	Jonas Harrington
Isaac Parker	Robt Patten	Jacob Tyler
Benj^{a} Kingsbury	Thomas Bartlet Ju^{r}	Saml Barnard
Wm Fairfield Ju^{r}	Jon^{n} Marsh Ju^{r}	Robt Duncan
Moses Davis	Jonas Noyes	Humphry Barret
Joshua Harrod	Ebenezer Nichols	Nathl Hall
Ebenezer Hall	Jobe Gage	Joseph persons
William Nickels	Andrew Black	Benj Mubb: Holmes
Charles Prescott	John Mico Wendell	Wm Watts
Eben^{zr} Hough	Bellingham Watts	James Erewing

Province of the Massachusetts Bay

To His Excellency Francis Barnard Esqr Capt Genl the Commander in Chief of said Province, to the Honourable his Majesties Council and the Representatives in Genl Court assembled at Boston Jan^{ry} 13th 1762

The Petition of the Subscribers hereunto on behalf of themselves and associates whose Names are Contained in the Several lists Accompanying this Petition Humbly Sheweth

That your Petitioners and Associates who by far are the Greatest part of them Persons Brought up to Husbandry and not having lands Sufficient for themselves and Sons — who are also Husbandmen — have been put Upon the enquiry for Wilderness lands to Exercise their Calling upon — And that in the course of their Enquiry, they have been lately inform'd that there is a considerable Tract of Unappropriated Wilderness Lands and Islands, lying between the Province of Nova Scotia and that part of this Province call Province of Main — of which this Goverment have the Inspection with Power of granting the Same, Sending home such grants for his Majesties approbation — And as your Petitioners and Associates Apprehend the Setling said Lands or Islands would be Agreeable to His Majesty Your Excellency and Honours - engage Many persons to become Setlers there that would otherwise go out of the Province — They Humbly pray you will please to grant them such a Quantity thereof as you May Judge proper for Such a Number of persons as your Petitioners and Associates consist of vizt 360 with Liberty of Viewing and reconoitering the Same — and to Plan and Pitch Upon Such Tract or Tracts or So much of it as they shall be Alow'd and find Suitable for their purpose — in Some place or places on the Sea Coast Rivers or Inland part, between the River St Croix or Passamaquoddy, and land Near Penobscut river belonging to the Heirs of Brigd^r Genl Waldo — or of said Islands on the Coast — and return to your Exellency and Hon^rs a plan or Plans of the Same Setting forth and Shewing it's Bounds and Extent; in Such time as you may See fit to Order them —

But inasmuch as the lands Pray'd for are at a considerable Distance from the respective homes of your Petitioners and Associates, And the preparing Habitations there and Transporting themselves and Family's to them will be Attended with Considerable Difficulty and expence — Your Petition^rs for themselves and Associates further Pray Your Excellency and Hon^{rs} will please to Grant Time Proportionable to those things for fulfilling Such Conditions as you may see fit to Injoin them, in case you should See cause to grant their request — And as in Duty bound will ever Pray

David Marsh	Enoch Bartlet	James McHard
James Duncan	Edmund Mooers	Dudley Carlton
Peter Parker	Benjn Harrod	

In the House of Representatives Feb^{ry} 20 1762.

Voted, That the Petition of David Marsh, Enoch Bartlet, James McHurd, James Duncan, Peter Parker, Edmund Moers, Dudley Carlton, Benjamin Harrod, and three hundred and fifty two Others their Associates, be so far granted, as that there be and is hereby Granted unto Him the said David Marsh & his Associates herein named vizt

Enoch Bartlet	James McHard	James Duncan
Peter Parker	Edmund Moores	Dudley Carlton
Benjamin Harrod	Wm Fairfield	James Duncan ju^r
Jon^a Buck	David Remmick	David Marsh ju^r
John Johnston	Jesse Johnston	Joshua Bayley
Edmund Morse	Jacob Morse	Theophilus Eaton
Ezekiel Eaton	Joseph Hadley	John Mills
Moses Morse	Maxey Hesseltine	John Hesseltine
William Marshall	John Hazen	Moses Hazen
Ebenezer Hale	Thos Johnston	Caleb Johnston
Oliver Knight	Tristram Knight	John Knight jun^r
Enoch Noyes	Samuel Little	Joshua Sawyer
James Sawyer	Peter Clements	Jon^a Kimball
Philip Clements	Jeremiah Pecker	Benj^a Clemons
Isaac Snow	John Dow jun^r	Isaac Bradley
John Dow 3^d	Nathl Rolfe	Nathl Johnston
Moses Marsh	William Lampson	Daniel Johnson
Willm Townsend	Robert Hale	James Winn
Alpheus Goodwin	Samuel Plummer	Kelly Plummer

Jasial Herriman	Peter Johnson	Jacob Sayer
Peter Morse junr	Ebenezer Mudgit	Joshua Howard
Moses Mudget	Hanes Johnston	Edmund Sayer
Joseph Sayer	Simeon Goodwin	John Goodwin
Joseph Pilsbury	Benjamin Pilsbury	Benja Morse
James Woodward	Asa Heath	Moses Little
Stephen Little	Charles Haddock	Josiah Fulsom
Edmund Herriman	Benja Moores	Saml Clements
Jno McHard jur	William McHard	Daniel Hills
Benja Kimball	Jona Kimball jr	Benja Pettingall
Cutten Marsh	Enoch Badger	Amiruhamah Moores
John Moody	John Eaton	Elias Johnston
John Ayers	John Woodman	Moses Swasey
Daniel Poor	Jona Poor	Daniel Poor junr
Moses Ketley	John Bayley	Ephraim Noyes
John Hazen junr	James Bricket	Samuel Bayley
James Cook	William Cook	Jona Webster jun
Samuel Ayers	James Pecker	Samuel Morrison
Samuel Ayers terts	Ezekiel Wilson	Mark Emerson
Joseph Johnston	Jacob Ayers	John Varnam
Asa Herriman	John Mullken	Joseph Tillings
Wilks West	David Pettangal	Nathaniel Purpey
Joseph Swasey	Stephen Coffin	Thomas West
William Page	Asael Herriman	Peter Herriman
Moses Bartlet	Lewis Page	William Page
Samuel Robie	Nathaniel Bartlet	Thomas Whitaker
Daniel Bartlet	Jacob Bayley	Ephraim Bayley
Joshua Springer	Nathl Marsh	Moses Chase
James Simonds	Joel Herriman	Samuel Souther
Benjamin Eaton	Jonathan Eaton	Andrew Frink
Ezekiel Belknap	Ezra Chase	David George
Israel Merrill	Timothy George	Josiah Brown
Jacob Buck	Jonathan Buck junr	John Whiting
Nathan Baker	Alexander Wilson	James Wilson

John Otterson	Samuel Fisher	John Duncan ye 4th
David Slorow	George Duncan ye 4th	John Bell
Adam Dickey	John Barnet	Samuel Hides
Matthew Slorow	Thomas Berverly	James Tood
Isaac Bruister	James Clemens	Peter Page
James King	Ebenezer Eaton	Ammy Hanes
Samuel George	Timothy Smith	John Pell
Samuel Trask	Barnard Kimball	Joseph Hanes
Evan Jones	Richard Ayers	Ebenezer Kimball
Richd Emerson jun	David Hanes	Jonathan Nelson
Dudley Lad	Samuel Moores	Enoch Marsh
Ebenezer Porter	Samuel Duncan	Samuel Foster
Ephraim Chandler	James Patterson	Matthew Patten
Joseph Bell	Peter Ewins	James Acken
Adam Wier	John Wier	David Stell
Samuel Cockran	John Gilman	Robert Stewart
John Cockran	Benjamin Cudworth	William Cockran
Nathl Cockran	Matthew Thornton	William Wallis
John McLaughlin	James Cockran	Joseph McCartney
Jonathan Gilmore	William Blair	Samuel Allison
Timothy Walker	Samuel Johnston	Reuben Mills
Benjamin Gage jun^{r}	Nathl Gage jun^{r}	Amos Mulliken
Moses Day	Benjamin Day	William Easman
Jacob Kimball	Eliphalet Marton	Samuel Johnston
Ebenezer Kimball	Samuell Kimball	Ebenezer Day
Daniel Jaques	Bezaleel Calton	Dudley Calton j^{r}
William Kimball	Stephen Knight	John Duncan
George Duncan	William Duncan	Willm Duncan j^{r}
George Duncan tert^{s}	Hugh Ramsey	John Hogg
Daniel Spauldin	William Hopkins	James Gregg
Joseph Boyes	Jeremiah Hasseltine	William Bradley
Daniel Page	Jabez Fisher	Jeremiah Fisher
Samuel Fisher	James Pecker jun^{r}	Eben^{r} Herrick
Isaac Osgood	Bayley Bartlet	Willm Greenleaf

William Maxwell	Simeon Parker	John Varnum
Wm Torye	Joseph Stevens	Nathan Parker
Peter Parker jr	Abraham Duncan	John Duncan terts
John Humphry	Samuell Bell	Benja Stevens
Nicholas Holt	Samuel Foster	Ward Noice
Abiel Freye	Samuel Blodget	James Lister
John Stinson	William Gooch	Simon Elliot
Nathan Jones	Ephraim Prerer	Nathl Allen
Elias Joans	Jona Bates	James Fowls junr
Nathl Frye junr	John Briggs	George Duncan
James Hall	John Farnum jr	Benj Harrod jr
Jonathan Stevens	Robert Parker	Joseph Frye jr
Saml Chickering	Jno Chickering jr	David Nevens
John Prince	Josiah Snelling	Benja Hammett
Jas Mulliken jr	Benja Cushing	Saml Hogg
John Truman	James Richardson	Rufus Clap
Ephraim Bounds	John Indicott	Nathl Brown
Nathl Brown jr	Samson Stoddard	John Warren junr
Benjamin Ingals	John Baker	James Harrod
Saml Barnard	Wm Fairfield	John Marsh jr
Robert Duncan	Moses Davis	Jonas Noyes
Humphry Barrett	Joshua Harrod	Ebenr Nicholls
Nathl Hall	Ebenr Hall	Jabez Gage
Joseph Parsons	William Nickells	Alexr Nickells
Andrew Black	Benj Mull: Holmes	Charles Prescott
John Mico Wendell	Wm Watts	Ebenr Hough
Isaac Parker	Robt Patten	Jacob Tyler
Benja Kingsbury	Thomas Bartlet junr	Bellingham Watts
James Vrewing	George Dum̄ar junr	John Duncan jr
John Dummer	John Cogswell jr	Jonathan Begley
David Dexon	William McHard jr	Samuel Glover
John Hall	Theophilus Mansfield	Benja Bond
Jonas Harrington		

their Heirs and Assigns for ever as Tenants in Common, six

Townships of Land, each to consist of the Quantity of six Miles Square, of the unappropriated Lands of this Province, between the River Penobscot and the River S[t] Croix; to be laid out in as regular and contiguous a Manner as the Land will admit of: That no Township be more than six Miles on the Sea Coast, or on Penobscot or other Rivers: That they return a Plan or Plans of the same (taken by a Surveyor and Chainmen on Oath) to this Court for further Confirmation, on or before the last Day of July next: That they within six Years after they shall obtain his Majesty's Approbation of this Grant (unless prevented by War) settle each Township with sixty good Protestant Families, and build sixty Houses, none to be less than eighteen Feet Square, and seven Feet Stud; and clear and cultivate five Acres of Land on each Share fit for Tillage or Mowing; and that they build in each Township a suitable Meetinghouse for the publick Worship of God, and settle a Learned Protestant Minister, and make Provision for his comfortable and honourable Support: And that in each Township there be reserved and appropriated four whole Rights or Shares in the Division of the same (accounting one sixty fourth Part a Share) for the following Purposes, Viz[t] One for the first settled or Ordained Minister, his Heirs and Assigns for ever; one for the use of the Ministry, one to and for the use of Harvard College in Cambridge, and one for the Use of a School for ever: And if any of the Grantees or Proprietors of any or each of said Townships respectively, shall neglect within the Term of six Years as before mentioned to do and perform according to the several Articles respecting the Settlement of his Right or Share as hereby enjoined, his whole Right or Share shall be intirely forfeited and enure to the Use of the Province.

Provided nevertheless, the Grant of the Above Lands is to be void and of none Effect unless the Grantees do obtain his Majesty's Confirmation of the same in eighteen Months from this Time.

And be it further Ordered as a Condition of the Grant aforesaid, That each Grantee give Bond to the Treasurer of this Province for the Time being, and to his Successors in said Office, for the Sum of Fifty Pounds for the Use of this Province, Conditioned for the faithful Performance of the Duties required according to the Tenor of the Grants aforesaid; And that a Committee or Committees be appointed by this Court to take said Bonds accordingly.

And further that said Committee be impowered to admit others as Grantees in ye room of such Persons contained in ye List aforesaid who shall neglect to appear by themselves or others, in their Behalf, to give Bonds at such time as ye Comm^e^ shall appoint.

Sent up for Concurrence. James Otis Speaker

In Council March 2^d^ 1762. Read and Concurred

A Oliver Sec^r^

Consented to Fra Bernard

Letter to Hon. Jere^h^ Powel. 1762.

New Glocester January the 14 1762.

To Jere^ah^ Powel Esqr

Honoured Sir these are to inform your Honour that we the Inhabitants of New Glocester are In danger of haveing our Town Spoiled by reason of the New-Boston Proprietors Runing their line in upon us and as we live a great distance from our Committee we would Apply ourselves to you desireing your Honour to be a friend for us in the Affair — and as your self is so well acquainted with the Affairs and Settlements of these three new Towns (viz) New Marblehead New Boston and New Glocester that it would be needless for us to write Every perticuler but ondly Enform you that New Marblehead has got by a late line a considerable quantity of land more then they ought to have for their Townshp which drives New Boston upon us.

And as one man (viz) Mr Edward King who was the Cheif Surveyor in laying out these three Towns first New Marblehead then New Boston and lastly New Glocester which line between New Boston and New Glocester is now fairly to be seen upon the Trees and that line was accounted to be a Right line between Town and Town, whereupon New Glocester Proprietors Immediately layed out their Town for the first division Into Sixty Acre lots and the land being more commodious for the first Settlement of the Town began the first division lots next to New Boston line and upon these lots the Town is now settled and as we have thus fairly and Honestly begun and Carried on our Town through the great dificuties of the Enemy and with great Cost and hard Labour have got our Town In a flourshing manner but if it be allowed that we shall be cut off from our first line then our Town will be wholly Ruined and the major part of the Inhabitants we therefore desire Your Honour to lay the Case before the great and Generall Court hopeing that they will as we are his Majesties Subjects let us Injoy the fruits of our own Labours and so we subscribe your Humble Servants

P S Sir if there be any thing that is Incorrect in this we desire your Honour to Correct it. Yours

Jabez True	Humphry Woodbery	John Tufts
Barnabas Winslow	Daniel Merrill	William Stevens
Sam^ll Lawrence	Jonathan Tyler	Thomas Tucker
David Millet	Samuel Parsons	Eliah Royall
William Harris	Moses Woodbury	Horton Mitchel
Benj^a Hamman	Nathaniel Eveleth	Robert Bayley
John M^cguire	Isaac Parsons	John Stenchfield juneo^r
Moses Stevens	Samuel Paul	Jonathan Row
Samuel Tarbox	John Prince	Moses Bradbury
Robert Burnam	Eben^r Mason	John Stenchfield

Indorsed — Capt Powell Mr Bradbury Dr Sayer

Report.

The report of a Committee appointed to take under consideration the bounds between this Province & Nova Scotia & also the claims of the Patentees of lands in the eastern parts of this Province

The Committee find that the Province of Nova Scotia by the Royal Patent to Sir Wm Alexander is bounded by the River St Croix to the head thereof & the remotest westernmost branch or stream & from thence by an imaginary line to run north to the river St Lawrence

That by the Royal Charter to this Province all the lands between the Province of Main & the said line of Nova Scotia from the Sea to the said river St Lawrence are undoubtedly within the jurisdiction of this government.

That by the first voyage made by the French who gave the name to the river St Croix as also by divers maps or charts which have been since published the said river may be ascertained.

The Committee are therefore of opinion that one or more gentlemen be appointed by this Court to join with such as may be appointed by the Province of Nova Scotia to repair to the said river St Croix & to determine upon the place where the said north line is to begin and to extend said line so far as the said Committee shall think necessary & to ascertain the same by mark'd trees or other boundary marks. And that his Excellency the Governor be desired to acquaint the Commander in chief of Nova Scotia with this proposal.

The Committee further report that no persons appear to claim any grant of lands to the Eastward of the lands contained in the Patent to Beauchamp & Leverett. That the said lands in s^d^ Patent are claimed by the representatives of the late Brigadier General Waldo and they upon conference with the Committee agree to release to the Province all their right & claim to lands east of Penobscot river provided the

Province release & convey to the said representatives a tract of six miles in breadth at the head of the said patent, to extend from the said river to the line from Muscongus after extending said line 36 miles from said Muscongus into the Country ∧ And the Committee are of opinion that such conveyance be made by persons to be authorized & impowered by the Court upon the terms & conditions aforesaid accordingly. All which is submitted in the name & by order of the Comittee

T. Hutchinson

In Council Feb[y] 18th 1762 — Read & sent down

In the House of Rep[ves] Feb[y] 18 1762

Read and Ordered that this report be accepted.

Sent up for concurrence James Otis Speaker

In Council Feb[y] 23, 1762 Read and Concurred with the Amendment at ∧ viz[t] Insert "provided the same do not interfere with any prior Grant And Provided the Line aforesaid extending from Muscongus into the Country do not interfere with any prior Patent

Sent down for Concurrence A Oliver Sec[r]

In the House of Rep[ves] Feb[y] 25 1762

Read and Concur'd James Otis Speaker

Consented to Fra Bernard

In the House of Representatives Feb[ry] 23[d] 1762

Voted, That the Petition of Wait Wadsworth and Sixty others his Associates be so far granted as that there be, and hereby is granted unto the said Wait Wadsworth & his Associates herein named x their Heirs and Assigns for ever as Tenants in Common, one Township of Land, to consist of the Quantity of six Miles Square of the unappropriated Lands of this Province, between the River Penobscot and the River S[t]

Croix: — That the said Township be no more than six Miles on the Sea Coast, or on Penobscot or other Rivers: That they return a Plan of the same (taken by a Surveyor and Chainmen on Oath) to this Court for further Confirmation, on or before the last Day of July next: — That they within six years after they shall obtain his Majesty's Approbation of this Grant (unless prevented by War) settle said Township with sixty good Protestant Families, and build sixty Houses, none to be less than eighteen Feet Square, and seven Feet Stud, and clear and cultivate five Acres of Land on each Share fit for Tillage or Mowing; and that they build in said Township a suitable Meeting house for the publick Worship of God, and settle a Learned Protestant Minister, and make a Provision for his comfortable and honourable Support. And that in said Township there be reserved the appropriated Four Whole Rights or Shares in the Division of the same (accounting one sixty fourth Part a Share) for the following Purposes, Viz[t] one for the first settled or ordained Minister his Heirs and Assigns forever; one for the use of the Ministry; one to and for the use of Harvard College in Cambridge and one for the use of a School for ever: and if any of the Grantees or Proprietors of said Township shall neglect within the Term of six Years as before mentioned, to do and perform according to the several Articles respecting the Settlement of his Right or Share as hereby enjoined, his whole Right or Share shall be entirely forfeited and enure to the Use of this Province:

Provided Nevertheless the Grant of the above Lands is to be void and of none Effect, unless the Grantees do obtain his Majesty's Confirmation of the same in eighteen Months from this Time

And be it further Ordered as a Condition of the Grant aforesaid, That each Grantee give Bond to the Treasurer of this Province for the Time, and to his Successors in said

Office for the Sum of Fifty Pounds for the Use of this Province, Conditioned for the faithful Performance of the Duties required according to the Tenor of the Grant aforesaid, and that a Committee or Committees be appointed by this Court to take said Bonds accordingly. And further that said Committee be impowered to admit others as Grantees in y[e] Room of such Persons contained in the List afores[d] who shall neglect to appear by themselves, or others in that behalf to give Bonds at such time, as y[e] Comm[e] shall appoint.

Sent up for Concurrence, James Otis Speaker

In Council March 2[d] 1762. Read and Concurred.

A Oliver, Sec[r]

Consented to Fra Bernard

x

Nath[l] Simmons	Joseph Freeman ju[r]	Jethro Sprague
Samuel Bradford	Ezekiel Bradford	Calvin Partridge
Peres Loring	Ebenezer Soule	Micah Soule
Elnathan Weston	Nath[l] Silvester	Sam[l] Brewster
William Clertey	Joseph Freeman	James Cobb jun[r]
John Maughton	Peleg Chandler	Micah Simmons
John Phillips	Simeon Bradford	Joshua Stanford
Blany Phillips j[r]	Joshua Shoanes	Ebenezer Dawes
Ambros Dawes	Zebedee Chandler	Bazaleel Alden
Silvanus Prior	Seth Weston	Eliphas Prior
Silvanus Dred	Zenas Dread	Paul Sampson
Abner Weston	Benjamin Prior jun[r]	Joseph Russell
Jacob Weston	John Hunt jun[r]	Robert Stanford
Blany Phillips	Levi Loring	Isaac Brewst_
Joseph Holmes	Edward Tintcham	Will[m] Drew
Jabez Washburn	Wrestling Alden	Nath[l] Loring
William Sprague	Judah Delano	Jedidiah Simmons
Enoch Freeman	Zebulon Drew	George Uffel
Joseph Brewster j[r]	Amos Samson	Peleg Wadsworth

Saml Additon
Ebenezer Moten
Seth Bradford
Peabody Bradford
John Fance
Phineas Sprague
Constant Southworth
Dr Nathl Cushing

In the House of Representatives Febr 23d 1762

Voted, That the Petition of Moses Twitchell and one Hundred and eighty Others his Associates be so far granted that there be and is hereby granted unto Him the said Moses Twitchell & his associates herein named viz their Heirs and Assigns for ever as Tenants in Common, three Townships of Land, each to consist of the Quantity of six Miles Square, of the unappropriated Lands of this Province, between the River Penobscot and the River St Croix; to be laid out in as regular and contigious a Manner as the Land will admit of: That no Township be more than six Miles on the Sea Coast, or on Penobscot or other Rivers: —

That they return a Plan or Plans of the same (taken by a Surveyor and Chainmen on Oath) to this Court for further Confirmation, on or before the last Day of July next: That they within six Years after they shall obtain his Majesty's Approbation of this Grant (unless prevented by War) settle each Township with sixty good Protestant Families, and build sixty Houses; none to be less than eighteen Feet Square, and seven Feet Stud; and clear and cultivate five Acres of Land on each Share, fit for Tillage or Mowing; and that they build in each Township a suitable Meetinghouse for the publick Worship of God, and settle a Learned Protestant Minister, and make Provision for his comfortable and honourable Support;

And that in each Township there be reserved and appropriated C four whole Rights or Shares in the Division of the same (accounting one sixty D fourth Part a Share) for the following Purposes vizt one for the first settled or Ordained

Minister, his Heirs and Assigns for ever; One for the use of the Ministry, One to and E for the Use of Harvard College in Cambridge, and one for the Use of a School for ever: And if any of the Grantees or Proprietors of any or each of said Townships respectively, shall neglect within the Term of six Years as above mentioned to do and perform according to the several Articles respecting the Settlement of his Right or Share as hereby enjoined shall be entirely forfeited and enure to the Use of this Province.

And be it further Ordered as a Condition of the Grant aforesaid, That each Grantee give Bond to the Treasurer of this Province for the Time being, and to his Successors in said Office for the sum of fifty Pounds for the faithful performance of the Duties required according to the Tenor of the Grants aforesaid; and that a Committee or Committees be appointed by this Court to take said Bonds accordingly. And further y[t] s[d] Comm[e] be impowered to admit others as Grantees in y[e] Room of such Persons contained in y[e] List afores[d], who shall neglect to appear by themselves or others in their Behalf, to give Bonds at such time as the Committee shall appoint —

Sent up for Concurrence James Otis Speaker

In Council March 2, 1762 Read and Concurred

A Oliver Sec[r]

Consented to Fra Bernard

In the House of Representatives Feb[ry] 23[d] 1762

Voted, That the Petition of Eben[r] Thorndike and fifty nine Others his Associates be so far granted as that there be, and hereby is granted unto Him the said Ebenezer Thorndike & his Associates herein mentioned viz.

Samuel Freeman	Ezek[l] Cushing	Ezekiel Cushing jun[r]
Jeremiah Cushing	Joseph Milliken	Sam[l] Cate

Nathl Harmon	John Trott	Samuel Trott
John Trott	Thomas Trott	Stephen Hutchinson
Samuel Osborn	Edward Milliken	Nathl Milliken
Joseph Brown	Mark Haskell	Anthony Dyer
Thomas Strout	Samuel Wood	Samuel Trask
Joshua Silvester j^{r}	Samuel Silvester	David Silvester
Samuel Silvester	Samuel Trask	Joseph Trask
David Trask	Spencer Bret	Rougles Colbe
Thomas Trask	Thomas Williamson	Benjamin Frissel
Adam Silvester	George Dyer	Benjamin Thorndike
David Alden	John Thorndike	Joshua Woodbery
Samuel Clark	John Robinson jun^{r}	Nathl Ingersoll
Nathl Jordon jun	Joseph Wilson	Edward Milliken jun
John Bicknell Junr	Benjamin Milliken	Lemuel Smith
Saml Elwill	Danl Mackey	Wm Masury
Henry Herrick	William Morgan	William Bartlett
John Roundey	Nicholas Thorndike	Andrew Thornkike
Joseph Wood	William Haskell	Daniel Noyes
Paul Thorndike	Jno Mulbery Milliken	Thomas Milliken
Benjamin Robbins	Benjamin Robbins	Archibald Henery
Josiah Henery	Stephen Combes	Joshua Combes
Andrew Simonson	William Dyer	

their Heirs and Assigns for ever as Tenants in Common, one Township of Land to consist of the Quantity of six Miles Square of the unappropriated Lands of this Province, between the River Penobscot and the River St Croix.— That the said Township be no more than six Miles on the Sea Coast, or on Penobscot or other Rivers: — That they return a Plan of the same (taken by a Surveyor and Chainmen on Oath) to this Court for further Confirmation on or before the last Day of July next: — That they within six Years after they shall obtain his Majesty's Approbation of this Grant (unless prevented by War) settle said Township with sixty good Protestant Families, and build sixty Houses, none to be less than eighteen Feet Square, and seven Feet Stud; and clear and cultivate five Acres of Land on each Share fit for Tillage or Mowing; and that they build in said Township a suitable Meeting-House for the publick Worship of God, and settle a Learned Protestant Minister, and make Provision for his comfortable and honourable Support:— And that in said Township there be reserved and appropriated four whole Rights or Shares in the Division of the same (accounting one sixty fourth Part a Share) for the following Purposes, Viz^{t} One for the first settled or Ordained Minister, his Heirs and Assigns for ever, one for the Use of the Ministry; one to and for the use of Harvard College in Cambridge and one for the Use of a School for ever: And if any of the Grantees or Proprietors of said Township shall neglect within the Term of six Years as before mentioned to do and perform according to the several Articles respecting the Settlement of his Right or Share as hereby enjoined, his whole Right or Share shall be entirely forfeited and enure to the Use of this Province.

Provided nevertheless, the Grant of the above Lands is to be void and of none Effect, unless the Grantees do obtain his Majesty's Confirmation of the same in eighteen Months from this Time.

And be it further Ordered as a Condition of the Grant aforesaid, That each Grantee give Bond to the Treasurer of this Province for the Time being, and to his Successors in said Office, for the Sum of Fifty Pounds, for the Use of this Province, Conditioned for the faithful Performance of the Duties required according to the Tenor of the Grants aforesaid: And that a Committee or Committees be appointed by this Court to take said Bonds accordingly.

And further that said Committee be impowered to admit Others as Grantees in the room of such persons contained in the List aforesaid who shall neglect to appear by themselves or Others in their behalf to give bonds at such time as the Committee shall appoint

Sent up for Concurrence James Otis Speaker

In Council March 3d 1761 Read and Concurred

A Oliver Secr

Consented to Fra Bernard

Grant to S. Waldo & others. 1762.

By the Governour, Council and House of Representatives of the Province of the Massachusetts Bay in New England in the Great and General Court Assembled

L.S.

Whereas their late Majestys King William and Queen Mary by their Letters Patent bearing date the seventh day of October in the third Year of their Reign, did give and grant unto the Inhabitants of the Province of the Massachusetts Bay (among other things) all those Lands and Hereditaments lying between the Territory of Nova Scotia and the River Sagadahoc, then and ever since known and distinguished by the Name of the Territory of Sagadahoc, together with all Islands lying within ten Leagues of the Main Land within the said Bounds, To Have and to Hold the same unto the said Inhabitants and their Successors, to their Own proper Use and Behoof forevermore: provided always That no Grant of Lands within the said Territory of Sagadahoc made by the Governour and General Assembly of the said Province should be of any Force or Effect untill their Majesties, their Heirs or Successors should signify their Approbation of the same.

The Governour, Council and House of Representatives of the said Province of the Massachusetts Bay in the Great and

General Court Assembled, have given and granted, and hereby do give and grant unto Samuel Waldo, Francis Waldo, Lucy Winslow Wife of Isaac Winslow Esqr Hannah Flucker Wife of Thomas Flucker Esqr Children and Heirs of the late Brigadier Samuel Waldo and Assignees of Thomas Leverett, (In Consideration of said heirs having released and Quit Claimed to the Province of the Massachusetts Bay, all their Right and Title to the Lands lying between the Rivers of Penobscott and St Croix), a Tract of Land of six Miles in Breadth at the head of the Patent granted to Beauchamp and Leverett the thirteenth of March One Thousand six hundred and twenty nine, and in the fifth year of the Reign of King Charles the first, which six Miles shall extend from the River Penobscott aforesaid to the Line from Muscongus, after extending said Line thirty six Miles from said Muscongus into the Country*; provided the same do not interfere with any prior Grant, and provided the Line aforesaid extending from Muscongus into the Country do not interfere with any prior Patent; To Have and to Hold the said Tract of Land with all and every its appurtenances unto the said Samuel Waldo, Francis Waldo, Lucy Winslow and Hannah Flucker and their Heirs, to the only Use and Behoof of the said Samuel, Francis, Lucy and Hannah as Tennants in Common and to their Heirs and Assigns forever; Yeilding and paying therefor Yearly unto his Majesty his Heirs and Successors, One fifth part of all Gold and Silver Oar and precious Stones which shall happen to be found and gotten in the Land aforesaid — provided always That the present Grant shall be of no Force or Effect untill his Majesty, his heirs or Successors shall signify his or their Approbation thereof.

Given in the Great and General Court and Sealed with the public Seal of the Province at Boston, this sixth Day of March in the Second Year of the Reign of his Majesty George the Third, by the Grace of God of Great Britain, France and

Ireland, King, Defender of the Faith &c and in the year of Our Lord One Thousand seven Hundred and Sixty two

By the Governour

By the Council by Order

By the House of Representatives by Order

* Six miles beyond ye Original Patent of Beauchamp & Leveret so as to make Thirty six miles including ye six miles hereby granted at the head of sd Patent

Dele the words Thirty six miles from said Muscongus

Resolve relating to Townships. 1762.

At **A** instead of the words River of Penobscot insert the Mouth of the River Penobscot At **B** instead of the words this House insert this Court At **C** add as follows viz the Person to be appointed as aforesaid giving seasonable Notice to the Petitioners in the Boston News Papers of the time and place when and where they may meet him.

In the House of Representatives March 2, 1762.

Whereas this **B** Court at their Present Sessions have Granted Twelve Townships of Land Lying between the Rivers of Penobscut and St Croix to Divers Petitioners On Certain Conditions therein Expressed referance thereto being had, and Whereas sd Towns are to be Laid Out as Contigious as May be, which Method is most Likely to be beneficial as well to the Province as to the Petitioners

Therefore Resolved that the sd Petitioners in Laying out sd Towns, begin at the mouth of the River **A** Penobscot, and to Exstend their Water Line Either on the sd River or Bay of Penobscut til they run out their Exstent,— And that the Six Towns lie adjoyning And when the Mater is so settled to be Desided by Lot, And to Prevent Any Difficulties or Disputes, that May arise Between the Petitioners, as well as that Justice May be done to the Province in Runing the Lines, there, be Some Suitable Person Skiled in those Matters Appointed by the Court, (to be paid by the Petitioners Accordin to their Interest, Reckoned as Townships) whose Duty shall be to Inspect the Several Surveyors Laying out the Various Townships And to Deside all Controverseys that may arise respecting their Lines as well as those between the Province & them, which Person So appointed, Shall on or Before the middle of June repair to the spot and attend that Duty, And in Case Any of the Petitioners should Neglect to appear at that time Such Delinquets to Lose their Chance by Lot and those on the Spots to Lay out their Towns and make their Pitch C The person to be appointed as aforesaid giving reasonable Notice to the Petitioners in the Boston News Papers of the time and place when and where they may meet.

Sent up for concurrence James Otis Speaker

In Council March 3, 1762

Read and Concurred A Oliver Sec[r]

Consented to Fra Bernard

Order, appointing a Committee. 1762.

In the House of Represen[tes], March 2[d] 1762 On a Motion made & Seconded

Ordered That Gen[l] Winslow and John Brown Esq[r] with such as the Hon[ble] Board shall appoint be a Comittee to receive the Release of the Representatives of Brigad[r] Waldo Dec[d] (& Others if any there be claiming with Them) of their right or Claim to any Lands East of Penobscott River by Virtue of the Patent made to Beachamp & Leverett and to prepare the form of a Grant to them to be passed by the

General Court of a Tract of Land six Miles in Bredth at the Head of the Same Patent on the West Side of the s[d] River agreable to the Vote of this Court of the 25th of February last provided s[d] six Miles of Land do not interfere with any former Grant.

The Comittee to report

Sent up for Concurrence James Otis Speaker

In Council March 3. 1762 Read and Concurred, and the hon[le] Tho[s] Hutchinson Esq is joined in the Affair

A Oliver Sec[r]

Consented to Fra Bernard

The Committee have prepared the form of a release or quitclaim which is herewith humbly offered. The Committee further report that they are of opinion that the form of the grant to be made by the Province be the same with that of the grant of Mount Desart to His Excellency the Governor mutatis mutandis all which is humbly submitted

March 6 1762 T. Hutchinson by Order

In Council March 6, 1762. Read & sent down

In the House of Rep[ves] March 6 1762 Read and Accepted

Sent up for concurrence James Otis Speaker

In Council March 6, 1762. Read & Concurred

A Oliver Sec[r]

Consented to Fra Bernard

Committees on Twelve Townships. 1762.

In the House of Representatives March 6th 1762

Whereas This Court at their Present Sessions in Granting the Twelve Townships to Divers Petitioners therein Named, which Lands are Lying between the Rivers of Penobscut and

S[t] Croix, Determined that a Committee should be appointed to Take Bonds of the Sundry Petitioners payable to the Treasurer and his Successors in that office for y[e] use of the Province in the Penalty of Fifty Pounds that they respectively Perform the Terms Mentioned in the Grant on which they are to hold s[d] Lands, which Committe are also Impower[d] In case aney of those Subscribers for their Lands are removed or shall refuse or Neglect to Give Bonds as afores[d] to Admit of Others in the room of such Persons til they Fill up the Number of Sixty to Each Town **A** and the House have Chosen on their Part, for their Committe to be Joyned by such as the Hon[ble] Board shall Joyne to Carry those Matters into Execution — viz[t]

For the Six Towns Petitioned for by Marsh & Others

Richard Saltonstal Esq[r] Benj[a] Mulliken Esq[r]

For the Petitioners that Dwell in the Town of Falmouth and Places adjacent

Jeremiah Powal Edward Mulliken Esq[r]

For those in and near York

John Bradbury Esq[r] Benj Chadburn Esq[r]

For those in and near Duxborough

Cap[n] Briggs Alden Cap[n] Rob[t] Bradford

and that the Charge of the Committe be paid by y[e] Petitioners and that they make report to this Court as soon as may Be.

A Dele & Insert — Therefore Voted That the persons herein after named with such as shall be joined by the hon[l] Board be the Committees for carrying these matters into Execution.

Sent up for concurrence James Otis Speaker

In Council March 6, 1762. Read and Concurred with the Amendment at **A** and Nathaniel Sparhawk Esq[r] is joined to the Committee for the Six Towns Petioned for by Marsh & Others, for those petitiond for by the Town of Falmouth and places adjacent & for those in and near York, and that Gam[l]

Bradford Esqr be joined for the Towns petitioned for by Inhabitants of and near Duxborough.

Sent down for Concurrence A Oliver Sec^{r}

In the House of Rep^{ves} March 6 1762

Read and Concurd James Otis Speaker

Consented to Fra Bernard

J. Frye & B. Harrod to prefer a Petition, &c.

We the Subscribers a Com^{tee} to Manage the Prudential affairs of the Grantees of the Six Townships Granted by the Genl Court to David Marsh and Others —

Sensible of Some Inconveniencys that may attend the Laying Out one Township on Account of a resolve Passed in the General Court on the 2^{d} of March Last — Do hereby desire and Direct Col: Jos Frye and Mr Benj^{a} Harrod who are of said Committee To Prefer a Petition or Memorial in Order to have Something Determined which we think Uncertain And Doubtful in Said Resolve — And to Obtain (if it may be) Some More favourable resolve and Instructions respecting the laying out or Taking Up s^{d} Township —

And we hereby recommend it to them to make enquiry in what Manner the other Grantees do Intend to proceed — And to Advise with some of them about the going down to lay Out the Township — And to move that a Superintendent be Spedily Appointed if Necessary —

Haver^{l} April 5th 1762

David Marsh
Enoch Bartlett
Isaac Osgood
Jonathan Buck
James Duncan
James McHard
} Com^{tee}

Copy of Record.

Biddeford April 12th 1762 At a Legal Town Meeting held by the Freeholders and other Inhabitants of sd Town Qualify'd to Vote in Town affaires.—

Rishworth Jordan Esqr was chosen Moderator Voted to sett of the Inhabitants on the East Side of Saco River in sd Town as a District and allow said District theire just proportion of the Towns personage, Lands with the Buildings thereon Bought for the Revd Mr Moses Morrill as Shall be adjudged by a Committee to be chosen by the Town, at said Meeting if they see fit; and the Value thereof be Assessed on the Inhabitants of the West Side of ye River To be paid to said District when they shall be so constituted by the General Court: on said Districts giving the Inhabitants on the West Side of ye River a Discharge in full of theire Interest in the aforesd personage Previledge Also

Voted that the Inhabitants on the East Side of the River shall have theire proportionable Benefit of other Priviledges, in common with ye Inhabitants on the West Side of said River as the Town now Stands or may hereafter collectively be benefited—

Attesd Rishwth Jordan Town Clerk

A True Coppy

Inspector of Surveyors chosen.

Prov: of Massa Bay April 17th 1762

The two Houses pursuant to agreement proceeded to the Choice of a person to inspect the Surveyors in laying out the several Townships granted the last Session, Eastward of Penobscot River; when Samuel Livermore Esq was chosen by a major part of the Votes of the two Houses

Attest A Oliver Secr

Consented to Fra Bernard

A dele & insert

all the Lands in the Town of Bideford lying on the East Side of Saco River in the County of York together with an Island in the said River commonly called and known by the Name of Indian Island.

B to **B** dele and insert and shall be notified of the time & place at election in like manner with the inhabitants of the said town of Biddeford by a warrant from the selectmen of the said town directed to a Constable or Constables of the said District requiring him or them to warn the Inhabitants to attend the meeting at time & place assigned which warrant shall be seasonably returned by the said Constable or Constables. And the Representative may be chosen indifferently from the said town or district the pay or allowance to be born by the town and district in proportion as they shall from time to time pay to the province tax.

Report of Committee.

The Committee to whom was refer'd the petition of David Marsh & others for them selves & Associates to whom the Six Townships wer_ Granted by this Court the 20th of Febu^ry^ last between the Rivers Penobscot & St Croix

Report That it be a Direction to Sam^ll^ Livermore Esqr Appointed by this Court to Inspect the Survey of the Twelve Townships Granted at or Near Penobscot; that the whole being first Survey'd, Marsh & his Associates draw One half the Same. And then the s^d^ Marsh and his Associates, as well as the proprietors of the Other Six Townships mentioned in the Courts Grant draw among them Selves, no preference being given to Either. and further after drawing the Townships afors^d^ Mr Livermore be directed to view Each of them, & report the Circumstance of the Land whether Ponds

Mountains or brocken in Order to the Courts makeing such allowance as they think proper: which is Humbly Submitted

p^r Order John Hill

In Council April 24. Read and Accepted and Ordered That Samuel Livermore Esq$_{\text{s}}$ be instructed to follow the direction above mentioned in laying out the twelve Towns East of Penobscot.

Sent down for Concurrence A Oliver Sec^{r}

In the House of Rep^{ves} April 24 1762

Read and Concur'd James Otis Speaker

Consented to Fra Bernard

The Draft of a letter to Jasper Manduit Esqr of London chosen Agent for the Province the 23^{d} Instant: Said Letter to be signed by the Secretary in the name of the General Court. viz

Boston April 24th 1762

Jasper Manduit Esqr

S^{r}

The Character the General Court has received of your integrity and Capacity, has induced them to make choice of you as public Agent for the Province in Great Britain, as youll observe by a transcript from the records of the Court of yesterday's date: And it is by their direction I now inform you of it. Your Comission signed by his Excellency Governor Bernard is sent you herewith. It is probable the General Court at their next May Session will instruct you fully upon the public Affairs of the Province that will be proper for your cognisance: But as it is necessary you should have the earliest notice of the circumstances of their principal Money-concerns, you are hereby informed that according to a Letter from Mr Bollan dated April 29. 1761 the Province's proportion of the Grant made by Parliament to the Colonies for their Services in 1759 is £60,634.— " — Sterling: on the credit of which, the Gen[l] Court order'd the Province Treasurer to draw upon M[r] Bollan for £60,000.St[g] Accordingly Bills were drawn by the Treasurer in favor of the Purchasers agreable to the form herewith sent. After the Bills were drawn Letters were received from M[r] Bollan acquainting the Court that the said Grant would be paid one half in money, and the other half in Exchequer tallies payable with Interest in March 1762.

It is probable these bills are paid by this time, or so many of them as the Province's share of s[d] grant would enable him to pay: And in case of deficiency of said Share, he was directed to pay the Overplus Bills out of the Province's proportion of the Parliamentary Grant for the Services of the year 1760. This last mentioned Grant it is apprehended M[r] Bollan has not yet received the Province's part of: And in that case there may remain some of said Bills unpaid.

As the General Court have empowered you to receive the Province share of the last mentioned Grant, as you'll find by an authenticated Act of the Court herewith sent: It is the desire of the Court, and you are hereby directed (on receiving the Province's share of said Grant, or a Sufficiency of it for the purpose) to pay the s[d] Bills that may remain unpaid; together with the Interest that may be due upon them Agreable to their tenor. **B**

With respect to the Province's Proportion of the last mentioned Grant, if it be not already Setled, M[r] Bollan can furnish you with the Accounts that have been transmitted him, of the Expence the Province incurred for his Majestys Service in 1760: and by those Accounts the proportion will be setled. In the Settlement of it, consideration ought to be had to this Circumstance: namely That a number of the Province Troops was detained in Garrison at Louisbourg &

Nova Scotia during the Winter of 1759 & Spring of 1760, occasioned by the reduction of Quebec, which prevented our troops being releived by the Regulars. As the other Colonies did nothing to balance this service we apprehend a distinct & seperate allowance ought to be made but if you cannot obtain that you will use your utmost endeavours that the whole expence of it be deducted out of the Grant before any apportionment be made of it among the Colonies. The Particulars relative to this matter, Mr Bollan can inform you.

The Act above mentioned empowers you to demand and receive of Mr Bollan whatever monies may be in his hands belonging to the Province, and to give him a discharge for what you shall receive of him. You will therefore make application to him pursuant to such power; and receive for the Province use what he may pay you. **C** You will also receive of him all Papers that relate to the Affairs of the Province committed to him: in particular those that respect the dispute between this Government and New York in regard to the boundary lines between us: also with Connecticut in regard to the Towns that have revolted to them; and with New Hampshire in regard to a Reimbursement for our maintaining Fort Dummer within that Province, and defending their Frontiers: / and obtain of him a state of these matters as they stand at present; and any information he can give you with regard to those or any other affairs of the Province. We would recommend to you that in all matters of Law you may be concerned in relative to the Province you consult with Richard Jackson jun^r^ Esqr

By order of the Great & Genl Court I have wrote the foregoing as Sec^r^ of the Province and am &c.

To be inserted at **B** – in Letter to Mr Manduit.

And in case you should not receive the Province share of said Grant by the time said Bills are returnable, you are desired to take up money upon Interest upon the credit of said Grant & pay off said Bills & by no means suffer them to be returned

dele at **C** & insert You will also receive of him all the Papers that respect the dispute between this Government and New York in regard to the Boundary lines between us. Also with Connecticutt in regard to the Towns that have revolted to them, and with New Hampshire in regard to a reimbursement for our maintaining Fort Dummer & N° Four &c within that Province and defending their Frontiers as also all Papers relative to the claim of the Earl of Sterling as to the Eastern parts of this Province and all other Papers that relate to the affairs of the Province.

Letter

The Draft of a Letter to Mr Bollan to be Signed by the Secretary in the name of the General Court, viz

Boston April 24th 1762

William Bollan Esqr

Sr

I am directed by the General Court to inform you that they have chosen Jasper Manduit Esqr of London, Agent for the Province in your stead: And it is their request, that you would pay the monies in your hands belonging to the Province to him; whose receipt will discharge you for what you shall pay him on account of the Province: as you'll observe by an authenticated Act of the Court herewith sent to you. **A** It is their request also that you would deliver Mr Manduit all the Papers you have relative to the public Affairs of the Province, particularly in reference to the disputes between this Province, and New York & Connecticut, and to our demand upon New Hampshire, on account of our maintaining Fort Dummer. You'll be pleased to furnish him with a state of these matters as they stand at present: and with any information he may want in regard to those, or any other affairs of the Province.

The Court desires also that you would send them your Account with the Province, in order that it may be setled. In their name & behalf I am

S[r] your obed[t] h[ble] Serv[t]

The Draft of the foregoing Letter was agreed on by the Great & Gen[l] Court.

A O Sec[r]

Petition of Joseph Webber & others

To His Excellency Francis Bernard Esqueir Captain General Governour and Chieff in and Over His Majestys Province of the Massachusatts Bay and Vice admiral of the same and the Honourable the Council and Honourable House of Repersintetives

Humbly Sheweth

that wee the Subscribers are Inhabitants of a tract of land laying on the west side of Kennebeck river within the Limits of the Kennebeck Purchas from the Late Colony of New Plymouth — and wee are Desirous of Good order & Government and that wee may have the Gospel preached to us and also to be inabled to Provid a School to Teach our Children and many Other Neceassarys which wee Cant Injoy in our Present Situation therefore wee most Humbly Pray your Excellency & Honours to Incorporate us into a Town by the Name of

as your Excellency shall think Proper and Grant us all the Priveledges of Other Towns in this Government by the following meets & Bounds Viz[tt] begining at the South West Eand of Brick Island which Island lays in Merremeeting Bay and to run from the South west Eand of said Brick Island a west North west Course Without the Varration of Compass which is the Southerly Line of James Bowdoin Esq^{rs} Lott and runs five miles from Kennebeck river — then to run Northly on the westerly Eand of Said Bowdoin Lott and Lotts N° 1: 2: 3: & 4 being about 6 miles to the South line of Lott N° 5 then to run an East southeast Course on the Southerly line of said Lott N° 5 to Kennebeck river and merremeeting Bay to the first mentioned Bounds which makes a tract of land of about five Miles and a half square as by the Plan anaxt & Prect lines thereon will more fully appear And wee as in Duty Bound Shall Ever Pray

Kennebeck river May the 20th 1762

Abraham Preble	Isaac Gillpatrick	Elihu Getchel
Elnathan Reaymand	Elijah White	Jonathan Preble
Joseph Webber	Samuel Malbune	Job Gelison
David	James Getchel	Neamiah Gecthel
Nathaniel Gellison	Jeames White	Solomon Goodwin
Moses Spncer	Samuel	Isaac Spencer
Francis Whitmore	James Cochran	Benjamin Shute
John Clarck	Iseck	Eleazar Crabtree
Agreen Crabtree	Abraham Preble ju^{r}	Samuel Getchel
Getchel	John Getchel	Robert Sedgley
Zacheus Beal	Zacheus Beal J^{r}	Josiah Tingley
Martin Haly	Thomas	Dominick Cavany
Philip Hodgkins Junr	David Thomas	

Memorial of sundry inhab^{ts} of Biddeford. 1762.

To His Excellency Francis Bernard Esq Capt General and Governour in Chief in and over his Majesties Province of the Massachusetts Bay in New England: The Hon^{l} his Majesties Council: and Hon^{l} House of Representatives in General Court assembled this 26 Day of May 1762

The Memorial of sundry Inhabitants on the East Side of Saco River in Biddeford in the County of York Humbly sheweth, That by reason of the many Difficulties naturally attending the crossing said River particularly to attend the necessary Duty of the Publick Worship of God, Your Memorialists did on the twelfth Day of April last past obtain a Vote of the Town of Biddeford that we should be a separate District, for the Purposes of transacting the necessary publick Affairs of a Community among our Selves, more especiall the Laudable Designs of the publick Worship of the Great God As by the Votes of said Town, herewith exhibited will fairly appear —

Wherefore your Memoriallists request that your Excellency and Honours Would at this Sessions invest said Inhabitants with the Powers and Priviledges of a District agreeable to the Votes of said Town annex'd hereunto —

At this Sessions of the honourable Court, We would with Submission, suggest, as We have an Opportunity with the greatest Unanimity of inviting an ingenious orthodox young Gentleman, to settle over us in the Gospell Ministry Who is also well affected among our Brethren on the West side of the River in said Town of Biddeford, and is in High esteem with the Revd Mr Morril Our present Town's Venerable Pastor. And Your Memorialists as in Duty Bound shall ever Pray &c

Biddeford May 20, 1762

Tristram Jordan	John Googins	Gershom Billings
John	James Gray	Robert Patterson Jr
Amos Chase	Beniamin Jellson	James Patten
Robert Patterson	Robert Edgcomb	William Jameson
Richard Berry	Joseph Libbey	Samuel Scamman
Thom^s^ Cutt	John Maine	Ezra Daves
Ebenezer Ayer	Samuel Dennet	

Petition of Heirs of Robt Jordan. 1762.

To His Excellency Francis Bernard Esqr Captain General Governor & Commander in Chief in & Over His Majesty's Province of the Massachusetts Bay The Honble His Majesty's Council and House of Representatives for said Province in General Court Convened the 26 Day of May 1762

The Humble Petition of Sundry of the Heirs & Legal Representatives of Robert Jordan late of Falmouth in the County of Cumberland Clerk Deceasd Shews.—

That the said Robert was in his life time Intitled to & Seizd of Sundry Tracts of Land in Scarborough Falmouth & other places within the County of York as then Limited, and in or about the Year 1679 Died so Seized — That by the Ravages & Destruction made by the Indians & the long Continuance of the Wars with them, the Descendants of the said Robert were Scatterd over Divers parts of New England & lost many of the Evidences of their Title to Sundry Parcels of Land in his right, which by Reason of the Minority of some, Coverture, Distance & Ignorance of such Right as to others of said Descendants, has hitherto Prevented a Prosecution for those Lands to which they have an Undoubted Title & ought to Recover.

That they are now so Multiplied Married Related & Connected That it is next to Impossible for them all to join in an Action at Law, both with Regard to the Description of those who should be Plats, and the various Descents thro' which the title must be Carried &c — and as they are in the Nature of Parceners Respecting such Estate, they coud not Pursue their Claims Separate by there being now about Sixty which Your Petitioners Remember, who are Descendants in the Right Line from the said Robert, so that without special Aid they seem to be under an Insuperable Difficulty in Recovering their Right —

Wherefore your Petitioner most Humbly Pray for the Aid

of this Honle Court that the said Descendants may be Incorporated Into a Propriety & Invested with the usual Powers & Privileges of Proprietors of Lands lying in Common, Enabled to Sue & be Sued to sell Purchase & hold by such Name as in Your Wisdom you shall Judge proper and that they may have Leave to bring in a Bill accordingly — Or Grant them such other Relief in the Premises as to Your Great Wisdom & Goodness appears proper and they as in Duty bound will Pray &c —

Jeremiah Jordan	John Jordn	Jeremiah Jordan Jur
Thomas Jordan	John Martin	Nathll his N mark Jordan
Samuel his X mark Jordan	Tristram Jordan	Samuel Jordan Ju
John Jordan thrd	Richard his X mark Jordan	John his C mark Jordan
James Jordan Juner	Ichabod Goodwin	Rishworth Jordan
Moses Morrill	Saml Jordan	

Act of Incorporation 1762

Anno Regni Regis Georgii Tertii Secundo.

An act for incorporating the East Side of Saco River in the Town of Biddeford, into a separate District by the Name of

Whereas the Inhabitants on the East Side of Saco River in the Town of Biddeford, in the County of York, have represented to this Court the great Difficulties and Inconveniences they labour under in their present Scituation, and have earnestly requested that they may be invested with the Powers, Priviledges and Immunities of a District.

Therefore

Be it enacted by the Governour, Council and House of Representatives, That **A** the East Side of Saco River in the Town of Biddeford in the County of York be and hereby are erected into a separate and distinct District by the Name of bounded with the same Bounds as the Town of Biddeford now is on the East Side of Saco River; and that the said District be, and hereby is invested with all the Priviledges, Powers and Immunities, that Towns in this Province by Law do or may enjoy, that of sending a Representative to the General Assembly only excepted; and that the said District shall have full Liberty and Right from time to time, to join with the Town of Biddeford in chusing a Representative to represent them at the General Assembly; **B** and that the said District shall from Time to Time be at their proportionable Part of the Expence of such Representative: and that the selectmen of Biddeford as often as they shall call a Meeting for the Choice of Representative shall from Time to Time give seasonable Notice to the Clerk of said District for the Time being, of the Time and Place of holding said Meeting, to the End that said District may join therein, and the Clerk of said District shall set up in some publick Place in said District a Notification thereof accordingly.**B**

Provided nevertheless, and be it further enacted That the said District shall pay their Proportion of all Town, County and Province Taxes already set or granted to be raised on the Town of Biddeford aforesaid as if this Act had not been made.

And be it further enacted, That Rishworth Jordan Esqr be and hereby is empowered to issue his Warrant to some principal Inhabitant of said District, requiring him to notify and warn the Inhabitants of said District qualified by Law to vote in Town Affairs, to meet at such Time and Place as shall be therein set forth, to chuse all such Officers as shall be necessary to manage the Affairs of said District.

In the House of Rep^ves May 31 1762 Read a first time June 1, 1762 A second time 2^d a third time and pass'd to be engross'd

Sent up for concurrence Tim^o Ruggles Sp^r

In Council 2d June 1762 Read a first time

Read a second time and passed a concurrence with the amendments at **A** & **B**

Sent down for concurrence A Oliver Secr

In the House of Repves June 2 1762

Read and Concur'd Timo Ruggles Spkr

Act to incorporate the Heirs, &c., of Robert Jordan. 1762.

Anno Regni Regis Georgii Tertii Secundo.

An Act to incorporate the Heirs and legal Representatives of Robert Jordan late of Falmouth in the County of Cumberland Clerk Deceased into a Propriety.

Whereas the said Robert Jordan was in his Life Time intitled to, and seized of sundry Tracts of Land in the Towns of Scarborough, Falmouth and other Places within the County of York, as then limited, and in and about the Year One Thousand six Hundred and seventy nine died so seized. And whereas by the Ravages and Destruction made by the Indians, and the long Continuance of the Wars with them, the Descendants of the said Robert Jordan were scattered over divers Parts of New England, and have lost many of the Evidences of their Title to sundry Parcels of Land in his Right, which by reason of the Minority of some, Coverture, Distance and Ignorance of such Right, as to others of said Descendants, has hitherto prevented a Prosecution for the Lands aforesaid:

And whereas the said Descendants are so multiplied, married, related and connected, that it is impossible for them all to join in an Action at Law, both with regard to the Description of those who should be Plaintiffs and the various Descents through which the Title must be carried

For Remedy whereof

Be it enacted by the Governor, Council and House of Representatives, That the Heirs and legal Representatives of the said Robert Jordan be, and they are hereby incorporated into a Propriety, & may sue and defend, claim and take by the Name of the Proprietors of common and undivided Lands held under Robert Jordan Deceased: And that Joseph Storer Esqr be hereby empowered to call the first Proprietors Meeting, appoint Time and Place, and to notify those Interested, by posting up Notifications in the Shire Towns of the Counties of York, Cumberland and Lincoln, and inserting the same in Two of the Boston News Papers, one Month before the Meeting of the Proprietors.

In the House of Rep^{ves} June 1 1762 Read a first time
2^{d} a second time
3^{d} a third time and pass'd to be engrossd
Sent up for concurrence Tim^{o} Ruggles Spk^{r}

In Council 4 June 1762. Read a first time.

June 5. Read a second time and the Question being put Whether the Board pass a concurrence with the House for the engrossing this Bill?

It passed in the Negative

A Oliver Sec^{r}

Act.

An Act for Incorporating The Plantation heretofore Call'd New Marblehead in the County of Cumberland into a Town by the Name of

It appearing to this Court that the Inhabitants of the s^{d} Plantation labour under difficulties & Inconveniencies by reason of their Not being invested with Priviledges of a Town —

Therefore be it enacted by the Governour, Council & House of Representatives, That the whole of that Tract of Land known by the name of New Marblehead, Bounded as follows Viz^{t} Begining at a pine tree marked **F.** standing Eight miles and ninety five Rods North west from a White Rock by the Water side in Casco Bay for the Northerly Corner of the Town of Falmouth, and from thence to run on a Straight Line to come fifteen Rods to the Eastward of a Brook calld Inkhorn Brook, below the Mouth of s^{d} Brook, where it enters into Pesumpscot River. To Run again from the s^{d} Pine Tree back on the Line of Falmouth ninety five Rods to the Westerly Corner of North Yarmouth, being a Stake, and from thence North East three miles, on the back of North Yarmouth to the Line of the Township called New-Boston, Westerly on the s^{d} Pesumpscot River to a greate Pond called Greate Sebago Pond, Thence North East four miles & 120 Rods, thence South East to North Yarmouth back line; Be, and hereby is Erected into a Town by the name of

And that the Inhabitants thereof be and hereby are invested with all the Powers, Priviledges & Immunities that Towns in this Province by Law do, or may enjoy And that Enoch Freeman Esqr be and hereby is Impowered to Issue his Warrant directed to some principal Inhabitant of s^{d} Town requiring him to Warn the Inhabitants of the s^{d} Town qualified by Law to Vote in Town affairs to Assemble at Such time & place as he Shall appoint then & there to Choose all Needfull Town officers to remain and Act til their Anual Town Meeting in March next and the s^{d} Inhabitants So Conven'd shall be & hereby are Authorized and fully Impowered to Choose such officers accordingly.

Provided Nevertheless that all Province & County Tax's already laid on the s^{d} Inhabitants Shall be Collected & paid in the same Manner, as tho this Act had not been made.

Permit.

Prov: of Mass[at] Bay June 11, 1762 —

For the Sloop Benjamin Torrey Master, bound to Kittery —

Permit the said Benj[a] Torrey to ship on board the Sloop bound to Kittery Fifty one barrels of Pork: He giving Bond to take in no other Provisions on board and to land the said Pork at Kittery and to return a Certificate thereof.

To the Officers of the Custom House and Naval Office.

Petition of Richard King

"Sloop Mermaid Fra' Haskell, 16 June 1762."

To his Excellency Francis Bernard Esq[r] Captain General & Governour in Chief in and over his Majestys Province of Massachusetts Bay in New England and Vice Admiral of the same

Richard King of Scarborough Humbly Sheweth

That he has ready to Ship on board the Sloop Mairmaid Francis Haskell Master bound to Scarborough aforesaid 30 barrells of Flour 5bb[ls] Pork, 2 barrells of Bacon, 2 Cask Rice and 50 bushells of Corn, for the use of the Inhabitants there but can't do it without leave from your Excellency and Honors —

He therefore prays your Excellency would permit him to Ship the Provisions aforesaid under the usual restrictions —

And as in duty bound shall ever pray &c[a]

Rich[d] King

Answer of the First Parish in Scarborough to a Petition.

Province of the Massachusetts Bay

To His Excellency Francis Barnard Esq[r] Captain General in Chief in and over his Majestys said Province to the Honourable his Majestys Council and to the Houn[ble] the House of Representatives in the Great and General Court assembled

The Inhabitants of the First Parish in Scarborough in the County of Cumberland in answer to a Petition Exhibited against said Parish to this Honourable Court in January or February last by Twenty one Persons who Call themselves Inhabitants of said Parish Humbly Sheweth,

The Petitionrs Say they have been Deprived of a Gospel Minister upward of five years past its true upwards of five years past the then Minister of the Parish was Remov[d] by Death but the Parish used all Propper Means to Get another Minister Settled and was at Great Expence in Journing as far as Boston and Sometimes further after one and another by which means we had several upon Probation one after another three of which had a Clear Call to Settle with us —

The Petititioners further Say they Could not Get one Settled because their is a party that would Compel whoever Settled with us to join in Fellowship with M[r] Clark which assertion is False for every Person agreed in Either of the three not a hand nor Tongue against Either of the three when at the same time all the People very well knew Neither of the three would have had Fellowship with M[r] Clark if they had Settled with us but they all refused but for what Reason we Never Knew.

The Petitioners Go on and Say when in Expectation of being Fined they made Application to the Presbetry to Send one who very Readily Sent M[r] Peirce it is a pitty Men had not More regard to Truth then to assert things that are falce for the Parish never made any application to the Presbetry neither did the Presbetry Send Mr Peirce but one of the Parish in Seeking after a minister heard of Mr Peirce & had a Promise of his Coming to Scarborough on Probation which accordingly he came and was so well Liked by the People that they Gave him a Call Notwithstanding he Told the Parish he Should not Settle on any other Constitution but as a Presbetrain the Petitioners themselves was as Willing to Settle him on that Constitution as any of the rest ware & as free in Voting his Settlement and Stating a Sallary upon him as any ware (them that was Voters of them) The Petitioners Complain of the Suddent and Rash Proceeding of the Parish in Calling and Settleing Mr Peirce the reason why Mr Peirce was settled in so short a time we Gave in our Former answer which we shall not mention here but shall answer other things but Supposing it had been a Suddent and Rash Preceeding of the Parish (as they say) the Petitioners themselves ware as Guilty as any of the rest was for they acted as freely therein. The Petitioners Pray they may not be Deprived of their other Priviledges in the First Parish and be set off to the Second Parish their seems to be Something in their Prayer Extraordanory they must thereby mean their Priviledges of Voting in the First Parish and be voters in both Parishes which would be a Great Priviledge indeed Meaning thereby to Get as Many as they Can to Follow them out at the same Door till they have Got the Major part of the voters on their side then they Shall Carry the Vote in the First Parish this is what some of the Petitinors has Honestly owned Intending thereby that Mr Peirce shall have no Sallary at all tho. they the Petitioners themselves did act as freely on Stating a Sallary on Mr Peirce as any in the Parish did Therefore your Respondants Can but wonder with what face the Petitioners Can ask to be freed from their Obligation when your

Respondants Look upon themselves Obliged by Law as well as by Concience to Make Good their Contract with their Minister — The Petitioners Complain of the Conduct of the Presbetery by a late Instance at the Eastward which dont concern us as we know of, the Presbetery Must answer for their own Conduct — The Petitioners further Pray that they may not be Compelled to pay any thing toward the Settlement & Support of Mr Peirce altho they Promised it and that they may have the money that has been taken from them — Meaning as we Suppose all of them that has freely paid toward the Settlement and Support of Mr Peirce Restored to them — Your Respondn^ts^ Suppose they mean that the Inhabitants that are not Set off must Restore their money to them againe let their Number be ever so Small which Number would be but Small if the Petitioners Could have their Will for without Doubt they will Pursuade as many as they can to Get off the same way they do by telling them they will thereby get Cleare of Paying Rates So that if the Prayer of their Petition be Granted their will be but a small Number to pay or Restore their money and to Support a minister the Parish being but a Small Parish when altogather and will find it hard enough to Support a minister Considering Other heavy Taxes Your Respondants Humbly Pray that if the Petitioners Must be Set off they may not Retain a Priviledge of Voteing in the First Parish and thereby to Maintain a quarrell in said Parish — The Major Part of the Inhabitants of said Parish are well Satisfied in our Minister and would be Glad to Enjoy him in peace but if any Considerable Number Should be Set off from us we Cant See how we shall be able to Support a minister at all and thereby must be without any which if no Other Motive would Engage us the Law will Compell us thereto Therefore your Respondants Humbly Pray that your Excellency and Honours would take the whole affair under your Wise Consideration and Dismiss their Petition all which we do Humbly Submitt and as in Duty Bound Shall Ever Pray

Sam^ll Small Solomon Bragdon Reuben Fogg	Committee in the Name and Behalf of the First Parish of Scarborough

At a Parish Meeting held in the first Parish in Scarborough September ye 6th 1762

Voted, agreed, and Concured with the Churches Votes in this Parish in Setling Mr Thomas Peirce in the Work of the Gospel Ministrey in said Parish in the Presbytery Order Agreeable to the Westminster Confession of Faith.

Voted to Give Mr Thomas Peirce in Case he Settles in the work of the Ministery in said Parish Eighty pounds Yearly During his Ministery or as long as he shall officiate in the office of a Minister in said Parish.

Voted to Give One hundred pounds as a Settlement to the said Mr Peirce in Case he Settles in s^d Parish in the work of the Ministery

A true Coppy of Record

Attest Sam^ll Fogg Parish Clark

At a Parish Meeting held in the first Parish in the Town of Scarborough March ye 19th day 1765 —

Mr Sam^ll Small, Capt Solomon Bragdon & Captn Reuben Fogg, Chose for a Parish Committe

Attest Sam^ll Fogg Parish Clark

Act of inncorporation. 1762.

Anno Regni Regis Georgii tertii Secundo.

An Act for incorporating a certain Tract of Land lying in the County of Lincoln into a Township by the name of

Whereas the Inhabitants of a certain Tract of Land lying on the West Side of Kennebeck River in the County of Lincoln are desirous of enjoying the Privileges that will arise to them by being incorporated into a Town.

Be it enacted by the Governor, Council and House of Representatives That the Tract of land aforesaid butted and bounded as follows viz: Beginning upon Kennebec river on the Northerly line of a Lott of land (Containing thirty two hundred Acres) being Lott Number Four, granted by the Proprietors of the Kennebeck Purchase from the late Colony of New Plymouth to William Bowdoin Esqr — The Line aforesaid being about four Miles above or to the Northward of a Point of Land called Abagadusett Point, Which makes the most Northerly part of Merry Meeting Bay in said River, and where said Bay begins on that side: From thence, viz: from the River aforesaid where said line strikes it, to run a West North West Course upon the Northerly line of the lott aforesaid five Miles; and from the end of said five Miles to run a South South West Course till it shall strike a line running from the South westerly end of Brick Island a West North West Course into land (this line being the Southerly line of a Tract of land granted by the Proprietors aforesaid to James Bowdoin Esqr) And from thence running an East South East Course upon the last mentioned line to the South Westerly end of the Island aforesaid which lies in Merry Meeting Bay And contains about ten Acres more or less; and from thence running (including said Island) to Abagadusett Point aforesaid, And from thence up the River aforesaid to the line first mentioned: be and hereby is erected into a Township by the name of

And that the Inhabitants thereof be, and hereby are invested with all the Privileges and Immunities which the Inhabitants of the Towns within this Province respectively do, or by law ought to enjoy.

And Be it further enacted that William Lithgow Esqr be and hereby is impowered to issue his Warrant directed to some principal Inhabitant in said Township to notify and warn the Inhabitants in said Township, qualified by law to vote in Town Affairs, to meet at such Time and place as shall be therein set forth, to choose all such officers as shall be necessary to manage the Affairs of said Township.

In the House of Rep[ves] Sep[t] 11 1762

Read three several times and passd to be engrossd

Sent up for concurrence Tim[o] Ruggles Spk[r]

In Council Sep[r] 11, 1762. Read a first time.

In Council Sep[r] 15, 1762. Read a second time & passed a concurrence to be engrossed

A Oliver Sec[r]

Act of Incorporation. 1762.

Anno Regno Regis Georgii tertii Secundo

An act incorporating a Certain Tract of Land in the County of Cumberland into a Township by the name of

Whereas the Inhabitants and proprietors of a certain Tract of Land lying on the back of the Township of Falmouth in the County of Cumberland heretofore known by the Name of Narragansett Number Seven alias Gorhamtown are desirous of enjoying the priviledges that will arrise to them by being incorporated into a Township

Be it enacted by the General Council and House of Representatives, That the Tract of Land aforesaid bounded agreeable to the Original Grant thereof be and hereby is erected into a Township by the Name of
and that the Inhabitants thereof be and hereby are invested with all the powers priveledges & Immunities which the Inhabitants of the Towns within this province respectively do or by Law ought to enjoy

And be it further Enacted that Alexand[r] Ross Esq[r] be and he hereby is impowered to issue his Warrant directed to some principal inhabitant in said Township to Notify & Warn the Inhabitants in said Town qualified by law to vote in town Affairs, to meet at such time and place as shall be therein sett forth, to choose all such Officers as shall be ,necessary to manage the Affairs of said Township —

In the House of Rep^{ves} Sep^{t} 11 1762

Read a first time

14 a second and third time and pass'd to be engross'd

Sent up for concurrence Tim° Ruggles Spk^{r}

In Council Sepr 15, 1762 Read a first & second time and passed a concurrence to be engross'd

A Oliver Sec^{r}

Message. Sept. 13, 1762.

Gentlemen of the House of Representatives.

Pursuant to a resolution of the General Court in last Session, I proposed this Summer to have gone to the Eastward and reduced the Garrisons of Fort Pownall and Fort Halifax in person. But before I could make that Voyage, Advice came of the French Invasion of Newfoundland; and then it became quite unadvisable to weaken either of those Garrisons. But as the danger from Newfoundland will probably soon be over, and the objection to the reduction arising from thence will cease; I would desire you to reconsider this matter, whether the reduction you propose is not too great for the present time. For this purpose I have detained Col° Lithgow that you may hear him concerning Fort Halifax. For Fort Pownall I have had no opportunity to confer with Brig^{dr} Prebble, but possibly may before the reduction can be safely made.

Council Chamber Sep. 13, 1762 Fra Bernard

Message. Sept. 14, 1762.

In Council Sepr 14th 1762

Voted y^t ye follow^g Message be sent to his Excell^y.—

May it Please Your Excellency

The Two Houses have consider'd Your Excellency's Message of the 9th Instant, and although they Apprehend it convenient that a Peace shou'd be concluded with the Penobscot Indians, yet inasmuch as they have not signified to the Government their desire thereof, The Two Houses are of Opinion that it would be too great a Condescension in Your Excellency to undertake a voyage for that purpose, And in case Those Indians are desirous of a Peace or labour under any difficulties in their present situation, that it will be more for the Honor of the Government that they, or a number of them properly Authorised, should wait on your Excellency at Boston to represent the same—

Voted that, Samuel Danforth, & Nath^ll Ropes Esq^rs with such as ye hon^ble House shall join be a Comm^e to present this Message to his Excell^y ye Gover^r

Sent down for Concurrence Jno Cotton D: Secry

In the House of Rep^ves Sep^t 14 1762

Read and Concurd and Mr Tyler Mr Waldo and Capt Thayer are Joyned in the Affair

Tim^o Ruggles Spk^r

Scarborough ye 10th Novem^br 1762

S^r/.

We the Inhabitants of the first Parish in Scarborough in ye County of Cumberland & Province of ye Massahu^sts Bay in New England have^g been desird to Attend Severeel Parrish meetings in s^d Parrish ℘ Notifications to see weather we ware willing to Mr Thomas Peirce having a Call to ye Ministry in sd Parrish and also to Settle him ye sd Peirce & Likewise to vote money for the Same & also to See weather we would vote him money to pay his bord and the Charge of his Ordination at Newbury Likewise ye Parrish in part have voted the Same that they will Settle Mr Thomas Peirce as A Minister Under the Presbiterian Goverment or Scotch Platform at the sd Newbury which we the Subscribers say is Contra to our Profession in Religion and Also Contra from what ever we have been brought up unto and Also we think Contra to the Laws of this Land in their Proceedure & Unless all have agreed, We have been most of us brought up & Settled under the Congregational Constitution in sd Parrish untill it Pleased God to take from us our Minister by Death and we think verry hard that we cant have A Proper time or Place to make A Defence to Support and Vindicate our Cause before the Presbitere but away we must go to Newbury near Eighty Miles Distant from Scarborough & Put to A Prodigious charge by their Voting away our Money to go to Newbury either to be a Presbiterion Rite or wrong or elce to Support those that are so minded we dont Pretend Sr to say any thing against ye Presbiterian Order for we are Strangers thereto but this we think that Mr Peirce never has known how many Persons have appeared against his being Settled at Newbury and in that Order which Perhaps may Disappoint Mr Peirces Expectations in Settling in that Order in this Place, but Sr our Cheif desire of you is this that you upon your Perrill would not Officiate in Settling Mr Thomas Peirce as our Minister in ye Affforesd Parrish for we are Determined not to pay one farthing of charge towards his Support or maintanance in Preaching or any other Charge that may arise or has Arose Unless he the sd Peirce will Settle According to ye Common Custom of New England As in Generell and according to ye Laws of this Goverment in that Respect Provided We Sr are of ye first Church and Par-

ish in Scarborough and hope for your Compliance & Sign our Names Accordingly.
To the Rever^{c} Mr John Morehead of Boston Suppos^{d} to be one of ye Presbitteree to be communicated to the Presbitere upon ye Suppos^{d} Ordination of Mr Thomas Pierce at Newbury —

Timothy Prout	Jos. Prout	Wm Tompson
Moses Plumer	William Plumer	Joshua Small
Elisha Lebbey	Richard Libby	Benj^{a} his ʊ mark Blake
Thomas Larrabee	Nathanel Libby	John Gilford
Sam^{ll} March	Samuel Jones	Peter Lebbee

P S. we have wrote to y^{u}Self & Mr Jon^{a} Parsons and Mr David Macgriger Sup^{g} they are all that belongs to ye Presbittere but if more pray to be Excus^{d} for not knowing it or else should have wrote them.

Reasons humbly offered to obviate an Objection to the Right of the Province of the Massachusetts Bay to Originate Grants of Lands between the Rivers Penobscot and St Croix.

It cannot be doubted that the Charter of William and Mary, which constituted the Province of Massachusetts Bay, contains, in the letter of its grants, All the lands lying between the River Sagadehock and the River St Croix by the Name of the Territory of Sagadehock. Under this Title the Government of this Province has defended and possessed this Country for upwards of 70 Years without any other interruption, than from Indians with Indianised French men intermixed with them and one invasion by a 20 gun french Ship, so momentory, that she did not wait the approach of the Massachusetts Forces, which were immediately sent against her.

During all this time, The Title of the Province hath never been impeached but twice: upon both of which occasions, the Attorney and Sollicitors general, to whom it was referred, reported in favour of the Province. Upon the last of these, The Attorney and Sollicitor general heard Council on both sides and thereupon made so full a report on the behalf of the Province, that Queen Caroline, then Regent, made an order in Council to prevent the further interruption of the Province in their right and Possession of that Country: which was immediately carried into Execution by all the Persons, whom this order concerned, removing from thence.

After this Public recognition, The Province considered their right to this Country so absolutely confirmed to them, that they entered into the most Vigrous measures for the protection of it, for proof of which they can show now standing in that Country 4 different Forts; besides Fort Pownall, erected in the heart of the Country of the Penobscot Indians. The Province in consideration of the great charge they were then at, beyond their proportion, were assisted by general Amherst in the expence of building this Fort; but they were at the whole charge of furnishing it with Artillery, Ammunition and small Arms; and have ever since maintained the Garrison there over and above their contingency to the Army. At the erecting this Fort Governor Pownall took and confirmed a formal repossession of this Country on the East side of the River for the Province Massachusetts Bay And now, When they expect to reap the fruits of 70 Years expence of blood and Treasure, from the possession of a Country convenient for their own People, continually increasing, to settle in, they find the right of the Province to originate grants of lands thereof like to be questioned by a New Objection to their title under the Charter: which is this, "That King William & Queen Mary at the time of their making this Charter were not in the possession of this Country and therefore could make no grant of it."

If this was true, and his Majesty upon this account should

be inclined to resume this country, there can be no doubt, but that the Province would be intitled to a reimbursement of all the expences they have been at in conquering and maintaining this Country for upwards of 70 years, acting all the while under a Royal Grant, which for upwards of 30 years has been formally confirmed by the Crown; which Expence would greatly exceed the present Value of this Country, tho it was to be put up to Auction and sold for the best price possible.

But in truth the Fact is quite otherwise: King William and Queen Mary, at the time of making their Grant, were in the Actual Possession of this Country. This will sufficiently appear from the following Narrative, which is wholly taken from Original and Authentic papers.

In the Year 1689 The Province of Massachusetts Bay having resumed their Old Charter Government upon advice of the revolution, soon afterwards found themselves attacked in the Eastern Country by Indians joined by Parties of French from Canada and Nova Scotia, War being then declared between France and England. They sent a Sloop express to England with advice of this irruption and immediately after determined to fit out a strong Armament against the French in Acadie and Nova Scotia, and appointed Sr William Phips to be General and Commander in Chief. Accordingly Sir William Phips sailed from Boston April 23rd 1690 having under his command 3 Ships and 4 other Vessels and in the whole 737 men. On the 1st of May they anchored at Mount desart and from thence sailed to Penobscot where there was an Indian Fort and the settlement of a French man, married to an Indian Squaw and then a profest Indian chief, one Casteen. They found the Fort which had been Garrisoned by Indians only, abandoned, and took possession of it. From thence on the 5th of May they Sailed to Machias near the Great Menan Island, (called in Southback's Map Mechisses) where they found only 2 Frenchmen, who Surrender'd and they took them and their goods on board and carried them off. On the 6th of May They went to Passimaquady where there were some French Planters, who refusing to treat with them, they burnt their Houses and brought off their goods. On the 9th of May they came before Port Royal which surrender'd on the 11th and on the 14th the Inhabitants took the Oaths to K. William &c and an English Government was appointed. On the 19th the Inhabitants of Menis and other places came in and took the Oaths. On the 21st Capt Alden in the Sloop Mary was left to cruise on those Seas and order'd to take possession of several parts of Acadie and Penobscot in particular and the rest of the Fleet returned to Boston, where they arrived on the 30th of May. From that time to the day of the date of the Charter, the Government of Massachusetts Bay kept possession of Port Royal and of consequence of all the Country before mentioned, including the whole Territory of Sagadehock; as appears by several orders of the General Court and particularly one dated June 2 1691 (4 months before the date of the Charter) whereby the Governor and Council are empowered to settle a Garrison in the Coast of Nova Scotia and Acadie lately subjected to the obedience of the Crown of England and for securing the Country and Trade thereof to the Crown. And in another Entry dated Decr 12th 1693 2 years after the date of the Charter) it appears that Port Royal was garrisoned at the expence of the Province of Massachusetts Bay.

Soon after this Conquest, Decr 10th 1690 an Address from the general Court to their Majesty's giving an Account of the Subjection of this Country (and also of the unsuccessfull attack of Quebec) was sent home by Sr William Phips who is mentioned in the Address to be the bearer of it. And on October 8: 1691 (within 10 months after the date of the address at Boston) Their Majesty's granted the Charter including therein All the Lands between the Province of Main and Nova Scotia by the Name of the Territory of Sagadehock and appointed Sr William Phips the first Royal Governor of the united Province.

From this Narrative It appears plain that King William and Queen Mary at the time of granting the Charter were really and actually possessed of the Country between Sagadehock and Nova Scotia in the strictest Sense of the Words which the Nature of this Country will admit; where All European possessions are incumbered with Indian Settlements and Subject to be interrupted by Indian incursions. It also appears (if not positively, at least to the highest degree of Probability) that the including this Country within the bounds of the New united Province of Massachusetts Bay was intended both as a reward and a reimbursement. And altho' Special Grace is allowed to be a sufficient consideration for a Royal Grant, yet where there happens to be also a Valuable consideration, The Grantee may with greater Reason expect to hold his Grant unimpeached, than if it was founded upon Special Grace alone.

As for the Conquest of this Country after the date of the Charter: if there had been such, Upon the reconquest and Cession of it to the English, The Province would have been restored to their right, jure Posthuimÿ according to the Opinion of the Attorney and Solicitor general in 1731, But there really never was such: If there was any revolt or Conquest of Port Royal and other parts of Nova Scotia yet this was not the Case of the Country Westward of St Croix. Indeed the Newport a small French Ship of War which had been taken from the English, stragling that way in 1696 Surprized the Fort of Pemaquid and demolished part of the Works; but was so far from attempting to keep possession, that she got away in hast before 3 Vessels of War, which were immediately sent from Boston could come up with her. This is all the Conquest of this Country that the French have to boast of: and Surely such a temporary Invasion can never be understood to divest the Province of any part of its constitutional Territories.

There seems to be no foundation for a distinction between the Lands Westward of Penobscot and those Eastward in regard to the Right of the Province: as in the Charter, so upon all other occasions, The Lands between Sagadehock and Nova Scotia or the River St Croix have been considered as one intirety; The Possession and Defence of one part thereof was the possession and Defence of the whole; And It is apprehended that at this day the Right of the Province on one side Penobscot and the other must stand and fall together. In this light it was seen by the Attorney and Sollicitor general in 1731, who considered the Forts erected by the Province as a performance of the tacit Conditions of their Grant, altho' such Forts were wholly on the Western side of Penobscot. But there is less occasion to press this Matter, as it appears from the foregoing Narrative that the Reduction of the Country the Year before the Grant of the Charter, by the Arms of Massachusetts Bay, and the actual possession of King William and Queen Mary arising therefrom was executed upon the Lands between Penobscot and St Croix only; beginning with the Fort at Penobscot which was on the last side of the River and ending at the Island of Passimaquady which lies in the bay of St Croix.

For these Reasons it is humbly submitted that the Objection to the Provinces Right to these Lands arising from the Supposition that King William and Queen Mary at the time of granting the Charter was not possessed thereof is fully answered by the state of the forementioned Facts, which prove an actual possession in the Crown of England at the time of granting the Charter, and that the Recovery of that

Country was the probable Reason that it was included in the Charter of the New united Province.

P. S.

As it appears afterwards that Casteen continued at Penobscot after Sr William Phip's expedition and was the only Frenchman left in that Country, It may be proper to give some further Account of him.

At the time of Sr William Phip's Expedition, Casteen, in the quality of an Indian chief, had joined a party of French from Canada against the English Settlement at Casco bay, which they took and plunder'd and carried off some prisoners to Canada [see Extract of Mr Davis journal] Casteen upon his return found his own Settlement broke up, his Daughter a Prisoner, the whole Country subdued by the English from Boston, and Port Royal in their hands. He therefore submitted to the English and took the Oaths of Allegiance to King William; which it appears he had faithfully observed to the Year 1694 3 years after the Charter. [See a Letter from Lieu^{t} Governor Stoughton to Casteen dated Jany 30: 1694/5 and sent by Wm Alden who was Mate of the Sloop sent from Port Royal by Sr William Phips against Penobscot, to whom probably Casteen submitted]. Casteen's Settlement therefore, from before the date of the Charter and for several Years after, was that of an English Subject, under the Province of Massachusetts Bay. It does not appear that any other Frenchman was settled in that Country at the time of the date of the Charter. If the French settlements in the Island of Passimaquady were resumed (which is not probable, as the Massachusetts kept possession of Port Royal) that Island is within the grant of Nova Scotia.

In Govr Bernards letter to M^{r} pownall. Decr 1. 1762

Petition of the Well Affected Inhabitants of Gorhamtown; 1763.

To his Excellency Francis Barnerd Esqr Captain General & Governour in Chief in & over his Majestys Province of the Massachusetts Bay in New England — The Honble his Majestys Council and House of Representatives in General Court Assembled

The Petition of a Number of the Inhabitants of a place Call'd GorhamTown Alias Narraganset N° 7 which are Generally distinguished from ye Rest of the Inhabitants by the Term well Affected — Humbly Sheweth

That whereas we are Informd that there is a Petition now Lying before the Genl Court of this Province of a Number of Inhabitants of s^{d} GorhamTown who are ye Disaffected — that ye Lands of Gorham Town might be Incorporated into a Town or District, and that the Inhabitants be Vested with Previledges as other Towns in like case, &c. Now as Such an Incorporation must Necessarily Effect us the well Affected, especially under our Present Division and Distraction, and Lay us Open to Oppression and Insults of the Disaffected, who have the Majority on their side, we being ye Minor Part; being about thirty, or five & thirty Mails from Sixteen years and Upwards. So that it will be in the power of the Disaffected by their Votes in their Publick Meetings to Subject us Your Humble Petitioners To Pay equal Taxes with the Disaffected for all their Ramble about the Country for to Seek out Lay Preachers and Introduce one into this place to Settle, All the Cost of his pretended Settlement and Annual Salarey. All the Cost of their Meeting-house And all and every Charge that they in their Present Frenzy may incline to Involve themselves and Neighbours in. and not only so but we must be expos^{d} to all ye Contempt and Slight that men in Such Rage and Temper are Capable to Cast. as we already in a Publick Meeting have had a Sufficient Taste of. That our Case will be Simelar to Slavery in Turkey and many more Diffecultys will arise Upon Our Incorporation — Your Petitioners therefore Humbly pray his Excellency and Hon^{rs} not to Suffer non_ in this place to be Incorporated while we Remain in Such a Temper for we Dread the Consequences of it.—

But if y^{r} Excellency & Honours in y^{r} Great Wisdom See meet to Grant their Petition, Your Petitioners Humbly Beg that his Excellency and Honours would enjoyn the Iubabitants to Settle a Learned well Quallify'd Minister in s^{d} Place as Provision is made by the Act of William and Marey in whom we may all Joyn as the Condition of Incorporation as has ben Usual for the Government in Similar Cases, on which our Minister will Chearfully Resign his Ministry. the Disaffected have Pretended to Settle one whom they Call their minister, whom we esteem every way Unquallify^{d} for the work and we think ought to be Taught Rather than to be a Teacher. your Humble petitioners have no Rellish nor likeing to an Illitrate and Ignorant Ministrey your Humble Petitioners further Humbly pray that they may be exempt from paying any Charges that the Disaffected have brought on the place already by Riding about ye Country to Seek out Lay preachers. There Settleing one — And Salery fixt on him — and Building a Meeting-house for their party^{s} Use. The Proprietors of Gorham Town are Under Obligation to Build a Meeting house and have Voted money for that Purpose and have the Timber now on the Spot and Propose Soon to Build the same —

But if his Excellencys and Honours should think propper to excuse them that are Disaffected that Common Condition of Settleing a Minister Qualifyd as by ye Act of W^{m} and Marey, your Humble Petitioners Pray that your Excellency & Hon^{rs} would Indulge your Humble Petitioners wth ye Priviledge of Being a Society by them selves Independent and free from any Relation to them as a Town District or Parish and that they may injoy a Learned Ministry and have Power to Transact their own Affairs by them Selves — And your Humble Petitioners as in Duty Bound Shall Ever Pray

Charles McDaniel	Robert McDaniel	hugh M^{c}lellen
William Mclellan	Karey Mclellen	Timothy Hamblen
James M^{c}lellan	Joseph Pilkinton	Duno Leay
Phinehas thompson	John M^{c}daniel	Joseph Brown
Samuel Bridges	Josiah Bridges	John Harding jun^{r}
Joseph Rounds	Jacob hamblen	Joseph Brown Junr
danieL Mosher	Elisha Cobb	Solomon Lombard Jr
Prince Davis	Wentworth Stuart	Joseph Hamblen
John MacDaniel Ju^{r}	James Low	Austin Alden
Zep^{h} Harding	Richard Lombard	

In the House of Rep^{ives} Jany 31 1763

Read again and revived and Ordered that this Pet^{n} be dismissed

Sent up for concurrence Tim^{o} Ruggles Spkr

In Council Feb^{r} 4. 1763 Read and Concurred

A Oliver Sec^{r}

Petition of a number of the Inhabitants of Gorhamtown. 1763.

Province of the Massachusetts Bay

To His Excellency Francis Bernard Esqr Governour & Com̄ander in chief in and over said Province the Honble his Majestys Council and House of Representatives in General Court assembled May 1762

The Petition of a Number of Inhabitants of Narragansett Township Number Seven alias Gorhamtown in the County of Cumberland Humbly Shews, That about two years past, We your Petitioners represented to this Honble Court, "That with great Difficulty and Hardship we had for many Years past lived in said exposed Frontier, and in Jeopardy of our Lives, and indeed with the Loss of Several Lives we had maintained our Ground there in Time of War; That Through the good Hand of Providence our Numbers were then increas'd to Sixty Families, since which the Proprietors of said Township (who were before very helpful to us) had neglected us. By means whereof and for Want of proper Authority among our Selves, we were then in a Suffering Condition particularly we had no Meeting House, or School; our High Ways were neglected, and in many Places impassable, our Fences, and Cattle without Regulation;" for which and Other Reasons we then petitioned the Hon[ble] Court to be imbodied into a Town, which Petition not being granted we have been Obliged to endure those Difficulties ever since. But as the Hon[ble] Court have in one of their last Sessions seen meet to lay a part of the publick Tax upon us, in the Act for which Provision is made that the Assessors shall be paid for their Labour in the same Manner, as those in corporate Towns are, which we imagine is by the Town Treasurer, which Officer we have no Right by Law to choose while unimbodied —

Therefore we humbly conceive we have some Pretensions to renew our Request again to be incorporated; In doing which we shall not trouble your Excellency and Honours with a needless Repetition of Grievances, which still are of the same Kind as before, but are increased in Degree. For we have since our last Memorial been at the sole Expence of Building a Commodious Meeting House, which the Proprietors have hitherto neglected to do and our Numbers being now increased to about Eighty Families, consequently our Distress for Want of having the Benefit of the good and wholesome Laws, which incorporated Towns have, increases in Proportion, of which those that respect the due Observance of the Lords Day, and the Support of Schools are not the least; Nor do we imagine it possible to remedy these Difficulties while we remain in such a loose and confus'd Condition — We are very Sensible that Some of the Proprietors opposed our Petition before, and we don't know but that they may now, but if they should, we are soberly of the Opinion, their Opposition will arise rather from some private Resentment, they have to some of us for Causes to us unknown, than from a View to the publick Good, and we humbly conceive there is no Other New Township in the Government whose Inhabitants are so numerous as ours, and have brought to their Settlements in the Manner we have, that have been opposed by the Proprietors in their Applying for Incorporation — We therefore humbly beseech your Excellency & Honours that we may be incorporated into a Town, to be bounded according to a Plan of said Township established by the Honble Court some few Years past, and that we may be invested with the Authorities and Priviledges of other Towns — and as in Duty bound will ever pray —

Richard edwards	Philip Gomman	John Phinney
Nathan Whitney	Briant Morten	John freeman
George Hanscom	Moses Whitney Junr	John Sawyer
Sawyer	Nathaniel Whitney Junr	Benj^{a} Skilling
Joseph Weston	John Wilyams	Abel Whitney
David Sawyer	Moses Whitney	Samuel Crocker
Moses Weston	Ebenezer Murch	Samuel Murch
Charles McDaniel	William Hodden	Joseph Cate
Wileam O	Joseph Morten	Nathaniel Whitney Junr
John	David Whitney	Amos Whitney
Benjamin ffrost	Samuel Libby	James Gilkey
Benj^{a} Stevens	Ebenenezer Mortor	Joshua Davis
John Phinney jun^{r}	Nath̄ael ffrost	William
James	Barnabas Bangs	Ebenezer Morton
Seth Harding		

In the House of Rep^{ves} Jany 13 1763

Read again and revived and Ordered that this Pet^{n} be dismissed

Sent up for concurrence   Tim^{o} Ruggles

In Council Feb^{r} 1, 1763 Read and Concurred

A Oliver Sec^{r}

Govr Bernard to the Lords Commissioners for Trade & Plantations.

Boston Ap. 8. 1763

My Lords

I write this to introduce to your Lordships the Grants of six townships laid out on the East side of the River Penobscot, made by the General Court of this Province & submitted to his Majesty for his royal confirmation according to the terms of the Charter. And tho' the soliciting of this confirmation is properly the Business of the Grantees only, yet the Event is so intresting, to the Province in supporting their Right to originating grants of lands in this Territory, & to the Nation in encouraging a speedy cultivation of the Wast lands of North America, that I think it my duty to lay before your Lordships my sentiments upon both these points.

In regard to the Province's originating these Grants, I shall not enter into any disquisition of their Right to do so: If that is made a Question, the support of it must not depend upon me. I have perhaps allready engaged too far in it, in what I have before wrote upon this subject. At present I only mean to show in what manner they have exercised this power in these instances which are the first of the kind; and from thence to show that this power is in hands, which are not like to abuse it.

1 These Grants have been made without any other consideration than a Covenant to settle the lands; not a farthing

has been paid or stipulated for on behalf of the province. 2. The Grants are not only made strictly conformable to the restrictions of the Charter, but there is also a limitation of the time in which the King's Confirmation is to be obtained, after which the Grants, which are in strictness only recommendations, for want of confirmation cease & determine. 3. The General Court has been so intent upon their main purpose, peopling the Country, that they have not trusted to the forfeiture for not settling, which in other grants has been the only obligation hitherto used, but they have obliged the grantees to give Security to settle their lands within a certain time after the Grants shall be confirmed; which bonds were lodged in the Secretaries Office, before the Grants were made. From this I would infer, That the general Court have had the strictest regard to the public good in making these grants has shown itself worthy to be intrusted with this power & therefore deserves to have its acts approved & confirmed, if weightier reasons not known here should prevail against it.

I need not urge to your Lordships the expediency of encouraging, by all proper means, the cultivation of the wasts of N America. The Sentiments of your Lordships have been fully shown by your unwearied endeavours to promote such purpose: And now the Motives to it have received much additional strength by the late great enlargement of his Majesty's N American Dominions. But perhaps It may be of use to endeavour to remove the obstructions which may lie in the Way of your Lordships approving this settlement, & arise from your doubts concerning the Province's right to originate Grants of land within this Territory: which Question, if it is to be discussed with that deliberation which its importance will require, may not be determined within the time necessary to resolve upon allowing or putting a stop to the proposed settlement.

Undoubtedly This Settlement must be of general advantage to the public, whether it shall appear hereafter to be in this or that province or in neither of them: and the undertakers deserve all possible encouragement to induce them to pursue their Scheme, which is certainly planned with good judgement for the neutral support of one another. The whole 6 Townships are laid upon a Neck of land lying between Penobscot River & a River called Mount desert river the Mouth of it being near the West End of the Island of that name. The whole Plan of the 6 Townships (each of which is intended to contain the Area of 6 miles square) extends not above 15 miles of longitude. This Spot is at present a Wilderness, & lies at a great distance from the settled parts of the Massachusets province & at a much greater distance from the nearest Settlements of Nova Scotia, & would, if duly promoted, be the means of connecting in time, one with the other. On the other hand if this settlement should now be prevented, It will cast a great damp upon undertakings of this kind, & may contribute to keep this great length of coast in the desert states in which It has hitherto continued.

I must therefore submit to your Lordships whether, in case your doubts concerning the right of the Province should still remain, It might not be advisable to disengage this Settlement from the dispute concerning the Right of the Province, and let the settlement go on to wait the determination of the right. To whatever province the Land shall be allotted, it will not be the Worse for having 360 families upon it. I urge this not on the behalf of the Province which will gain nothing by such a proceeding, but for the sake of the settlers, many of whom are embarked so deep in this Adventure that the disappointment may be their ruin. And with great submission I conceive, that this Method of favouring them is very practicable, as it seems to require nothing but that in the Kings confirmation there be a recital of the doubts concerning the Provinces Right to these lands and a proviso that this Grant & confirmation shall not prejudge the same, but that It shall still remain to be considered & decided, this Grant & confirmation notwithstanding.

I have been the more particular and indeed the more earnest in this representation, as I think it would be a great pity that a Settlement so compact & so well calculated for the public Utility should be prevented. There was an application made to the general Court for 6 other Townships; but they do not go on: 3 of them are drop't already; one of the other 3 proceeds and I believe the other two will, if they are encouraged. These 3 Townships adjoin to the other six, & will help to strengthen them. The whole if they are allowed to proceed, will form a settlement of 540 families. The first settling of a wast Country is so hardy a work that a little Discouragement is apt to defeat it. I therefore hope that this undertaking will meet with your Lordships favour.

I am, with great respect, My Lords Your Lordships
Most obedient and Most humble Servant
Fra Bernard

Govr Bernard to the Lords Commissioners for Trade & Plantations.

Boston Ap 25. 1763

My Lords

By a Letter dated the 8th inst I informed your Lordships that the general Court had passed a Grant for 6 Townships on the East side of the river Penobscot to be submitted to his Majesty for his Confirmation: and I humbly offer'd to your Lordships such observations and reasons as have induced me to recommend this settlement to your Lordships favour.

About a week after this packet was sent away, I received your Lordships letter of Dec. 24, which has given me a most sensible Mortification; for I had flatter'd myself that I stood in such a degree of credit with your Lordships, that I should not easily have been suspected of acting, with intention, in opposition to your Lordships opinion or in prejudice of his Majesty's right. As I am persuaded that upon a full & true state of this affair, Your Lordships will readily acquit me of this imputation, I was desirous of being discharged from it as soon as possible. I therefore by the return of the Post to New York sent a short defence of my Conduct inclosed in a letter to Mr Pownall, desiring him to lay it before your Lordships at such time as he should think it fit and necessary. I should have addressed myself immediately to your Lordships, if the hurry I was in had not made me prefer the form of a Memorial. And as upon a revisal I find it contains the chief substance of my defence, I shall avoid repeating, as well as I can, &, in this, explain such proofs, as I shall think proper to introduce in support of my allegation.

The Proofs I have to submit to your Lordships are these: a Copy of the order of the general Court for the settlement of the line between the Massachusets & Nova Scotia; a Copy of the report of the Committee appointed for that purpose; a Copy of my letter to The Lt Govr of Nova Scotia, in pursuance of the report of the Committee, wrote in Council & recorded there; A Copy of the record of the election of Commissioners to join those of Nova Scotia to repair to St Croix & ascertain the line &c; a Copy of my Letter to the Lieut Governor of Nova Scotia, in pursuance of the last mentioned act of the general Court, wrote in Council &c

From these will appear; 1 That I was not a mover of this intended Survey, and that, if I am blameable for any thing, it is only for consenting to the resolutions of the two houses: with what propriety I could refuse my consent thereto will be considered hereafter. 2. That the deliberation of the general Court turned solely upon these questions; which stream was the river S[t] Croix? and from what part of that river the Northern Line was to be run? and that they were not aware of an objection to their title arising from any other consideration. 3 That in my consenting to these resolutions & consequentially communicating them to the L[t] Gov[r] of Nova Scotia, I judged for the best, if nothing then appeared to me to invalidate the report of the Committee, which I found to be agreable with the the letter of the Charters of Nova Scotia & Massachusets Bay.

I cannot say whether at that time the boundary of Acadia as ceded by Charles the second to France was in my thoughts or not: but this I am sure of, that I had not the least apprehension that such boundary was applicable to the limitation of King William's Grant to Massachusets Bay. As a presumptive proof thereof (the only kind of proof which such an asseveration is capable of) It appears that my immediate predecessor Gov[r] Pownall, altho' he came to this Government directly from England, was not acquainted with this objection to the Provinces right. If He had, I am sure that He who was never reckoned inattentive to his Duty, would not have taken a formal & monumental possession of the East side of Penobscot on behalf of the Province of Massachusets Bay; as it appears, from the inclosed Copy of the record of that transaction, that he did. This Transaction alone, which I must suppose was communicated to your Lordships board & was never, that I have heard of, excepted to, must justify me in presuming that the East side of Penobscot was allowed to belong to Massachusets Bay.

In regard to my consenting to the grant of the 6 Townships, I believe I might, after what I have allready said, safely trust my justification to the grant itself, in which so much care has been taken to provide for the Kings rights &

the public Emolument. But It may be necessary to state to your Lordships the time & manner in which it was made. The first Grant originated in the House of Representatives Feb 20. 1762; (see the Votes pa 265) & having been concurred by the Council received my Consent. This Grant amounted to a positive assurance of 6 Townships, of the contents of 6 miles square each, to the 360 Grantees, altho' it was incomplete, untill by an actual survey, the boundaries of the Townships could be ascertained. This Survey was not perfected till the end of the Summer following; and it was certified upon Oath to the general Court at the first Session after; when on Feb 24 1763 a positive Grant was ordered to be passed under the Province Seal to be laid before his Majesty for his approbation. (See the Votes pa 277)

Between the times of the originating the grant & the completing of it by an Authentic instrument, I was advised that probably an Objection arising from the bounds of Charles the seconds cession might be urged against the Provinces right; and the general Court received the same intimation from the Province-Agent. But I was so far from thinking that that would authorise me without an order from your Lordships, to put a stop to this business, that I was rather inclined to forward it as much as might be, thinking it the best & the Easiest Way of bringing this right into Question. And I still persuade myself, that, when your Lordships have perused this grant, you will think that the general Court has introduced their claim, in as respectful & proper a manner as they could well have done. Nevertheless upon the first notice of these doubts concerning the Provinces right, I resolved to consent to no more grants 'till the present shall be determined upon.

I am very unwilling to extend the trouble I now give your Lordships unnecessarily; and therefore for the rest I shall only refer to my former letters upon this subject; from the whole tenor of which I flatter myself your Lordships will perceive that from the first time I had reason to think that this Question was like, to be controverted, I have expressed an earnest desire that I might be engaged in it as little as my station would permit: and tho I have thought it my duty to lay before your Lordships such arguments as I knew would be urged in favour of the Provinces right; yet your Lordships must have observed that the general Service of his Majesty in extending the population of his Dominions has been my chief purpose.

I am, with great respect My Lords, Your Lordships most obedient & most humble Servant

Fra. Bernard

Petition of T. Westgatt & others.

To His Excellency Francis Bernard Esq[r] Governor & Commander in Chief of the Province of the Massachusetts Bay

The Petition of Thomas Westgatt and others inhabitants of a Tract of Land known by the name of Majabaagadoose in said Province Humbly Sheweth

That most of your Petitioners were Soldiers in his Majesties Service in the Pay of this Province & were Dismissed from the Service after the Peace was settled & being Humbly of opinion that some of the Lands they had Conquered would be as likely to fall to their Share as to others they settled upon the afores[d] tract of Land a Place where no English inhabitants had ever before settled & at Great Peril Labour & Expence they Cleared & cultivated Some Small Spots of Land & have got themselves Comfortable houses Suffering beyond Expression the Last winter & after having grappled through those Difficulties they have been able this Summer to Raise sauce & a few necessaries to Support their families & have been in hopes to have had their Settlements confirmed to them & accordingly Petitioned to the General Court for this purpose Long before the s[d] Land was granted to 60 others but your Petitioners being Poor & not able to attend and further their Petition they are informd it never reachd the General Court & that now the fruit of their heavy toil & Labour is like to be reapt by others unless your Petitioners will Submit to very hard terms offered them by the new proprietors your Petitioners are glad of an opportunity to lay their Distress Before your Excellency & Humbly Pray you wo[d] take it into your Wise Consideration & Lay the Same Before your Assembly for their Consideration and Grant them Such Relief as your Excellency & their Honours shall think Just & Reasonable & your Petitioners shall Ever Pray

Dated at Majabragadoose October y[e] 3[d] 1763

Thomas Wasgatt	John Trott	Sam Trott
Matthew Toben	hateviel C	Ichabod C
		Thomas Wasgatt jun[r]

We whose Names are underwritten Do Sign the Within written Petition.

John Moore	John Corson Soldier	Samuel Matthews
Stephen Littlefield	Jacob D	Samuel Westcot
Joshua Gray	John Gray	Andrew **X** Gray
James **8** Gray	Andrew Westcot	Joseph Lowel
John Daley	David Daley	John Daley Junr
Jonathan Stover	John Hanson	Stephen Goodwin
Nathan Lankester	Thons Simon	John Smart
Thomas Laighton	Samuel Leighton	Thomas Laighton Jun
Thoder Laighton	Hatuel Laighton	Thomas Laighton
Trustram Pinkhan	Josiah Tucker	Eyod Howard
James Howard	Benj Howard	ArChibell haney
Joseph Sessions	Jeremiah Springer	John Grindal
Jeremiah Veasey	William Westcot	John Dame
Jonathan Swett	Joshua	Ebenezer Low

Speech. Dec. 21, 1763.

Gentlemen of the Council and Gentlemen of the House of Representatives

At the opening of the last Session, We exchanged our mutual congratulations upon the late happy conclusion of the peace & the fair prospect, which it opened, of the extensive improvement of his Majesty's American Dominions. But this View has been since overclouded by an insurrection of the Savages, as ungrateful & unprovoked as it has been merciless & inhuman.

This must create an Alarm throughout all North America. It is not an Attack of this or that province a Dispute about boundaries; or a Resentment of private injuries: but it is an open War begun indeed by particular Nations only, but avowedly designed to be improved to a general Confederacy of the Indians against the British Empire.

To put a stop to these Mischiefs, to punish the perfidious promoters of them & to establish a general & durable peace with the Indians, General Gage, now Commander in chief proposes to Assemble a respectable body of troops at Niagara early next Spring. To effectuate this He finds himself obliged to call upon the provinces north of the River Delaware to raise provincial troops to join his Majesty's regular forces & carry the war into the Indians own Country upon the lakes; whilst the Southern Provinces are performing the like service on the Ohio. The Number required of this Province is 700 men, to be doubly officer'd upon Account of the Service they are designed for, to be clothed in an uniform short Coat and other light cloathing; & to be ready to march to Albany by the first of March next: They are to be provided with Arms & tents & furnished with provisions at the Kings expence; the time of their Service may be limited to the first day of Novr next; but it is to be hoped that they will be dismissed much sooner.

It is surely (to use the Generals own words) consistent with true policy humanity & brotherly Affection, that ev'ry Province should in times of Calamity contribute to the mutual assistance of each other: I may add, it is also agreeable to his Majesty's royal instructions to his Governors in America. . And therefore the General may reasonably hope from you a favorable reception of this requisition, when he Considers the readiness this Government has shown on former occasions in forwarding & promoting the public service. Consider, Gentlemen: if this flame is not soon extinguished, who can tell how far it will extend? We are at present at a Considerable distance from it: Yet if it is suffered to rage much longer, We may well expect that it will soon come to our own homes. But it is not self intrest alone that should dictate to us upon this occasion. The principles of Humanity, the reciprocal tyes which connect fellow Christians & fellow subjects must afford strong incitements for us to assist in putting a Speedy end to this horrid war & inflicting exemplary punishment upon the abominable beginners of it.

But Gentlemen, whilst I am recommending to you to Assist your neighbours, I must also desire you to take care of your selves. It seems to me to be absolutely necessary that some immediate measures should be taken for the Security of the Eastern Country. The Indians now living within that part of this Province are not numerous, but enough (even without their being joined by others) to spread wide desolation thro' the dispersed & defenceless settlements of that Country.

At present indeed they profess themselves to be friends to the English; and it is undoubtedly their intrest to be so. But will you risk so great a stake as the growing improvements of that Country upon the words of Indians? Will you put any Confidence in their faith or their discretion? It has been frequently observed that they always give the first blow, which with them is the best part of the Battle. This may be sufficiently accounted for from their total disregard of public faith joined with the jealousy, inhumanity & rapaciousness which mark their Character. But I have sometimes thought that the Inattention & Remissness of some English Governments have contributed a good deal to Indian invasions; they have been, as it were, invited to plunder by the defenceless state of a Country. Let not this be our Case but let Us be suspicious in our turns; & show our selves prepared for them before they have formed their plan for attacking us.

Gentlemen of the House of Representatives

The Forces I want you to enable me to raise for the protection of the Eastern Country should not be less than 200 Men formed in 2 Companies with a Captain & 3 Lieutenants to each & a field Officer to Command in Chief. They should be made appear as like regulars as possible, as part of their business is to keep the Savages in Awe. They should be inlisted to serve during the Indian War; that, if that should not be determined next summer, you may not be put to the expence & trouble of reinlistments. With this force I think that Country will be secured from real danger & the Apprehensions of it; Without it, I can not be Answerable for the Effects of one or the other. As for the present state of the Forts there, I shall lay it before you in separate papers by which you may be enabled to judge what is wanting to the proper support thereof.

Gentlemen

It is ever with much regret that I propose to you any measures that will be attended with extraordinary expence: A Consideration of what is due to your Honor & necessary to your Welfare is always my motive for such a proposal. The present intended Armaments will not be very expensive in fitting out nor, I hope, will be of any continuance. At least I will Assure you for myself, that such part thereof as shall depend upon me, shall not be kept up one day longer than the Safety of the Country shall require.

Fra Bernard

Council Chamber Dec 21 1763

Resolve. 1764.

In the House of Rep[ves] Jan[y] 1764

The House took under Consideration the Petitions of the Officers and Soldiers who have been in the service of the Province in the late Wars & pass'd the following Resolve Viz

Resolved That Surveyors be appointed to survey the Country for six Miles of Latitude above the North Line of the new Townships on the East Side of Mount Desart or Union River, noting the exact Courses of the principal Rivers and their Navigability, the Nature of the Lands and other Things remarkable, including the Western Side of Union River, and the Eastern Side of the River at the End of the sixth Township. That an exact Account of the Expence of such Survey be kept, to be defreyed by the Grantees of any Townships or Tracts of Land which shall be hereafter granted in such Proportions as shall be ordered by the General Court.

That the same Surveyors shall also survey the Lands lying between the six Townships on the West Side of Union River, and the said River beginning at the North Point of the said Townships and running **A** due East by Compass to the said Union River & to the east Point of Number Six of the said Townships, the Expence to be born by the future Grantees as before.

That the Grantees of all the aforementioned Townships be obliged to have the boundary Lines of their several Towns, and also the Courses of the principal Rivers therein carefully run and noted by able surveyors to be approved of by the Governor and Council and to be returned within a certain Time.

That Surveyors be appointed to survey all the Islands belonging to the Province from Penobscot Bay to the End of the granted Townships (excepting Mount Desert and its Dependencies) with their Distances and Bearing from each other and from the Continent: And that the Expence thereof be born by the publick Sale of one or more Islands that will be sufficient to pay the Charge thereof: And that the further Consideration of the said Petitions and ye claims of such officers & soldiers as have served in ye late war who have not petitioned be referred until the above said survey be had, and the Plans of the abovementioned Lands be returned to this Court.

Sent up for concurrence Tim^o^ Ruggles Spk^r^

Resolved that publick Notice be given in the Boston News papers that **B** this Court have under their consideration a number of Petitions from Officers and Soldiers praying some reward in Lands for their services and sufferings in the late Wars And that the consideration thereof is referd to the Sessions of **C** this Court in May next to the end that those who have the like claims may then (if they see cause) prefer their Petitions.

Sent up for concurrence Tim^o^ Ruggles Spk^r^

In Council Jany 31, 1764. Read and Concurred with the Amendments at **B** & **C**.

Sent down for Concurrence. A Oliver Sec^r^

In the House of Rep^ves^ Feby 1, 1764

Read and Concur'd

A dele due

B dele this insert the General

C dele of this Court

In Council Jany 31, 1764 Read and Concurred with the Amendment at A

Sent down for Concurrence A Oliver Sec^r

In the House of Rep^ves Feby 1 1764

Read and Concurd Tim^o Ruggles Spk^r

Consented to Fra Bernard

Grant to Paul Thorndike & others 1764

By the Governor, Council, and House of Representatives, of the Province of the Massachusetts Bay, in New England, in the Great and General Court assembled.

Whereas their late Majesties King William and Queen Mary, by their Letters Patent, bearing date the Seventh Day of October, in the third Year of their Reign, did Give and Grant unto the Inhabitants of the Province of the Massachusetts-Bay (among other Things) all those Lands and Hereditaments, lying between the Territory of Nova Scotia, and the River Sagadahock, then and ever since known and distinguished by the Name of the Territory of Sagadahock, together with all Islands lying within ten Leagues of the Main Land, within the said Bounds. To Have and to Hold the same unto the said Inhabitants and their Successors, to their own proper Use and Behoof for evermore. Provided always, That no Grant of Lands within the said Territory of Sagadahock made by the Governor and General Assembly of the said Province, should be of any Force or Effect, until their Majesties their Heirs and Successors, should signify their approbation of the same:

The Governor, Council and House of Representatives of the said Province of the Massachusetts-Bay, in the Great and General Court assembled, have given and granted, and hereby do Give and Grant unto Paul Thorndike, Samuel Freeman,

David Alden, Samuel Cates, Andrew Siminton, Joseph Wilson, John Thorndike, Joshua Woodbury, Nathaniel Jordan Junr, Ezekiel Cushing Esqr, Jeremiah Cushing, Ezekiel Cushing Junr Robert Thorndike Junr, Stephen Hutchinson, John Bradbury, Stephen Hutchinson, Theophilus Herrick, Ebenezer Thorndike, Nicholas Thorndike, Benjamin Thorndike, Anthony Dyer, George Dyer, William Dyer, Nathaniel Milliken, Joseph Milliken, Thomas Milliken, Jonathan Milliken, John Robinson Junr, Joseph Wallis, Benjamin Robbins, John Mulberry Milliken, Edward Milliken Esqr, Edward Milliken Junr, Nathaniel Ingersol, Benjam Milliken, William Meserve, Joseph Brown, William Morgan, Robert Haskell, Paul Thorndike, Ebenezer Ellingwood, Henry Herrick, Lemuel Smith, Edward Milliken Esqr, John Roundy, William Bartlet, Joseph Herrick, Isaac Woodbury, Ebenezer Thorndike, Ebenezer Thorndike, Nathaniel Harmon, Thomas Milliken, Joshua Herrick Junr, Henry Herrick Junr, Jer. Powel, Jer. Powel, Jer. Powel, Elisha Jones, Elisha Jones, Elisha Jones and their Heirs, all that Tract of Land lying in said Territory of Sagadahock, on the East Side of Mount-desart River now called Union River, beginning at a Spruce Tree marked about Eight Miles up said River on the East Side thereof, and marked **A** on the Plat exhibited, and thence extending due East by Compass, Six Miles, from thence South to the Sea about five miles then Westerly along the Sea Shore to the said River, and up said River to the Spruce aforesaid: To Have and to Hold the said Lands with their Appurtenances, to them and their Heirs, to the only Use and Behoof of them and their Heirs forever, as Tenants in Common: Subject nevertheless to the Reservations, Provisoes and Conditions hereafter mentioned.

And the said Governor, Council, and House of Representatives assembled as aforesaid, have also given and granted, and hereby do Give and Grant unto David Banė, James

Gowen, Nathaniel Harman, Benjamin Prebble, Mathew Austin, Jonathan Farnham, Thomas Moody, James Sayward, John Norman, Joseph Shaw, Joseph Moody, James Horn, Jonathan Nowell, Alexander Mackentier J^r^, Saml Addams, Joseph Baker Abr̃a Chapman, Jos^h^ Maine, Danl Grant, John Bane, Benj^a^ Donell, John Bradbury Jr, Joseph Horn, Abraham Lunt, Elisha Horn, Joshua Simpson, Mathias Whitney, Henry Sympson, Charles Bane, Jon^a^ Bane Esqr, John Frost J^r^, Tim. Frost, Silas Nowell, Saml Bane, Joseph Bragdon, David Bane, Josiah Simson, Saml Paul, James Carlisle, Eben^r^ Cook, Saml Simpson J^r^, Webster Simpson, Dummer Sewall, Saml Adams J^r^, Tobias Allen, Josiah Black, Jer^h^ Bragdon J^r^, Josiah Black Junr, Nathl Prebble, Peter Grant J^r^, Humphry Chadborn, Mathew Austin, Saml Mane, Joshua Grant, Danl Grant, Job Lyman, Jon^a^ Bane, Joshua Maclucas, and their Heirs, all that Tract of Land adjoining to the Tract of Land beforementioned, and beginning at the North East Corner of N° one, and running due East, along a Line which is to be continued as a General Boundary Line North of all these Towns Eight Miles, thence due South, untill it meets the North Side Line of N° Three, then due West along said Line to the Sea Shore and along the Same to the South East Corner of N° One; thence North by the same to the first Point. To Have and to Hold the said Lands, with their appurtenances, to them and their Heirs, to the only Use and Behoof of them and their Heirs forever, as Tenants in Common, subject nevertheless to the Reservations, Provisoes and Conditions hereafter mentioned.

And the said Governor, Council, and House of Representatives assembled as aforesaid, have also Given and Granted, and hereby do Give and Grant unto Nathan Jones, Francis Shaw, & Robert Gould and their Associates and their Heirs, all that Tract of Land, adjoining to the Tract of Land beforementioned, and beginning at a Point on the West side of a

Creek marked **K**, ten Chains below the Falls, at N° 841 of the Survey, and running West seven Miles to another Bay of the Sea, and from thence along the Sea Shore Easterly to the first Point, To Have and to Hold the said Lands, with their appurtenances, to them and their Heirs, to the only Use and Behoof of them and their Heirs forever, as Tenants in Common. [Provided that one fourth Part of the said Township shall be Separated, and set apart unto the said Nathan Jones and his associates in Manner following. A Line shall be run from the Mouth of a Stream which falls from a large Pond, into the Bay next to N° Two, marked in the Plan **D** East by Compass unto the Bay in which Capt. Frost is settled; That the said Line be equally divided, And at the Point of the Division, another Line be run North by Compass to the bounding Line of the Township, on the North Side, and South indefinitely; which Line shall be determined to the Southward by a Point from which a Line being run Westward, to the first mentioned Bay, may together with the said North and South Line as to the East, and the said Bounding Line of the Township to the North, and the Shore of the said Bay to the West, Inclose one equal and equitable Fourth Part of the Township, Regard being had to the Quality as well as the Quantity of the Land so Inclosed. And Mr Jones and Mr Frye the Surveyors heretofore employed in Surveying those Towns, shall run the said Lines, and determine the said South Boundary of the said Fourth Part as aforesaid: & shall make their Return upon both if the same shall be requir'd. And if they cannot agree concerning the settling and running the said South Line, they shall call in a third Person, by whose Arbitration the Thing shall be finally determined. And the said Nathan Jones and his Associates shall do and perform one fourth Part of the Duties of the said Township] Subject nevertheless to the Reservations, Provisoes and Conditions hereafter mentioned. And the said governor, Council and House of Representatives assembled as aforesaid have also given and granted, and hereby do Give and Grant unto Edward Small, Jacob Sawyer Junr, Benj^{a} Thacher, Jonas Woodbury, Nath. Jordon J^{r}, John Woodbury, Isaac Lovet, Jonathan Fickett, Saml Woodbury, Joshua Woodbury, Joseph Strout, Saml Fowler, Robert Mayo, Ephraim Dyer, Paul Thorndike, Andrew Siminton, James Siminton, Jon^{a} Lovet J^{r}, Henry Dyer Junr, Henry Dyer, David Alden, Moses Young, Aaron Chamberlain, Robert Mitchel, Benj^{a} Jordon, Wil. Plummer, Henry Johnson, William Webb, Saml Cobb J^{r}, John Jack, Thos Armstrong, Thomas Ficket, Peter Woodbury, Jed^{h} Soul, Arch^{o} Stone, Jon^{a} Dyer, Eben^{r} Jordon, Oliver Bowley, Ephraim Dyer, Benj^{a} Waite, Andrew Siminton J^{r}, John Strout, Joseph Sterrat, Stephen Randall, Elisha Parker, Eben^{r} Smith, Simon Armstrong, William Dyer, Henry MacKenny, Elisha Parker J^{r}, Richard Williams, David Alden, Jerah Sprague, Dan. Merret, Jon^{a} Lovet, Wil. Dyer J^{r}, Jer^{h} Sebins, Benj^{a} Dyer, Noah Jordon, Elisha Berre J^{r} and their Heirs all that Tract of Land adjoining to the Tract of Land aforementioned, and beginning at a Point on the East Side of the Creek marked **K** opposite to the Point that makes the North East Corner of N^{o} Three at N° 845 of the Survey, and from thence along the Sea Shore Easterly to the West Side of the Mouth of a Creek marked **X** N° 1138 of the Survey, and from the first mentioned Point, and also from the last mentioned Point by Lines due north unto the Great East and West boundary Line, and along the same till the Lines meet To Have and to Hold the said Lands with their Appurtenances to them and their Heirs, to the only Use and Behoof of them and their Heirs forever as Tenants in Common, subject nevertheless to Reservations, Provisoes and Conditions hereafter mentioned —

And the said Governor, Council and House of Representatives, assembled as aforesaid have also given, and granted, and hereby do Give and Grant unto Josiah Sawyer, John Small Jr, John Small, Danl Small, David Strouts, Nathl Knowles, Peter Woodbury, John Emery, Moses Fowler, Wil Siminton, Andrew Siminton, John Siminton, Jona Siminton, Ebenr Cole, Elisha Small, Jona Winkell, Joseph Wallis, Jesse Brown, Wm Webb Jr, Jona Kendall, Anthony Dyer, Jesse Brown Jr, Moses Plummer, David Brown, Noble Maxwell, Saml Webb, Ebenr Sawyer, Jona Elvil, Wm Strout, Aaron Plummer Jr, Wm Maxwell, Joshua Mayo, Benja Ficket, Christopher Dyer, Elisha Brown, Ephraim Dyer, Dominicus Jordon, Ebenr Cox, Josh Cobb Jr, Wm Ray, Edwd Small Junr, Manwarren Beal, Manwarren Beal Jr, Elisha Berry, David Strout, Samnel Freeman, Saml Freeman, Saml Freeman, Jereh Powell, Jer. Powell, Jer. Powell, Jer. Powell and their Heirs all that Tract of Land adjoining to the Tract of Land before mentioned and beginning at the North East Corner of No Four, and running by the great East and West boundary Line unto the East End of the thirty third Mile from Union River, from thence South unto the Sea, and from thence along the Sea Shore Westerly to the East Side Line of No four, and along that Line to the first Point. To Have and to Hold the said Lands with their Appurtenances to them and their Heirs, to the only Use and Behoof of them and their Heirs forever, as Tenants in Common, Subject nevertheless, to the Reservations, Provisoes and Conditions hereafter mentioned.

And the said Governor, Council and House of Representatives, assembled as aforesaid, have also given and granted and hereby do Give and Grant unto Nathl Parker, George Deake, Josiah Stanford Jr, Daniel Merritt, Joseph Weston, William Hix, Charles Woodbury, Wm Siminton Jr, Walter Siminton Jr, John Duggen, Saml Knowles, Theos Siminton, John York Jr, Wm McLellan, John Armstrong, Ebenr Robinson, Benja Wallis, John Robinson Junr, Isaac Small, Moses

Plummer Jr, Moses Plummer, Micah Dyer, Danl Merrett, Charles Peoples, Joseph Tebbut, Ebenr Roberts Junr, Jabez Sawyer, Jona Sawyer, Saml Cash, Reuben Dyer, John McCreet, John Dyer, Benja Small, Eleazer McKenny, William Bucknam, Wm Doliver, John Doliver, Nichr Blazedil, David Vickery, Samuel Doliver, Ebenr Roberts, John Brown, Daniel Sawyer, Alexander McLelland, Apollos Robinson, Joshua Robinson, Saml Sergent, Job Small, Eliza Starbord, Benja Mussey, George Strout Junr, Joshua Strout, Wm Siminton, Benja Milliken, Solomon Bragdon, Benja Milliken, Nathan Jones, James Gowen, Jonas Cutler, Nathan Jones, and their Heirs, all that Tract of Land adjoining to the Tract of Land beforementioned, and beginning at the North East Corner of No Five, and running along the great East and West Boundary Line five Miles, and from thence South about Seven Miles, to the West Side of a River, near to which is a stooping Spruce marked **W** on the Plat, and down the said River, and along the Sea Coast Westerly to the East Line of No Five, then North up that Line to the first Point. To Have and to Hold the said Lands, with their Appurtenances, to them and their Heirs to the only Use and Behoof of them and their Heirs forever, as Tenants in Common, Subject nevertheless to the Reservations, Provisoes and Conditions hereafter mentioned. Reserving nevertheless, to be yielded and paid unto his Majesty his Heirs and Successors, by the several Grantees and their respective Heirs and Assigns, one fifth Part of all Gold and Silver Oar and precious Stones, which shall happen to be found and gotten on the said Tracts of Land, or any of them, or any Part thereof. Provided, that these Grants, or any of them, shall be of no Force or Effect, untill his Majesty, his Heirs and Successors, shall signify his or their Approbation thereof. And it is hereby provided and declared that the foregoing Grants, and each of them are and is made upon these express Considerations and Conditions, that the several Grantees of the said several Tracts of Land hereafter to be made so many several Townships, and each of them shall within six Years after they shall have obtained his Majesty's Approbation of such Grants (unless prevented by War) settle each Township with Sixty good Protestant Families, and build sixty Houses, none to be less than Eighteen Feet Square, or of Equal Area, and seven Feet Stud, and clear and cultivate five Acres of Land on each share; fit for Tillage or Mowing: and that they build on each Township a suitable Meeting House for the public Worship of God, and settle a learned Protestant Minister, and make Provision for His comfortable and honourable Support. And that in each Township there be reserved and appropriated four whole Shares in the Division of the same (accounting one sixty fourth Part a Share) for the following Purposes, viz. one for the first settled or ordained Minister, his Heirs and Assigns forever, one for the Use of the Ministry, one to and for the Use of Harvard College in Cambridge, and one for the Use of a School forever. And if any of the Grantees or Proprietors, of any of the said Townships respectively, shall neglect, within the Term of six Years as aforesaid, to do and perform the Conditions aforessid, as shall respectively belong to his Share or Right as aforesaid, such Share or Right shall be entirely forfeited, and shall enure to the Use of this Province, this Grant or any Thing therein contained to the contrary notwithstanding.

Provided nevertheless, that if the aforenamed Grantees, their Heirs and Assigns, shall not obtain his Majesty's Confirmation of these Grants before the Expiration of eighteen Months, to be computed from the Day of the Date hereof, then the said Grants or such thereof as shall remain unconfirmed, shall cease and determine, and be null and void, this present writing or anything therein contained to the contrary notwithstanding.

Given in the Great and General Court, and Sealed with the public Seal of the Province the 27th of Jany in the Fourth Year of the Reign of his Majesty George the Third by the Grace of God, of Great Britain, France and Ireland King Defender of the Faith &c. and in the Year of our Lord One Thousand seven Hundred and Sixty four.

In the House of Representatives January 27 : 1764 —

Resolved That the Grant of the Six Townships East of Penobscot be, and hereby is Confirmed to the several Grantees mentioned in the Draft hereunto annexed respectively, in manner as is therein mentioned in the Draft hereunto annexed respectively, in manner as is therein mentioned, and that his Excellency the Governor be desired to cause the Province Seal to be annexed to a fair Draft and sufficient duplicate thereof and to sign the same; and that the Secretary be directed to sign the said Grant in the name of the Board, and the Speaker to sign it in the Name of the House.

Sent up for Concurrence   Tim^{o} Ruggles Spk^{r}

In Council Jan^{r} 27, 1764 Read and Concurred —

A Oliver Sec^{r}

Consented to   Fra Bernard

Line between Maine & New Hampshire.

The Committee Appointed by this Honble Court in their session^{s} in January A. D. 1763 to Perambulate ye line between that part of the Province Called the Province of Main & the Province of New Hampshire with Such as Should be Appointed by that Government to Joyn us therein, and upon their refusall to proceed Ex parte.

beg leave to Report that the s^{d} Province of New Hampshire was seasonably advised of the Time we should proceed on the affaire, and upon Our Arrival at Portsmouth Gave Govr Wintworth notice thereof and of our Commis^{n} who Signified that he had Communicated Govr Barnerds Letter to the Assembly but had Rec^{d} No Answer. he directed the Sec^{ry} to give us Copys of what had been don by the Surveyers appointed by Govr Belcher A D 1741 w^{c} are herewith Exhibited, and finding matters in this Scituation and no junction of their Province with ours Relative to the Above perambulation, we then inform'd the Sec^{ry} of New Hampshire of Our intention to proceed Ex parte and of the Time thereof, but finding by the return of the afores^{d} Surveyer that he had left the first pond Supposed to be the head of Newichwewoneck or Salmon fall River, and pass'd through a Second and Continued upon a branch of the River about Thirteen miles from the first Pond before he began his line and being inform'd that the river which he Should have Observed (if the first pond was left) run as much to the west^{d} as the Branch above mentioned did to the East^{d} we Judg'd it necessary to take a Survey of s^{d} River & branch North^{d} of the s^{d} first pond with their Distance &c a plan of w^{c} is herewith Presented under Oath, and we beg leave to Observe that from the view we had On the Spot the Quantity of water flowing from the s^{d} River Contains Two parts in three more than what runs from the s^{d} Branch & having taken all possable pains to Collect Evidence^{s} from the most Knowing and Ancient people in those parts with respect to the Head of Newichwewoneck or Salmon fall River, & finding they did not Appehend from what Could be Collected from the Indiens or from their Own knowledge that the River Afors^{d} extended further then the Two first ponds noted On the plan We beg leave further to Offer it as Our Opinion that the place from whence the Surveyer took his departure as the Head of the s^{d} Newichwannock or Salmon fall river when this line was run by Order of Govr Belcher in the year

A. D. 1741 is not and as we think Cannot be understood to be the place intended by Order of his late Majesty in Council for settling that line; but as the present Controversy between the Two Governments must depend upon the place where in Right the line should begin or the Head of the River afores[d] we must beg leave to refer that Determination to this Hou[ble] Court

All w[ch] is Humbly Submitted

Benj[a] Lincoln
Samuel Livermore
Joseph Frye

In the House of Rep[ves] Jan[y] 28, 1764.

Read and Ordered that Maj[r] Livermore Cap[t] Chadburne and Gen[l] Winslow with such as the Hon[ble] Board shall Joyn be a Comm[ee] to take this report under consideration and make report thereon

Sent up for concurrence

Tim[o] Ruggles Spk[r]

In Council Jan[y] 28th 1764 — Read & Concur[d] & Thomas Flucker, & James Otis Esq[rs] are joined in y[e] affair —

Jn[o] Cotton D. Secry

Topsham. Act of incorporation. 1764.

Anno Regni Regis Georgii Tertii Quarto —

An Act for erecting a Town in the County of Lincoln by the Name of

Whereas the Inhabitants Settled on a Tract of land Scituate on the Easterly Side of Androscoggin river, lying convenient for a Town hitherto called & known by the name of Topsham within the County of Lincoln have humbly petitioned this Court that for the reasons therein mentioned they may be incorporated into a Town & vested with the powers and Authorities belonging to other Towns

Therefore for the Encouragement of said Settlement

Be it enacted by his Excellency the Governour Council & house of Representatives in general Court Assembled — that the Said Tract of Land described as follows viz — to begin upon the Southerly line of the Town of Bowdoinham where Said line Strikes the water & from thence to run a West north west course upon said Bowdoinham line as far as it goes & from thence on the Same Straight course to little river so called which is about eight miles from the Water Aforesaid & from thence Southward down said little river to Androscoggin river to Merry meeting Bay & from thence to the line of Bowdoinham aforesaid including Several Small Islands or Islets lying in said Androscoggin river between the said Little river & the falls at Brunswick fort, be & hereby is erected into a Town to be called
and the Inhabitants thereof Shall have & enjoy all Such Immunities & priviledges as other Towns in this province have and do by law enjoy.

And be it further enacted, that Aaron Hinckley Esq[r] be & hereby is Impowered to Issue his Warrant to some principal Inhabitants of the said Town of
requiring him in his Majesty's Name to warn & notify the said Inhabitants qualified to vote in Town Affairs to meet together at such Time & place in said Town as Shall be Appointed in said warrant to choose such Officers as the law directs & may be Necessary to Manage the Affairs of Said Town & the Inhabitants being So met Shall be & hereby are Impowered to choose such Officers Accordingly.

In the House of Rep[ves] Jan[y] 28 1764

Read three several times and passed to be engross'd

Tim[o] Ruggles Spk[r]

In Council Jan[y] 28 1764 Read a first & second time and passed to be engrossed.

A Oliver Sec[r]

Petition of inhabitants of Townsend. 1764.

To His Excellency Francis Barnard Esqr Capt General and Commander in Chief in and Over his Majesties Province of the Massachusetts Bay in New England together with his Majesties Council &c —

The Petition of us the Inhabitants of Townsend so called Humbly Sheweth —

That Whereas we have for a Number of Years Lived in this Place till we have Increased to about the Number of Seaventy five Ratable Poles and as we have a Desire of Setleing the Gospel among us Labour under a Great deal of Difficultie on account of Not Being Incorporated into town Order we would Humbly Beg Your Honnours would be pleasd to take our Case into Consideration and for that End set Off as a town the Land Lying on the East Sid of Sheepscut River Extending as farr to the Northerd as a Place Called the Cross River and from thence about E. S. E across the Neck to Dammarascotty River to the Northly Part of the Land in Possession of Samuel Kelly and so Running Southerly down Damarascotty River to the Sea with all the Lands Adjacent Your Compliance in this will Greatly Oblig Your Very Serv^{ts} and we as in Duty Bound Shall Ever Pray

Given at Townsend this 31st Day of January 1764

Nal^{el} Tebbets	Thomas Kenney	Joseph Crosby
Joseph hosden	Ichabod pinkham	James Cromwell
Sam^{ll} Adams	Joseph Farnam	Abner foord
John Young	Cornelius Cook	Willm Fullerton
Ephraim ^{mc}farland	Joseph Beath	James fullerton
William M .	Robert	Samuel McCobb
Samuel B	John Beath	Willm his O mark Kenedy
Andrew Reed	Israel Davis	Paul Reed
James Montgomrey	Robert Montgumery	Joseph Reed
Samuel Kenney		

At the Council Chamber Whitehall the 4th of February 1764

By the Right Honourable the Lords of the Committee of Council for Plantation Affairs —
His Majesty having been pleased by His Order in Council of the 21st of December last to refer unto this Committee the humble Petition of James Duncan, Benjamin Harrod, John Wier, Edmund Morse, Peter Parker and David Marsh on behalf of themselves and several others, humbly praying, for the reasons therein contained, that His Majesty will be graciously pleased to ratify and confirm a Grant made by the Governor Council and House of Representatives of the Province of the Massachusets Bay, to the Petitioners and others, of six several Tracts of Land or Townships within the Territory of Sagadehock, particularly mentioned and described in the said Grant. The Lords of the Committee this day took the said Petition and Grant into their Consideration, and are hereby pleased to refer the same (Copies whereof are hereunto annexed) to the Lords Commissioners for Trade and Plantations, to consider thereof and Report their Opinion thereupon to this Committee.—

Phil: Sharpe.

To the King's most Excellent Majesty in Council

The humble Petition of James Duncan, Benjamin Harrod, John Wier, Edmund Morse, Peter Parker and David Marsh on behalf of themselves, and the several other Grantees named in the Grant hereunto annext
Sheweth —

That their late Majesties King William and Queen Mary by their Letters Patent bearing date the seventh Day of October in the third Year of their Reign did give and grant unto the Inhabitants of the Province of the Massachusets

Bay (among other things) All those Lands and Hereditaments lying between the Territory of Nova Scotia and the River Sagadehock then and ever since known and distinguished by the name of the Territory of Sagadehock together with all Islands lying within ten Leagues of the Main Land within the said bounds To have and to hold the same unto the said Inhabitants and their Successors to their own proper use and behoof for ever More Provided always that no grant of Lands within the said Territory of Sagadehock made by the Governor and General Assembly of the said Province should be of any force or effect untill their Majestys their Heirs and Successors shou'd signify their Approbation of the same.

That the Governor, Council and House of Representatives of the Province of the Massachusets Bay in New England in the Great and General Court Assembly by an instrument in writing Date the Twenty fourth Day of February last hereunto annext sealed with the public Seal of the Province at Boston Dive give and grant unto your Petitioners and the several other persons in the said Instrument named and their Heirs six several Tracts of Land or Townships in the said Instrument particularly mentioned and described — To hold to and to the use of your Petitioners and the said several other Grantees and their Heirs as Tennants in Common Subject to the Reservations Provisoes and Conditions in the said Instrument mentioned.

That your Petitioners humbly apprehend that the said grant if confirmed by Your Majesty will be of general publick Utility and tend to the Benefit and Security of your Majestys American Dominions.

Your Petitioners therefore most humbly pray your Majesty to ratify and confirm the said grant so made to your Petitioners in manner and form aforesaid

And your Petitioners shall every pray &c.

Tho[s] Life Soll[r] for the Pet[rs]

Ye Request

Woolwich March ye 20th 1764

To the Select men of Woolwich—

The Request of us the Subscribers is that you put into a warrant that ye People Assemble at ye meeting house on monday the Ninth of April at three a clock in ye after Noon to Consider whether it Shall be thought best to Chuse a man, to go to the General Court in ordor to maintaine our English Preveleges and Liberties.

A true Coppey of ye Request Lawfulley Requested as appeares on Reccord

pr Joshua Farnham { town Clerk

Letter, to English hunters

Fort Pownall March 24 1764

Gentlemen

The Indians complain heavily of the injury you do them, in hunting upon a Stream which they had taken up, there is a Law against English hunting at all, but it is hardly yet in force still I cant but hope that you are so friendly to the Commonwealth that you won't give the Indians any just cause of complaint, the little advantage you may make will will be a poor compensation to you if by this means you should be the Authors of disturbing the Peace and quiet of your Country. Therefore I earnestly intreat you to quit the Stream you are upon, and which it plainly appears the Indians have the best right to, but if you will not and any mischief ensues, I cannot see how you can acquit yourselves. If you are apprehended after the Act takes place, you are liable to a fine and forfeit your Fur, and I shall certainly use my endeavours to have the Act duly executed.

I am yours &c

To the English hunters on Quontabagook pond

Their Answer received upon a piece of Birch Bark mark'd with a Pin —

Letter, Han^{s} Robinson to Capt. Goldthwait.

Capt Goldthwait

S^{r}

This comes to let you know that I have seen the Indians you sent your Letter with, and they have given it to us, and we have not set any Traps where they have any, and we would be very glad, you would tell the Indians that we would hunt upon the Pond, that we were upon it first, and there was no Signs of any Indians upon it when we came here, if there were any Traps upon it we wou'd not have sat any here, and as we were here first we think it is our Right to hunt here, but if they are not Satisfied we will go home

So I remain your hum^{ble} Servant

Han^{s} Robinson

Whereas a Request hath ben made to us the subscribers select men of Georgetown by sixten of the Inhabitants freholders in said town desiring us to call a meting as sone as may be of the said Inhabitants of said town to act upon the artacels therein and hereafter mentioned —

these are therefore in his majestys name Required you or any of you forthwith to warn the Inhabitants in Georgetown aforesaid qualified to vote in town meetings to assembel themselves at the metin hous or arrowseek Ilaud in said town on munday the twenty first day of May next at two of the clock in the afternone —

first To chuse a moderrator of said meting —

2ly To Know their minds relating to a petition which silvanus garderner Esqr have put into the general court in behalf of those that call themselves the Kenebeck proprieters for the removing the land cases in this county to some distant county in this province for trial and whether they will petition to the general court to continue our priviliges to us other counties in this province —

3ly To chuse som fitt person to prer said petition.

hereof fail not and make return of this warrant with your doings therein unto ourselves at or before the said twenty first day of may next. Dated at georgetown in said county the 30 day of April 1764 and the fourth year of his majestys reign.

Thomas Moulton
Solomon Page

Lincoln georgetown May 21 – 1764

persuant to the within warrant to me directed I have warned the Inhabitants of the within town to appear at the time and plase within mentioned by putting up a copy of the within warrant at three publick plases in said town fourten days before the day and date above mentioned

by me Henry Totman Constable

the above warrant and return are trew copies

as attest Samuell Denny Town Clk

Lincoln ss at a town meting warned and held at the meting hous on arrowsick Iland in georgetown this twenty first day of May A. D. 1764

first Voted that Samuell Denny be Moderrator.

2ly Voted that the town is willing and desirous that a petition be preferred to the general court to pray his Excellency and honours not to grant the petition prefared by the plimouth company for the removal of the trials of all land actions Reletive to their patant to som distant county for trial said vote parsed by 22 to 2 in the negitive —

3ly Voted that the petition now presented and red to us and signed by the select men of woolwidge be the petition that we would have prefered to the general court as this towns petition and that the select men of this town or the major part of them sign the same in behalf of said Town.

4ly Voted that Capt Samuell Harndan be the person desired and impowered to prefare the said petition and by all proper ways to Indavour to gitt it granted.

Samuell Denny Moderator

the above are trew copies as attest

Samuell Denny town cl'k.

Letter, Thos Goldthwait to Mr. Robinson & others

Fort Pownall March 28: 1764

Gentlemen,

I received your Note by Arexes, and am sorry to tell you, that there is an absolute occasion for you to leave the Pond, which you are upon, and which the Indians say and demonstrate they have the best right to, I wish you cou'd accomodate yourselves otherwise for the little Time which you have a Right to hunt, but if you are determined to continue where you are I fear what will be the Consequence.— It is as much as I can do now to pacify the Indians, and I hope you'll consider what injury may be done the Province by your not complying with my request, I am Gentlemen

Your very good Friend &c

Tho: Goldthwait

Message. June 5, 1764.

Gentlemen of the Council, and Gentlemen of the House of Representatives

I promised you at the opening of the Session that I would give you my Sentiments upon the present State of the Eastern Country in regard to taking proper Measures for defending the Settlers against the Indians, or rather for preventing the Indians attacking the Settlers. I am convinced that people who are not acquainted with that Country have formed very wrong Ideas of the Indians living in it, imagining that it is not worth while for this Government to give itself any trouble about them: But it is not so: For the Indians are not so powerful as to be able to maintain a War with this Province assisted, as it would now be with the force of Canada; they are still capable, whenever their Passions get the better of their Reason (no uncommon Case with them) to depopulate a fine growing Country for 100 miles length of Coast.

You may remember that some time ago I represented to the general Court the expediency of this Governments holding a general Treaty with the Indians in the Eastern Country, as well to establish a formal peace with them & obliterate the ill impressions which the late hostilities had occasioned, as, by giving them an opportunity to explain their complaints & suspicions, to prevent any future misunderstanding. I recommended this Measure not without good advice from others as well as due deliberation with myself: but the proposal was declined; and the given Reason was that the Indians had not sollicited this interview in a manner suitable to the dignity of the Government. I call this the given Reason; for I cannot think that the Safety of the people settled in that Country any ways depended upon having or not having such an interview; that it would have been prevented upon account of Ceremonials only. I believe that the true reason was that the Indians were thought to be too contemptible & insignificant to deserve so public a notice from this Government. Had I been of the same opinion, probably the Error of it would before now have been evidenced by woful experience.

The Indians settled within the territory of Sagadehock are of 3 tribes: 1 The Norridgewocks living at Norridgewak; these have been encreasing ever since the peace & have probably now more than 30 Warriors. 2 The Penobscots living at Passadonteag; these have at least 60 Warriors. 3 The Passimaquodies living at Passimaquody; these are supposed to have at least 30 Warriors. The two former tribes belong to the General Nations of Arasigunticokes, of which (among others) there are two tribes settled at Wewenock upon the river Puante, & the other upon the river S[t] Francis both of which keep a constant communication with our Norridgewoaks & Penobscots. The Passimaquody tribe belongs to the Nation of S[t] Johns Indians a large people consisting of many hundreds (the Indians say some thousands) of Warriors. This will give you an Idea of the Power of the Indians in that Country, tho' they should confine themselves to their own Nations only without seeking foreign alliances.

I have therefore taken all the pains in my power to keep the Indians in good humour, as well as by redressing & preventing injuries, as by soothing their fears & removing their jealousies. Last Summer I received 3 of the Penobscot chiefs at Boston at their own desire, held a public conference with them, heard their grieviances & have since, according to their own confession, redresst them in the fullest manner. In the fall I had another conference with two other Penobscot chiefs at Fort Pownall; in which I endeavured to satisfy them in evry thing that was in my power to grant or to promise. Last year I received a letter from the Norridgewoaks complaining that some of their people had been robbed of goods to a very large value by some English Hunters. I pursued the offenders & with the assistance of the Attorney general obliged them to restore the goods or otherwise make full satisfaction: for this the Indians have since returned me thanks. The Passimaquody Indians wrote to me last Summer complaining among other things of the English hunting and Settling: I gave them the most favorable Answer I could without giving up our Right to settle that Country, as We should see occasion. I could mention several other things that have been done to conciliate the affections of the Indians to the People of this Government: and yet I find there still remains much more to be done. These partial Negotiations have had partial effects: there still subsists Uneasiness among the Indians in general which shows itself in frequent instances.

At the beginning of the Spring the Indians about Penobscot behaved so insolently, that some of the principal settlers in the New Towns were going to quit the Country, not thinking it safe to remain there any longer. It was afterwards discover'd by Cap[t] Goldthwait that a formal Motion had been made in the general Council of the Penobscots to rise against the English, first by surprising the Fort & massacring the Garrison & then laying wast the whole Country. It is true this proposal was readily & allmost generally rejected by the means of those Chiefs which came to Boston last Summer: but yet we see it made an impression upon the minds of the Indians as to render them surly & insolent to such a degree as spread a terror among the English Settlers. Some of the Norridgewoak_ told Col Lithgow that this Spring they would stop up the river (Kennebec) & block up the Fort (Halifax). It is probable that the Indian was drunk when he spoke this at the Fort itself; but undoubtedly he took his Notion from sober Conversation among his own people. The Passimaquody Indians have also declared that they will not suffer any English to go up their Rivers: at present they have nothing to complain of but illegal settlers but it may not be long before this may become a matter of serious Dispute.

It seems to me that all the uneasiness of the Indians arises from two things, the settling of the English & their hunting; which indeed are but one cause, as they fear the one only because it is productive of the other. And indeed they have great reason to be alarmed at the extension of English hunting; their very existance depends upon its not being permitted; and it is with great justice they complain how hard it is that the English who have many ways of living will interfere with the Indians in the only business by which they subsist. For this purpose at last Session an Act was passed to prevent English hunting: but it was enacted only for one Year and the Activity of it was postponed to such a distant day, that the very Mischiefs it was intended to prevent had like to have been produced by that defect only. This Spring before the Act took place, a Quarrell happened between some English and Indian hunters at a pond near Fort Pownall. Happily Capt Goldthwait got timely notice of it: the Act had not gained its activity; and therefore he could use no other Authority than persuasion, which luckily had the effect: If Blood had been drawn in this quarrel, it would probably have turned the Scale in favour of an Indian insurrection: so nicely are the politicks of those people at this time ballanced.

It is therefore high time that these Matters were finally adjusted: & I make no doubt but that the jealousy of the Indians may be removed by very easy and plain means. If They were to be called together and had liberty to unbosom their minds; if they were patiently heard & their grievances readily redressed; if they were assur'd that English hunting would be effectually prevented; if they were told that the Settlements in those parts being chiefly intended for fishery

& not for husbandry — were not likely in ages to come to extend up into the Country So as to incommode them; if they were treated in such a manner as would show that We did not neglect or despise them; & if at the same time they were given to understand that we should insist upon our right to settle the Country in such parts as were convenient for us; I make no doubt but that a firm & lasting accommodation with the Indians might be established & that Country be intirely freed from the apprehension of danger from Indian irruptions. If for this purpose a General Conference should be had, It would be most proper to hold it at Fort Pownall: nevertheless I should make a point of confining them to send Deputies only & not suffer them to bring in their whole tribes. The Norridgewoak Indians have lately sent to desire leave for their Deputies to come to Boston: but I have deferred giving an Answer, 'till it shall be considered whether it would not be best for them to meet together with the Deputies of the Penobscot & Passimaquody Indians at one time at Fort Pownall; that the Policy of that Country in regard to Indians may at once be finally & uniformly Settled.

Fra Bernard

Concord June 5 1764

Message. June 6, 1764.

Gentlemen of the Council and Gentlemen of the House of Representatives

At the last Session The General Court made an order that the Grantees of the six Townships east of Mountdesart-river should cause the inland lines of the said Townships & also the principal rivers running thro' the same to be accurately surveyed at their own expence: and also that the Lands above the said Townships for 6 miles of latitude should be surveyed from Mountdesert river to the river on the East side of the said Townships, at the expence of the Province. As these several Works must necessarily interfere with one another, It was proper they should be both done by the same surveyor. I therefore engaged Mr Frye a Surveyor employed by the Grantees in the former survey to do the business of the Province; & directed him to keep an exact account of the time employed in running the several lines that by distinguishing which of them belong to the Grantees & which to the Province the Accounts might be separated and adjusted. But Mr Frye has lately informed me, that having applied to the same Gentlemen, who before employed him in the former survey to give him orders for this, they declined employing him, saying that the other Grantees would not raise money for this or any other expences belonging to those Townships; and that they could not get in the money they had expended in the former Survey. So this Business stands Still & is like to stand still untill the General Court takes further order upon it. And what is hard Mr Frye has depended upon this employment, & has put himself out of all other business. I recommend this to your consideration: Mr Frye attends for this purpose.

Fra. Bernard

Concord June 6, 1764

Message. June 6, 1764.

Gentlemen of the House of Representatives.

Being impower'd by the general Court in their last Session to appoint two parties to explore the inner parts of the Eastern Country, I got them fitted out with all possible expedition; and one of them is, I hope, now on their Way from Fort Pownall to Quebec; and the other is employed in Surveying the Bay and River St Croix, and exploring the passage between the head of that River to the River Penobscot a great way above Fort Pownall. They will be obliged to discontinue their operations during the heat of the Summer, and will resume their employment, early in the fall. I shall take the best care to save all unnecessary expence: but I observe, that the establishment for this Service is extended only to the first of October. The Month of October is the most proper time in the whole year for traversing Woods; and the Expeditions of that kind cannot well be resumed before the beginning of September: It will be therefore necessary to include the chief part if not the whole of October in this Work. Also it may be necessary to the Service to survey some Rivers and Waters, especially those lying between Fort Pownall and Fort Halifax by Actual measures; but the only time for measuring Waters exactly is when they are froze over: It would therefore be of great utility to continue one of these Companies thrô the Winter, for the making mensurations upon the ice in those parts more immediately under our care. I therefore recommend these matters to your consideration.

Fra Bernard

Concord June 6 1764

The Committee are of opinion that it is not expedient to enlarge s[d] Establish[t] at present

J Otis p[r] order

"*Answer of Nath[l] Donnel, 6 June 1764.*

To his Excellency Francis Bernard Esq[r] Governour & Commander in Chief of the Province of the Mass[a] Bay The Hon[ble] his Majesty Councill & the Hon[l] House of Representatives

The Memorial of Nathaniel Donnell Esq[r] in answer to the

Petition of the Proprietors of the Kennebeck purchase from the late Colony of Plymouth —

The Respondent conceives very little need be said with respect to the two first Pages of the Petition, as it appear a preamble but little connected with the Prayer, and whether true or false cannot avail them. Only in general, that Swearing allegiance, or taking an Oath of fidelity is no uncommon thing in any Government, and if the respondent is not much Mistaken there is a Law of this Province now in Force that requires it. They Suggest they gave a large sum for the purchase, more than the Province of the Mass[a] Bay gave for the late Province of Main all things considered did the Mass[a] when they purchased the Province of Main Expect any advantage from the Towns laid out more than the right of Jurisdiction? Was there any Trade with the Indians in the Province of Main, that would Rent for £40 Ster[g] p[r] Annum? The Respondent could did he apprehend it necessary; give your Excellency and Honours a long, detail of Ancient Entry and Possession of his Lands at George Town, and the hardships his Grantees and Tenants have suffered by the Indian Enemy. That as to giving away Town Ship after Township as the said Petitioners suggest he would observe that in case these Townships are below Cobersecontee as he has been informed, he imagines they have no occasion to Boast of their Generosity. The Petitioners say they left their Settlements in 1675, when a resettlement appeared remote, but as soon as a resettlement could be made with success & safety to the Lives &c. they began again; But Whether they began after the Inhabitants at the Expence of their Lives and Substance for 70 years, & more had kept and defended them, and made them Valuable by selling near to them? — or Whether they began sooner; from their Petition does not appear. The respondent is quite at a loss to find the Town them Gentlemen Setled that paid one hundred and Forty Pounds to the Province in 1762. If they Intend Pownalborough the Respondent would Query whether that Town was all, setled by the Plymouth Company. or rather whether it was not done by other Persons long before, they pretended to give the present enormous stretch to the Lymits of their Pattent? And did not the Province Garrison their Fortifications, and Expend large Sums for them.— That instead of his wanting to avail himself of these Gentlemens "great Expences" the very reverse true from their own shewing for they say "to put a Stop to these outrages against all peace & order" The Respondent commenced an Action against one John Lemont for cutting Timber &c which the Plymouth Company Justify (and they might have added, ordered him) said Lemond in doing. The Petitioners say they were at great Expence to attend a Court with a Lawyer & Witnesses, the Respondent was likewise, and that since that Time they have brought many other Actions to the said Court which being under the same circumstances with this, are likely to meet with the same Fate viz. a Continuance for want of a Court, and if by any means, a court could be found they must be continued for want of a Jury, and, therefore they are in dismal circumstances, without Law, having their Property Exposed without remedy to every Invader, which leads the Respondent to enquire, how a County came to be made where there were not People, in it, sufficient to put the Laws in Execution. He would observe from the Printed Votes of the Honble House, That a Bill was read the 17th Day of June 1760 for dividing the County of York into three Countys, & upon the Questions being put, Whether it should be read a Second Time? it passed in the Negative, Whereupon a Committee was appointed to bring in a Bill for dividing the County of York into Two Countys; That but Two Days after in the forenoon (about one or Two Days before the rising of the Court that session) the same Bill for dividing the County of York into three Countys passed to be engrossed, and in the afternoon of the same Day the said Bill passed the House to be Enacted, from Whence, & from some other Circumstances, the respondent has reason to Collect, that from the pressing instance and request of them Gentlemen, the said County of Lincoln was first made; at which Time the difficultys the People Inhabiting the now County of Lincoln, underwent in being so remote from Courts of Justice, was by them Gentlemen magnified, increased and exaggerated, The hardship it was so numerous a People, should not have the Priveledge of a County by themselves for which they, the Inhabitants, were fully Ripe, was their declaration and now it seems the Plymouth company are deprived of Law by unhappily having their Property placed in a County where their is neither Court nor Jury, and now the Inhabitants of the County of Lincoln are Invading their Property against all Peace & Order, and since this is their unhappy case to have all the County in a Manner some how or other Interested in their causes (as they would claim all the Incorporated Places in A manner in the County) and Whereas they say us Probable the Inhabitants of the Countys of Cumberland and York "are some way or other concerned in the Event" of their causes, as the Inhabitants of York and Cumberland were till lately in the same county with those of Lincoln. Therefore they pray their causes may be removed to some remote county, Where the Nature of the dispute and the Witnesses Testifying cannot be known. The Respondent humbly concieves Your Excellency & Honours will not belive all the Inhabitants of the late Province of Main to be interested merely because these Gentlemen Conjecture that to be the case, nor Will your Excellency & Honours Imagine all the Inhabitants of the Province of Main unfit for Jurymen, because they once lived in one County together, Thay are not all related, there are few very few in Cumberland or York that lay Claim to Lands in the County of Lincoln, how they can all be Interested, the Respondent cannot concieve. The Respondent would not Willingly Imagine Those Gentl^{n} would harrass Men Hundreds of Miles, till causes must be lost for Want of Ability to defend them; and on the Whole — it appears to him that the prayer of the Petition being big with fatal and destructive consequences would necessarily Your Excellency and Honours to dismiss it if nothing was said by way of answer, and without being further Tedious for the following reasons among many others that might be offered —

1. Because he apprehends some matters suggested & asserted therein are False in Fact.

2^{ly} Because their own restless unwearied importunity has brought the Supposed Calamity, on themselves, by Misrepresenting the State of the Inhabitants of the County of Lincoln, at the Time it was constituted.

3^{ly} Because Improbable, Probabilitys can have no Weight.

4^{ly} Because the Remedy proposed is more than adequate (& indeed much Worse) than the disease, For if the causes mentioned are removed to Cumberland, or York the Respondent avers an Impartial Jury may be found.

5^{ly} Because great Numbers of Persons in Suffolk, Middlesex, Essex & Worster, are some way or other Concerned in the Event of these Causes. The said Proprietors being Rich Numerous & having large connections.

6^{ly} Because it will be subversive of the end and design of Tryals, and is unconstitutional, and will Introduce a precedent which if followed, will have a direct Tendency to Enable the longest Purse and not the Justest Cause to prevail. Wherefore the said Nathanael prays the said Petition may be dismissed, and that the causes he is concerned in may be removed to the Inferiour Court at Cumberland, or York Where they would have been tryed in case no such County as Lincoln had been made, agreable to a Petition he some Time since preferred to your Excellency & Honours, or that said Causes may be bro't forward by Demurrer to the Superiour Court at Falmouth Where by Law they must finally be determined in case either Party appeals.

Nath[l] Donnell

Petition of Proprietors of Kennebeck purchase from late Colony of New Plymouth.

To His Excellency Francis Bernard Esquire Captain General and Commander in Chief, the Honourable the Council and House of Representatives in General Court Assembled–

The Petition of the Subscribers, Proprietors of the Kennebeck purchase from the late Colony of New Plymouth,

Humbly Sheweth,

That in the Year 1620, a Number of People came from Plymouth in England, and settled at a place they called New Plymouth, and after residing there for nine Years the Council of Plymouth in England gave them a Patent for that Tract of Land where they then lived (being the Colony of New Plymouth, and as a further Reward for their Hardships and Sufferings, and in Consideration of their making the above Settlement, They the said Council of Plymouth, by the same Patent gave them a Tract of Land at Kennebeck to accommodate them for Trade and Fishing.

The Plymouth People soon after receiving their patent began a Settlement at Kennebeck which became so numerous as that in the year 1654, they Erected a Government there, Subordinate to, and dependant upon the said Colony of New Plymouth, to which each of the Settlers was obliged to take an Oath of Fidelity) which was the Condition of their being allowed to be Inhabitants there.

In the year 1661. the Government of New Plymouth sold all their Kennebeck Tract to Antipas Boyes, Edward Tyng, Thomas Brattle and John Winslow for Four hundred pounds Sterling (a greater sum all Things considered than the Province of the Massachusetts gave for the Province of Main) and they the said Boyes and Company carried on said Settlement untill the Indian War in the year 1675. which broke up and destroyed all the Settlements Eastward of Piscataqua.

The Indians at that Time were so very numerous and the English so few that the Resettlement of your Petitioners Tract with any Success appeared very remote at that time, but as soon as there was a probability that a Resettlement could be made with Success and with Safety to the lives of the King's Subjects, your Petitioners began to resettle the same, and that no Person might Suffer that had settled there without leave from the Proprietors, altho' the design of such Settlers had been more to make Strip and Waste of the Timber, than to bring to and subdue the Land, that even those should not have cause to complain, the Proprietors pass'd a Vote (N° 1.) quieting every person in their possessions, that did not disturb the Quiet and Peace of the Settlement; and to encourage the Settlement of that part of the Country they Voted to give away twelve Townships of five Miles Square each (N° 2.) on no other Condition than settling a certain Number of Families thereon & clearing a certain Quantity of Land within a limited Time, besides giving away a great Number of Lotts on both sides the River between Pownalborough and Fort Halifax on the same Conditions (N° 3.) which has had so good an Effect that within these few Years. your Petitioners have extended their Settlements Thirty Miles higher up the River than they were before.

Besides giving away Two hundred thousand Acres of Land, your petitioners have expended near Four thousand pounds sterling in building defensible Houses for the Security of the Settlers, and supporting them with the necessaries of Life, untill they were able to support themselves, the good Effects of which the Province already begins to feel, one Town only which they have settled) paying a Province Tax of £140—the last year.

These Exertions of your petitioners having brought that part of the Province to be very valuable, many persons now want to avail themselves of our Expenses, and have entered and are daily entering into your petitioners Tract (in Opposition to your petitioners) some of whom have built Mills, and are making great Waste and destruction of the most valuable Timber, and that done after many and repeated Admonitions; and to put a Stop to these Outrages against all Peace and Order, We have been obliged to bring an Action of Ejectment against Capt James Cargill; besides which an Action of Trespass was brought by Nathaniel Donnell of York Esqr; at the Inferior Court of Common Pleas held at Pownalborough in the County of Lincoln on the first Tuesday of June 1762, against one John Lamont of George Town in said County for cutting Timber and Trees off of a Tract of Land adjoining to Stevens's River in said George Town; and the said Lamont holding under your Petitioners, your petitioners were Obliged at a very great Expence to attend said Court with a Lawyer from Boston, Witnesses at the same Time giving their attendance; but when said cases were called, the Judges declined trying the same, because they were interested in Lands lying within the Plymouth Patent, so that said cases stand continued to this day.

Since the foregoing divers other actions have been brought Vizt;—David Jeffries Lessee of Silvester Gardiner Esqr; who holds under the Kennebeck Proprietors, against James

Springer of George Town who has lately built Mills within your Petitioners Tract thô: not within the Limits of any Town, and makes great Strip and Waste of the most valuable Timber, being an action of Ejectment.

Silvester Gardiner Esqr; Lessee of said Kennebeck Proprietors, against Benjamin Woodbridge of New Castle in an Action of Ejectment.

David Jeffries Lessee of Silvester Gardiner Esq[r] who holds under said Kennebeck proprietors against Joseph Sergeant of George Town who holds under Nathaniel Donnell of York Esq[r], being an Action of Ejectment.

Silvester Gardiner Esq[r], who holds under said Kennebeck Proprietors against John Clarke and James Whitehouse not within the bounds of any Township, in an Action of Trespass — said actions to be tried at the Inferior Court to be held at Pownalborough in the County of Lincoln on the first Tuesday of June next.

As the Judges of the Court declined trying the two first cases abovementioned, as they did likewise the Third and Fourth case in September last, because they were interested in the Plymouth Kennebeck Patent, it is probable they will also, for the same reason, decline trying the two Actions last abovementioned in which Case your Petitioners will be deprived of the benefit of the Law of the Province, and their property exposed, without Remedy, to every Invader, unless they are relieved by your Excellency and Honors.

Your petitioners beg leave to represent, that as great numbers of Persons in the late County of York, within which the actions aforesaid are by Law to be tried, are some way or other concerned in the Event of them, they humbly apprehend it very difficult if not impossible that your Petitioners should have impartial Juries in either of the three Countys which have been formed out of the said late County of York.

Wherefore your petitioners humbly pray your Excellency

and Honors that the said Actions may be removed for Trial to the Inferior Court of Middlesex, Suffolk, Essex or Worcester more especially as divers persons in the hope and Expectation that the said Actions and any other that may be brought by your petitioners may be for a long time continued are yet entering into your petitioners Tract, erecting Saw Mills and making great Strip and Waste of the most valuable Timber within the same — Your petitioners also humbly pray that in all Cases of Trespass or Ejectment relative to your petitioners aforesaid Tract, they may be enabled to bring their Actions in one or other of the Counties aforesaid, vizt either in Middlesex, Suffolk, Essex or Worcester; or otherwise relieve your petitioners as to Your Wisdom may seem meet; and your petitioners as in duty bound shall ever pray &c

Boston December 1763

Ja^{s} Boutineau	W: Temple	Jno Temple
Guardian to	Wm Tayler	Silv: Gardiner
John Jones	Gersham Flagg	Benj^{a} Hallowell
William Vassall	Nat: Wheelwright	att^{y} to Chas W^{d}
Apthorp Esqr		

In the House of Representatives January 4: 1764 Read and Ordered that the Petitioners serve the adverse Parties Viz^{t} Nathl Donnel of York Esqr James Springer of GeorgeTown Joseph Sergeant of George Town, James Cargill of Sheepscut Benjamin Woodbridge of Sheepscut John Clark and James Whitehouse without the bounds of any Town with copies of this Petition that they shew cause if any they have on the 31st of January Instant if the Court be then sitting if not on the first Tuesday of the next Session of this Court why the Prayer thereof should not be granted.

Sent up for Concurrence

Tim^{o} Ruggles Spk^{r}

In Council Jan[ry] 4: 1764 Read and Concurred

A. Oliver Sec[r]

A true Copy Examined

ꝑ Jn[o] Cotton D. Secy

In Council January 14th 1764. Whereas an Order passed the two Houses on the 4th Instant upon the Petition of John Temple Esq[r] and Others, Proprietors of the Kennebeck purchase, that they serve the Adverse Parties in the said Order named with Copies of the said Petition that they shew cause (if any they have) on the 31st of January Instant, if the Court be then sitting, if not on the first Tuesday of the next session of this Court why the Prayer thereof should not be granted: and it being represented that there will not be time for the Adverse Parties to make Answer on the 31st Instant. Ordered that the Petitioners serve the Adverse Parties in said Order named with a Copy of the said Petition, that they shew cause if any they have) on the first Tuesday of the next Session of the General Court why the prayer thereof should not be granted —

Sent down for Concurrence

A Oliver Sec[r]

In the House of Representatives Jan[ry] 16: 1764

Read and Concurred —

Tim[o] Ruggles Spk[r]

A true Copy Examined

ꝑ Jn[o] Cotton D. Secry

York 21 Feb[y] 1764 Delivered a Coppy of the within Petition & order to Nathaniel Donnell Esq[r]

J[a]: Flagg

Georgetown 27th Feb[y] 1764 then left a Copy of the within Notification at M[r] Joseph Sergeant's House & also left another Copy of the within with M[r] James Springer of Georgetown —

Ja: Flagg

Lincoln Sc February 29th 1764 Then the abovenamed Mr James Flagg made Oath that he delivered a true Copy of the within Petition and Order to the within named Nathaniel Donnel Esqr and left a True Copy at Mr Joseph Sergeants dwelling house and also another at the dwelling house of the with named James Springer

Before me Jona Bowman Justo ad pacem &c

Sheepscutt 2th March 1764 then left a true Copy of the within Notification at Mr Benjamin Woodbrige & also left another true Copy of the within Mr Jams Cargill of Sheepscutt.

Samll Goodwin Jr.

Lincoln Sc March 3d 1764 Then the above named Mr Samuel Goodwin Junr made Oath that he left a true copy of the within Petition and Order at the dwelling house of the within named Benja Woodbridge; and also a true Copy thereof at the Dwelling house of the within named James Cargil

Before me, Jona Bowman Justo ad pacem &c

Lincoln Sc March the 6th 1764 Then I left a Copy of the within Petition and Order at the Dwelling of Samll Whitehouse and One at the dwelling house of John Clark both of Sheepscutt the persons against whom Silv. Gardiner Esqr hath brought an Action of Trespass

Samll Goodwin Junr

Lincoln Sc March 7th 1764 Then the abovenamed Mr Samuel Goodwin Junr made Oath, That he left a true Copy of the within Petition & Order at the dwelling house of the above named Samuel Whitehouse; and also another true copy thereof, at the Dwelling house of the above named John Clark —

Before me, Jona Bowman Justo ad pacem &c

In Council June 6, 1764 — Read again together with the several Answers: And Ordered That there be a Hearing on friday next, at 3 o'clock in ye afternoon before the two houses, & that the Parties be directed to attend accordingly–

Sent down for Concurrence

Jno Cotton D. Sec̃ry

In the House of Rep^{ves} June 6, 1764

Read & Concur'd

S: White Spk^{r}

In Council June 8, 1764. A hearing having been had on the Subject matter of the within Petition, and the affair having been duly considered by the Board. Ordered That the Petition be dismissed

Sent down for concurrence

A Oliver Sec^{r}

In the House of Rep^{ves} June 8, 1764

Read and Concur'ed

S: White Spk^{r}

Petition. 1764.

To His Excellency Francis Bernard Esqr Captain General Governor and Commander in Chief in & over his Majestys Province of the Massachusett Bay and to the Honourable the Council and House of Representatives in General Court assembled. The Humble Petition of the Inhabitants Settled up Kennebeck River, from this, & the neighbouring Colonies, being Encouraged thereto to Provide for our selves & Families but the expence of removing there, and building such Houses as are only necessary to keep us from the weather & providing our Selves and Families in this uncultivated frontier Country has so far exhausted the Little we had, that, had it not been for Some well disposed people that assisted us with Stores in the winter Season we must have Perished and what has added to our distresses is, that the Town of Pownalborough has tax'd us to releive themselves Tho' none of us were Settled there when their Valuation was taken, nor any of us are Settled within Six Miles of their Town and many of us are Settled from 12 to 20 Miles from it, therefore we humble Pray your Excellency & Honours that we may be Exempted from the Taxation of Pownalborough and from paying Taxes till our Ground Shall be Subdued that we shall be able to Maintain our Selves & Families from it by our Labour or other wise releive your Petitioners as you in your Wisdom Shall think most proper, & in Duty bound we Shall ever pray

Daniel his C mark Sopers	John Estes	Simeon Wyman
John Ward	M Wheeler	John his X mark Shannon
Jabez Cowing	Peter his X mark Brown	Jabez Cowing J^{r}
Abisha Cowing	Adam Carson	Wm Bacon
James Cocks	Benjn White	Hezekiah Cloutman
Beniar D	Moses Bickford	Samuel Bullin
Job Philbrook	Rob^{rt}	Mathew Hastings
Ezekiel Page	Jon^{a} Philbrook	

In the House of Representatives June 1764

Read & Resolved that the Petitioners notify the Town of Pownalborough of the Contents of this Petition by leaving a Copy thereof with the Town Clerk, that the Town may make Answer to ye same (if they see Cause) the first Tuesday of the next sitting of this Court & that all Proceedings with respect to the Taxing the petitioners as also of Collecting the Taxes already assessed be stayd till the further order of this Court

Sent up for concurrence T Clapp Spk^{r} Pro Temp^{re}

In Council June 12, 1764 Read and Concurred
A Oliver Sec^r^

Consented to Fra Bernard

In Council Feb^r^ 19 1765 Read again and Sent down it appearing that the Town of Pownalborough had been duly notified

In the House of Representatives Feb. 27, 1765. Resolved that the prayer of this Petition be granted, and that the Petitioners with their Poles and Estates be Exempted from paying any Taxes to the Town of Pownalborough. And the Taxes already assessed on them or their Estates are hereby declared Void, & shall not be Collected. and the assessors of said Town are hereby forbidden to Assess or tax any person or persons that are Setled, or may Setle upon Lands not within the bounds of said Town, till the further Order of this Court.

Sent up for concurrence S. White Spk^r^

In Council March 1, 1765 Read and Concurred
A Oliver Sec^r^

Consented to Fra Bernard

*Govr Bernard to John Pownall Esqre*

Boston, July 11 1764

S^r^

I find myself obliged to state to you a complaint against Mr Waldo & partners proprietors of the lands on the West side of Penobscot river & bay under an old grant purchased by their father Brigadier Waldo; desiring you to lay it before their Lordships at such a time & in such a manner, as you shall think most proper: as I would not at this time of hurry trouble their Lordships with business that does not require their immediate consideration.

You know that Fort Pownall upon Penobscot was built at the expense of the Crown, the Province of Massachusetts

Bay undertaking to protect the Work & afterwards to Garrison the Fort. It was built on a Neck of Land on the West side being Brig^{r} Waldo's property, he himself assisting at the reconnoitring the place & dying there of an Apoplexy. The neck of land on which it stands contains in the whole 1800 acres: but there was no stipulation made on behalf of the Crown (as far as I can learn) that the said Neck of Land or any part of it should belong to the Fort. And yet the Advantages of building a Fort on that Spot were so great to the Proprietors, that if they had granted to the King the quantity of a Township that is 24,000 acres, they would have had a great bargain. But nothing of this kind was done & so the matter rested.

About 2 years ago I learned that Col Prebble who commanded the Fort had purchased this neck of land: & upon enquiry I found that he declared that he had purchased evry foot of Land about the fort, & that the fort itself stood upon his ground. I took the first opportunity of going there & found such Acts of separate ownership, that the garrison had not a foot of land to raise vegetables for their necessary subsistence. I remonstrated so strongly upon this that he agreed to quit so much land as should be wanted for the Garrison, if the Proprietors would make him a compensation elsewhere. I thereupon reconnoitred the Place & fixed upon a part of the neck next the Fort containing about 130 acres, to be annexed to the Fort: & upon my return to Boston I proposed this to some of the Proprietors with a plan of the land: & they seemingly agreed to it. But upon my proposing to them to execute a conveyance to the King, they fell off & said that they only intended to let the garrison have the use of it whilst the fort was kept up in garrison. When it was not, they should expect to have the fort themselves. I told them that this was so ill a return to the King & the Province for having defended & improved their Estate at so great an expence that I should represent the matter to his

Majesty's Ministers, & in the mean time should order the Garrison to keep possession of that tract, it being greatly within point blank & necessary for the defence of the Fort. Upon which the two proprietors said that they would consent to the conveyance of this tract to the King, if the elder Brother Mr Waldo would; and they would recommend it to him so to do. I acquiesced in this & have waited half a year for his coming & compleating this Agreement: And now upon my seeing him for the first time since & calling upon him to join in a conveyance of the 130 acres to the King, He sayes he is willing that the Garrison should enjoy this piece of land; but he will make no conveyance to the King in the manner which I require. Upon which I told him, The Business was now quite open, & I should represent it accordingly, which I do in the following manner.

When the Fort was built, undoubtedly the whole Neck of 1800 acres ought to have been conveyed to the King & probably such a requisition, if it had been then made, would have been readily complied with.

The whole Neck should be now conveyed to the King, as it would be of great public Utility to apply it to the purposes hereafter mentioned, & it is equitably due to the King; as the advantages arising from the building is the Fort to the proprietors Estate are of more than ten times the Value (I might say an 100 times the Value) of the land in question.

This conveyance is very practicable now, as the former bargain is not completed by the payment of the purchase Mony & an actual conveyance of the land, and the Proprietors might easily make the purchaser a compensation by a grant of other lands lying near to the Neck.

The use I would propose for this land would be to lay it out (after setting apart a sufficient part for the Garrison) in lots of 20 or 25 acres each & give them away on condition of settling & maintaining for a certain time, a family on each lot.

By these means a close Town very easy to be fortified might be soon formed by 64 or 80 families, which would be a good ground Work for defending the passage of the River from foreign Enemies in future times, as it would immediately become a support to the Fort & a Barrier against the Indians for the present.

Such a Support & Barrier are very much wanted as there is no Town now within 40 miles of the Fort on that side of the river nor is there like to be any, whilst the Proprietors hold their lands up at such a price as must necessarily keep that part of the Country wholly unpopulated.

Such a settlement would be of great Advantage to the proprietors, infinitely beyond the value of the lands in question, altho' most probably their narrow & contracted Views of their property there, will in this Case as in others make them blind to their own intrest.

For these reasons I must recommend that, if it may be, a Conveyance of this whole Neck to the King may be procured, that it may be settled in the manner aforesaid or some such like way. But if this cannot be obtained, It will be quite necessary to insist upon a Conveyance of the 130 acres to the King for the use of the Fort.

It must be observed that if ever it should be thought proper to fortify this Point against foreign Enemies, the whole Neck will be wanted: and therefore in Case of settling It will be proper to make a reserve of the liberty of fortifying at pleasure. The River is Navigable for near 30 miles above the fort for large Ships.

I am with truth & regard

S[r] Your most faithful & obedient Servant

Fra Bernard

I shall send another Copy of this by the next Ship as it may be proper to submit it to my Lord Halifax.

Govr Bernard to Earl of Halifax.

Boston, Aug. 18th 1764.

My Lord

I hereby inclose to your Lordship the Copy of a note I received from a chief of the Penobscot Indians being an answer to their request to Govr Murray that they might have a priest from Canada, which they transmit to me with a prayer that I would give leave for such a priest to come among them. It is above a year ago since the Passimaquody Indians applied to me for a Romish Priest & near a year ago since the Penobscots made the like application. I could only give them a general Answer, not having a priest at my command: and if I had had one of the Romish Communion, I should not have sent him thither without a greater authority than my own. And now the Question comes home to me, I must beg directions how I am to act.

These Indians are very religious & great Zealots for the Church of Rome. A Romish Priest would immediately enter into full authority over them; and if he would confine himself to matters of religion, would be of great use in reforming their manners & keeping them in order: But there are many things to be guarded against in such an appointment. A french Priest would probably be attached to french Policy as well as to the Romish Religion; & would endeavour to alienate them from the English Government as well as the Protestant Religion; and perhaps might feed them with the hopes of a french Revolution in that Country: for such Notions the Indians are still continually receiving from Canada. So that if they were to have a Romish Priest, I had rather that he should come from Ireland than Canada.

I will admit that with Indians, who are not capable of abstract reasoning, The Utility of their religion is rather to be consulted than the truth of it. Facility of Admission &

Implicitness of obedience are all the Advantages of a Romish Priest. The latter forms a kind of objection; for the more absolute the power of the priest the more dangerous would he be to civil Goverment if he should be a latent Enemy to it. And this leads to another objection: I dont think that the dispersed Settlers in that Country where there is at present no public place of Worship (except the Chapple at Fort Pownall) for the lenght of 60 or 80 miles, would be safe from perversion, if the Zeal of the Priest should exceed his discretion.

On the other hand I dont think that the difficulties of getting them to accept a protestant Minister are at all unsurmountable, provided they could have a Priest of the Church of England. They distinguish between the Church of England & the Independent Worship; and have too high an Opinion of the priestly Character to receive a self constituted Minister as an ordained priest. And as their Religion has consisted hitherto entirely of Ceremonies, It is too great a transition to pass to a Worship with no ceremony at all. And therefore I am of Opinion that an Independent or a Presbyterian Minister would make but a slow progress among them. But I think otherwise of a Priest of the Church of England: By a judicious use of the habit & Ceremonials of the established Worship, He would probably very soon get the better of their prejudices. He must speak french, which they understand.

As such a Missionary must come from the Society for propagating the Gospel if at all, I'll mention another use that may be made of him. There are Eastward of Penobscot & Westward also, a Number of Settlers, whose dispersed condition will make it difficult for them for some Years to establish any settled Ministry among them; many of whom would prefer the Church of England, & many others tho' not professing the Church of England would be glad to have a

Church to resort to. The proprietors of one Township east of Penobscot have applied to me to recommend them to the Society for a Missionary: which I have promised to do, when they are capable & ready to receive one. Now if a Missionary was appointed for the double purpose of ministring to the Indians & also to such of the new settled Towns as shall desire him, He would be of great use not only as a Minister of Religion but also as a civil Mediator between the Indians & English.

I have got to such a length upon this Subject that I begin to wish that a proposal of this kind was made to the Society for propagating the Gospel. If your Lordship shall think this letter a ground for such a proposal I must beg leave to assure your Lordship that I will assist such appointment to the best of my power. I will take care that he shall be well lodged & accommodated at Fort Pownall, & also at other convenient houses along the Coast. I will, if I can make it advisable, as I think it may easily be, recommend him to the London Society for propagating the Gospel in New England, for an additional Salary from them: as I have before done for a Catechist professing the Church of England now living among the Mohawks & Oneidas. And anything else, by which I can assist this undertaking I will readily engage in.

All which is humbly submitted to your Lordships Decision: in expectation of which I shall postpone giving a positive Answer to the Indians, whom I shall see in their own Country in about a fortnights time.

I am with great respect My Lord, Your Lordships most obedient & most humble Servant

Fra Bernard

A Conference with Indians.

A Conference between his Excellency Gov[r] Bernard & Aleser a chief & others of the Penobscot Indians held at Fort Pownall September 26, 1764.

Aleser. All the young men that you wanted to go to Canada & Norridgewalk immediately went at your desire, & now we hope you'l mind what we desire, & assist us. We are poor.

There is one God, & we have a Religion among us that we cannot part with, & we want a Father to baptize our Children, & marry us, & administer the Sacrament to us, & confess us, & shew us the way to Heaven; That is, to keep us from what is bad, correct our lives, & absolve our Sins. It is a few years since Canada was taken, & since we have had no father among us; our People grow loose & disorderly, drink too hard, & run into many bad practices, which a Father (if we had one among us) would remind us of & correct. It is usual to help the poor; We are poor, & therefore help us in the matter of Religion.

I am a young man & therefore would not talk too much, lest the old men should dislike it. I would say no more upon this.

Gov[r] I am very glad to hear you express so great a regard for Religion: If you are sincere in it, it will be for your good in this World & in the World to come. It's now about a year since you first exprest your desire to me upon this head; I have been mindful of it ever since, but have been doubtful concerning the means to bring it about: I then told you that the Fathers which you have been used to were enemies to our people, & would endeavour to make mischief betwixt us & you, & therefore it behoves me to take care not to introduce secret enemies to our Country; That is one considerable difficulty in providing a Father for you; another is, that a Father would want a support & I have no fund to provide it for him. About two months ago I received a letter from Govr Murray of Canada & I also received another letter which was directed to Toma one of your Chiefs: From those letters I learnt that Toma had applied to Govr Murray for him to send a Father from Canada; Govr Murray answered that he would consent to a Father going from Canada if I appled for one; By these means a difficulty was put upon me. I am the Kings deputy, & came immediately from his presence, & am answerable to him for evry thing I do. If I should apply to Govr Murray for a Father, or should consent to one going from thence, I should be answerable for him tho' he will be a stranger to me; If he was to do mischief among us, I should be asked how I came to consent to this mans going among you, & I should be answerable to the King my Master for the Mischief he did, by trusting to a man whom I did not know. I therefore thought proper to send Govr Murray's letter to the King himself together with an account of all that had pass'd between me & you concerning a Father; & I have desired that a Father may be sent to you, such an one as the King can trust, & then I shall not be answerable for what he does. I will now repeat to the King your request as soon as I get home, & will transmit to him all that passes at this time, & I will do my utmost that you shall have a Father proper for you, Who (whether french or english) will be such an one as will be capable to administer to you all you want.

Aleser If any difficulty arises on account of a Fathers maintenance, We will provide for that ourselves; He shall live well.

Govr I have represented to the King, that you are poor, & that some Salary should be provided for him, as he will want mouy as well as Victuals; however if he has a Salary, it will be kind in you to give him some Share out of your hunting.

Govr Bernard to Earl of Halifax.

Boston Sep. 29. 1764

My Lord

By my letter of Aug 18 I informed your Lordship that I was very much pressed by the Indians in the Eastern parts of this Province to provide them a Romish Priest, & that I had many doubts & difficulties about it: also that I intended in a Voyage I was going to take to the Eastward to see the Passimaquoddy & the Penobscot Indians, & talk with them about this business. I am now returned from that Voyage; & what I have observed upon this occasion is the Subject of this letter.

At Passimaquoddy The chief Indians & allmost the whole tribe were fishing at such a distance that I could not wait their return: However I saw 4 or 5 of them; who, tho' they were not of consequence enough to take upon them to talk upon public business, again & again reminded me of their great want of a priest. I gave them for answer that I must wait for the King's commands before I could do anything in this business. And I signified the same to their cheif (who applied to me for this purpose above a year ago) by a Message sent by a Captain of rangers, whom I dispatched with a surveyor & two others, under the direction of these Indians, to explore the Way from Passimaquoddy River to Penobscot.

At Penobscot I found but few Indians but amongst these one of their cheifs a Man of the first Sense among them. I had a conference with him; & what related to a Priest I had put down in writing as it was spoke; that I might transmit it with more exactness to your Lordship & also that it might be communicated to the Indians as an Answer to the Message they sent me 2 months ago. The next day I had another conference with him which I did not put into writing. In this I used my utmost endeavours to engage them to accept of a Priest of the Church of England, offering to send one to them for the present purpose of baptizing & marrying such as stood in present need of it. But I could make no impression upon him. He said God would be very angry with them, if they should desert the religion he had sent among them. That it was the first they received & they knew it to be good; and it would not be right for them to change their religion as often as the power of the Country changed; God would be much offended with them, if they trifled with his religion in such a manner.

In the course of these conferences, I took notice of one of the low arts which their priests had used to estrange them from the Government of England. I observed that the Interpreter when he mentioned the King of Great Britain, he called him King James. I asked him the meaning of it: he said that the Indians allways called the King of England King James & that they had done so at all public treaties at some of which he had been present. This was confirmed by another Interpreter who was by & had known the Indians many years. He said it was from James 1st in whose reign New England was first peopled. I was convinced that this distinction could not be derived so high as from James 1st. I therefore asked the Indian why he called the King of England King James. He readily answered that they learnt it from the French who allways called the King of England so. I asked him if by King James he meant the same person as I did by King George. He either did not or would not understand the question. I then askt him if by King James he meant that King who had lately conquered Canada; being pressed for an answer he at length said he did & added that he knew of no other King. So here has been a system of verbal Jacobitism at least (tho' I suspect it to be more). kept up among the Indians from the revolution to this day.

[After all I am as much at a loss what to propose as ever.

The Indians must have a Priest of some kind or other: if he be a true Romish Priest, He will keep them estranged from & inimical to Great Britain; flatter them with the expectation of a french Revolution; and have them ready to rise upon the least foreign invasion or internal Canadian commotion: & all this by means of their religion. On the other hand a Missionary of the Church of England will meet with great difficulties; but I am far from thinking that they will be insurmountable. He will have a safe & convenient residence at Fort Pownall; & by exercising his functions in the Chapple there (which I have had built there this year) with as much show and form as our Religion will admit of, I am satisfyed that the Indians would by degrees be reconciled to it. I mentioned before that a french protestant in English orders would be most suitable upon account of his language (which is generally understood by the Penobscot Indians & universally by the Passimaquoddies) as well as of his Nation. But one who has been a Romish priest & has conformed to the Church of England, if he was sincere & discrete would be more suitable. Canada must afford many such persons: but in general the Priests there are very ignorant & illiterate. Ireland must have such; but he must be Master of the french tongue if not a frenchman.]

All which is humbly submitted.

I am, with great respect My Lord, Your Lordship's
most obedient & most humble Servant
Fra Bernard

Pownalborough. Answer to Pet'n of Adam Carson & others. Oct. 1764.

To his Excellency Francis Bernard Esq[r] Governor and Commander in chief in and for his Majestys Province of the

Massachusetts Bay in New England, and to the Honble the Council and House of Representatives in general Court assembled.— Humbly sheweth, the Select Men of the Town of Pownalboro', that said Town was served with a Copy of the Petition of Adam Carson, Isaac Farwell and about thirty others Inhabitants in Kennebeck River complaining of the Taxation of Pownalboro' and praying to be relieved therefrom by reason of their Poverty and new Settlements.

In Answer to which, we your Petitioners the said Select Men of Pownalboro' being desired thereto by a vote of said Town, humbly beg leave to say, that we conceive Poverty is no just Excuse to free said Petitioners from their Province Tax as it is laid on them only in proportion to their Estates, and so he that has nothing pays for nothing: — and we humbly apprehend that it ought to have no weight in favour of the said Petitioners in the present Case, as the direct Effect of it would be to ease them of a burthen which they now only bare in equal Proportion with us, and to lay it upon the Town of Pownalboro' by no means able to bare it, as many of its Settlements are as now, and almost all its Inhabitants as poor as said Petitioners are. Tho' we have the advantage above them, of being an Incorporated place, which is the only one we can boast of, yet that can't be supposed much to increase our real wealth in so short a Time as four or five Years. We humbly apprehend the desire of said Petitioners to be excused from their Taxes, does not arise solely from their Poverty, but must be from something else. For Isaac Farwell one of said Petitioners milks sixteen or Eighteen Cows, and hath about forty head of Cattle and can cut Hay Enough to keep them beside many others are supplied with large Quantities of fresh Medows and the best of Lumber handy and had at their first settling twenty Acres and upwards of Upland cleared almost fit for the Plow; neither did any of them as we have heard lose any of their Cattle in the hard Winters after the late dry Summers; while none of the Inhabitants of Pownalboro are able to keep a stock any ways equal to said Farwells, and many of them thro' the scarcity of Hay after the late dry Summers lost a considerable part of the small stoek they were able to keep. The family of James Howard Esq[r] who live up Kennebeck River, and expect as we suppose to be excused their Tax by said Petition, tho' not signed by 'em, own two Sloops about eighty Tons each, and have two Saw Mills which employ at least twenty hands and have besides a large stock of Cattle, and carry on a considerable Trade.—

At Cobbaseconte a place up said River where many of said Petitioners lived, there is a considerable of ship building carried on, and a double Sawmill and Grist mill which employ thirty or forty hands, many of 'em Young Men, who have 250 acres of land granted 'em by the Kennebeck Propriety, and have also very good Stocks of Cattle.

It is suggested by said Petitioners that they were not settled in their present places when our Valuation was taken; or within six miles of this Town.—

In answer to which we beg leave to say, that Numbers of them were living then in Pownalboro' and moved up Kennebeck River to better their Circumstances as there were greater Advantages to be had there than here, and some who expect, as we suppose, to be excused their Province Tax by said Petition instead of being six miles and more distant from this Town, are within one Mile.

These in general are the Circumstances of the Inhabitants up Kennebeck River, while those of Pownalboro' by the repeated wars that have been since its first Settlement, and two late dry Summers and hard Winters which rendered Hay so scarce that many of 'em lost near half their Cattle, are reduced to very low Circumstances.

When we Petitioned the Great and General Court to be incorporated into a Town for the sake of Rule and good Order, they were pleased the first year to lay a heavy Tax upon us considering our then Circumstances, but which we chearfully paid tho' very unable, and the Court have every Year since been pleased to lay a heavy Tax upon us, yet we never complained but ever did the utmost in our Power to pay it, as we were willing to pay our full proportion of Charge for the Support of Government, the benefits of which we so largely partake of.—

Besides, before we were incorporated into a Town, one part of us was Taxed by Georgetown, and the other part by Newcastle which we then tho't it but just and equal to pay.

We therefore humbly conceive the said Petitioners have no just Cause of Complaint: and that the Town of Pownalboro' had a just Right to tax them their proportionable part to the Province as they are adjacent paying no where else, as it is agreeable to Law and the Precept from the Province Treasurer, and as it is but just and Reasonable that they should help with us to bear the Charges of Government as they in Proportion share the Benefit, especially considering many of us are no new Settlers and poorer than they, not having equal Advantages, and have the additional weight of a large Town Tax —

Wherefore we most humbly pray your Excellency & Honours not to excuse said Adam Carson Isaac Farwell and others Inhabitants up Kennebeck River, from paying their Province Tax as Assessed upon them by the Town of Pownalboro'— but if your Excellency and Honours should think proper so to do, we most humbly pray your Excellency and Honours would be pleased to take our low Circumstances into your wise Consideration and excuse the Town of Pownalboro' the full Sum which the adjacent Persons up Kennebeck River are taxed to the Province by said Town, or otherwise

relieve them as in your wisdom you shall think proper.—
and your Petitioners as in duty bound shall ever pray &c

Jon[a] Williamson
Michal Sevey
John Decker
} Select Men in behalf of the Town of Powalborough

Pownalborough Oct[r] 1, 1764

Petition of Ezekiel Cushing & others to be restored to the Second Parish in Falmouth.

Falmouth October 10th 1764.

To his Excellency Francis Barnard Esq[r] Captain General and Commander in Chief in & over his Majestys Province of the Massachusetts Bay in New England and Vice Admiral of the same And to the Honourable his Majestys Councel & House of Representatives in the Great and Generall Court Assembled The Petition of Us the Subscribers, humbly Sheweth your Excellency and Honours that at the time of the Rev[d] M[r] Ephraim Clark's being setled in the second Parish in the Town of Falmouth, We your petitioners belonging to said Parish petition'd Your Excellency and Honours that We might be sett to the first parish in said Town, the prayer of which petition your Excellency and Honours were pleas'd to grant—

But We your Petitioners haveing since discovered many Inconveniencys which we now suffer on account of our being so sett off humbly pray your Excellency and Honours would, if in your great Wisdom you should think fitt, restore us again with our Estates to said second Parish, and your Petitioners as in Duty bound shall ever pray Ez Cushing

Samuel Dunn	Nathaniel Jordan ju	George Roberts
John Robinson	Josiah his X mark Stanford	Simon Lovett
Samuel Dyer	Israell Lovett	Josiah his X mark Stanfoare Junor
Paul Thorndike	Vallentin Wieman	Robert Stanford
Ebnezr his X mark Cobb	Ezekiel Cushing Ju[r]	Loring Cushing

In the House of Rep^ves^ Feb^ry^ 14, 1765
Read and Ordered that the Pet^rs^ serve the first Parish in Falmouth with a copy of this Petition that so they shew cause if any they have on the second Wednesday of the next Session of this Court why the prayer thereof should not be granted.

Sent up for concurrence

S. White Spk^r^

In Council Feby 15, 1765 Read and Concurred.

A Oliver Sec^y^

Anno Regni Regis Georgii Tertii Quinto

An Act for erecting the Plantation called Goreham Town into a Town by the name of

Whereas it has been represented to this Court, that the erecting the Plantation called Goreham-Town, in the County of Cumberland into a Town will greatly contribute to the Growth thereof, and remedy many Inconveniences to which the Inhabitants and Proprietors may be otherwise subject.

Be it enacted by the Governor, Council and House of Representatives, That the Plantation commonly called and known by the name of Goreham-Town, in the County of Cumberland, bounded as follows, vizt Begining at a marked Tree on the Westerly Side of Presumpscot River in a Course South West twenty three Degrees from the Hemlock Tree, on the other side of the said River, which is fifteen Poles below Inkhorn Brook; and thence runing South twenty three Degrees West on the Head of Falmouth two Miles and two Hundred and twenty six Poles to a Spruce Tree marked, standing about two Poles Westward of an old Mast-Path being the Corner Bounds of Scarborough, Falmouth and Gorham-Town, thence runing on the Head of Scarborough nine Hundred and fifteen Poles to a large Hemlock Tree marked N: G.; thence runing North thirty three Degrees West seven Miles and one Quarter of a Mile by Narraganset Number One to a Fir Tree marked and from thence runing North East Seven Miles and two Hundred Poles to said Presumpscot River to a large Hemlock Tree about two Rods from the said River marked G: P: and bounded Northeasterly by said River; be and hereby is erected into a Town by the Name of and that the Inhabitants thereof be and hereby are invested with all the Powers, Priviledges and Immunities which the Inhabitants of the Towns within this Province do or may enjoy.

Provided that none of the Inhabitants or Proprietors of said Town be held by Virtue of this Act of Incorporation to pay any part of the ministerial Charges heretofore Arisen in said Plantation to such they were not Obliged (by their own Contract) to pay previous to such Incorporation.

And be it further enacted, That Stephen Longfellow Esqr be and hereby is empowered to issue his Warrant directed to some principal Inhabitant in said Town, requiring him to warn the Inhabitants of the said Town, qualified to vote in Town Affairs, to meet at such Time and Place as shall be therein set forth, to chuse all such Officers as are or shall be required by Law to manage the Affairs of the said Town.

In the House of Rep^ves Octr 25, 1764

Read a first and second time 27th a third time and passd to be engrossed

Sent up for concurrence S: White Spk^r

In Council Octr 27, 1764. Read a first time. Octr 29, Read a second time and passed a concurrence to be engrossed

A Oliver Sec^r

Consent of Propʳˢ of Kennebeck Purchase.

To His Excellʸ Fraˢ Bernard Esqʳ Govʳ of the Province of the Massᵃ Bay,—To the hon: his Majesty's Council & the honᵇˡᵉ House of Representatives

The Proprietors of the Kennebeck Purchase from the late Colony of New Plymouth humbly join in the Prayer of the foregoing Petition

Silv. Gardiner James Pitts Benjⁿ Hallowell Wᵐ Taylor Gershom Flagg	For themselves & Partners of the Kennebeck Purchase

In the House of Repᵛᵉˢ Octʳ 31 1764

Read and Ordered that the Petʳˢ have liberty to bring in a Bill for the purpose mentioned.

But that the incorporating them as a Town is not to be understood to give countenance to any Persons claiming property in said lands

Sent up for concurrence.

Petition, Narraganset No. 1. 1764.

To his Excellency Francis Bernard Esqʳ Commander in Chief in and over the Province of the Massaᵗˢ Bay, the Honᵇˡᵉ his Majesty's Councill & House of Representatives in General assembly Convened

Humbly Shew

The Subscribers Inhabitants of Narraganset Nᵒ one in the County of York That the said Settlement being a Frontier Were under Continual Fears of the Indian Enemy, and were obliged to keep Watch and Ward till the Reduction of Quebeck in 1759 —

That before the two late Years of Drowth & Scarcity they were few in Number, and very Poor, being Scarcely able with their utmost Diligence in the Improvement of such Means as their Situation afforded to procure the Necessarys of Life — That the two Years of Scarcity, almost reduced them to Famine: in Addition to which in the Year 1762, a desolating Fire Ravaged their Small Improvements, Burnt several of their Dwellings and much reduced the very little the Drouth had left 'em That these repeated Calamitys obliged many of the then Inhabitants for the preservation of Life to pluck up Stakes and leave the Settlement, and those that remained were Just preserved from Perishing with Want, by the Relief afforded from some of the Neighbouring Towns — That Your Excellency and Honours did lay a Tax on the said distressed Inhabitants in the Year 1762. To the amount of Forty four Pounds seven shillings & six pence, Which they are Unable to pay, as many of the then Inhabitants are reduced to Penury by the Calamitys aforesaid, and removed to other places — And those that remain are in a Condition but little Better —

Wherefore Your Poor Petitioners Humbly pray your Excellency & Honours to Compassionate their distressed Circumstances & Remit to them the said Tax and Grant 'em such other relief in the Premises as Your Wisdom shall direct & Your Poor Petitioners as in duty Bound shall ever Pray &c

Joseph Woodman	Joshua Woodman	Nathan Woodman
John Boynton	Will hancock	Job Roberts
Beniamen Donel	John Donel	John Nason
John Brooks	John Cole	Ephraim Sands
Timothy Hasaltine	John Lane	Samuel Roaf
John Elden	Joseph Leavit	Samuel
Umphery Atkeson	Daniel Leavit	James Emery
John Elden	Samuel Merrill	Amos Hood

In the House of Representatives October 31st 1764

Read & Resolved that the prayer of this Petition be granted by remitting the Tax of Forty Four pounds seven shillgs & six pence laid on Narragansett Township Number One in the Year 1762, and that the Treasurer be directed to stay the Execution gone forth against them therefor.

Sent up for concurrence S: White Spkr

In Council Novr 1st 1764 Read & Concurred

Jno Cotton D. Secry

Consented to Fra Bernard

Act of Incorporation

Anno Regni Regis Georgii Tertii Quinto

An Act for Erecting a Town in the County of Lincoln By the Name of

Whereas the Inhabitants of Land lying between Sheepscut & Dammerascota River within the County of Lincoln known by the Name of Townsend have Petitioned this Court that for the reasons mentioned they may be Incorporated into a Town, and Vested with the Powers and Authorities belonging to other Towns

For the Encoragement of sd Settlement — Be it Enacted by the Govr Council & House of Representatives That the sd Tract of Land Discribed and bounded as Follows vizt Beging at the Most Northerly Side of the Ovens Mouth So Called on Sheepscut River thence to run an East South East Course to Dameras Scota River then Southerly Down sd River to the Sea or Western Ocean then to run Westerly on the Sea Coast as the Coast lyes to the mouth of Sheepscot River then to run Northerly up Sheepscot River, between Jerymy Squam Island and Barter's Island to the Cross River at the

Head of Barters Island and From thence North Easterly to the ovens Mouth being the First Mentioned bounds, with all the Islands in Dameras Scota River from the Oven's Mouth Downward: And also all the Islands lying within Six Miles from ye Main Land to the South between the aforemention^{d} Rivers of Sheepscot and Dameras Scota — Be and Hereby is Errected into a Town, by the Name of
and the Inhabitants thereof Shall have & Enjoy all such Immunities & Priviledges as Other Towns in this Province have & do by Law Enjoy —

And be it Further Enacted that Samuel Denny Esqr be and Hereby is Impowered to Issue his warrant to some Principal Inhabitant of the s^{d} Town of
requiering him to Warn & Notify the s^{d} Inhabitants Qualified to Vote in Town Affairs to Meet togather at Such time and Place in s^{d} Town as he shall appoint in a Warrant to chuse such Officers as the Law Directs and may be Necessary to Manage the Affairs of s^{d} Town & the Inhabitants so met Shall be and are hereby Impowered to Chuse Such officers accordingly.

In the House of Rep^{ves} Novr 2 1764

Read three several times and passed to be engross'd.

Sent up for concurrence S. White Spk^{r}

In Council Novr 2, 1764 Read a first time Read a second time and passed a concurrence to be engrossed.

A Oliver Sec^{r}

The description of the town to be as follows viz

Beginning at the most northerly part of a Bay called the Oven's Mouth; & from thence to run an East South East Course to Damariscotta River; thence Southwardly down s^{d} River to the Sea or Western Ocean, then to run Westerly on the Sea Coast as the Coast lies to the Mouth of Sheepscot River, then to run Northerly up Sheepscot River between Jeremy Squam Island and Barter's Island to the Cross river at the head of s^d^ Barter's Island & from thence over the water to the most northerly part of the Oven's Mouth aforesaid, with all the Islands in Damariscotta River below or to the Southward of the first described line &c

Govr Bernard to Earl of Halifax.

Boston Novem^r^ 9. 1764

My Lord

Being apprehensive that very soon, if it is not at present, a New Arrangement of New England may be taken into consideration, I think it is my Duty to make your Lordship acquainted with my Sentiments upon this subject. I have long had it in my thoughts, having been convinced that the present Distribution of the lands between New York & Nova Scotia must, sooner or later, be put under new Establishments. This Business seems only to have waited for a proper time; & probably that time is now come.

The Country Westward of Boston is sufficiently well known; & so is that to the Eastward as far as Casco bay, & also in some degree to Kennebeck river, & beyond it, to the West side of Penobscot Bay. But further it is but late that the Land has been explored; only since the Reduction of Quebec, & the submission of the Indians in consequence thereof has made it safe for Englishmen to visit it. And all the surveys by actual measure of the Country between Penobscot & St Croix that I know of, have been taken by my directions, & some of them under my own Eye.

The Division of New England into Governments of suitable size & with proper boundaries, is by no means a difficult task, if it was unimbarrast with the politicks, prejudices, & humours of the people. These create some apparent difficulties, but in my opinion, no more that what, Conduct, Perseverance, & Authority will easily get the better of. At present I will waive the consideration of these, and only regard the topographical state of the Country, & from thence conclude what would be the most convenient Division of it into separate Governments, if the People in general were indifferent about it.

And first I will suppose that the two Republicks of Connecticut & Rhode Island are to be dissolved: Without that a New Arrangement of New England would be impracticable at least Very imperfect. I will also suppose that it would be most agreable to his Majesty that the Government of New York should be extended as far as Connecticut river. The Dividing Connecticut in this manner will create some internal Difficulties, which are obvious to those who know the temper & disposition of the people of that Colony. But certainly the River Connecticut is the most proper boundary to New York: and therefore I will suppose in the New Arrangement that River to be the boundary of New York.

The first province then (reckoning from the Westward) would be thus composed. That part of the Colony of Connecticut which lies on the East side of the River Connecticut, all the Colony of Rhode Island, that part of the province of Massachusetts Bay lying Westward of Newhampshire, & all the Province of Newhampshire. The Breadth of this united Province, reckoning by roads, & not by a geographical line, would be 160 miles. But by a parallell drawn from the Connecticut & the Nichywannock being the two boundary river it would not be above miles wide. Boston would be a very convenient Capital, as it is as much in the Centre as can well be. And tho' this would be one of the finest provinces in America, It would be so by populousness

& close settling, & not by extension of boundaries, which would be very sufficiently confined.

The next province should consist of the Province of Maine, & such part of Acadia or the Territory of Sagadehock as lies Westward of the River Penobscot, that is all the Country between Piscataqua & Penobscot. The length of this in a right line along the Coast is about 150 miles; tho' by a geographical paralell between the divisional line at the head of Nychiwannock & the river Penobscot It would be considerably less, not above miles. The Town of Falmouth in Cascobay here offers itself as a very proper Capital, being 60 miles from Piscataqua, & 90 from Penobscot bay. This Town is now growing with great rapidity; it has a large trade in Ship building, & is becoming a principal Seaport for masts: & if it was made the Seat of a Government, it would soon become worthy of being one. This would make a good province, & would show at present the middle state of one, between infancy & maturity.

The third Province would contain the remainder of the Territory of Sagadehock with so much of the Continent of Nova Scotia as shall be thought proper to add to it: for instance, from the River Penobscot to the river St. Johns. They would be not less than 180 miles in a strait line, due West & East, which is the Course of great part of the Coast. This would truly be an infant province, & a very helpless one too. The whole of this Tract would at this time have been an uninhabited Wast, if it had not been for the efforts of the Province of Massachusetts bay about 3 years ago to settle 13 Townships on the East side of Penobscot, the grants of which still want his Majesty's Confirmation, upon account of the Provinces title to make such grants being questioned. In some of these towns there are several settlers, at a considerable expence; at one particularly, where Money and spirit have not been wanted, 60 families, the whole required by the Terms of the grant, are settled at the expence of 1000 pounds sterling out of the pockets of 2 or 3 persons only. Nevertheless I dont believe there are above 150 families in all these townships, (including the Island of Mountdesert where there are at present about 20 families) which together with about 30 families in the bay of Machias, who are settled under no Authority at all, make in the whole 180 families. All these except 1, 2 or 3 leading men in each township, are extremely poor & worth nothing but their lot of land, & the miserable dwelling with the little clearances they have made upon it. This is a true state of the Country between Penobscot & St Croix, the whole length of which I have reconnoitred in person.

It seems therefore too early to make a separate Government of this Country at present; tho' it may be Very proper even now to make a designation of it, & even to form the plan, to be executed when it has a sufficient population. In the mean time it may be best to let the parts which are to compose this Government be divided by the bounds of Nova Scotia; that is, that Country which lies on the East of St Croix to remain to the Government of Nova Scotia, & that Country which lies on the West of St Croix to remain to the Government of Main & Sagadehock: And let them be settled under these respective Governments, untill they have acquired a sufficient Number of people to make one of their own. As for a Capital, It would be too early to determine upon that now: it would be perhaps the best way to let the sevral towns advance themselves as they can & then to pick & choose among them. At present, for the situation of a Capital we should ballance between the Bay of St Croix (or more properly the bay of Passimaquoddy) & the Bay of Machias. The former I know very well having lived there at Anchor 4 days & having had the whole of it to the Westward of the River. St Croix surveyed & planned. The Bay of Machias I know only by report & a sea View of it, not being able to go in for want of a pilot who knew it.

Having gone thro the Topography of the Country, I must return to the Westward to take notice of the difficulties, which the politicks, prejudices, & humours of the people may create there. And these seem all to arise from the bad policy of establishing republican forms of Government in the British Dominions. It was a strange oversight in Charles the second, when Monarchy was restored in Great Britain, to confirm the republicks in America. Hence has arisen a Notion that The people on one side of a river have a right to a greater degree & a different mode of liberty than their fellow subjects on the other side. Hence it probably will be, that the Western part of Connecticut will be unwilling to be united to New York, & the Province of Main will be unwilling to be seperated from the Massachusets. But If the Form of the Massachusets Government should be so far altered as to remove the little remains of its republican cast, the Distinction between that & the adjoining Governments would be less regarded. As for the Religious Divisions, they are become so entirely subservient to politicks, that if the State of the Government is reformed, & a perfect toleration secured, Religion will never give any trouble.

Your Lordship knows perhaps, that it is my opinion, that the most perfect form of Government for a mature American Province remains still to be designed. The Desideratum is a third legislative power, which shall be, or at least appear to be, independent of the King & People. Without this, the Constitution of an American Government is not made so similar to that of the Mother Country as it is capable of being, & therefore hath not received its greatest possible perfection. To effect this, The Functions of the present Council should be separated, & that Body divided into a legislative Council & a privy Council: the former to be appointed by his Majesty for Life, removeable only for misdemeanours by the Judgement of their own body; the latter to be appointed by his Majesty during his pleasure, & to be composed of the Members of either house, or of persons belonging to neither, as there shall be occasion.

To show what steadiness such appointments would give to a Government, & in what manner & by what means they would operate, would exceed the bounds of this letter. It is sufficient for the present purpose to say that the Province of the Massachusets, united as aforesaid, will afford a fine opportunity for trying the experiment; (if a regulation founded upon fixed & certain principles & allready fully proved & approved can be called an Experiment) as it would certainly be an improvement of the Government of the Massachusets, whatever it might be to others. It is well known that the appointment of the Council by annual Election is a very faulty part of the Government of the Massachusets It cannot be denied but that to have the Members of the middle legislative body removeable at pleasure by the people is unconstitutional. But then the people will say that it is as unconstitutional for such members to be removeable at pleasure by the King: to answer the purposes of a mediating power they should be independent both of King & People. If therefore the alteration of the appointment of the Council was made in the manner before proposed, The Arguments in favour of it would be unanswerable: It might be truly said, that thereby, the Form of the Government was meliorated upon principles of independence. And yet the Crown would receive a considerable accession of strength therefrom: but it would be of constitutional strength, such as could give no just cause of umbrage to the People.

But this is not all that is wanting: it will be absolutely necessary to establish a certain & sufficient Civil List for the support of such officers of the Crown as fall under that establishment in Great Britain; that they who hold the reins of Government & the ballance of justice, may no way be subject to popular influence. And this is wanting, not only to make them independent, but to pay them adequately; the appointments in this, & all other Governments where they are paid by the people, being scandalously unequal to the rank & business of their sevral offices: and this will never be remedied but by a superior power. Such an establishment will not only give firmness to the Governments for the future, but will greatly assist the reforming them at present. It is now no secret that Honours and Posts of Profit are the chief Weights in the Scale which keep the ballance of political power in Equilibration: and It is not too much to say that to this influence Great Britain at present owes its very being. Why then should not the application of the same influence be equally beneficial to America? It certainly will: & I will venture to say that the Honours & places of profit incidental to a mature Government established upon the foregoing principles will be sufficient to support all the powers & faculties of it; & will place the Seat of the Governor (provided his administration is conducted with some prudence, much patience, & a little publick spirit,) upon a Rock.

As to the manner of conducting the new Arrangement of these Governments, I shall not presume to offer my thoughts upon it, any further than what relates to the part the people here are allowed to bear in it. It seems that there are but two ways of proceeding, 1, by the King in Council, 2, by the King in parliament. In the first Case the Consent of the Colonies will be absolutely necessary; in the second Case, It will not be necessary, tho' Very expedient. Where it is necessary, it will be harder to obtain, & will require perhaps a good deal of time as well as some Management. Where it is not necessary, it will probably come more easily, will be best conducted in a public manner, & may soon be brought to a conclusion. In this last case all that the Provinces & Colonies can expect, will be to have the plan laid before them, & time given them to make their objections to it. It will go down more hardly with the two Colonies: I cannot think, if it is anything like what is before proposed, that it will meet with much difficulty in this Province, being manifestly greatly for its advantage.

I have before informed your Lordship that I have taken great pains to make myself well acquainted with the Territory of Sagadehock. I have made three Voyages thither at my own Expence, & this year I went to the Extremity of it, to the Bay of St Croix; which is 350 miles from Boston. I have kept up a continual correspondence with all the Indians living in that Territory, & have gained their Confidence by means of deeds as well as of Words. Last Winter I prevailed upon the Assembly to authorize me to employ Surveyors as many as I wanted, for surveying & reconnoitring that Country: and by these means I have this Summer done the following Works.

I have sent a party, associated with Indians, from Fort Pownall up Penobscot river thro' the river Chaudiere to Quebec, who returned part of the way by a different rout from what they took going. They made observations for drawing plans of both passages by taking the sevral bearings & computing the distances & noting the particulars of land & Water. The same party afterwards went from Fort Pownall thro' the river Sebesticook to Fort Halifax on Kennebeck, & took observations as before. Another party took a survey of the Bay of Passimaquoddy with the Islands therein as far as the Mouth of St Croix & some few miles beyond it; & also went up the rivers St Croix & Passimaquoddy for about 15 miles each. Afterwards part of the same party associated with Indians went up the River Passimaquoddy to the head of the West branch, & thence thro' a multitude of lakes to the river Penobscot about 70 miles above Fort Pownall & down the river to the Fort; & took all necessary observations for a plan. This last passage together with that from Fort Pownall to Fort Halifax, make an inland line from passimaquoddy to Kennebeck, not less than 300 miles in length. I have also run a line from Fort Pownall to George's River, being the most easterly settlement on that side of Penobscot, & have had an horse-road cut thro' the whole, being the length of 50 miles: this addition makes a clear land passage from Boston to Fort Pownall, which will be soon continued, whenever the Settlements on the East side of 'Penobscot shall be allowed to be improved.

At Sea I have had two parties of Surveyors employed all this Summer in surveying the Islands on the East Side of Penobscot Bay, called the Fox Islands, which are very numerous, & some of them considerably large. They have also connected those Islands with the Continent by trigonometrical lines, by which means, & by the survey of the Sea Coast in the laying out the 12 Townships granted by this Province, We shall have a regular Chart of all the Sea Coast for near 50 miles East of Penobscot. In the mean time there has been another party of Surveyors, being the fifth employed this Summer, engaged in running inland lines thro' & above the said townships, by which the rivers & principal inland waters will be made known. After this there will be only wanting the Sea Coast between the East end of the 12 townships into the Bay of Passimaquoddy, which is about 70 or 80 miles more, to compleat the survey of the whole Coast between the rivers Penobscot & St Croix; which would have been an easy Summer's Work, if I could go on with it; But this must be deferred untill the designation of the Country is determined: as I cannot now ask our Assembly for more money for this business.

It will be the work of great part of this Winter to get all these Surveys protracted, & copies of them made: the first I can get properly finished, I shall transmit to your Lordship together with more particular accounts of the Country thro' which these routs have been made. And I shall at the same time, as I do now, make an offer of my best Services for the settling & improving this great Wast, whether it shall be allowed to be within my Government or not.

I am, with great respect, My Lord, your Lordships, Most obedient & most humble Servant,

Fra Bernard

Letter to Jasper Manduit, Agent

Boston 27th November 1764.

Sir

The Massachusetts government has been so unfortunate in all their controversies about boundaries that we have but little courage in undertaking the defence of any of our lines however plain the justice of our cause may appear to us.

A dispute had long subsisted between the Colony of Massachusetts and the heirs of Mason who claimed the Province of New Hampshire. At length in 1677 it was determined by K. Charles the 2d in Council that the Massachusetts boundary should extend three miles north of Merrimack river as far as the river went, and then a line would run West to the extent of their limits. Until then the Massachusetts had exercised jurisdiction over the whole Province of New Hampshire but afterwards supposed themselves bound by this determination. The river Merrimack was known at that time to extend to Winnepeseaukee lake as fully as it is at present. The whole of the Massachusetts Colony was expressly included in the new charter to the

Massachusetts Province in 1691 when this settlement was fresh in the mind of the ministry. Notwithstanding this the Province of New Hampshire, it was determined by determination, in the year 1738, upon a new claim set up by his late Majesty in Council that the line of the Massachusetts Province should run no farther upon the river Merrimack than to Patucket falls and the west line to begin upon a parallel with them and to run &c[a] This cut off more than half the river and a large tract of Country great part of which had been granted to private persons most of whom were deprived of their property, as well as the government of it's jurisdiction. This however it was necessary to submit to. A war with French and Indians coming on soon after M[r] Shirley the then Governor before he removed the garrison from a Block house called Fort Dummer west of Connecticut river desired the governor of New Hampshire to place a sufficient garrison there but he declined it, and upon representation made to the ministry, His late Majesty's royal order was sent to this Province recommending to the Assembly to make Provision for the continuance of a garrison at that fort and assuring them that New Hampshire should reimburse the expence or otherwise that an equivalent in territory should be assigned to this Province. The government thereupon continued the garrison for several Years and disbursed large sums for the pay and support thereof and of other Forces employed in the defence and protection of that part of the Country which had been taken from the Province.

The account of this expence was prepared and transmitted to England but has lain many years without any consideration nor could we ever hear of any reason for the neglect besides a suggestion of the Agent of New Hampshire that this fort was a place of no importance and that M[r] Shirley had misrepresented the case, a suggestion which if it had been true as we suppose it was not yet ought not to affect the government seeing the provision they made was in consequence of the Royal order which did not leave it to their discretion whether it was expedient to comply with it or not.

Rhode Island encouraged by the success of New Hampshire set up a new claim upon the South boundary of the Massachusetts and applied to his late Majesty that Commissioners might be appointed to determine it. Their request was soon granted and four or five gentlemen of New York with which Province the Massachusetts was then in controversy were of the number and although a few Years before Rhode Island made pretence only to a small gore of land a corner of a township yet the Commissioners now established a line never before thought of which cut off from this Province half a dozen of the best towns which had been deemed part of the colony of New Plymouth and jurisdiction had been exercised over them as such above an hundred years.—

Connecticut had settled a line with this Province in 1713. Four towns planted by Massachusetts People fell within Connecticut but by Agreement, at the desire of the inhabitants were to remain under the jurisdiction of the Massachusetts, and for the property an equivalent was given to Connecticut in lands which that government received and Sold and put the money into their Treasury. Notwithstanding this in the year 1748 when the taxes of this Province were much higher than those of Connecticut the inhabitants of these four towns revolted and applied to Connecticut to receive them which they accordingly did in violation of a solemn agreement to the contrary.

Instead of any compulsory measures which might have been attended with ill consequences, the governor of that colony having intimated that the People would stand upon their defence it was thought most adviseable to make humble application to his Majesty for his Royal order to that government to forbear any further exercise of jurisdiction over those towns, and we have ever since been encouraged that so reasonable a request could not fail of being granted and yet it has lain fourteen or fifteen years without our being able to obtain any determination.—

New York having from time to time extended their grants upon the lands of this Province obtained a very favorable report of the board of trade which cut off from this Province several hundred persons who presumed they had settled within the bounds of it. We thought it a hard case for us, and yet even this was excepted to by New York before the King in Council and it has lain several Years without a final determination, and we are lately informed that the Agent for that Province is now endeavouring to have all the proceedings set aside and Commissioners appointed to hear and determine the controversy upon the Spot.

The whole Province of Nova Scotia is expressly included within the charter of this Province. The great difficulty of defending a Country so remote from our center made it a lesser hardship than otherwise it would have been for the Crown to take it from us after Peace of Utrecht and to settle a distinct government there; but for the Country between the Rivers Kennebeck and S[t] Croix we have been at continual expence in defending it, never imagining our right of jurisdiction and our right of granting the Property conditionally would ever be disputed, and yet as soon as that Country is freed from the danger of Enemies our title both to jurisdiction and property as to great part of that Country is questioned and all our grants made in order to forward the settlement of it are disapproved.—

This is a true state of our case. Notwithstanding all these discouragements we are bound in faithfulness to our trust to go on, as long as there shall be any room left for it, defending our cause and preventing if possible this Province which formerly was one of the first from being made the last in rank and importance of any of his Majesty's Colonies.—

We do not know what evidence can be transmitted to you in defence of the lines which still remain controverted further than what you are already possessed of. The printed states of our title as it respects New York, Connecticut and Nova Scotia we think cannot be answered. The documents to support our allegations have been sent properly authenticated except those historical facts which from the nature of them can be no otherwise evidenced than by the general credit they have obtained among mankind of all nations. In general, if any new difficulties be started as to either of the Governments which you are not able to remove we desire you to move for time to communicate them to us as we do not doubt we shall be able to give further satisfaction.— For the territory east of Kennebeck we suppose Lord Sterling's claim is over as we hear nothing lately said about it and indeed it never had the least foundation. Nor can we well conceive what exception can be taken to our title under the limitations in the charter. We know that none of our grants will be of any validity without the Royal confirmation. Our principal view in making grants of the townships was the cultivating and improving His Majesty's dominions which otherwise must remain a Wilderness and can be in no respect beneficial to the nation. We should be glad to be informed whether the exception be to our right to originate any grants, or whether it be to the particular grants either as to the Persons to whom the townships were granted, the conditions of the grants or to any other matter either in point of form or substance. If there be any prospect of the grants obtaining his Majesty's Confirmation we doubt not the General Court will do everything proper on their part in order to promote the settlement of so considerable a part of the Province. By a proper application for that purpose you will no doubt be able to satisfy yourself and as upon these points.

The People of Connecticut for many Years past have had but little expectation of finally holding the revolted towns and the inhabitants of the towns or a great part of them are well enough disposed to return. We should be glad to be informed what the obstacles are which prevent the success of the application so long since made by this government.

It will be extremely disagreeable to us to engage again on this side the water in the controversy with New York especially to submit the decision of it Commissioners to whose characters and connections we are altogether strangers. We are sure it will be expected by the General Court that you should oppose in all the ways you are permitted to do it, the issuing of such a Commission for although the report of the Board of trade was much more unfavorable for us than we expected, having never imagined that New York would be allowed more than twelve miles from the River yet we had rather submit to this unexpected line than to open the controversy anew, perhaps the rumor spread by the New York People concerning such an intended Commission may be without sufficient grounds.

As for our demand upon New Hampshire it has been so long suspended that we suppose one of the alternatives the assigning us part of that Province is now impracticable most if not all their lands being granted away; the other being a reimbursement of the expence of this government, we have no way of obtaining except by a Royal Order for that purpose. It is certain that the inducement to advance so large a Sum was a Royal promise that in one way or the other a full recompence should be made for it.

The line with Connecticut as settled between the two governments in 1713 having been perambulated by Commissioners in 1734 we think it necessary to send you a copy of this perambulation it having been taken notice of in the State of the Case formerly sent you. It will undoubtedly be of use if the Colony of Connecticut shall persist in their claim to jurisdiction. A copy of the vote of the General Court authorizing us to correspond with you we shall also send under the same cover. We are S^r

Your very humble Servants

To his Excellency Francis Barnard Esqr Captain General and Commander in Cheife in and over his Majesties Province of the Massachusets Bay in New England &c. To the Honble his Majesties Council, And the Honble House of Representatives in General Court Assembled the Day of A D 1764

The Pettition of John Bezune and Margret his Wife (said Margret being Daughter to Henry Harmson late of Marblehead Dec^d) And Stephen Chapman Guardeen to three Grand children of the said Henry Harmson Humbly Sheweth

That the said Henry Harmson did in his life Time (some short time before his Death) Purchase of Thomas Bartlet of said Marblehead, (for a Considerable Sum of Money) All his Right, Title and Property in and to a Township Granted by this Honble Court in the year 1734 To Sixty of the Inhabitants of said Marblehead & laid Out on the Back of the Towns of Falmouth and North-Yarmouth in the County of Cumberland: of the Which, said Thomas Bartlet was one of the Original Granttees. And in the first Division of home Lots Drew N° 25: Soon after Which he sold said Right or Grant as aforesaid. And from that time to this, the Said Henry Harmson and his Descendants has paid all the Taxes or Dues laid on said Right, For clearing of Roads, Building of Bridges, laying out future Divisions, Setleing and maintaining of Ministers: And all other Charges ariseing for the performing the Conditions laid on said Grant, by this Honble Court (which is now perfected) all which time the said

Thomas Bartlet never concerned himself with the Premises. And on the Division of the Real Estate of the said Henry Harmson Pursuant to the Order and Commision of the Judge of Probates for the County of Essex, the said Right or purchase was Sett off to us the Said Margret and the said Grandchildren as part of the said Real Estate (although at that time the Deed of said Purchase could not be found) Presuming it was in the Registers office in the County of York:)

But on further inquiry, and lately Searching at said Registers office after said Deed, it Could not be found. nor any record thereof. (it is Presumed that it is either Mislaid or Lost) and cannot at present be found.

And the said Thomas Bartlet Departing this Life about Six Years Since and leaveing Several Children some of them being in their Minority whereby a Quit claim cannot be obtained from them.

We therefore Humbly Pray that Your Excellency and Hon^rs Would be pleased to take this Our Pettition under Your Mature Consideration. and Confirm the said Grant (of Thomas Bartlet) unto the said Henry Harmson, his Heirs and Assigns for ever, any former Grant to the Contrary Notwithstanding.

And Your Petitioners as in Duty Bound Shall Ever pray

John Bezune

Margret X Bezune's
mark

In the House of Rep^ves Octr 23 1764

Read and Ordered that the Pet^rs serve the Heirs of Thomas Bartlett with a copy of this Pet^n that they Shew cause if any they have on the second Wednesday of the next Session of this Court why the prayer thereof should not be granted

Sent up for concurrence S: White Spk^r

In Council Octr 25, 1764. Read and Concurred.

A Oliver Sec^r

In Council Jany 19, 1765 Read again, and it appearing to the Board That the heirs of Thos Bartlet within mentioned have been prevented by some mistake in the Affair, giving in an Answer to this Petition.

Ordered That John Choate Esqr with Such as the hon^{le} House shall join be a Committee to take the same under consideration, hear the Parties and report.

Sent down for concurrence A Oliver Sec^{r}

In the House of Rep^{ves} Feby 9 1765

Read and concur'd and Col^{o} Powell and Col^{o} Bourn are Joyned

James Otis Speak^{r} pro Tempore

In Council 9th Feby 1765. Read and Concurred and James Otis Esq$_{s}$ is appointed in the room of John Choate Esq$_{s}$ who is absent.

Sent down for Concurrence A Oliver Sec^{r}

In the House of Rep^{ves} Feb^{ry} 9 1765

Read and concur'd James Otis Speak^{r} pro Tempore

Report of Committee. 1765.

The Committee to whom was referred the Petition of John Bezune and Margaret his Wife, and Stephen Chapman Guardian to three of the Grand children of Henry Harmson Deceased, have met and considered the same: and find the Facts set forth therein to be true:

And whereas it appears the said Henry and Successors (and not the said Thomas Bartlett or his Heirs) have fulfilled the Orders of the General Court for thirty Years last past, relative to the bringing forward ye Settlement of the said Town of Windham, and wholly compleated the same, (so far as respects the Right said to be sold the said Harrison by the said Bartlet:

The Committee, therefore, are of the Opinion, That the Prayer of said Petition be granted, and that the Grant made to the said Thomas Bartlet is become void, as he never did any one Thing towards fulfilling the same; and that the Share of Lands in said Town intended for said Bartlet (on Conditions) be, and hereby is confirmed unto the Heirs and Assigns of the said Henry Harmson for ever, who with his Heirs have fulfilled the Conditions of said Grant.

All which is humbly submitted,

James Otis ꝑ order

In Council Feby 12, 1765 Read and Accepted — And it appearing that Thomas Bartlett one of the original Grantees of the Township now called Windham hath never done anything towards fulfilling the Conditions of the Grant upon which his Right or Share therein was to have been confirmed to him. It is hereby ordered that the Share of Lands in the said Town intended, on certain conditions, to have been for the said Bartlett be, and it hereby is confirmed to the Heirs and Assigns of the said Henry Harmson forever; the said Henry Harmson & his Heirs having fulfilled the Conditions upon which the said Grant was made, on the right of the said Thos Bartlet, who as is alledged in the said Petition had sold the same to him —

Sent down for Concurrence A Oliver Sec^r

In the House of Rep^ves Feby 22^d 1765

Read and concur'd S: White Spk^r

Consented to Fra Bernard

Petition of sundry Inhabitants of the First Parish in Scarborough.

Province of the Massachusets bay To His Excellency Francis Barnard Esqr Captain General and Governour in

Chief in and over his Majesties s[d] Province To the Honourable his Majesties Council and to the Honourable House of Representitives In the Great and General Court Assembled

The Petition of Sundry Inhabitants of the first Parish in the Town of Scarborough In the County of Cumberland Humbly Sheweth That Your petitioners has for upwards of Five Years Past been Deprived of a Gospel Minister. And the parishoners Ever since been in Great Divisions and Contentions about Getting Another Minister Although we have had Several Worthy Candidates upon Tryal with us Could not get one Settled because there is a party among us would compel whoever Settles with us to Joyn in Fellowship with one M[r] Clark a Lay Minister of a Neighbouring Parish. In opposition to the Rest of the ministry of the Land, and as they Could not get one to Settle on those Terms, and in Expectation of being fined for want of one, They made application to the Presbiterey [to] Send one, Who very Readily Sent one M[r] Peirce, Whom a Majority Very Suddenly & Rashly after Two or Three times hearing him, choose to be their Minister, and Voted [to] alter the Church Goverment, and Invest it in the power [of] Three or four Men. The Presbetery being Sundenly ordain'd Ordaind him at Newbury and Sent him to be A Minister in this Place although a Considerable number Sent Up to desire that it might not be done Since Which we think the Said M[r] Peirce does not behave himself as A Minister of the Gospel ought to do in his Cariage and behaviour. They are also Distraining & Compelling us to pay Taxes against our minds to Support him which makes very Great Trouble Among us. We also find it will be very Difficult to get any Disorder Settled by The Presbetery by A Late Instance of A Church to the Eastward of us to Settle A Disorder there of the Same Nature as is among us, and also by their Late Votes Concerning us. Now your Petitioners Would Intreat Your Excellency & Honours, that they may Not be deprived of the Other Privilidges of the Parish and Set off to the Second Parish in said Scarborough, and not be compelled to pay any thing towards the Settlement or Support of the said Mr Peirce or any charge thereof and that what they have taken from Us may be Restored although we are over Ruld by a Larger Majority of People though not So in porportion in Estate & that we may if possible be Retreav'd from those disorders or in any Other way your Excellency & Honours as in Your great Wisdom shall See meet & Your petitioners as in Duty bound shall Ever pray &c.

Peter Libbee	Wm Tompson	Alex. Kirkwood
Kezia Libbee	Abrm Clark	Israel Cloke
Abraham Tyler	Eben Prout	John Radman
George Meserve	Joseph Ring	John Gilford
I McKeny	Nathanel Libbey	Jo Prout & atty
Samuel Goodwin	Joshua Small	to Timothy Prout
Samll March	Elisha Libby	

Instructions to Capt. Gideon Smith April 20, 1765.

By his Excellency Francis Bernard Esq Captn General and Governor in Chief in and over his Majestys Province of the Massachusetts Bay in New England and Vice Admiral of the Same.

Instructions to be observed by Gideon Smith Master of the Schooner Thankful bound for the Gulph of St Lawrence and the Streights of Bellisle.

Having upon application made to me for that purpose, granted You License to carry on a Trade with the Indians under his Majestys Protection for a term not exceeding six months from the date hereof; and you having given bond in all things to conform to such regulations as are or shall be prescribed to You by his Majesty or his Commissaries for the benefit of the said Trade; and also that You will not trade with the Norridgewalk or Penobscot Indians or any other Indians residing on or frequenting the Rivers Kennebec or Penobscot or usually trading with the Provincial Truck houses established on the said rivers —

You are to consider the forementioned Conditions of your Bond as Instructions to You for the carrying on the said Indian Trade; and You are to treat such Indians with whom You may carry on any Trade or Dealings with that Justice, good faith and kindness as may conciliate them to his Majestys Government and serve to fix them in their obedience and subjection to it.

Given under my hand at Boston the twentieth day of April 1765. In the Fifth Year of his Majestys Reign.

Copy of Instructions rec^d from his Excell^y Govr Bernard.

Gideon Smith

Gorham, Petition 1765.

To his Excellency Francis Barnard Esqr Capt General and Governour in Chief in and Over his Majesties Province of the Massachusets Bay in New England, The Honourable His Majesties Council and House of Representatives in General Court Assembled

The Petition of the select men of Gorham in the name and in behalf of the Inhabitants of said Town Humbly sheweth, That being in expectation of being incorporated into a Town last May Sessions of the Great and General Court of this Province, in Consequence of which we in our Annual Meeting in 1764 thought it expedient to defer the Choice of Assessors Collector &c till the Act of Incorporation should be Obtained which we hop^d would not be Long and therefore adjourned our March Meeting to a future Day, which unhappy Mistake incapacitated us to make any Choice at all so that the Last years Province Tax remains uncolected, which we are very unable to pay in as much as we have been great sufferers by fires Drought and severe frost Last Year that Numbers of families in this Place are in extreme want of bread Moreover we are on the Point of settleing a Good Minister which will we trust be to universal acceptance both in this Place and all around us, the charge whereof will be a very heavy burden on our shoulders. Your Petitioners therefore Humbly pray That the Province Tax of 1764 may be Abated or remitted And Your Petitioners as in Duty bound shall ever pray

Gorham May 20 1765

Briant Morton, Benj[a] Skilling, Amos Whitney } Selectmen of Gorham

In the House of Rep[ves] June 20 1765

Read and Ordered that the Province Tax laid on Gorham for the Year 1765 be superseded — And that the same be added to their Province Tax in the Year 1766 and the Treasurer is directed not to Issue his Execution ag[t] said Town in the mean time

Sent up for concurrence S: White Spk[r]

In Council June 20, 1765 Read & Concurred

A Oliver Sec[r]

Consented to Fra Bernard

Bond. 1765.

Know All Men by these presents

That we Henry Young Brown of Canterbury in the Province of New Hampshire in New England Esquire Joseph Fry of Andover in the County of Essex in the Province of the Massachusetts bay in New England aforesaid Esquire and Richard Saltonstall of Haverhill in the County of Essex Aforesaid Esquire are Holden and Stand firmly Bound and Obliged unto Harrison Gray of Boston in the County of Suffolk in the Province of Massachusetts bay Aforesaid Treasurer and Receiver General of the said Province of Massachusetts bay in the full and just Sum of Two Thousand Pounds Lawfull Money of the same Province of Massachusetts bay to be paid unto the said Harrison Gray Treasurer as Aforesaid or his Successor in the said office to and for the Use of the said Province of Massachusetts bay to the which payment well and truly to be made we Bind ourselves our Heirs Executors and Administrators Jointly and severally in the whole and for the whole firmly by these Presents Sealed with our Seals. Dated the Sixteenth day of February Anno Domini one thousand seven hundred and Sixty five And in the Fifth Year of His Majesty King George The Thirds reign.

The Conditions of the above written Obligation are Such That Whereas the Great and General Court of the Province of the Massachusetts bay at their Sessions in January 1764 Granted unto the Above bounden Henry Young Brown Liberty to Lay out a Township of the Contents of Six Miles Square in some Place on each or either side of Saco River Above Col° Frys Purchase where it might not Interfere with any former Grant And Whereas the said Township has been Laid out Conformable to said Grant and a Plat thereof returned to the General Court of the said Province of Massachusetts bay who have Accepted thereof and have on the Seventh day of June Anno Domini 1764 Confirmed the same Township to him the said Henry Young Brown and his Heirs and Assigns forever on Condition that he gave Bond with Sufficient Security to the Province Treasurer or his Successor to Settle the same with fifty nine good Families, each of which in the Term of Six Years from the date of said Grant, to have Built a good House of Twenty feet by Eighteen, and Seven feet Stud, and have Cleared for Pasturage or Tillage Seven acres each, and that they Also out of the said Township Grant one Sixty fourth part to the first Protestant Minister duly Settled there, one Sixty fourth part for the Use of the Ministry forever two Sixty four parts for the Use of Harvard College, and one Sixty fourth part for the use of the School forever within the said Town and shall within Ten Years have a Protestant Minister Settled among them.

If therefore the within Bounden Henry Young Brown his heirs Executors Administrators or Assigns shall Grant one Sixty fourth part of the said Township to the first Protestant Minister duly Settled the one sixty fourth part thereof for the use of the Ministry forever, two Sixty four parts for the use of Harvard College and one Sixty fourth part for the use of the School forever within said Township and shall within the Space of five Years from the date of said Grant Settle the said Township with Fifty nine good Familys each of which in that Term shall have Built a good House of twenty feet by Eighteen and Seven feet Stud and have Cleared for Pasturage or Tillage Seven Acres each and shall also within Ten Years from the Date of said Grant have a Protestant Minister Settled there Then the Aforewritten Obligation shall be Void otherwise shall remain in full force.

Henry Young Brown Seal
Joseph Frye Seal
Rich[d] Saltonstall Seal

Signed Sealed & Deliv[d] in
p[r]sence of
Jonathan Bagly
Josiah Wolcott

Answer of First Parish in Scarborough.

Province of the Massachusetts Bay To His Excellency Francis Barnard Esq[r] Captain Gene[l] and Governor in

Chief in and Over his Majesty– Said Provincc To the Honourable his Majestys Councel and House of Representatives in General Court Assembled the 29th Day of May 1765 —

The Inhabitants of the First Parish in Scarborough in the County of Cumberland in Answer to a Petition Exhibited to this Honour^{ble} Court in Feb^{ry} Last by Twenty one Persons who Call themselves Inhabitants of Said Parish Humbly Sheweth

That had the Petitionrs been So Honest as to have Set forth in their Petition or Complaint in a True Light your Respondants would have had less to Say in Answer to it The Petitioners Say they have been Deprived of a Gospel Minister upward of five years past That was not in the Power of the Parish to avoid In Answer to that we would observe it pleased God in his holy Próvidence to Remove the Minister of the Parish by Death upwards of five years Since but the said Parish as soon as they Could Sought after Another Minister and being advised to a young Gentleman at a Distance wrote to him and waited a Considerable time for him but at last had an answer we Could not have him but in the mean time we hired a Gentlemen to Preach for us who had been a Settled Minister before but he being advanced in years we thought it not adviseable to Settle him but Still the Parish was in Pursute after another which accationed Great Expences having a Great Distance to journey time after time at Length having had three or four young Candedates upon Probation one after another three of which had a Clear Call both by Church & Parish but all Refused to Settle but for what reason is unknown to us So that the Petitioners Saying the Parish would Compell whoever Settled with us to Joyne in Fellowship with Mr Clark is Groundless and false for the Parish knew very well that neither of the three would in case they did Settle with us

Notwithstanding the whole Body of the People agreed in the Call of Each of the three not one hand against either of the three — The Petitioners go on and Say that the majority very Suddenly and Rashly after two or three times hearing him meaning as we Supose M[r] Peirce Chose him to be their Minister and that the Presbitary Suddenly ordained him at Newbury In Answer M[r] Peirce Came to the Parish about the Twelfth or Thirteenth of Augus— 1762 and was ordained the latter part of November. Following the reason why m[r] Peirce was so soon Called and Settled was Because the Church had been So long without the Ordanances of the Gospel which was two or three years and the People was so well Satisfied in him that they ware Desireous to have— Settled as soon as might be and reason that the Minister was Ordained at Newbury was because it was so late in the Year as November the Presbittery Could not Come Down to Scarborough at that Season of the year otherwise it must be put off till another year which the Church and People ware not Willing too The Petitioners Say that M[r] Peirce doth not behave him self as a minister of the Gospel ought to in his Carrage & behavour.

Answer that it is well known that a man in the Midest of his Enemies Must be very upright Otherwise they take all accations against him and will overlook no failing at all in him — The Petitioners Pray your Excellency and Honours they may not be Deprived of the Other Priviledges of the Parish and be Set off to the Second Parish in Scarborough their Seems to be Something in their Prayer we Do not understand what they mean by not being Deprived of their Other Priviledges in the First Parish wheither they mean in attending the Publick Worship of God in the First Parish that the most of them or their Families do and have done ever Since M[r] Peirce Came into the Parish or wheither they mean to Retain their Priviledges as Voters in the First Par-

ish if that be what they mean that would be a Priviledge Beyond what we Can Conceive of and Must be Voters in both Parishes and if so they may be hurtfull to the First Parish in Opposeing the Parish in Supporting the Minister in case they ware able or thereby Lay Burdings on the Parish when they paid no part of it themselves —
Therefore your Respondants Pray that if the Petitionrs must be set off they may not remaine Voters in the First Parish Your Respondants would observe that the Petitioners all that ware Voters Except two viz[t] William Tompson & Joshua Small acted and Voted as freely in Calling and Settleing M[r.] Peirce as any in the Parish and it seems Strange to us they should have the face to ask to be freed from Supporting him Several of the Petitioners are Tenants and have no Estates in the Parish nor no where Else that we know of and others of them only Single Poles But in the whole we are but a Small Parish when altogather and if part be Set off we know not how the rest Can Support A minister at all —

Therefore your Respondants Pray your Excellency and Honours to take this our Answer under your Wise Consideration and Dismiss their Petition and your Respondants as in Duty Bound Shall Ever Pray &c

Sam[ll] Small
Reuben Fogg
Solomon Bragdon
} Committe of the First Parish in Scarborough

Petition of Proprietors of Cox Hall. 1765.

To his Excellency Francis Barnard Esq[r] Captain General and Governour in and over his Majestys Province of the Massachusetts Bay and To the Honourable his Majestys

Council and House of Representatives in General Court assembled the Twenty ninth Day of May 1765 Humbly Shew

The Proprietors of a Tract of Land in the County of York called Cox Hall about Four Miles wide & Six Miles long being Forty two (in Number) viz Benjamin Jones Ebenezer Ellingwood Michael Farley Wm Bakers Heirs John and Thomas Masten John Low Samuel Harris Benjamin Cleaves Junr Joshua Cleaves John Chipman Stephen Whipples Heirs Francis Goodhue John Kinsman John Baker Nathanel Conant Jacob Brown, Wiglesworth & Tupper John Jones Dodge John Fellows Nathan Smith Richard Walker Heirs, William Brown Nathan Brown Junr John Higginson Daniel Standifords Heirs Jonathan Low Nathl Low David Heirs Robert Lords Heirs Wm Jones And^w Woodbury John Harris Ichabod Woodman Jacob Toppans Heirs Abraham Tilton Francis Burnum Samuel Brown Moses Titcomb & Jacob Thorndike

That they are Extreamly desirous of brining forward a Settlement of said Tract that it may be beneficial to the Community but upon a Carful View of it find a Great part of it so barren and Rocky That it is almost useless for Most Purposes And They find that they shall be unable to Compass their Ends unless they can have some other Lands Annexed thereto And Inasmuch as there is a Tract of Province Lands about Two Miles wide adjoining to the North West side of said Tract not within the bounds of any Town or Place Your Petitioners Humbly pray That your Excellency and Honours in order to help forward the purposes aforesaid Will be pleas^d to Grant or Sel_ to Your Petitioners the said Tract of Province Land to be equally divided among them in Forty Two shares over and above those Shares Which your Excellency & Honours shall please to be ordered to be Reserved for Publick Uses They also pray That your Excellency & Honours Will place your Pet^rs under such

Regulations as will compel them to bring on a Speedy Settlement of said Lands—

And whereas Divers of Your Petitioners viz Benjamin Jones David Titcomb John Thorndike Samuel Harris John Low Moses Titcomb And^w Woodbury Stephen Whipples Heirs John Harris Daniel Standifords Heirs Abraham Tilton Thomas Masten John Chipman Nathl Conant John Kinsman John Jones & Nathan Brown & Michael Farley hold Rights in said Tract which were sold at Vendue for the Nonpayment of Taxes Assessed on them Legally to pay for the Division of the same but it so happened that those Rights were divided & Drawn before such sale so that a Doubt hath Arisen whether such sale be Legal Your Petitioners further pray that your Excellency & Honours would be pleasd to Confirm to your Petitioners that hold as last mentioned the Land so purchased as aforesaid in as full and Ample manner as if such Rights had not been Divided and Drawn as aforesaid before their sale And Your Petitioners as in Duty bound shall ever pray

In the Name & by order of the Prop^rs

John Chipman
John Baker

At a Meeting Lawfully warned and held in Falmouth on the 10th Day of June 1765 By the proprietors of the township N° 6. Laid out to the Eastward of mount Desert River and in their 2^d Article Voted that there be a Petition Provided to send to the General Court to pray the Court to Renew the Grant of the township. also to give the Proprietors Power to sell those Proprietors Rights that have not Paid their part of the charges that has arisen or to Direct us what we shall do and that Daniel Merritt be the Person to Provide the Petition in Behalf of the Proprietors

Daniel Merritt } Clerk to s[d] Proprietors

At a meeting Lawfully Warned held in Falmouth on the 11th day of June 1765 By the Proprietors of the township N° 5 Laid out to the Eastward of Mount Desert River and in thier 2[d] article Voted that thier be a petition Provided to send to the General Court to pray the Court to Renew the Grants of the township also to Give the proprietors power to Sell those Proprietors Rights that have not paid thier part of The Charges that has Arisen or to Direct us what we shall do and that Sam[ll] Webb be the Person to Provide the Petition in Behalf of the Proprietors

Sam[ll] Webb } Clerk to said proprietors

At a meeting lawfully warn'd & held in falmouth on the 11th day of June 1765 By the Proprietors of the township No 4 Laid out to the eastward of mount desert River and in their 2[d] Article Voted that there be a Petition provided to send to the general Court, to pray the court to Renew the Grants of the township; also to give the proprietors power to sell those proprietors Rights that have not paid their part of charges that has arisen or to direct us what we shall do; & that Peter Woodbery be the Person to Provide the petition in Behalf of the proprietors —

Peter Woodbary } Clerk to s[d] proprietors

Petition. 1765.

Province of the Massachusetts Bay

To His Excellency Francis Barnard Esq[r] Governor in Chief in & over his Majesties Province of the Massachusetts

Bay and Vice Admiral of the same; and the Honourable his majesties Council and house of Representatives in General Court Assembled 1765

The Petition of the Proprietors of the townships Number four: five & six Laid out to the Eastward of mount desert or Union River.—

Whereas it Pleased your Excellency and Honours in Council in January the 27th 1764 to Grant unto us the three above mentioned townships which we Humbly thank your Excelcency & Honours for: and as your Excellency and honours was Pleased to give your Petitioners Eighteen months time to get his majesties approbation; and if we did not obtain the same (in that time); then those grants to be Void &c; and the time being almost Expired & your Petitioners has not obtained his majesties approbation your Petitioners Prays your Excellency and Honours to grant us some longer time to get his majesties approbation, on those grants.— Also your Petitioners Desires to acquaint your Excellency & honours that there has been several Dollars Laid on each Right to defrey the Charges for surveying &c and a great part of the proprietors has Neglected to Pay their Part of the charges; & we Cannot find any means to oblige them to pay. your petitioners Prays your Excellency & honours to Grant to us Liberty to Sell the Rights of those that neglect to Pay their part of the charges Laid on each Right: or direct us what we shall do in that case so that we may Recover the money that is due: to Pay our just Debts.—

And your Petitioners as in Duty Bound Shall ever Pray —

Peter Woodbary in Behalf of N° four
Saml[l] Webb in Behalf of N° five
Daniel Merritt in Behalf of N° six

Falmouth June the 12th 1765

Act of Incorporation. 1765.

Anno Regni Regis Georgii Tertii Quinto

An Act for erecting a Town in the County of Lincoln by the Name of

Whereas the Inhabitants of a Tract of Land on the Eastern Side of Damariscotty River, in the County of Lincoln known by the Name of Walpole, Herrington and Pemaquid, so called, have petitioned this Court, that for the Reasons mentioned they may be incorporated into a Town, and vested with the Powers and Priviledges belonging to other Towns:

For the Encouragement of said Settlement, Be it enacted by the Governor, Council and House of Representatives, That the said Tract of Land described and bounded as follows; Viz[t] Beginning at a Heap of Stones at the Head of Brown's Cove, near the great Salt water Falls in Damariscotta River, on the Eastern Side of the said River, running a Southeasterly Course to a Heap of Stones at a Place called Round Pond, five Miles and an Half; from thence to run a Southwesterly Course to Pemaquid Point as the Shore lies: and from Pemaquid Point as the Shore lies up Damariscotta River to the first mentioned Bounds. And also all the Islands lying within Six Miles from the Main Land to the South, between the Afore Mentioned River Damariscotta and Pemaquid point, be and hereby is erected into a Town by the Name of

and the Inhabitants thereof shall have and enjoy all such Immunities and Priviledges as other Towns in this Province have, and do by Law enjoy.

And be it further enacted, That Thomas Rice Esq[r] be and hereby is empowered to issue his Warrant to some principal Inhabitant of the said Town of

requiring him in his Majesty's Name to warn and notify the said Inhabitants, qualified to vote in Town Affairs, to meet together at such Time and Place in said Town as shall be appointed in said Warrant, to chuse such Officers as the Law directs, and may be necessary to manage the Affairs of said Town, and the Inhabitants so met shall be, and hereby are empowered to chuse such Officers accordingly.

In the House of Rep[ves] June 14 1765

Read a first time 14 a second and third time and passd to be engross'd

Sent up for concurrence S: White Spk[r]

In Council 16. June 1765 Read a first time Read a second time and passed a concurrence to be engrossed

A Oliver Sec[r]

Message. June 18, 1765.

Gentlemen of the House of Representatives

I have laid before me the Establishments which have been made by You for Castle William, Fort Pownall and Fort Halifax; and find them so inadequate to their purposes that I can by no means consent to them. I must therefore desire that You will continue the present Garisons until I can apply to his Majesty for Orders for garrisoning the Same; it being my determined Resolution not to make myself answerable for the Consequences of an improvident Reduction of Garrisons so as to leave fortified Posts indefensible

Fra Bernard

Council Chamber June 18th 1765

Act, erecting Second Parish of Falmouth into a District. 1765.

Anno Regni Regis Georgii Tertii Sexto

An Act for erecting the second Parish of Falmouth in the County of Cumberland into a District by the Name of

Whereas the second Parish of Falmouth in the County of Cumberland, labour under many and great Difficulties by Reason of their not being erected into a distinct and separate District: Wherefore,

Be it enacted by the Governor Council & House of Representatives, That the said second Parish of Falmouth, lying and being on the South Side of Fore River in Falmouth, running up said River towards Stroudwater River, until it comes within half a Mile of the Mouth or Entrance of said Stroudwater River; and thence on a due West Course, or Line, across to Scarborough Line, be, and is hereby incorporated into a District, by the Name of
and that the said District be, and hereby is invested with all the Priviledges, Powers and Immunities that Towns in this Province by Law, do or may enjoy, that of sending a Representative to the General Assembly, only excepted: And that the Inhabitants of said District, shall have Liberty, from Time to Time to join with the Town of Falmouth in the Choice of a Representative or Representatives, and that the Selectmen of the Town of Falmouth give seasonable notice to the Inhabitants of s[d] District of the time & place for the choice of such Representative or Representatives which Representatives may be chosen indifferently from said Town or District

And be it further enacted, That Samuel Waldo Esq[r] be, and hereby is directed and empowered to issue a Warrant, directed to some principal Inhabitant within said District, requiring him to warn the Inhabitants of said District, qualified to vote in Town Affairs, to assemble at some suitable Time and Place in said District, to chuse such Officers as are necessary to manage the Affairs of said District.

Provided nevertheless, The Inhabitants of said District of shall pay their proportionable Part of all such Town, County and Province Charges as are already assessed, in like Manner as tho' this Act had not been made.

In Council June 20 1765. Read a first time P. M. Read a second time and passed to be engrossed

A Oliver Sec[r]

In the House of Rep[ves] June 21 1765

Read and referd bill next Session for consideration.

Sent up for concurrence S: White Spk[r]

In Council June 25, 1765 Read and Concurred

A Oliver Sec[r]

Resolve. 1765.

In the House of Represent[ves] June 24 1765

On the Petition of the hon[ble] James Otis Esq[r] and M[r] Nathaniel Gorham, in behalf of themselves and the rest of the Heirs and Assigns of Cap[t] John Gorham and Others, to whom was granted a Township of six Miles Square, in consideration of their Sufferings and Services in the Expedition against Canada in 1690; which Township (a small Part only excepted fell within the Government of New Hampshire, on running the Line between this Province and New Hampshire, and the Part excepted remained in this Province, for which they have received no Consideration, excepting eight Shares which was purchased by the late Colonel Blanchard of some of the Grantees & for which he the said Blanchard, as it is apprehended received a Consideration from the Province of New Hampshire, and is therefore excluded.

Resolved, that in Lieu thereof there be granted to the Proprietors, and legal Representatives or Assigns of said Cap[t] John Gorham and his Company, excepting the eight Shares aforesaid; and in Lieu of those eight Shares there be admitted the following Persons who have lost their Rights by the runing of the Line in other Townships — be and are placed by the Committee in this Township, which is to consist of seven Miles Square, Viz[t] W[m] Blair Townsend Esq[r] in the Right of Capt Moseley; the Reverend Mr Hull Abbot in the Right of Richard Way; Deacon Jonathan Williams in the Right of his Father Jonathan Williams; John Williams in the Right of Caleb Stedman, one Share each, all in Narragansett Number Five; James Prescot and Others, the Heirs of Benjamin Prescot, Esqr for two Shares in a Township called Suncook; Nathaniel Parker for one Share lost in said Suncook in the original Right of Benjamin Parker; and to the said Nathaniel Parker in the Right of Joseph Lakin for a Share of Land in a Town called Tyngs Town; which with the publick Lotts make the Complement of sixty four Shares, in the unappropriated Lands belonging to this Province.

Provided, That the Grantees within six Years settle Thirty Families in said Town, build a Meeting House, and settle a Learned Protestant Minister, and lay out one sixty fourth Part of said Town for the Use of the first settled Minister, and one other sixty fourth Part for the Ministry, and one other sixty fourth Part for a Grammar School, and one sixty fourth Part for the Use of Harvard College.

Provided also, That the said Township be laid out on such Part of the unappropriated Lands belonging to this Province, adjoining to some former Grants to the Eastward of Saco River; and that they return a Plan thereof into the Secretary's Office within twelve Months from this Day for Confirmation.

Sent up for concurrence S White Spk^r

In Council June 25th 1765 Read & Concurred

A Oliver Sec^r

Consented to Fra Bernard

Grant to Saml Gerrish & others 1765.

In the House of Rep^ves June 24 1765

On the Petition of Samuel Gerrish Esqr on behalf of the Proprietors of a Township of the Contents of six Miles Square granted to the Officers and Soldiers of the Companies under the Command of Capt John March Capt Stephen Greenleaf and Capt Philip Nelson commonly known by the name of Baker's Town, who were in the Expedition against Canada in 1690; that the whole of said Township fell within the Limits of New Hampshire, on the runing the Line between this Province and New Hampshire; for which the Grantees have received no Consideration, either from this Province, or the said Government of New Hampshire.

Resolved, That in Lieu thereof, there be granted to the Petitioner, and the legal Representatives or Assigns of the Original Grantees, a Township of the Contents of seven and an half Miles Square in the unappropriated Lands belonging to this Province

Provided, That the Grantees within six Years settle Thirty Families in said Town, build a House for public Worship and settle a Learned Protestant Minister, and lay out one Sixty fourth Part of said Town for the Use of the first settled Minister, and one other sixty fourth Part for the Ministry, and one other sixty fourth Part for a Grammar School, and one sixty fourth Part for the Use of Harvard College:

Provided also, That the said Township be laid out on such a Part of the unappropriated Lands belonging to this Province, adjoining to some former Grants to the Eastward of Saco River; and that they return a Plan thereof into the Secretary's Office within twelve Months from this Day for Confirmation.

Sent up for concurrence S: White Spk^r^

In Council June 25th 1765. Read & Concurred

A Oliver Sec^r^

Consented to Fra Bernard

We Whose Names are Subscribed Being Agents for the Grantees before Mentioned Duly Autherised Do promais **And**

Engage that if the afores[d] Grant shall be Confirmed We the Grantees Will Settle Ninety families on the said Township Including the Thirty Mentioned in the said Grant

Jonathan Bagly } Agents
Moses Little }

Grant to Joseph Sylvester & Company. 1765.

In the House of Representatives June 24 1765

On the Petition of James Warren and Joseph Josslyn Esq[rs] and M[r] Charles Turner, Agents for the Proprietors of a Township granted to Cap[t] Joseph Sylvester and Company who served in the Expedition against Canada in 1690; which Township was known by the Name of Sylvester Canada; and that the whole of said Township (on runing the Line between this Province and New Hampshire) fell within the Government of New Hampshire.

Resolved, That in Lieu thereof there be granted to the Proprietors, and the legal Representatives or Assigns of the said Joseph Sylvester & Company a Township of the Contents of seven Miles Square in the unappropriated Lands belonging to this Province.

Provided, That the Grantees within six Years settle thirty Families in said Town, build a house for public Worship, and settle a Learned Protestant Minister, and lay out one sixty fourth Part of said Town for the Use of the first settled Minister, and one other sixty fourth Part for the Ministry, and one other sixty fourth Part for a Grammar School, and one sixty fourth Part for the Use of Harvard College.

Provided also, That the said Township be laid out on such a Part of the unappropriated Lands belonging to this Province, adjoining to some former Grants to the Eastward of Saco River, and that they return a Plan thereof into the Secretary's Office within twelve months from this Day for Confirmation.

Sent up for concurrence S. White Spk[r]

In Council June 25th 1765 Read & Concurred

Consented to Fra Bernard

We whose names are subscribed being Agents for the Grantees before mentioned duly authorized, do promise & engage that if the aforesaid Grant shall be Confirmed, We will Settle Eighty one Families on the said Township including the Thirty mentioned in the said Grant.

for myself & as agent for James Warren Esq[r] and Charles Turner

Joseph Josselyn

Resolve. 1765.

In the House of Representatives June 24, 1765.

On the Petition of the Agents of the Proprietors of a Township granted to Cap[t] Will[m] Raymond and others who served in the Expedition against Canada in 1690 which Township (on running the Line between this Province and New Hampshire fell within the Government of New Hampshire

Resolved that in Lieu thereof there be granted to the Petitioners, and the legal Representatives or Assigns of the said William Raymond a Township of the Contents of Six Miles and three quarters of a Mile Square, in the unappropriated Lands belonging to this Province.

Provided that the Grantees within six Years settle thirty Families in said Town build a House for Public Worship settle a learned Protestant Minister, and lay out one sixty fourth part of said Town for the use of the first Settled Minister, and one other sixty fourth part for the Ministry, and one other sixty fourth part for a Grammar School, & one sixty fourth part for the use of Harvard College.

Provided also, that the said Township be laid out on such a part of the unappropriated Lands belonging to this Province adjoining to some former Grants to the Eastward of Saco River, and that they return a plan thereof into the Secretarys Office within twelve Months from this day for Confirmation

Sent up for concurrence S White Spk[r]

In Council June 25th 1765 Read & Concurred
A Oliver Sec[r]

Consented to Fra Bernard

We whose names are subscribed being Agents for the Grantees before mentioned duly authorized do promise and engage that if the aforesaid Grant shall be confirmed, we will Settle Seventy four Families on the said Township including the Thirty mentioned in the said Grant.

John Chipman
Tho: Porter

Order. 1765.

In Council June 25, 1765 —

Whereas divers Grants of Townships have this day passed the General Court to be laid out upon Province Lands to the Eastward of Saco River; and Plans of said Grants to be returned to the said Court within twelve months for Confirmation.

Ordered That the said Grantees, besides particular plans of their respective Grants shall exhibit to the General Court a Plan of the whole Tract within which the said Grants shall be laid out; and thereon delineate the said Grants together with the Lines of those Towns which may lye within the said Tract.

Sent down for Concurrence A Oliver Sec^r

In the House of Rep^ves June 25 1765

Read and concur'd S. White Spk^r

Letter, Mr. Nathl Noyes to Mr. Wm Tompson.

Mr Willm Tompson

S^r

Upon your desire to me to manifest Whether it was or was not any matter of discouragement with me to my setling in the work of the Ministry in the Parish at Black point I Answer —

I remember, that it then appeared to me, so many of the People where zealiously Set for Mr Clark, that it was attended with real difficulties for any Man to Settle in the Ministry at that place — & the division & disputes concerning Ministerial Communion with Mr Clark, would have been a great & I think, I may say a sufficient reason with me to give my Answer to ye people invitation for my Setling with them in the Negative, If I had no other reason — & I do not remember that any Gentl^n enjoined it upon me as a term of Settlement, that I should not have Ministerial Communion with Mr Clark, but they would leave their Minister to act as prudence should direct — these S^r

from yours Nath^el Noyes

North hampton July 19, 1765

Petition of Selectmen of Boothbay. 1765.

Province of the Massachusetts Bay in New England

To His Excellency Francis Barnard Esqr Governor in Chief, the Honble the Councill & House of Representatives in General Court Assembled,

The petition of the Select Men of the Town of Boothbay in the County of Lincoln Humbly Sheweth,

That the Inhabitants of said Town soon after Their Incorporation by Virtue of a Special Order of this Court Assembled, & Chose Town Officers In February last. that they Imagined the Officers so chosen might serve a Year Insuing & so Neglected to Chuse Officers in March following. That the Officers so Chosen have Acted in their several Capacities Rates have been Made a Meeting House is Contracted for, & in Building, and all this before Your Petitioners & the Other Inhabitants were sensible of their Mistake & that they Had not Complyed with the Letter of the Law, so that without the aid of Your Excellency & Honours the Town must be Greatly Distressed thereby & all Publick Business Cease.

Your Petitioners Therefore Humbly pray that the Town Officers so chosen in the Month of February may be Declared to be the Officers of said Town untill new ones shall be Chose in March 1766 & that all the Doings of the Officers so chosen in February shall be as Valid and Effectual as if they had been Chosen in March, or that Your Petitioners may be Other wise Releaved as you in your Wisdom shall seem Meet. & as in Duty bound shall ever pray &c

Boothbay 3d September 1765

Ephraim Mcfarland
John Beath
Jno Alley
} Selectmen

We the Subscribers being Inhabitants of the Said Town of Boothbay do Acquise in the Petition of the within Mentioned Select Men of said Town

David Reed	Paul Reed	Joseph Beath
Joseph Reed	Andrew Reed	Samuel Adams
Thomas Boyd	Thomas Reed	Willem mcCoob
Joseph Crosby	Samuel mcCoob	Willem Mour
John Willey	Ebeneser Smith	Joseph
Samuel Berto	Samuel Mountgomery	John Reed

In the House of Representatives Octr 24: A. D. 1765

Resolved that the Prayer of the foregoing Petition be so far Granted that the several Town officers Chosen in February last as mentioned in said Petition, and their Proceedings in Consequence of their Respective offices for the time Past be held good and vallid to all Intents & Purposes as much as tho they had been Chosen in the month of march last & that said officers retain their respective offices and Excersice the same in said Town untill others shall be Chosen in their room to ye respective town offices in ye month of march next any thing in ye Law to ye Contrary notwithstanding —

Sent up for concurrence S: White Spk^r

In Council Octr 25. 1765 Read and Concurred,

A Oliver Sec^r

Consented to Fra Bernard

Petition of Henry Young Brown. 1765.

Province of the Massachusetts Bay

To His Excellency Francis Bernard Esqr Governor and Commander in Chief of said Province, To the Honble His Majestys Council and House of Representatives in General Court Assembled October 1765 —

The Petition of Henry Young Brown Humbly Sheweth —

That Your Petitioner In Consequence of a Grant of the General Court Dated the 23^d of January A D 1764 Laid out a Township on Each side of Saco River above Colonel Joseph Frye's Town and return'd a Plan of the same to the Court for Acceptance which was Accepted and the Land contained therein was Confirmed to your Petitioner on Certain Conditions as by said Grant & Confirmation will more fully appear

That your said Petitioner has exerted Himself to the utmost of his ability in bringing forward the Settlement of said Township, has been at the Expence of Clearing Land, of

Building a House & Barn for himself, and has moved with his Family into said Town and got Several other Families therein, and was going to Compleat the Settlement of s[d] Township agreeable to the Grant, But is now Interrupted by one Daniel Foster & others who appear as Grantees of a Township Granted them By his Excellency Governour Wentworth, which they have laid out (as they say) upon the line between the Province of New Hampshire and the Province of Main, by which they have taken off the greatest part of the Township your said Petitioner has began the settlement of. And as your said Pet[r] used his best endeavour to avoid runing into the said Province of New Hampshire and really thinks, that if the line was Rightly Ascertained the Township will very little if any part of it fall within that Province he is at loss what to do without the aid of this Court. Therefore Humbly Prays your Excellency & Honours would take his Case under Consideration and Grant Him such Releif with regard to the Premises as your Excc[y] & Honours shall think Proper and as in Duty bound will ever Pray —

Henry Young Brown

In the House of Rep[ves] Oct[r] 29 1765

Read and Ordered that Col[o] Powell Col[o] Saltonstall Col[o] Gerrish Cap Gowen and M[r] Sayward with such as the Hon[ble] Board shall Joyn be a Comm[ee] to take this Pet[n] under consideration and report

Sent up for concurrence S: White Spk[r]

In Council Oct[r] 29 1765 Read and Concurred and Benj[a] Lincoln, Will[m] Brattle Gam[l] Bradford Nath[l] Sparhawk and John Bradbury Esq[rs] are joined in the affair.

A Oliver Sec[r]

Petition of Inhab[ts] of Pownalborough. 1765.

Province of the Massachusetts Bay

To his Excellency Francis Bernard, Esquire, Governor &c.

the Honorable his Majestys Council & house of Representatives, in General Court Assembled — Octobr 31, 1765 —

The petition of a Number of the Inhabitants of the Town of Pownalborough, in the County of Lincoln, inhabiting part on the East & part on the West side of said Town, humbly sheweth,

That the said Town is of very large Extent, situated between the two Rivers of Kennebeck and Sheepscutt, Bounded Westerly on the former and Easterly on the latter That the Inhabitants of said Town, consisting of near two hundred families, are cheifly settled upon the aforesaid Rivers, nearly equal in Number upon each river, by reason whereof there remains a large Tract of Land between the Inhabitants settled upon the Rivers as aforesaid, a perfect Wilderness extending from the North to the South Lines of said Town & near five miles wide: & no prospect of its being settled for many years to come — That, the said Town being situated and the Inhabitants settled in manner aforesaid, it is impossible for them to attend Publick Worship together on either side of said Town; to settle a Minister or transact any business relative thereto in Concert.— That it it very inconvenient, expensive & difficult for the Inhabitants upon both sides to attend the Annual Town Meetings in March, and frequently impossible, The distance, for the Inhabitants of one side or the other, being Ten miles, to travel; and at a Season when the Snow thro' the Wilderness between the aforesaid Rivers, is generally very deep, and but very little travell in the Winter season, By reason whereof the Inhabitants of one side of the Town are of necessity deprived of attending said Meetings & of giving their Voice in any Affairs of the Town, while the Inhabitants of the other side of the Town have it in their power to impose unreasonable Taxes upon the whole, for their Benefit without any Regard to the

Interest of the whole, & only by the voice of a far less Number than the Major Part of the whole; which has already greatly disturbed the peace and good Order of the said Town & Greatly tends to involve them in many Difficulties and to bring them into the greatest disorder & Confusion —

Wherefore to remedy the great Inconveniences & difficulties The Inhabitants labour under, especially in transacting the Business of the Town, and in making suitable Provision for the publick Worship of God amongst us We humbly beg your Excellency and Honors that we may be divided into two Towns by a line running from the South to the North line of said Town near the Center; so as Each Town may have an Equall number of Acres, which Division, we Apprehend the Situation of the Town & the Number of Inhabitants, will admit of & which will be very much for the Interest of the whole, And your Petitioners as in Duty bound, shall ever pray &c —

John Small	Philip Call	G
James Cooper	Dennis his X marks Lines	Moses hilton
Elisha House	Asa Smith	Christopher Erskin
David Nellson	Joseph Carleton	Moses Carleton
Samuel Ball	J	J
Richard Kidder	Jean George Goud	George Mayer
Abiathar Kendall	Jorge Pocherd	Jaques Bugnor
Jonas Fitch	Roger Chase	Edr Bridge
George Lierce	Ezra D	John Spaldin
Willard Spalding	Abner Marson	John Andrews
John Lindsy	Timothy Whidden	Robert Reed
John Noble	James Scott	John Stain Juner
Michel S	Jaque Goud	Stephen Marson
Josiah Davis	Chas Cushing	Jona Bowman
Samuel Goodwin	Samll Goodwin Jnr	Adino Nye
Abiel Lovejoy	Thos Allen	Obadiah Call

Philip Call	John his X mark Cavilear	Jean George Pechin
Mark his X mark Carney	Samuel Emerson	Carr Barker
Davi^{d} C	Lazarus his X mark G	Samuel White
William Wyman	Charles Estienne Houdelette	Daniel goud
John Barker Junr	John S	John his X marke ^{mc}Gown
his X marke Holland	John his X mark	John Mirick
Goerge goud junior	Ralph Chapman	Joseph Cleaveland
Seth Soper	Seth grele	Thomas Dinsmore
Thomas White	James Patterson	Stephen Goodwin
Wm Cushing	Uzziah Kendall	Jon^{a} Bryant
John Herin	Charles Callahan	Samuel Reed
James Meilbon	Abram Pochard	Peter Pouchard
Danel		

House of Rep^{tives} 31 Jany 1766

Ordered, That the Petitioners give Notice to the non Petitioners of the Town of Pownalborough of this Petition, by serving each Select man of s^{d} Town with a Copy of s^{d} Petition and the Order of this Court thereon and by posting up a Copy of the Same at each House of publick Worship in s^{d} Town, that they may shew Cause (if any they have) on the second Wednesday of the next May Sessions of the General Court why the Prayer of s^{d} Petition should not be granted

Sent up for concurrence S: White Spk^{r}

In Council Feb^{ry} 1, 1766 Read and Concurred

A Oliver Sec^{r}

In Council June 6th 1766 — Read again together with the Answers thereto, & Ordered that Royall Tyler & Jeremy Powell Esq^{rs} with such as the hon^{ble} House shall joine be a Comm^{e} to take s^{d} Pet^{n} & Answers thereto, hear the Parties & report

Sent down for Concurrence Jno Cotton D. Secry

In the House of representatives June 6 1766

Read & concurrd & M[r] Spooner M[r] Johnson & M[r] Dexter are joynd in the Affair

T Cushing Spk[r]

In the house of rep[s] June 16, 1766

Ordered that M[r] Dudley be on this Committee in the room of M[r] Johnson absent

Sent up for Concurrence T Cushing Spk[r]

Power of Attorney. 1766.

Know all Men by these presents That we the Subscribers Inhabitants of a place called Machias in the Province of the Massachusetts Bay Have And by these presents do Nominate Constitute Ordain and make and in our place and Stead put our Trusty friend Cap[t] Ichabod Jones of Boston in the province aforesaid to be our and each of our true Sufficient and Lawfull Agent and Attorney for us and in our names to appear at and before the Great and General Court or Assembly of the Province aforesaid at their next Session or at any other Session, and there present our petition for a Grant of a Tract of land called Machias to be made to us And also for our being Incorporated into a Town or Vested with priviledges equal thereto, And to sollicit by all lawfull ways and means that the prayer of our said petition may be granted; and We do hereby Give and Grant unto our said Attorney full Power and Authority to sign in our Names, any other Petition and in our behalf present the same to the said Great and General Court as he shall think Necessary for the Obtaining a Grant of the Tract of land aforesaid, and for having the same Incorporated Hereby giving and granting unto our said attorney our full and whole Strength power and authority in and about the premises with full power to Substitute one or more Attorney or Attorneys under him our said Attorney and the same again at pleasure to revoke; And Generally in and concerning the premisses with the dependences thereof to do say and Execute and cause to be done and Executed all and whatsoever We the Constituants might or could do or cause to be done if we were then and there personally present Hereby promising to Allow approve and hold Valid and good all and whatsoever our said Attorney or his Substitutes shall Lawfully do or cause to be done in the premisses by Virtue of these presents In Witness whereof We have hereunto set our hands and seals Att Machias the 26th day of July Anno Dom: One Thousand Seven hundred and Sixty six, And in the Sixth Year of his Majesty's Reign —

Signed Sealed & Deliv^{d} in the presence of

Benj^{a} Foster in Behalf of Jacob Foster Amos Boynton
Stephen Jones **X** John Scott Jonathan Longfellow
X Wesbruck Berre in the behalf of Jo^{n} Berri George Sevey
David Libby Joseph **X** Getchel Georg Libby Ju^{n}
X Japeth Hill in Behalf of Sam hill Morris Obrian
Jonathan Carlton Nathan Longfellow Jonathan Carlton Junr
Archelaus Hammond in Behalf of Elijah Bent Samuel Lebbee
Thomas Buck Jacob Lebbee Thos Buck Ju^{r}
Joseph Munson in Behalf of Step^{n} Munson John Manchestere
Joseph Dubuisont John Underwood Benj^{a} Foster Jur
Daniel Stone In Behalf of John Stone Archelaus Hammond
Joseph Sevey Joseph Munson Gideon Obrian
X Wooden Foster Jr for Behalf of John Woodon Foster
X John Knight Jonathan Woodruffe **X** Josiah Libby
Wesbruck Berre Ebenezer Libby In Behalf of **X** Josiah Libby
Daniel Stone Obediah Hill John Stone
X Wm Martin Ebenezer Libby Daniel Stone in Behalf of Solomon Stone Samuel Holmes Reuben Libby
Eleazer his **X** mark Bryant **X** Joseph Libby Sarah her **X** mark Libby Widow
Samuel Davis Bryant Thaddeus Trafton in Behalf of John

Crocker	Daniel Stone in Behalf Gorge Libby	
X Japeth Hill	X John his X mark Beers in Behalf of Jethro	
Timoth Libby	Sam[ll] Kenney	Jonathan Longfellow
in Behalf of Stephen Parker		X Ephraim Andrews
Wooden Foster	James Elliot	Abiel Sprague Jur

James Elliot Signed in Behalf of the three } Bengman Stone, Jeremiah Obrian, Joel Booney

John Wieland	Nath[ll] Davis	Abiel Sprague
Job Burnum	Reuben his X mark Crocker	Thaddeus Trafton
Morris OBrien	John his X mark Barre	Jones Dyer
Jeremiah Jeuks	Samuel Burnum	Daniel Longfellow Seal
Isaac Larrabee	Sarah Fogg	Nathaniel Young
Will[m] his X mark Kelly	Joshua Webster	Aaron Hanscom
Solomon Meserve	Joseph Holmes	Samuell Rich

Memorial of Earl of Catherlough & others. 1766.

To his Excellency Francis Bernard Esq[r] Governor the Hon[ble] the Council, and Hon[ble] House of Representatives of the Province of the Massachusetts Bay in general Court Assembled

The Memorial of Robert Earle of Catherlough Hugh Viscount Falmouth, and Florentius Vassall Esq[r] in behalf of themselves and several others Sheweth That his Majesty having exhorted and incouraged all his good Subjects to use the best means to people his Dominions in north America and having recommended To the Governors thereof to assist and promote in such good Purposes as far as in their Power

Your Memorialists being desireous to contribute their Services in a Work so necessary to the welfare and Security of Great Britain have joined themselves together with several Other Gentlemen to indevor to forward the same and considering that the Increase of the Wealth and Power of Great Britain must arise from the Augmenting the Number of its Subjects and Your Memorialists being informed that the Territories of the Massachusetts Bay laying eastward of Penobscott contain a large Tract of Land abundantly more than can Possibly for Ages to come be peopled except Persons of large Fortunes in Europe will be assisting in So laudable an Undertaking, They have determined to make the first Offer of their Services to the Province of the Massachusetts Bay

Therefore Your Memorialists propose to the General Court of the Province that if they will grant them that Tract of Land lying Twelve Miles on each side of the River Machias and to be continued the same distance from the River Fifty Miles into the Continent according to the Course of the said River or beyond the Head of it in the same Course together with all Islands laying in the Frontage of the said Tract according to the General Course of the Sea Shore thereof Your Memorialists and their Associates will engage to People the said Lands in such Manner and Time as may be thought Reasonable for so great an Undertaking and as shall be approved by our Agent Doct^{r} Silv. Gardiner

Catherlough Falmouth Flo. Vassall

(Indorsed)

Catherlough and others Jan 24 1766

Col^{o} Partridge Mr Lee Mr Otis

Mr Brown Salem Mr Cushing

Feby 4 1766 Allowed to be withdrawn.

Feb 20 1766 revived and referd till May Session.

Report.

The Committee to whom was referred the Petition of William Tompson and Others of the first Parish in Scarborough, have attended that Service, fully heard the Parties, and beg Leave to report as follows:

That from the first Settlement of the Colony of the Massachusetts Bay, for fourteen Years they had no Platform of Church Government, but the famous John Cotton's Book of the Keyes, wherein was contained Substance of the present Church Discipline in this Province, as much opposing the Form of the Presbyterian Government as possible: That A. D. 1646, It was agreed upon by the magistrates that a Synod should be called for composing and publishing a System or Platform of Church Government according to the Directions of Our Lord Jesus Christ in his blessed Word: That on the eighth of March A. D. 1649, a Platform of Church Discipline was agreed upon by the Elders and Messengers of the Churches then assembled in the Synod at Cambridge, and was accordingly presented to the Churches and General Court for their consideration and acceptance in the Lord, and was approved: Afterwards it was unanimously approved by another Synod, and by the General Assembly, who explicitly desired that the Churches might continue stedfast in the Order of the Gospel according to what is therein contained.— Upon this then established Form of Church Government, and this only, which is entirely Congregational were Laws made from time to time under the Old Charter, for the Support of the Congregational Ministers, and for procuring them suitable Habitations to dwell in, the Taxes to be raised by a Town Rate; and all of every Denomination paid to the Support of said Ministers in every Town in the Colony:— These were the Church Privileges, and these their Laws — all which were confirmed to the

Churches in the Province of the Massachusetts Bay under the present Charter; A.D. 1692 by Law and by King William and Queen Mary, Confirmation of the same; wherein it is expressly declared that the respective Churches in the several Towns within this Province, shall at all Times hereafter use, exercise and enjoy all their Privileges and Freedoms respecting divine Worship, Church Order and Discipline; and shall be encouraged in the peaceable and regular Possession and Practice thereof — All which Churches were Congregational — And in the same Act there is Provision made for the Support of said Ministers: Whereby it manifestly appears to your Committee, that there is not, or ever was either in the Colony or Province any Law obliging Congregationalists in any town or Precinct, to pay one Farthing to the Support of a Presbyterian Minister, and that there is no Law now subsisting, or ever was, whereby a Town or Precinct may tax the Inhabitants therefor, and that the Law ought to be so understood: So far from that was it, that Persons of every Denomination paid to the Congregational ministers, 'till within a few Years those of the Episcopal Denomination the Baptists and Quakers by express Acts of the General Court were exempt; and all that are of the Presbyterian Church at Newbury were under the like Obligation, 'till alike relieved by the General Court: All which your Committee humbly apprehend justifies their Opinion as aforesaid: The Committee are further of Opinion that when Baptists or Friends living in a Town where there is a Congregational Church, that they shall be exempted from the Support of the Congregational Ministry; And Yet that Congregationalists living in a Town where there is a Presbyterian Church Settled, shall be obliged to pay to the Support of the Minister thereof is against Law, against Reason and Practice immemorial; which if allowed directly repeals the Law before mentioned made 1692—and was furthest from the thought of the Legislators under the old Charter, or of those who so expressly confirmed their Acts relative to the Church Privileges and Freedom, respecting Church Order and Discipline under the new Charter.—Wherefore inasmuch as the Church in the first Parish in Scarborough is Presbyterian and consequently Seperates, the Minister a Presbyterian, ordained by the Presbytery in Newbury, against the explicit Desire and Remonstrance of fifteen of the first Parish in Scarborough, signified to said Presbytery in Writing under their Hands before Ordination; inasmuch as a Number in said Parish previous to the Ordination of Mr Peirce the Presbyterian Minister there, was imposed upon by being made to believe that there was no Difference between the Congregational and Presbyterian Forms of Church Government; and inasmuch as said first Parish by Law could not make any Tax or assessment upon the Inhabitants of said Parish, for defreying any charges arising, either for the Settlement or Support of said Presbyterian Minister there, it is the Opinion of the Committee that said Petitioners are not liable by Law to pay the Taxes assessed upon them for the support or Settlement of said Minister: And further that all such who in said Parish shall within three months from the acceptance of this Report, and the Order thereon signify their Desires in Writing, to be lodged in the Secretary's Office, to be set off to the second Parish in Scarborough as aforesaid, with their Estates lying in said first Parish in Scarborough, that they with their Estates as aforesaid, shall be annexed to, and made Part of the second Parish in said Scarborough, there to do Duty and receive Privilege in every Respect until the further Order of this Court, that of voting for the Removal of the Meeting House in said second Parish in Scarborough or building a new one in said second Parish only excepted in which they shall have no vote at all.

W Brattle by order

In Council Jany 29. 1766. Read and Accepted. And Unanimously

Resolved That the Petitioners are not by Law lyable to pay the Taxes assessed upon them for the Support or Settlement of Mr Peirce the Minister in s^d Petition Mentioned. And thereupon Ordered That all such of the s^d Parish who shall within three months signify their Desire in writing and lodge the same in the Secretary's Office, to be set off to the second Parish in Scarborough with their Estates lying in the first Parish in said Town; They with their Estates as afores^d shall be annexed to and made part of the second Parish in Scarborough, there to do duty & receive priviledge in every respect, until the further Order of this Court, that of voting for the removal of the Meeting House in said second Parish in Scarborough, or building a new one in said second Parish only excepted, in which they shall have no vote at all.

Sent down for Concurrence.

A Oliver Sec^y

In the House of Rep^ives Jany 30, 1766

Read and Non concur'd and Ordered that this Petition and Report be recommitted to the same Committee.

Sent down for concurrence.

S: White Spk^r

In Council Jany 31, 1766

Read & Concur'd

Jno Cotton D. Sec̃ry

Province of the Massachusetts Bay

In Council February 11th 1766

The two Houses according to Agreement proceeded to the choice of Civil officers for the present year, when Thomas Goldthwait Esqr was chosen Truckmaster for Fort Pownall and William Lithgow Esqr for Fort Halifax by a Major vote of the Council and House of Representatives

Attest A Oliver Secr

Consented to Fra Bernard

Letter, Andrew Oliver Secy to Gov. Wentworth

Boston 20 Febr 1766.

Sr

The General Court of this Province in their present Session have appointed a Committee to join with Such persons as may be appointed by your Government to run the Line between the Province of Maine & New Hampshire, and the two Houses have desired me to write to you upon the Subject. I have directed a Copy of the Resolve of the Court hereupon to be made out wch comes herewith inclosed.

This will be delivered you by Mr Bradbury one of his Maj. Council for this Province who is appointed to be one of the Comittee, and will be able to give your Excelly a further Explanation of the matter, if you shall think proper to make any Inquiry of him concerning it. I am

Petition of Inhab'ts of Boothbay. 1766.

Province of the Massachusetts Bay

To his Excellency Francis Bernard Esq[r] Governour & the Honorable his Majestys Council and house of Representatives in General Court Assembled March 4th 1766 —

The Petition of the Inhabitants of the Town of Boothbay in the County of Lincoln Humbly Sheweth

That Frankfort in the West side of Pownal in said County the place where the Courts of General Sessions of the Peace and Inferiour Courts of Common Pleas are now held is very near the Westren side of said County and quite remote from, by far the Greatest part of the Inhabitants of said County that there are but two or three Houses near said Place in which People who have Necessary business at said Court can have lodging and Entertainment so that a great part of the People during their necessary Attendance on said Courts are much distressed for Necessaries and are Oblidged to lodge on a floor or Barns or Sit all night by the fire during their whole stay at said Court — Wherefore your Petitioners humbly Pray Your Excellency & Honors that said Courts may be Removed to the Eastren Side of Pownalborough aforesaid which is much nearer the Center of said County both as to Land and Inhabitants and where those who have Business at said Courts may be sufficiently Provided for there being a Sufficient number of Houses there in which to Entertain and lodge them and for the Reasons aforesaid if Pownalborough should be divided into two Distinct Towns agreable to a Petition as we understand now before Your Excellancy and Honors for that Purpose We humbly Pray your Excellancy and Honors that what is now the Eastren side of Pownalborough may be made the Shire Town of said County it being a Place well Situated for the Courts to be held at —

And your Petitioners as in Duty bound shall ever Pray &c

Tho: Kenney	Cornelius	William M
John Alley	Joseph Giles	Samuel
Andrew R	Willm	Robert Wylie
Thos Reed	Reed	John Wiley
S	Nath:	John Death
T	J	David Reed
C	Reed	Joseph
Robert Wylie	Willm Wiley	N Wylie
Israel Davice	Benjeman	George Shearman
Joseph Crosby	John McC	Joseph
Joseph Barter	Samuel	Samll Barter
A Ford	Soln Pinkham	Pat: Magregor
John Alley Junr	Dl McCurdg	Jas Kennedy

Petition of Inhabts of Freetown. 1766.

Province of the Massachusets Bay

To His Excellency Francis Bernard Esqr Governour &c the Honble his Majestys Council and House of Representatives in General Conrt assembled March ye 9th 1766 —

The Petition of the Inhabitants of a Plantation called Freetown in the County of Lincoln Humbly Sheweth

That Frankfort in the West side of Pownalborough in said County the place where the Courts of General Sessions of the Peace and Inferiour Court of Common Pleas are now held is very near the westren side of said County and quite remote from, By far the greatest Part of the Inhabitants of said County and that there are but two or three Houses near said Place in Which People who have necessary business at said Court can have lodgings and Entertainment so that a great part of the People during their necessary attendance on said Courts are much distressed for Necessaries and are oblidged to lodge on a floor or in Barns or sit all night by the fire during the whole stay at said Court.

Wherefore Your Petitioners humbly Pray your Excellency & honors that said Courts may be run over to the Eastren Side of Pownalborough aforesaid which is much nearer the Center of said County both as to land and Inhabitants and where those who have Business at said Courts may be sufficiently provided for there being a sufficient Number of houses there in which to Entertain and lodge them and for the Reasons aforesaid if Pownalborough should be divided into two Distinct Towns agreeable to a Petition as we understand now before your Excellency and Honours that what is now the Eastren side of Pownalborough may be made the Shire Town of said County it being a Place well situated for the Courts to be held at and Your Petitioners as in duty bound shall ever Pray & &c

Solomon Trask	Samll Trask	Ebenezar Gove Junr
Nchem Herrinden	Thomas Trask	John Cuningham
Samll	Samuel Trask Junr	William Cliford
Nathan Gove	William Cliford junor	Abel Colby
David Trask	Jonathan Williamson	Jonathan Albee
William Cuningham	Stephen Barker	Nehemiah Haraden
james day	Ebenezer Gove	John Gray
Edmun Colby	Caleb	Solomon Baker
Hezekiah Herrenden	hery Colby	Benjamin Allbee
David his Y mark Torry	Lemuel	Asel Gove
John	James Thomas	A
Samuel chamberlain	Nathan Knight	Thomos ions
Benjamin Curtis	Temothy Dunton	Samuel Dunton

Timothy brown	John Knight	Wesbruck Knight
Joseph Trask	Joseph Dunton	Samuel Webber
Edmond hatch	Eleacer Sherman	Simon Pearl
John Laighton	Solomon Laighton	bengaman laighton
joseph brown	joseph m	nickles canady
bengaman day	Daniel carter	nathan Webster
jonathan day	james richards	dodeford richards
james chase		

In the House of Represetatives Nov[r] 3 1766 Read & Orderd that this Pet[n] be referrd for Consideration to the

(Indorsed) Oct 29 1766 read & ordered to lye

Nov[r] 4 referrd to

License to trade with Indians. 1766.

Whereas I Andrew Worth of Nantucket in the Province of Massachusetts Bay Mariner have applied to his Excellency Francis Bernard Esq[r] Governor of the Province aforesaid in pursuance of his Majestys Royal Proclamation for a License to Trade with the Indians on the Labrador Coast.

And Whereas by an Act of Assembly of the said Province whereby all persons are forbidden to Trade with the Indians in the s[d] Province, it is provided that the Governor of the Province may with the Advice of the Council grant unto any Person a License to Trade with the Indians under such Regulations, Limitations & restrictions as the s[d] Governor with the Advice of the Council shall determine. And Whereas the Council of the said Province hath Advised the said Governor to grant such License unto me; provided that I be restrained from Trading with the Norridgewalk or Penobscot

Indians, or any other Indians residing upon or frequenting the River Kennebec or penobscot or usually Trading with the provincial Truck houses established on the said Rivers.

I do hereby promise and Agree to conform to the said Restrictions and will observe such Regulations as his Majesty shall at any time think fit by himself or his Commissaries to direct and appoint for the benefit of the said Trade.

And I do likewise promise to pay to his Excellency Francis Bernard Esqr aforesaid the Sum of Two hundred pounds Sterling money of Great Britain, provided I do not comply with the Restrictions abovementioned.

Dated 2^d of April 1766 Andrew Worth

Signed in Presence of
Jno Cotton Fra^s Skinner

Instructions.

By his Excellency Francis Bernard Esqr Captain General and Governor in Chief in and over his Majestys Province of Massachusetts Bay in New England and Vice Admiral of the same —

Instructions to be observed by Andrew Worth Master of the Barrington bound for the Coast of Labrador

Having upon your application made to me for that purpose, granted you License to carry on a Trade with the Indians under his Majesty's protection for a term not exceeding one year from the date hereof; and you having given security in all things to conform to such Regulations as are or shall be prescribed to you by his Majesty or his Commissaries for the benefit of the said Trade; and also that you will not trade with the Norridgewalk or penobscot Indians or any other Indians residing on or frequenting the Rivers Kennebec or Penobscot, or usually trading with the provincial Truck houses established on the s^d Rivers.

You are to consider the forementioned Conditions of the security by you given as Instructions to you, for carrying on the said Indian Trade: And you are to treat such Indians with whom you deal or Trade, with that Justice, good Faith and kindness as may conciliate them to his Majesty's Government and serve to fix them in their Obedience and subjection to it.

Given at Boston the second day of April 1766 In the Sixth year of his Majesty's Reign.

Copy of my Instructions received from his Excel^y Governor Bernard

Andrew Worth

Memorial of S. Downe and M. Thornton. 1766.

Province of the Massachusets Bay

To His Excellency Francis Bernard Esq Governour & Commander in Cheif. The Honble His Majestys Council & Representatives of said Province in General Court assembled in Boston. May 28th 1766 —

The Memorial of Samuel Downe and Mathew Thornton in behalf of the Grantees of Six Townships in the Territorys of Sagadehock lately Granted to David Marsh, James Duncan,

Benjn Harrod, Edmund Morse John Wier & Peter Parker and others, whose names are in their respective Grants —

Humbly Sheweth —

That whereas by the Grants of their severall Townships made in February, 1763 it was Provided that in Case his Majesty should not in Eighteen months next coming approve of said Grants they should be null & void — and whereas upon application made to Your Excellency & Honors By Benjn Harrod in behalf of said Grantees, at the Expiration of said Term — Your Excellency & Honors were pleased to allow a further time of Eighteen months from 3^{d} Novr 1764 which Time being expired, and they not being able yet to Obtain his Majestys Approbation —

The said Grantees Beg leave to Acquaint Your Excellency & Honors that they have been at a still Greater Expence in Carrying on the Settlements of said Township, & likewise in their Application at Home for His Majestys Approbation, then when they presented their last memorial. & Having lately received a Letter from their Agent in England, signifying the great Encouragement he has received from the Ministry, whereby he Assures them of his hope for success on their behalf, and of his further Diligent Application to the board of Trade & others concerned in American Affairs. They therefore Humbly pray that they may have a further Time allow^{d} them for obtaining His Majestys Approbation,

Saml Downe
Mathew Thornton

In the House of Rep^{ves} June 6th 1766

Resolved That the Grantees of twelve Townships lying between the Rivers Penobscot and St Croix granted by this Court in March 1762 be allowed the further Term of Eighteen Months to obtain his Majesties Approbation of the Grants mentioned —

Sent up for Concurrence T Cushing Spk^{r}

In Council 9 June 1766 Read and Concurred —

A Oliver Sec[r]

Consented to

Petition of Henry Y. Brown 1766.

Province of Massachusetts Bay

To His Excell[y] Francis Bernard Esquire Governour & Commander in chief of said province to the Honb[le] His Majestys Council and House of Representatives in General Court Assembled this fourth day of June 1766

The Memorial of Henry Young Brown Humbly shews

That in consequence of purchase from the Province of a Township on Saco river, and the Resolves of the Great and General Court thereon Your Memorialist has been at great trouble & expence in order to bring forward the Settlement of the Town, notwithstanding which, he is now himself as likewise two of his settlers sued by persons claiming lands under the Governm[t] of New Hampshire, although said Lands lye on the easterly side of their claim.

Your memorialist therefore humbly prays Your Excell[y] and Hon[rs] would enable him to defend that part of said Lands which they think belong to this Province, as likewise to proscente any persons, who have, or may attempt to molest him for the future, and if it should be judg'd by this Hon[ble] Court that any of said lands do not belong to this province that he may have an equivalent therefor, in other lands belonging to the Province, or be otherways relieved as they in their wisdom shall think fit, and your memorialist as in duty bound shall ever pray.

Henry Young Brown

Nov 1st 1766

A Return and true Representation of the East side of the Town of Pownalboro' with Regard to the Number of Houses & Inhabitants &c taken in pursuance of an Order of the General Court June 19, 1766

Names of Families	No of Families	No Framed Houses Inhabited	No Logg Houses Inhabited	No one Story Houses	No 2 Story Houses	No Rooms with fire places	No Brick Chimneys	No Cellars Stoned	No squares of sash Glass in each House	No new Frames partly covered	No new Houses not finished so as to be inhabited	No of intended Rooms in each new house not partitioned off	No Persons under 16 years of Age	No Persons above 16 years of Age	Whole Number of Inhabitants	No of Males	No of Females	No small old Log Houses not inhabited
Moses Hilton	1	1	—	1	—	2	1	—	—	—	—	—	6	3	9	5	4	—
William Hilton	1	1	—	1	—	1	—	—	—	—	—	—	5	3	8	6	2	—
Joseph Hilton	1	1	—	1	—	1	—	—	—	—	—	—	—	2	2	1	1	—
Ephraim Grant	1	1	—	1	—	2	1	—	30	—	—	—	8	2	10	6	4	—
Gabriel Hamilton	1	1	—	1	—	1	—	—	—	—	—	—	2	2	4	1	3	—
[illegible]	1	—	1	1	—	1	—	—	15	—	—	—	3	2	5	1	4	—
John McKinney	1	—	—	—	—	—	—	—	—	—	—	—	1	2	3	2	1	—
Daniel McKinney	1	—	1	1	—	2	—	1	—	—	—	—	1	2	3	1	2	—
John [illegible]hel	1	—	1	1	—	1	1	—	—	—	—	—	2	2	4	2	2	—
Abraham Nason	1	1	—	1	—	1	—	—	—	—	—	—	3	2	5	1	4	—
Henry Kowman	1	1	—	1	—	2	—	—	—	—	—	—	1	3	4	3	1	—
Israel Honeywell	1	—	1	1	—	1	—	—	—	—	—	—	2	3	5	3	2	—
Benja Honeywell	1	—	—	—	—	—	—	—	—	—	—	—	—	2	2	1	1	—
John Honeywell	1	1	—	1	—	2	—	1	—	—	—	—	4	3	7	1	6	—
John Baker	1	—	1	1	—	2	1	1	—	—	1	2	2	5	7	3	4	—
Richard Bailey	1	—	1	1	—	1	—	—	12	—	—	—	1	3	4	2	2	—

John Plumer Junr	1	1	—	1	—	1	—	—	12	—	—	—	1	8	4	3	1	—
belonging to said Plumer	1	1	—	—	1	—	—	—	—	1	1	2	—	—	—	—	—	—
Christr Erskins	1	1	1	1	—	1	—	—	2	—	1 log	1	3	3	6	4	2	—
Moses Carlton	1	1	—	—	—	—	—	—	—	—	—	—	—	3	3	2	1	—
Peter Dow	1	1	—	1	—	2	1	—	40	—	—	—	2	2	4	3	1	—
Asa Smith	1	1	—	1	—	1	—	—	—	—	—	—	—x	2	2	1	1	—
Benja Dow	1	1	—	1	—	1	—	—	18	—	—	—	3	2	5	2	3	—
Stephen Haselton	1	—	1	1	—	1	—	—	—	—	—	—	2	3	5	3	2	—
Samll Hilton	1	—	1	1	—	1	—	—	—	—	—	—	3	2	5	4	1	1
Moses Gray	1	—	1	1	—	1	—	—	—	—	—	—	5	7	12	6	6	1
Israel Averell	1	1	—	1	—	1	1	—	21	—	—	—	3	6	9	5	4	—
James Clarke	1	1	—	1	—	2	1	1	10	—	—	—	7	2	9	5	4	—
Jeremiah Bran	1	—	1	1	—	1	—	—	2	—	—	—	2	3	5	3	2	—
Thos Murphy	1	1	—	1	—	3	1	1	91	—	—	—	4	2	6	4	2	—
William Clarke	1	—	1	1	—	1	—	1	—	—	—	—	5	2	7	3	4	—
Benja Averell	1	1	—	—	1	2	1	1	107	—	—	—	1	3	4	2	2	—
Samll Ball	1	1	—	1	—	1	—	—	—	—	—	—	4	2	6	3	3	—
Ezra King	1	1	—	1	—	2	1		78	—	—	—	6	2	8	3	5	—
Job Averell	1	—	1	—	1	4	1	1	94	—	—	—	3	6	9	5	4	—
James Hodge	1	—	—	—	—	—	—	—	—	—	—	—	1	3	4	2	2	—
Solomon Hearsey	1	1	—	1		1	—	—	—	—	—	—	—	2	2	2	—	—
Samll Perham	1	—	1	1	—	1	—	—	—	—	—	—	2	2	4	3	1	—
Joshua Hilton	1	—	1	1	—	2	—	—	—	—	—	—	—	3	3	2	1	—
Joseph Hutchins	1	1	—	1	—	3	—	1	105	—	—	—	4	4	8	2	6	—
Abraham Preble	1	1	—	1	—	2	1	1	—	—	—	—	6	4	10	3	7	—
Bartholow Fowler	1	---	1	1	—	1	—	—	—	—	—	—	3	2	5	2	3	—
William Jackson	1	---	1	1	—	1	—	1	—	—	—	—	1	1	2	2	—	—

Names of Families	No of Families	No Framed Houses Inhabited	No Logg Houses Inhabited	No one Story Houses	No 2 Story Houses	No Rooms with fire places	No Brick Chimneys	No Cellars Stoned	No squares of sash Glass in each House	No new Frames partly covered	No new Houses not finished so as to be inhabited	No of intended Rooms in each new house not partitioned off	No Persons under 16 years of Age	No Persons above 16 years of Age	Whole Number of Inhabitants	No of Males	No of Females	No small old Log Houses not inhabited
Thos Jackson	1	—	—	—	—	—	—	—	—	—	—	—	2	3	5	3	2	—
Sam^{el} Kincade	1	—	1	1	—	1	—	—	—	—	—	—	7	2	9	5	4	—
Elisha Kinney	1	—	1	1	—	1	—	—	—	—	—	—	1	3	4	2	2	—
Benj^{a} Coffin	1	1		—	—	2	1	1	36	—	—	—	2	3	5	4	1	—
Jon^{a} Munsey	1	—	1	1	—	1	—	—	—	—	—	—	6	3	9	4	5	—
John Decker	1	—	1	1	—	2	—	—	—	—	—	—	—	4	4	3	1	—
——— ———	—	—	—	—	—	—	—	—	—	—	—	—	—	—	—	—	—	4
Widow Kingsbury	1	1	—	—	1	5	2	1	291	—	—	—	1	3	4	1	3	—
John Huse	1	—	—	—	—	—	—	—	—	—	—	—	3	2	5	1	4	—
Benj^{a} Frizel	1	1	—	—	1	6	1	1	110	—	—	—	3	4	7	5	2	—
Daniel Tuckerman	1	—	—	—	—	—	—	—	—	—	—	—	4	3	7	2	5	—
William Groves	1	1	—	—	—	5	2	1	112	—	—	—	2	3	5	2	3	—
Eben^{r} Whittier	1	—	—	—	1	—	—	1	—	1	—	5	5	3	8	5	3	—
James Stewart	1	1	—	—	—	2	1	1	—	—	—	—	—	3	3	3	—	—
Janea Molatto woman	1	1	—	—	—	1	—	—	—	—	—	—	2	1	3	1	2	—
Josiah Bradbury	1	—	1	1		5	1	1	230	—	—	—	1	3	4	2	2	1
John Decker Junr	1	1	—	—	1	3	1	1	186	—	—	—	2	4	6	4	2	—
John Sevey	1	—	—	—	—	—	—	—	—	—	—	—	—	2	2	1	1	—
Joshua Fowler	1	—	1	1		1	—	1	27	—	—	—	4	2	6	4	2	—

Abiel Wood	1	1	—	1	1	—	1	1	50	—	—	—	1	3	4	2	2	—
Robert Jameson	1	—	1	1	—	1	—	—	—	—	—	—	5	2	7	3	4	—
Sam^{ll} Silvester	1	—	1	1	—	1	—	—	—	—	—	—	1	2	3	2	1	—
Nath^{ll} Rundlett	1	—	1	1	—	2	—	—	15	—	—	—	2	6	8	4	4	—
Niodemus Place	1	1	—	1	—	1	—	—	—	—	—	—	5	2	7	4	3	—
David Silvester	1	—	—	1	—	1	—	—	—	—	—	—	—	—	—	—	—	—
Stephen Young	1	—	1	1	—	1	1	1	19	—	—	—	3	2	5	2	3	—
John Groves	1	—	1	1	—	1	—	—	—	—	—	—	5	2	7	4	3	—
David Nash	1	—	1	1	—	1	—	—	—	—	—	—	—	—	—	—	1	—
Robert Foy	1	—	1	1	—	1	—	—	—	—	—	—	6	4	10	5	5	—
John Blackdon	1	—	1	1	—	1	—	—	—	—	—	—	2	3	5	2	3	—
William Arnold	1	—	1	1	—	1	—	—	—	—	—	—	7	2	9	3	6	—
Ambross Colbey	1	—	1	1	—	1	—	—	—	—	—	—	2	2	4	3	1	—
Charles Blackdon	1	—	1	1	—	1	—	—	—	—	—	—	8	2	5	2	3	—
Thos Homan	1	1	—	1	—	1	—	1	13	—	—	—	—	3	3	3	—	—
Widow Tomson	1	—	—	—	—	—	—	—	—	—	—	—	1	1	2	1	1	—
Roger Smith	1	—	—	—	—	—	—	—	—	—	—	—	1	3	4	3	1	—
Nath^{ll} Spofford	1	—	1	1	—	2	—	—	6	—	—	—	1	4	5	4	1	—
Moses Tomson	1	—	1	1	—	1	—	—	—	—	—	—	8	2	5	2	3	—
James Forester	1	—	1	1	—	1	—	—	—	—	—	—	6	2	8	3	5	—
Isaac Young	1	—	1	1	—	1	—	—	—	—	—	—	6	2	8	3	5	—
William Sevey	1	—	1	1	—	1	—	—	—	—	—	—	—	2	2	1	1	—
Joshua Silvester	1	—	1	1	—	1	—	—	12	—	—	—	2	4	6	2	4	—
Sam^{ll} Silvester Junr	1	1	—	1	—	1	—	—	12	—	—	—	2	3	5	3	2	—
Jon^{a} Williamson	1	—	1	1	—	2	—	—	8	1	—	—	2	3	5	2	3	—
Sam^{ll} Williamson	1	1	1	1	—	1	—	—	—	—	—	—	4	2	6	1	5	—
Thos Williamson	1	1	1	1	—	1	—	—	—	—	—	—	3	2	5	1	4	—

Names of Families	No of Families	No Framed Houses Inhabited	No Logg Houses Inhabited	No one Story Houses	No 2 Story Houses	No Rooms with fire places	No Brick Chimneys	No Cellars Stoned	No squares of sash Glass in each House	No new Frames partly covered	No new Houses not finished so as to be inhabited	No of intended Rooms in each new house not partitioned off	No Persons under 16 years of Age	No Persons above 16 years of Age	Whole number of Inhabitants	No of Males	No of Females	No small old Log Houses not inhabited
Ebenr Gray	1	1	1	1	—	2	—	—	—	—	—	—	5	2	7	4	3	—
Abijah Dickinson	1	1	1	1	—	2	1		—	—	—	—	—	2	2	1	1	1
Widow Fairfield.	1	—	1	1	—	1	—	—	—	—	—	—	4	3	7	4	3	—
John Gray	1	1	—	1	—	1	—	—	—	—	—	—	2	2	4	1	3	
Amasa Dilleno	1	—	1	1	—	1	—	—	—	—	—	—	1	2	3	1	2	
Francis Gray	1	—	1	1	—	1	—	—	—	—	—	—	7	5	12	6	6	
Widow Boyinton	1	—	1	1	—	1	—	—	—	—	—	—	—	2	2	1	1	
Joseph Taylor	1	—	1	1	—	2	—	—	—	—	—	—	6	4	10	5	5	
Jacob Medcalf	1	—	1	1	—	1	—	—	—	—	—	—	3	2	5	2	3	
William Boyinton	1	—	1	1	—	2	—	—	—	—	—	—	7	2	9	4	5	
Caleb Boyinton	1	—	—	—	—	—	—	—	—	—	—	—	1	2	3	1	2	
Robert Man	1	—	1	1	—	1	—	—	—	—	—	—	4	2	6	4	2	
Widow Blackl dge	1	—	1	1	—	1	—	—	—	—	—	—	1	2	3	2	1	
John Chapman	1	—	1	1	—	1	—	—	—	—	—	—	7	5	12	4	8	
Joseph Young Junr	1	—	1	—	1	2	—	—	—	—	—	—	8	4	12	5	7	
Benja Pomeroy		—	1	1		1	—	—	—	—	—	—	2	3	5	2	3	
Benja Pomeroy Junr		—	1	1		1	—	—	—	—	—	—	2	2	4	2	2	
John Bie	1	1	—	1	—	1	—	—	—	—	—	—	2	2	4	2	2	
Joshua Young	1	—	1	1	—	1	—	—	—	—	—	—	4	3	7	5	2	

Joseph Greenleaf	1	---	1	1	---	1	---	---	---	---	---	---	6	2	8	4	4	
Michael Sevey	1	---	---	1	---	4	1	1	159	---	---	---	3	3	6	3	3	
John Moore	1	---	1	1	---	1	---	1	---	---	---	---	6	2	8	4	4	
Richard Holbrook	1	---	1	1	---	1	---	---	---	---	---	---	7	2	9	5	4	
Robert Lambert Junr	1	---	---	---	---	---	---	---	---	---	---	---	1	2	3	2	1	
Robert Lambert	1	---	1	---	1	2	---	1	5	---	---	---	1	3	4	1	3	
Shearbiah Lambert	1	---	1	1	---	2	---	---	---	---	---	---	6	2	8	4	4	
Eben^r Dean	1	---	---	---	---	---	---	---	---	---	---	---	2	2	4	2	2	
Barth^w Bryant	1	---	---	---	---	---	---	---	---	---	---	---	3	2	5	1	4	
Widow Chapman	1	---	1	1	---	1	---	---	---	---	---	---	---	1	1	---	1	1
	114	39	61	94	9	155	26	23	1908	3	4	10	330	309	639	318	321	9

Chas Cushing Sheriff of ye County of Lincoln

Jon^a Williamson }
Thos Rice } Select Men for the Town of Pownalborough
Michal Sevey }

Lincoln ss. Oct^o 15th A. D. 1766 Then the said Jonathan Williamson, Thomas Rice & Michael Sevey made oath that the above return & Representation is a true one according to the best evidence they could obtain in going almost to every house in said town, before me Willm Cushing

Just. ad pacem &c

A Return and true Representation of the West side of the Town of Pownalboro' with Regard to the Number of Houses & Inhabitants &c taken in pursuance of an Order of the General Court June 19, 1766

Names of Families	No of Families	No Framed Houses Inhabited	No Logg Houses Inhabited	No one Story Houses	No 2 Story Houses	No Rooms with fire places	No Brick Chimneys	No Cellars Stoned	No squares of sash Glass in each House	No new Frames partly covered	No new Houses not finished so as to be inhabited	No of intended Rooms in each new house not partitioned off	No Persons under 16 years of Age	No Persons above 16 years of Age	Whole Number of Inhabitants	No of Males	No of Females	No small old Log Houses not inhabited
Ralph Chapman	1	—	1	—	1	9	3	1	216	—	—	—	7	2	9	4	5	—
——— ———	—	—	—	—	—	—	—	—	—	—	—	—	—	—	—	—	—	1
John [illegible]er Junr	1	—	—	—	—	—	—	—	—	—	—	—	3	2	5	2	3	—
John Andrews	1	—	—	—	—	—	—	—	—	—	—	—	4	2	6	3	3	—
[illegible]o [illegible]n	1	—	—	—	—	—	—	—	—	—	—	—	5	2	7	2	5	1
i[illegible]w Cheney	1	—	—	—	—	—	—	—	—	—	—	—	3	1	4	1	3	1
Stephen [illegible]n	1	—	1	1	—	1	—	—	6	—	—	—	2	2	4	2	2	—
John Barker	1	1	—	1	—	1	—	1	72	—	—	—	—	7	7	6	1	—
John Herin	1	—	1	1	—	1	—	—	8	—	—	—	1	2	3	2	1	—
Widow [illegible]in	1	—	—	—	—	—	—	—	—	—	—	—	3	1	4	1	3	—
Jona Bryant	—	—	—	—	—	—	—	—	—	—	—	—	—	1	1	1	—	—
Richard Kidder	1	1	—	1	—	2	1	—	96	—	—	—	—	2	2	1	1	—
Mark Carney	1	—	1	1	—	1	1	1	4	—	—	—	4	2	6	2	4	—
David Clancey	1	—	1	1	—	1	—	—	—	—	—	—	5	2	7	3	4	—
Samll Emerson	1	—	1	1	—	1	1	—	15	—	—	—	4	2	6	1	5	—
Daniel Goud	1	—	1	1	—	1	—	—	8	—	—	—	—	2	2	2	—	—

Michael Stilfin	1	—	1	1	—	1	—	—	8	—	—	—	6	3	9	6	3	—
John McGown	1	—	1	1	—	1	—	1	8	—	—	—	5	2	7	1	6	—
Adam Couch	1	—	1	1	—	1	—	—	4	—	—	—	3	2	5	4	1	—
——— ——— ———	—	—	—	—	—	—	—	—	—	—	—	—	1	—	—	1	—	2
Joseph Mcfarland	1	—	1	1	—	1	—	—	14	—	—	—	1	2	3	2	1	—
Chas Ettiene Houdlet	1	—	1	1	—	1	—	—	4	—	1 log	1	4	3	7	2	5	—
Abraham Pouchard	1	—	1	1	—	1	—	—	6	—	—	—	4	2	6	2	4	—
Uzziah Kendal	1	1	—	1	—	1	—	—	—	—	—	—	6	4	10	4	6	—
Benja Kendal	1	—	1	1	—	2	—	—	6	—	—	—	5	2	7	4	3	—
Philip Miers	—	—	1	1	—	1	—	—	2	—	—	—	—	1	1	1	1	—
George Mier	1	—	1	1	—	1	—	—	—	—	—	—	—	3	3	1	2	—
Casemise Miers	—	—	—	—	—	—	—	—	—	—	—	—	—	1	1	1	—	—
James Goud	1	1	—	1	—	2	—	—	36	—	—	—	4	2	6	2	4	—
George Pouchard	1	—	1	1	—	1	—	—	4	—	—	—	4	2	6	3	3	—
George Lillie	1	—	1	1	—	1	—	—	12	—	—	—	2	2	4	3	1	—
Jona Reed	1	—	1	1	—	1	—	—	10	—	—	—	—	3	3	2	1	—
Abiather Kendal	1	—	1	1	—	1	1	—	24	—	—	—	—	3	3	1	2	—
John George Goud	1	—	1	1	—	1	—	—	8	—	—	—	1	3	4	3	1	—
Amos Paris	1	—	1	1	—	1	—	—	12	—	—	—	4	3	7	3	4	—
Jacob Carlow	1	—	1	1	—	1	—	—	4	—	—	—	5	2	7	3	4	—
Dennis Lines	1	—	1	1	—	1	—	—	—	—	—	—	5	2	7	4	3	—
Frederick Pechin	1	—	1	1	—	1	—	—	12	—	—	—	2	2	4	2	2	—
Chas Calihan	1	1	—	1	—	3	1	1	100	—	—	—	1	3	4	3	1	—
James Paterson	1	—	1	1	1	1	8	1	443	—	1 Fr.	8	4	4	8	5	3	1
Philip Call Junr	1	1	—	1	—	3	1	1	90	—	—	—	4	2	6	3	3	—
Philip Call	1	—	1	1	—	1	1	—	12	—	—	—	1	3	4	2	2	—
Obadiah Call	1	1	—	1	—	3	1	1	132	—	—	—	2	4	6	4	2	—

Names of Families	No of Families	No Framed Houses Inhabited	No Logg Houses Inhabited	No one Story Houses	No 2 Story Houses	No Rooms with fire places	No Brick Chimneys	No Cellars Stoned	No squares of sash Glass in each House	No new Frames partly covered	No new Houses not finished so as to be inhabited	No of intended Rooms in each new house not partitioned off	No Persons under 16 years of Age	No Persons above 16 years of Age	Whole Number of Inhabitants	No of Males	No of Females	No small old Log Houses not inhabited
Joseph Cleveland	1	1	—	1	—	1	1	—	35	—	—	—	2	3	5	3	2	—
Abiel Lovejoy	1	1	—	—	1	3	1	1	152	—	—	—	7	10	17	11	6	—
House belonging to said Lovejoy on which Wm Cushing Eq lodges & keeps his Chamber	—	1	—	—	1	2	1	—	44	—	—	—	1	—	—	1	2	—
Samll Reed	1	1	—	1	—	2	1	—	34	—	—	—	4	2	6	2	4	—
Widow Wyman	1	—	—	—	—	—	—	—	—	—	—	—	2	1	3	1	2	—
William Wyman	1	—	1	1	—	2	—	—	30	—	—	—	4	3	7	5	2	—
Stephen Goodwin	1	—	1	1	—	1	1	—	—	—	—	—	2	4	6	3	3	—
Samll White	1	1	—	1	—	3	1	1	96	—	—	—	2	2	4	2	2	—
Thos Densmore	1	1	—	1	—	2	1	1	64	—	—	—	6	3	9	6	3	—
John Stain	1	—	1	1	—	1	—	—	12	—	1 log	1	—	3	3	2	1	—
Lewis Cavalier	—	—	1	1	—	1	1	—	5	—	—	—	—	1	1	1	1	—
John George Pochin	1	—	1	1	—	1	—	—	—	—	—	—	—	2	2	1	1	—
Francis Kittal	1	—	1	1	—	1	—	—	7	—	1 Fr.	2	5	2	7	4	3	—
Jaques Bugnon	1	—	1	—	1	2	—	1	18	—	—	—	1	2	3	—	—	—
John Pouchard	1	—	1	1	—	1	—	—	4	—	—	—	—	3	3	2	1	—
Daniel Malbone	1	—	1	1	—	1	—	—	—	—	—	—	—	2	2	2	—	—
Widow Jacequeer	1	1	—	1	—	1	—	—	6	—	—	—	—	2	2	1	1	—

Family in Sam[l] Boman Esq[r] House	1	1	—	—	1	8	2	1	660	—	—	—	2	5	7	3	4	—
Jonas Fitch	1	—	1	1	—	2	1	—	51	—	—	—	5	2	7	3	4	—
John Small	1	—	1	1	—	1	1	—	—	—	—	—	4	2	6	4	2	—
John Spearin	1	—	—	—	—	—	—	—	—	—	—	—	5	2	7	4	3	—
Jacob Bailey	1	—	1	1	—	3	2	1	78	—	—	—	1	3	4	1	3	—
House in which Sam[ll] Goodwin dwells & Courts are held	1	1	—	—	st'ry 3	6	1	1	858	—	—	5	2	9	11	5	6	—
Sam[ll] Goodwin Jun[r]	1	—	1	—	1	2	1	1	58	—	—	—	4	4	8	3	5	1
Abner Marsor	1	—	1	1	—	1	1	—	10	—	—	—	3	2	5	4	1	1
John Mirick	1	—	—	—	—	—	—	—	—	—	—	—	1	2	3	1	2	—
Widow Spaulding	1	—	1	1	—	1	—	—	—	—	—	—	1	4	5	3	2	—
Roger Chase	1	—	1	1	—	2	1	—	18	—	—	—	2	2	4	2	2	—
Mathew Chase	1	—	—	—	—	—	—	—	—	—	—	—	—	2	2	1	1	—
George Pierce	—	—	1	—	1	5	1	1	180	—	—	—	—	1	1	1	—	—
John Hankerson	1	—	—	—	—	—	—	—	—	—	—	—	4	2	6	4	2	—
Ezra Davis	1	—	—	—	—	—	—	—	—	—	—	—	3	2	5	3	2	1
Sam[ll] Eastman	1	—	1	1	—	1	—	—	12	—	—	—	3	2	5	3	2	—
Edmund Bridge	1	1	—	1	—	2	1	—	64	—	—	—	1	2	3	2	1	—
			45				35	18	3852		4	17	190	190	380	99	181	7

Cha[s] Cushing Sheriff of y[e] County of Lincoln

Jon[a] Wn Tds Rice Ml Sevey Selectmen for the Town of Pownalboro

Lincoln ss. Oct[o] 15th A D 1766 Then the said Chas Cushing Jn Wn Ths Rice

& Ml Sevey severally made oath that the above Return & Representation is a true one according to

the best de dy old of tain in going mst to every be in said wn fe me

Wm Gg Just. ad pacem &c

INDEX

B

D

E

G

H

K

O

P

S

T

Y

This Index was made by Mr. Edward Denham, of New Bedford, Mass.—J. P. B.

Lightning Source UK Ltd.
Milton Keynes UK
UKHW021206110219
337100UK00010BA/968/P

9 781330 884805